Sarah Pitt

RESTORING SANCTUARY

Restoring Sanctuary

A New Operating System for
Trauma-Informed Systems of Care

Sandra L. Bloom, M.D.
Brian Farragher, M.S.W., M.B.A.

OXFORD
UNIVERSITY PRESS

Oxford University Press is a department of the University of Oxford.
It furthers the University's objective of excellence in research, scholarship,
and education by publishing worldwide.

Oxford   New York
Auckland   Cape Town   Dar es Salaam   Hong Kong   Karachi
Kuala Lumpur   Madrid   Melbourne   Mexico City   Nairobi
New Delhi   Shanghai   Taipei   Toronto

With offices in
Argentina   Austria   Brazil   Chile   Czech Republic   France   Greece
Guatemala   Hungary   Italy   Japan   Poland   Portugal   Singapore
South Korea   Switzerland   Thailand   Turkey   Ukraine   Vietnam

Oxford is a registered trade mark of Oxford University Press in the UK and certain other
countries.

Published in the United States of America by
Oxford University Press
198 Madison Avenue, New York, NY 10016

Library of Congress Cataloging-in-Publication Data
Bloom, Sandra L., 1948-
Restoring sanctuary : a new operating system for trauma-informed systems of care /
Sandra L. Bloom, Brian Farragher.
  p. ; cm.
Includes bibliographical references.
ISBN 978-0-19-979636-6 (hardback : alk. paper) — ISBN 978-0-19-979649-6 (updf) —
ISBN 978-0-19-997667-6 (epub)
I. Farragher, Brian J. II. Title.
[DNLM: 1. Mental Health Services—organization & administration.   2. Delivery of Health
Care—organization & administration.   3. Models, Organizational.   4. Organizational
Innovation.   5. Stress Disorders, Post-Traumatic—therapy. WM 30.1]
LC Classification not assigned
362.2068′5—dc23   2012029880

9 8 7 6 5 4 3 2 1
Printed in the United States of America
on acid-free paper

My heart is moved by all I cannot save:
so much has been destroyed
I have to cast my lot with those
who age after age, perversely,
with no extraordinary power,
reconstitute the world.

Adrienne Rich, 1977
From "Natural Resources" [1]

Contents

List of Figures and Tables

TABLES

Prologue

In 1980, when we started down the path that has led to *Restoring Sanctuary*, Sandy had just completed her psychiatric training and had transformed a medical-surgical unit into a psychiatric unit within a small general hospital. Like Brian, who was about 10 years behind her, she had learned nothing about child abuse, domestic violence, or other kinds of trauma. The knowledge we have gained along the way has been life-altering for both of us and potentially revolutionary for our fields of endeavor and for our society as a whole.

By "revolutionary," we mean a social, economic, and scientific revolution that is both nonviolent and politically transformative. Every revolution must stand upon new knowledge that moves humanity in the direction of a better life within a complex and endangered ecological system. The understanding that we have gained across the last three decades, usually referred to as "Trauma Theory," provides the beginning of such a framework for the critical spheres of activity related to human psychology and sociology. Trauma Theory offers an integrative, scientifically based, and developmentally grounded framework for all human systems. The psychobiology of trauma points us toward knowledge that heals the Cartesian split between mind, body, and spirit and, in doing so, "puts Humpty-Dumpty back together again." The simultaneous burgeoning of knowledge about the importance of early childhood attachment and the impact of toxic stress exposure offers developmental continuity between childhood and adulthood and therefore the very real possibility of preventing most of the problems that plague humanity. Using the concept of "allostatic load," we can now connect the psychobiology of trauma and disrupted attachment to many of the social determinants of health such as racism, gender-based discrimination, and poverty. Never before have we had an integrative framework that allows extensive and specialized bodies of knowledge to be connected to each other within a human rights context as a public health challenge.

This book represents decades of lived experience on the part of numerous administrators, physicians, social workers, psychologists, counselors, nurses, direct care workers, educators, secretaries, finance staff, maintenance staff, housekeeping staff, children, adults, and families. When asked who our target reader is, we had a difficult time answering that question because we realized that our target reader is anyone who is interested in helping humanity to survive and thrive. However, the experiences we draw upon, the vignettes we use for illustration, and the knowledge base with which we are both most familiar draw upon our understanding of human service delivery systems that include health care, mental health care, educational institutions, shelters, child welfare, and other social service entities. We thank all of those hard-working, dedicated people, past and present, who have shared their wisdom and experience with us.

RESTORING SANCTUARY

Chapter 1

It Starts with a Dream

It all begins with make believe.
A sudden spark of inspiration.
And every note of everything
Started with a dream in some imagination

"It Started with a Dream"

Music and Lyrics by Cy Coleman

If you want to bring about significant change in anything or anybody, the place to start is not the present or the past. The place to start is the future. As the gifted American song writer Cy Coleman observed, everything worth doing, having, or being begins with someone's imagination. One of the great paradoxes of existence is that destroying something takes relatively little energy. There is a built-in aging to everything in the world around us, even to our universe. Creating and restoring require tremendous energy, commitment, and will, but only after the work of imagination has already occurred. You have to be able to imagine a future that is different from the reality of the past and present.

In this book, and in the work it is based upon, we challenge our readers to use their imaginations. We use the word "Sanctuary" to describe a place where injured people—and that includes all of us in some way or another—are able to heal through the supportive care of others. Sanctuary® is a place where our tendencies toward violence and vengeance have been subdued, where individual and collective powers are used to bring about a better life and a better world. Sanctuary is a place of joy and creative innovation, of sympathy and solace, and of transformation. In Sanctuary, people:

- are sufficiently physically, psychologically, socially, and morally safe that, as individuals and in a group, they are able to make good decisions and think creatively without becoming destructive;
- know how to deal with each other in a way that respects and enhances emotional development as well as cultural diversity;

- are constantly learning together how to peacefully resolve problems and conflicts;
- have a voice, and each person is expected to contribute to the well-being of the whole;
- do work that expresses their own individuality and their sense of responsibility for the common good;
- are learning together how to adapt to changing conditions without losing what is most spiritually important to them;
- use their vision of a better future to determine what to do in the present and are willing to give up today's comforts in order to work toward a future goal

As we said, we challenge you to use your imagination because the idea of Sanctuary is largely make-believe. There is no perfect organization. Few of us have experienced emotionally intelligent environments of perfect safety, where honesty and openness prevail and there are no secrets, where continuous learning from conflict is the norm, where decisions are routinely made by democratic consensus balancing individual needs with the common good, where justice is accorded to everyone, or where loss is compassionately understood and honored as a key factor in change and everyone shares in a drive toward a better future.

And yet, we can imagine such an organization, such a society, such a world. Utopian visions are not new; yet we would argue that in today's world, they are in short supply and are usually greeted with scorn. After eons of intergenerational violence, degradation, confusion, irrationality, deceit, and disaster, humanity is at a crossroad. There is an urgent need for us to adapt in a different way, to change the way we do things, the way we think, how we manage our emotions, and, perhaps most importantly, how we treat each other and the complex ecological system in which we are all embedded. We live in a traumatized world that needs to heal if we are to survive.

The twentieth century gave birth to unimaginable horrors, but with the Universal Declaration of Human Rights in 1948 it also produced a new mental model of the world, a vision of human rights for everyone that is the basis for a peaceful, nurturing, and life-sustaining world.

It's one thing to have a vision, but it is quite another thing to bring that vision in line with reality. That is where the work of *Restoring Sanctuary* has something to offer. Today, around the country and in several other parts of the world, thousands of people, children and adults, are striving to turn make-believe into a living reality. They are striving together to heal themselves, to heal their organizations, and in doing so, to heal this traumatized world. In the next chapters we will describe some of the steps we are taking together to move from imagination to practical reality. Let's start by broadly outlining some of the basic ideas that need to be shared in order to get a group of people "on the same page."

Creating Sanctuary

This work is the third part of a trilogy that explores what it means for people to come together and create organizations within which traumatized clients are given opportunities to heal. In the first volume of the trilogy, published in 1997, *Creating Sanctuary: Toward the Evolution of Sane Societies*, "Creating Sanctuary" refers to the shared experience of creating and maintaining safety within a social environment—any social environment [2]. The recognition that a past history of exposure to childhood adversity lay at the heart of many psychiatric diagnoses challenged our mental models for understanding our patients, our relationship with them, and the way we understand our world. In the next few pages, Sandy will describe the key findings that she and her colleagues made in the first years of understanding what it meant to treat trauma survivors.

Trauma-Organized Individuals

In 1980, we created an acute care psychiatric unit in a general hospital. Around 1985, we began to recognize that most of the adolescents and adults we had been treating for a variety of different problems had histories of exposure to childhood adversity. From 1985 to 2001, when we closed the program, we (Bloom and her colleagues) treated several thousand adults and adolescents who had been subjected to all kinds of childhood abuse, trauma, and adversity. Many of them had also experienced the traumas of war and interpersonal violence as adults as well. They taught us a great deal about the impact of those experiences of multiple disrupted attachments.

First of all, the primary reason for their even being admitted to a psychiatric unit was a lack of safety. Sometimes they were suicidal and just wanted to die. But for many others, the struggle to be safe in the world meant a struggle with substance abuse, eating difficulties, chronic anxiety, and self-mutilation. For others, safety in relationships was a serious problem. Independent of their gender, age, race, economic status, or educational achievements, they had challenges with managing distressing emotions and would become overwhelmed by anger, fear, and sadness, and these feelings would often lead to the unsafe behavior. Cognitive function and judgment were altered, particularly when they were in the grip of an emotion. Despite the enormity of their experience, we saw that they were unlikely to make connections between their present problems and those previous experiences, as if the present and the past had become completely disconnected from each other. Early in our learning process, we were exposed to the memory problems associated with trauma and saw that our patients were often unable to remember, much less talk about, the worst parts of their experiences, while at the same time they were behaviorally reenacting the problematic relationship dynamics, so that they ended up being hurt again and again. They usually had great difficulty communicating directly and openly about their needs, feelings, or perceptions. Self-functions, so important for success in our complex, demanding culture, were often compromised, leading to problems with self-control, self-discipline, and self-esteem. Moral development had frequently followed a complicated and confused pathway because of the enormous contradictions they had been compelled to live with and adapt to. By the time they reached our level of care, they were weighted down by repetitive tangible and intangible losses that left them unable to even imagine a better future. Their lives had become organized around their past histories of trauma and adversity (Figure 1.1).

A Humbling Experience

Throughout those 15 years in the psychiatric unit, we learned a great deal about the people we were working with and we learned much about ourselves. We realized that with all we had learned in our various training programs, we did not *really* understand what had happened to our patients, nor had we fully grappled with how their negative experiences in childhood had evolved into the symptoms we were trying to treat—sometimes successfully, sometimes not. In part because we had not actually defined the correct problem, we did not understand what worked and what did not work at all. We discovered that our "goals of treatment" were vague and insubstantial and did not necessarily

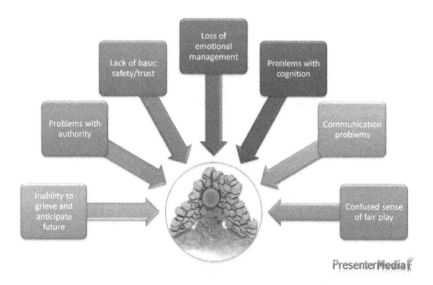

Figure 1.1 Trauma-organized individual.

directly address the very real problems and dilemmas confronting our patients every day, largely because we did not understand the underlying causes of their symptoms. We were not truly committed to recovery because we did not know what recovery actually was, much less if it were possible. We often struggled with our patients for control, sometimes setting unreasonably rigid limits, sometimes too few limits. At times we behaved as if our patients were children, both helpless and hopeless, and at other times as if they should just behave like everyone else. We denied the ways in which we were at times violent toward them and toward each other and failed to take into account the impact of our own past traumatic experiences. We failed to fully comprehend how trauma impacts systems as well as individuals, creating a reverberating cycle of dysfunction, and therefore failed to recognize what we have come to call "parallel processes." The result of our ignorance and confusion, that were also typical of our field, was that our patients had often experienced "sanctuary trauma"— expecting a protective environment and finding only more trauma [3].

Trauma Theory

As we gradually came to terms with new knowledge about trauma, adversity, and disrupted attachment, our treatment approaches changed, and as that happened, our patients began to make much more progress. We were no longer standing in their way—we were truly helping them to recover. At the time, research about traumatic stress and toxic stress, as well as normal and disrupted attachment, was beginning to find its way into the scientific literature, and we discovered that we were not the only people who were questioning the foundations of established wisdom. We discovered that those of us who were studying trauma, dissociation, and attachment in children and adults had more in common with each other than with many of our mainstream connections and that knowledge was beginning to offer a long-sought integrative framework. That was important because we had begun to see the lack of integration as a primary cause of problems everywhere.

The science of understanding what happens to people who are exposed to overwhelming events is called "Trauma Theory." Trauma Theory describes a scientifically informed and complex biopsychosocial understanding of what goes wrong for human beings under conditions of overwhelming stress. Trauma Theory presupposes a cause for one's difficulties, and that cause is not an individual character flaw, a moral weakness, or innate malevolence, but a result of injury. This is especially important if those injuries have occurred in childhood because normal development of body, brain, and mind is likely to be derailed.

Trauma Theory provides us with an opportunity to integrate large bodies of knowledge—a process called "consilience"—that have previously remained in knowledge silos to great disadvantage [4]. Ideally, our growing understanding of the interaction between stress and development will provide us with an

ramework for all human systems and, in doing so, heal the tradi-
ian split between mind and body that still is a significant barrier to
medicine. Similarly, this knowledge base provides an opportunity
meaningful continuities between childhood and adulthood, conti-
..... _n the surface appear entirely logical but in practice are rarely considered; adult health, mental health, and social services remain almost entirely
segregated from what happens to children, as if they were an entirely different species. Deriving from new research in sociology, economics, and public
health, we are learning a great deal about the social determinants of health and
the multiple ways in which class, race, and socioeconomic status interact with
individual and social health and child development. This kind of consilience
within all of our human services has never happened before, and the resultant
fragmentation of services has meant that our outcomes are not even remotely
as positive as they could be were our services integrated along a true continuum
of care.

Attachment and the Loss of Integrated Experience

Every experience we have is actually the product of complex brain operations
that automatically integrate behavior, emotions, sensations, and knowledge into
a coherent whole, so rapidly and smoothly that under normal circumstances we
are unaware of any separation of components [5].

This very smooth operation is what allows us to remember all of the components of an experience as a whole; experience events from the past as being situ-
ated in the past, not the present; and store that entire experience as a memory.
It also explains why our recall of an event is usually subject to "weathering," the
normal erosion of accurate remembrance in the course of everyday experiences.

As we learned about the study of attachment relationships, we came to
understand that a healthy attachment between a child and a primary caregiver
plays a vital role in determining healthy development and how children interact with the world around them. Over the course of childhood and in the context of healthy caregiving relationships, the brain gradually becomes capable of
high-level integration of very complex information.

Exposure to abuse, neglect, or other adversity in childhood interferes with
healthy brain development and shatters experience into its component parts,
preventing normal integration of experience. This failure of integration may
manifest in a wide variety of ways including flashbacks, nightmares, overwhelming and inappropriate emotional arousal, unrelenting physical sensations, too
much or too little memory, and misinterpretation of reality (Figure 1.2).

Under these circumstances, people are compelled to use whatever coping
measures they can to survive. Over time, coping measures that were initially
helpful can become extremely problematic—such as substance abuse, avoidance,

A SHATTERING OF EXPERIENCE

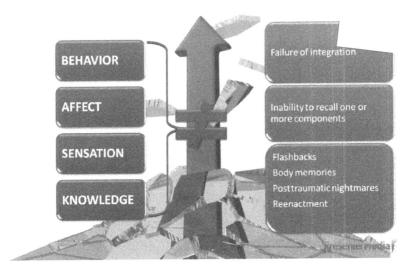

Figure 1.2 Failure of integration.

and aggression. The more a behavior is used in the service of survival, the more likely it is that the behavior will be repeated and will resist change. In other words, it becomes a habit. Then the more problematic the habit is for other people, the more likely it is that the previous coping measures will be called "symptoms" and the result will be one or more "diagnoses" (Figure 1.3).

Some symptoms will get people assigned to mental health services, and they will be labeled in some way as "sick." Other symptoms will result in contact with law enforcement and the criminal justice system, and they will be labeled "bad." Some unfortunates will end up being both "sick" and "bad." The labels and the assumptions that support them turn out to cause significant problems for everyone. We discovered that the reality was that all of the problems we saw were in fact related to "injury."

Neither Sick Nor Bad, But Injured

As a result of this growing knowledge base, we came to see our clients as neither sick nor bad, but as injured, and as a result the fundamental question for any kind of intervention switched from "What's wrong with you?" to "What has happened to you?" (Foderaro, as cited in [6]). This simple change in question represented a shift in basic assumptions that changed assessment, treatment, interpersonal styles of relating—everything. The most important thing is that we got better outcomes: more people recovered from their experiences and set out on a road to true healing than we had ever seen happen before.

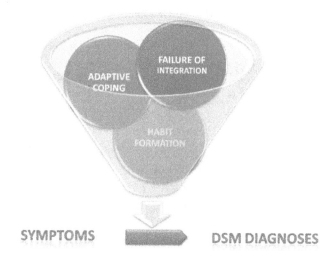

Figure 1.3 Symptoms and diagnoses.

As in physical injury, people who have been psychologically injured may be temporarily wounded, seriously wounded, or even disabled by their injuries, but their injuries are not their fault. The injuries may have started before they were born; they may be physical, psychological, social, and moral injuries. Whatever the case, they did not want to be injured, nor did they have any control over their injuries. If they have been repeatedly injured, then the continuing cycles of injury probably started when they were young. After that time they may have indeed used bad judgment and made poor decisions, but we understand this as yet another effect of the original injury and its impact on subsequent development.

After all, human service delivery and education is about *relationship*, and the base of that word is "relating." But psychiatric jargon can be mystifying. We might not know firsthand what it means to be a "conduct disorder" or a "schizophrenic" or a "borderline" but we all know what it is like to get our feelings hurt, to feel betrayed, to not know who to trust, to be scared, and to have experiences so shocking that our normal processes of thinking and feeling are overwhelmed. We all know what it is like to do or say something we know we should not have done or said. Sometimes we know it is wrong when we are doing it, but at other times, we don't even realize that it was wrong, or mean, or thoughtless until after it has already happened.

The ability to identify with somebody in pain, regardless of what form that pain takes, is vital in our world. People who are unable to imagine themselves in someone else's shoes, people who lack empathy, should not do this work. Given the prevalence of trauma and adversity in our society, there is a high likelihood that most consumers of mental health and social services have been the victims of past trauma and adversity, regardless of what their presenting problems are today. Sometimes they are engaged in harmful behavior that is directed at themselves, and they tend to end up in the mental health system. At other times, they are doing things that harm others and therefore become involved in the criminal justice system. But whatever the case, we look at the problem as originating in some kind of injury. It is this fundamental change that is at the heart of what are now called "trauma-informed" approaches to human services. This very basic change from "sickness and/or badness" to "injury" represents a major shift in the underlying assumptions called "mental models" (see Figure 1.4). These changes in basic assumptions lead to different ways of thinking and behaving toward others.

A Stress Continuum

In the last few decades, we have learned a great deal about what can be called a "stress continuum" moving from positive stress to tolerable stress, toxic stress, and traumatic stress, all complicated by allostatic load. Put together, this is why exposure to stress can be seen as our number one public health problem, particularly when too much stress is experienced in childhood.

Positive stress produces short-lived physiological responses but promotes growth and change and is necessary for healthy development. Tolerable stress, particularly in childhood, may trigger enough of a physiological response to dis-

SICK	BAD	INJURED
Mental health system	Criminal justice system	Every system
Fundamental defect	Fundamental defect	Something happened
Not your fault	Entirely your fault	Not your fault
Stabilization	No recovery	Recovery
Listen to experts	Obey orders	Active role
No accountability	Total accountability	Mutual accountability
No real choice	Total choice	Many choices
No one else can really understand	No one else willing to understand	Everyone knows what it is to be injured

Figure 1.4 Changing mental models.

rupt brain processes, but with sufficient social support, the child has sufficient buffering to prevent any damage.

The children and adults who are the subject of this book have been exposed to toxic stress and, in many cases, traumatic stress. "Toxic stress" is associated with prolonged and intense activation of the body's stress response to such an extent that it can change the way a child's brain develops, the very architecture of the brain, with problematic long-term consequences.

"Traumatic stress" occurs when a person experiences an event that is over-whelming, usually life-threatening, terrifying, or horrifying in the face of help-lessness [7]. "Allostatic load" is the term used to describe the wear-and-tear on the body and brain that can be a result of conditions such as poverty, bigotry, chronic hunger, and lower socio economic status. All can have a profound effect on a child's development and later health outcomes secondary to the constant allostatic load on the child and on his or her caregivers, even in the absence of perceivable traumatic events [8, 9].

Healing = Integration

Over time and after working with so many survivors of terrible life events, we recognized that their past experiences had produced the symptoms of post-traumatic stress and the chronic hyperarousal that accompanies it, but for many of them so long ago that no memory existed for how they had reacted to those childhood events. But the symptoms we were supposed to treat were the remnants of original and necessary attempts to cope with overwhelming stress. The coping skills had become bad habits over time, firmly entrenched in their styles of relating to themselves and the world around them. As a result, their capacity to create and sustain interpersonal trust was severely compromised. Hence, the challenges presented to us as helpers were significant and, without this new understanding, incomprehensible.

As we began to understand that most of the symptoms we were seeing were secondary to a failure to fully integrate past experiences, we began to under-stand how we could meaningfully help our clients to recover. We had to teach them safety skills so that they could have experiences that would build the capacity for trust. They had to learn how to manage intense emotion in safe and secure ways and to learn to use reason and judgment even in the face of emotional arousal. We had to teach communication and leadership skills so that they would be able to clearly assert their needs, create safe boundaries, and exercise self-control and self-discipline. We had to promote fair play and show them how to balance individual needs with the needs of the larger community. And we had to help them mourn for what was lost, prepare for the losses associ-ated with change, and imagine a future that would make all of this new learning and habit change worthwhile (Figure 1.5).

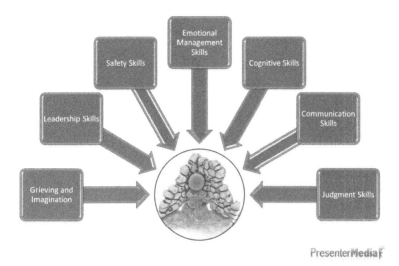

Figure 1.5 Trauma-informed treatment.

This then was what we came to understand as "trauma-informed" treatment. As we saw it unfolding, developing these cognitive-emotional-behavioral skills set the stage for trauma-specific treatment approaches that had a cathartic effect and helped people to integrate the fragmented bits of experience into a cohesive whole that then allowed the past to reside safely in the past, rather than continuing to haunt the present. This was RECOVERY.

Broad Definition of Safety

Experience in creating healing environments for trauma survivors taught us that we had to have a very broad definition of what it means to be safe and secure. We learned that there is a wide variety of human behaviors that are violent and that all violence is interconnected. Our clients reacted violently to a multitude of toxins, some from their families, some from others, and some from dysfunctional systems that were supposed to help them. All of this represented a loss of social support that is the only barrier any of us have against the cruelties that life can engender.

In order to create safe environments for healing, we needed to concern ourselves not just with physical safety but with psychological, social, and moral safety as well. That meant that as staff, we had to truly "walk the talk" if we wanted our clients to trust us. When we grasped the enormous power behind the reenactment dynamic, the powerful inclination to repeat the past that is so typical of human behavior, we realized that interpersonal trust was vital. If our clients were to change, they would have to make significant decisions to go against their own instincts and listen to us instead. For this to happen, there had to be trust between us. But we recognized that we were not always trustworthy. As we came to understand the impact of the injuries our clients had sustained, it become harder to deny our own vulnerability to the impact of stress, strain, and trauma. Things had happened to us as well, and those injuries had in part shaped who we had become as helping professionals. If we wanted our clients to change, then we were going to have to change as well.

Grappling with Complexity and Democracy

We learned that the problems our clients had were complex. They all had complicated and interconnected difficulties for which there were no simple solutions. The first problem was that any helping solution required interpersonal trust, and when someone has been serially betrayed, it can take a long time to place even a rudimentary sense of trust in helpers. And then, because of the complex array of problems they had, we saw that they did not need medication *or* psychotherapy, but the integration of medication AND psychotherapy. And not just verbal psychotherapy, but expressive therapies AND new innovative body-oriented therapies AND family therapy AND cognitive-behavioral therapies AND exposure therapies. And we had to collaborate with clients and each other in deciding what to do with whom, when, and in what order at a time when the push from regulatory authorities and managed care companies was going in exactly the opposite direction, with reduced lengths of stay and reduced services.

We could only find one way around that complexity and that was to put our heads together. That's how we discovered that democratic participatory processes are critical in dealing with complex problems, because no one mind is sufficient to deal with this level of complexity. We discovered informally what researchers had developed numbers for: what the client brings into a help-seeking environment accounts for only about 40% of the outcome of giving that help. The other 60% of the influence is determined by what helpers do and don't do within helping environments, most importantly the ability of a helper to be empathic, warm, and nonjudgmental, which accounts for a whopping 30% of therapeutic influence. Offering people hope that they can improve, that life will get better, accounts for about 15% of the outcome. Providing people with an explanation for their difficulties and a method for resolving those difficulties, a viable theory, accounts for about another 15% of the outcome [10].

As a result of what we experienced with our traumatized adult patients, we developed considerable optimism that we could achieve much better outcomes in the populations we serve in all of our helping services. But this would not happen by continuing to use the same strategies and methods that have failed in the past. To be successful, educational, social service, mental health care, and health care programs would have to become what was just beginning to be thought of as developmentally grounded, trauma-informed, and, in many cases, trauma-focused.

Destroying Sanctuary

In the years between *Creating Sanctuary,* service delivery for the most vulnerable members of the population shifted dramatically. Clients presented at the doors of mental health, healthcare, educational, juvenile, and criminal justice systems and other social service programs seeking remedy for their problems, but they often left with few solutions and sometimes with even more difficulties than they brought with them. Staff members in many programs were suffering physical and psychological injuries at alarming rates, were demoralized and often hostile, and their counter-aggressive responses to the aggression in their clients created punitive environments. Leaders became variously perplexed, overwhelmed, ineffective, authoritarian, or avoidant as they struggled to satisfy the demands of their superiors, to control their subordinates, and to protect their clients. When professionally trained and nonprofessionally trained staff gathered together in an attempt to formulate an approach to complex problems, they were not on the same page because they lacked a common theoretical framework for problem-solving. Without a shared way of understanding the problem, what passed as treatment often looked like little more than labeling, the prescription of medication, and behavioral "management." When troubled clients failed to respond to these measures, they were labeled again, given more medication, and termed "resistant to treatment." A core problem throughout these years was what has become known as extreme biological reductionism or "mindless psychiatry"[11].

Living Systems

Destroying Sanctuary: The Crisis in Human Service Delivery System, the second part of the trilogy, was the outcome of our shared understanding of what was happening to our systems of care [12]. We voiced a practical goal for that book: to provide the beginnings of a coherent framework for organizational staff and leaders to more effectively provide trauma-informed care for their clients by becoming trauma-informed themselves. This meant making the rather profound assumption that our systems of care, and all the organizations that are a part of those systems, are alive, functioning as interconnected living systems and therefore subject to the stresses, strains, and trauma of being alive. For us this meant becoming sensitive to the ways in which managers, staff, groups, and systems are impacted by individual and collective exposure to overwhelming and toxic stress and how they adapt to these stressors. But when we examined our own professional literature, we found that there was little research to draw upon. Most research about organizational dynamics and the process of change is not to be found in the mental health literature or in most health and social service training programs. For that, we had to look to the worlds of business management, organizational development, and communication, and we observed that little of that knowledge had made its way into clinical or social service settings over the course of the last few decades.

Systems Under Siege

In *Destroying Sanctuary*, we looked at the mental models that shape our organizations, especially health care and human service delivery environments. Looking through the lens of mental models enabled us to see the ethical conflicts that lie at the heart of many caring environments today. We then focused the lens on the mental health system as an example that we are both very familiar with and discussed the ways in which the chronic and disabling conditions that affect the mental health system represent a "system under siege."

We began the discussion of a system under siege by exploring the impact of workplace stress as a major determinant of the way in which our human service delivery system functions. It is impossible to understand the full impact of the last 30 years of changes in human service delivery without understanding the impact of acute and chronic stress on workers at every level of the system. We reviewed what we know so far about the magnitude of stress impacting daily existence with a specific focus on workplace stressors. We saw the issue of workplace stress as a public health problem of enormous proportions, not dissimilar to the threat to health that existed 200 years ago before we understood that microbes cause disease, only now the infectious agent is violence in all of its forms.

We came to the conclusion that if there is a solution for the multiple crises facing human service delivery systems—and humanity, for that matter—it requires a different way of understanding human nature and human dysfunction. But we recognized that we need an understanding that incorporates 150 years of accumulated scientific knowledge and clinical wisdom. Based on our own clinical and organizational experience, we made the claim that if we are going to diagnose and prescribe for our troubled social service and mental health organizations, everyone involved would need to have a working knowledge of the psychobiology of trauma and adversity: what it does to individuals, particularly when trauma is repetitive, occurs in early development, and is a result of interpersonal violence.

Workplace Stress, Bad Habits, and Parallel Process

Since we were making the case that organizations are not machines, but are living complex systems and as such are every bit as vulnerable to the impact of trauma and chronic stress as the people who receive and deliver service, we had to show how our physical health, mental health, and social service systems have been profoundly impacted by chronic and unrelenting stress that has extended for decades.

We used the concept of "parallel process" taken out of the individual context and applied to organizations as a useful way of offering a coherent framework that serves to connect different system levels showing that in a system, everything is connected to everything else and behaviors, thoughts, and feelings are mirrored at each level. The definition we use for parallel process derives from work done in industrial settings: "when two or more systems—whether these consist of individuals, groups, or organizations—have significant relationships with one another, they tend to develop similar thoughts, feelings and behaviors (p. 13) [13].

We went on to more thoroughly describe and summarize some of the impacts of chronic, toxic, traumatic stress, and adversity on individuals and groups. Given our premise that organizations are complex living systems, we next went on to explain the multiple ways in which organizations are vulnerable to the impact of trauma and chronic stress. We explored how groups respond and adapt to stress and suggested that as a result of acute and chronic organizational stress, destructive processes routinely occur within and between organizations that mirror or "parallel" the trauma-related processes for which our clients seek help. We described the social defense mechanisms such as denial, coercion, avoidance of conflict, and scapegoating that come to dominate the environment, often replacing actual service delivery or treatment. In the subsequent chapters of *Destroying Sanctuary*, we fleshed out this concept of parallel processes so that they could be named and understood within the context of our present knowledge of individual and group psychology. In the next few pages we will simply summarize some of our key conclusions. Figure 1.6 illustrates the interactive nature of these parallel processes.

Organizational Hyperarousal

We know what chronic stress does to an individual: the central nervous system changes so that the person stays in crisis mode so long that it starts to feel normal, a phenomenon called "chronic hyperarousal." The result is the development of some very bad habits. What started out as coping skills become destructive routines.

We saw similar dynamics occurring within every component of the human service delivery system. Functioning under conditions of chronic stress, repetitive trauma, and chronic crisis, the staff and the administration in many helping organizations are left feeling unsafe with their clients or even with each other. This lack of safety may present as physical violence, abusive behavior on the part of managers and/or staff, and a pervasive mistrust of the organization. A perceived lack of safety erodes trust, which is the basis for positive social

Figure 1.6 Organizational stress.

relationships. As a result, these organizations are very tightly wrapped and tensions run high. Under such unrelenting stress, helping professionals and the agencies themselves become highly reactive and readily see threat rather than opportunity, pathology rather than strength, and risk rather than reward. We called this state of chronic crisis "organizational hyperarousal."

Loss of Emotional Management

We had seen that our clients had significant difficulties managing emotions as a result of what had happened to them, and their symptoms could often be understood as methods for coping with overwhelming distress. Similarly, we saw that a core difficulty for staff members serving these clients was their own challenges in managing the constant demands for empathy, caring, concern, and tolerance—what is known as "emotional labor." Research has demonstrated that emotions are contagious and that under any conditions, human service delivery environments demand the highest levels of emotional labor from workers. Stress and trauma exacerbate those demands. The problem is that atmospheres of recurrent or constant crisis severely constrain the ability of staff to manage their own emotions or even acknowledge their emotions, and this makes it difficult to provide healing environments for their clients. Atmospheres of chronic crisis and fear contribute to poor services. Under these circumstances, conflict escalates and both relationships and problem solving suffer. We framed this situation as the loss of emotional management and containment at an organizational level and asserted that this organizational dysfunction paralleled the very problems for which the clients were seeking help.

Organizational Learning Disabilities and Organizational Amnesia

Under the conditions we described, we summarized research showing that stress interferes with a number of cognitive processes that are essential for both individual and organizational learning. Organizational memory is lost, organizational amnesia affects function, and service delivery becomes increasingly fragmented. Decision making becomes compromised and reactive so that short-sighted policy decisions are made that appear to compound existing problems. Dissent is silenced, leading to over simplification of decisions and lowered morale. When we stepped back and looked at all of these interactive and problematic processes, it was easy to see how the organization as a whole had become learning disabled at the same time that many components of the system had forgotten a wide variety of strategies and approaches that had served them well in the past. These cognitive disabilities were moving our social service system ever further from the goal of becoming "learning organizations" that could readily adapt to changing conditions.

Miscommunication, Conflict, and Organizational Alexithymia

We also saw that there were grave problems with communication networks among and between our organizations. We learned that under conditions of chronic stress, breakdowns in organizational communication networks occur. The feedback loops that are necessary for consistent and timely error correction no longer function. Without adequate networks of communication, the normal conflict that exists in human groups will escalate and increasing amounts of important information become "undiscussable"—all of the things that get discussed in the meetings-after-the meetings but never at a time when problems could actually be addressed. As these "elephants in the room" accumulate, the organization as a whole becomes increasingly alexithymic, unable to talk about the issues that are the most emotionally evocative, that are causing the most problems and that remain, therefore, unsolvable. One of the consequences of this situation is the emergence of collective disturbances that readily evolve into chronic unresolved conflict and violence.

The Uses and Abuses of Power

We recognized that as communication breaks down, errors compound, and the situation feels increasingly out of control, organizational leaders are more likely to become more controlling and authoritarian. Under these circumstances, workplace bullying is likely to increase at all levels, and the organization may become vulnerable to petty tyrants, paving the way for multiple experiences of injustice and abuse of the use of power.

As the organization becomes more hierarchical and autocratic, there is a progressive and simultaneous isolation of leaders and a "dumbing down" of staff, with an accompanying "learned helplessness" and loss of critical thinking skills. The organization and the individuals in it, become highly risk avoidant, an enormous problem since avoidance of all risk necessarily results in avoidance of all change. Efforts to empower workers may pay only lip service to true participation, a process called "bogus empowerment." In this way, power becomes steadily more centralized and bureaucratic.

Punishment, Revenge, and Organizational Injustice

We also recognized the connections between stress and the desire for more punishment. As leaders become more authoritarian and their efforts to correct problems are ineffective, organizational stress increases and the organization is likely to become more punitive in an effort to control workers and clients. Organizational practices that are perceived as unjust evoke a desire for vengeance. As in the case of the chronically stressed individual, shame, guilt, anger, and a desire for justice can combine with unfortunate consequences. When this happens, the organization may become both socially irresponsible and ethically compromised. We explored what happens when good people do bad things, including when otherwise decent people become bystanders, watch unjust behavior, and do nothing.

Unresolved Grief, Reenactment, and Decline

In light of this sequence of events, it was easy to see how chronic and unrelenting stress could wear out a system, just as the clients the systems are meant to serve became worn down, exhausted, and depressed. Exposure to trauma always means loss, even if it is the loss of invulnerability that protects us from feeling helpless. People in organizations and organizations as a whole suffer many kinds of loss. Staff and leaders depart and programs end. Neighboring systems close. Standards of care deteriorate and quality assurance standards are lowered in an attempt to deny or hide this deterioration. Over time, leaders and staff lose sight of the essential purpose of their work together and derive less and less satisfaction and meaning from the work. People begin to question whether they are actually successful at what they do or just permanently failing. When this occurs, staff members feel increasingly angry, demoralized, helpless, and hopeless about the people they are working to serve: they become "burned out." Unresolved loss increases the tendency of human beings to repeat the past and hopelessly reenact tragedy and loss, a tendency that we recognized as a major barrier to any kind of change and a source of the decline that we were seeing in individuals, in organizations, in communities, and in our society as a whole, accompanied by a failure to imagine anything else.

Trauma-Organized Systems

Regardless of whether we are talking about families, organizations, or entire systems, there are parallel similarities. Just as the encroachment of trauma into the life of an individual client is an insidious process that turns the past into a nightmare, the present into a repetitive cycle of reenactment, and the future into a terminal illness, the impact of chronic strain on an organization is insidious. As seemingly logical reactions to difficult situations pile upon each other, no one is able to truly perceive the fundamentally skewed and post-traumatic basic assumptions upon which that logic is built. As an earthquake can cause the foundations of a building to become unstable, even while the building still stands, apparently intact, chronic repetitive stress or sudden traumatic stress can destabilize the cognitive and emotional foundations of shared meaning that are necessary for a group to function and stay whole. Organizations then unwittingly reorganize themselves around their own adaptations to traumatic experience. Over time these behaviors develop into a whole system of bad habits and routines that become self-perpetuating. Organizational behavior that may have previously been understood as pathological can come to seem normal, or just the way things are, as illustrated in Figure 1.7.

Figure 1.7 Trauma-organized organizations.

The result is what we see all around us:

- lack of a clear, consistent, comprehensive, and coherent theoretical model for delivering services that can be shared by staff, clients, and families;
- lack of safety;
- communication failure and broken feedback loops between and among component parts of the system;
- conflicts between various levels of staff as to what defines treatment;
- hierarchical management structures that encourage obedience to authority but do not encourage initiative, innovative problem-solving, or direct conflict resolution;
- a relative inability to sufficiently address the enormity, frequency, and complexity of trauma-based problems in people's lives;
- only partially effective methods for dealing with aggressive acting out;
- unclear ideas about what constitutes success in these programs.

To complicate this matter further, organizations are usually under a variety of pressures deriving from fiscal, reporting, and legal concerns, many of which spring directly from social and political forces that exist in the larger environment.

From the staff's point of view, working in human services is often difficult, frustrating, and stressful. Everyone working in a caregiving environment is simultaneously leading their own life and going through their own struggles. These struggles often compound the stress of the workplace. Because of the exposure to adverse childhood conditions that so many people face, staff members are likely to have their own histories of experiences that consciously or unconsciously, for good or for ill, collide and intersect with those of the clients in their care, as illustrated in Figure 1.8. They may come to an organization with their own bad habits of thinking and relating that are then frequently reinforced by the organizational culture. Funding reductions for human services usually also result in decreases in training and supervision as well as in salaries and benefits, so the opportunity to alter problematic routines is missed.

As a result, complex parallel process interactions occur between traumatized clients, stressed staff, pressured organizations, and economic, political, and social forces in the wider environment. In this way, human service delivery systems become trauma-organized, uncannily and inadvertently replicating the very experiences that have proven to be so toxic for the clients in their care, as illustrated in Figure 1.9 [14, 15].

Sanctuary Trauma

As we pointed out earlier, the outcome for clients is "sanctuary trauma"—expecting a protective and caring environment and finding only more trauma

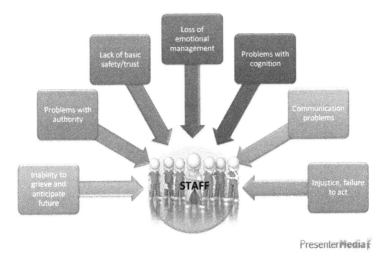

Figure 1.8 Trauma-organized staff.

and stress [16]. The result for providers of service is a collective kind of trauma as the organizations within which they work cease fulfilling a fundamental social role, that of containing anxiety in the face of suffering, defeat, uncertainty, and death. In such cases, social defense mechanisms come to dominate whatever therapeutic activity is supposed to be occurring in the social service environ-

Figure 1.9 Parallel processes.

ment, and providers tend to deny and rationalize just how bad things actually are.

Unfortunately, our social service network is functioning still largely unaware of the multiple ways in which its adaptation to chronic stress has created a state of dysfunction that in many cases seriously limits or even prohibits the recovery of individual clients and thus undermines the very mission of the system. This dysfunction damages many of the people who work within the system as well. This hurts clients, frustrates and demoralizes staff and administrators, and leads to worker burnout and the workforce crisis we are now facing. Ultimately, the inefficient or inadequate delivery of service, and the toll this takes on workers, wastes money and resources. This vicious cycle also lends itself to a worldview that the clients receiving the services are the cause of the problem and that their situations are hopeless and they cannot really be helped.

Restoring Sanctuary: Focusing on Organizational Culture

And that brings us to this book, the third part of the trilogy, which is designed to lay out a practical system for changing this situation at the deepest level within organizations—the "organizational culture." Our task has been to integrate a wide survey of existing knowledge about organizational dynamics with our understanding and experience in human service delivery environments. We hope that this expansion in knowledge will ultimately improve clinical outcomes, increase staff satisfaction and health, increase leadership competence, and enable human service delivery systems to develop an advanced technology for creating and sustaining healthier systems.

A shift in mental models is a critical first step in enabling the mental health system and its allied social service systems to make effective contributions to the healing of traumatized children, adults, and families and therefore contribute in a positive way to the overall health of the nation.

Can Computers Be a Useful Metaphor?

Mental models are the largely unconscious ideas and beliefs that structure what we think about—and what we do not consider. Mental models represent mental shortcuts and limitations. Understanding trauma, adversity, and exposure to toxic stress means changing your mental model about how the world works.

It is only when we all understand the nature of psychobiological adaptation that we are able to truly embark on creating trauma-informed cultures because doing so requires what is often radical change in thinking, behavior, and attitudes. The impact of organizational stress that we described in *Destroying Sanctuary* broadens our understanding of what it really means to have a "developmentally grounded, trauma-informed culture." In this current volume we will go much further in describing what a trauma-informed culture must include.

To even begin grasping the enormity of the shifts in thought and behavior that are required in order for organizations to be developmentally grounded, trauma-informed" systems, we need a different metaphor. We use the metaphor of computers and human brains to help guide our thoughts and to serve as a bridge between a mechanistic and living systems model of the world we live in. This shift in basic assumptions or mental models that we are going to describe in *Restoring Sanctuary* is analogous to the kind of change represented by changing "operating systems" in computers, and we all know how challenging that kind of change can be!

Hardware, Software, and Operating Systems

You don't see something until you have the right metaphor to perceive it.

Robert Stetson Shaw, American physicist, pioneer in chaos theory
As quoted in James Gleick, *Chaos: Making a New Science,* 1987,
New York:Viking, p. 262

Computers and human brains share some interesting qualities, and in fact, the brain is being used as a model for improving computer functions, just as computer technology is being used to enhance human functions. Both computers and people have memory, can learn, require energy to function, can change, and can be damaged. Computers and people have hardware and software. Hardware in a computer includes microchips, hard drives, input devices, and a motherboard. People have hardware that includes our DNA, genes, cells, and all of our organs, including our brains. This analogy shows the relationship between computer hardware and our human "hardware."

But neither computers nor people can do anything without software programming. There are basically two kinds of software: foundation software and application software. In a computer, the foundation software is called an "operating system," a master program that controls a computer's basic functions and allows other programs to run on a computer *if* they are compatible with that operating system. Operating systems are complex integrated software programs that function largely in the background of the computer, allowing many tasks to be accomplished at once, managing memory, and controlling the way the software programs of the computer works together in an integrated way. Examples of operating systems include Microsoft Corporation's various versions of Windows, Apple's Mac OS, and the open source operating system, Linux.

All the things that a computer can do, such as word processing, photography programs, and spreadsheet development, are "application software." In order to function properly, the application software must be compatible with the operating system. But this leaves us with a question: What is the "operating system" for people?

The Human Operating System: Healthy Attachment

Over the last few decades, research on the nature of attachment relationships has made it clear that for human beings, loving attachment is a fundamental requirement for healthy physical, emotional, social, and moral development. Attachment—the vital connection to other human beings that originates in the mother/child bond—is the operating system for human beings. It is the literal motherboard for human development.

We are "wired," even before birth, for attachment, but only in the last few years has the neurobiological basis of relationship been researched and the parts of the brain involved in relational development pinpointed. In order for human beings to develop properly, every child needs a primary attachment, a person who provides protection, support, security, and basic needs for food and shelter. The primary caregiver does not have to be the biological mother, of course, but in most cases today she still remains so, and therefore in some places in this book we refer to the primary caregiver as "mother." Most brain development occurs after birth and is powerfully influenced by what is going on in the environment as normal development unfolds.

The human brain is distinctive not just because of the sheer number of brain cells, but also because of the level of integration required to perform complex tasks. It is not simply that children have smaller bodies. From birth until well into the early 20s, our brains are becoming integrated, meaning vastly interconnected. The attachment relationship between caregiver and child determines how smoothly that interconnection occurs.

The grandfather of attachment studies, John Bowlby, called this primary operating system the "internal working model" long before computers became a useful analogy for human functioning. But similarly, he saw this internal working model as determining much of what would go on throughout individuals' lives, how they would relate to others, what they would remember and forget, how they would manage emotions, how they viewed themselves, and what kind of parent they were likely to be many years later [17].

The Bad News: Trauma Is the "Virus" That Disrupts Attachment

Like people, computers can get "sick." A computer virus is a small piece of software that piggy backs onto real programs. Each time the program runs, the virus has a chance to spread and to wreak havoc on the entire computer. Computer viruses masquerade as other things and are transmitted through personal contact. They are hard to diagnosis, difficult to treat, malevolent, and contagious. They may lie dormant for years and then attack the system. As anyone who has been violated by a computer virus knows, they represent a form of violence since they are created with the intention of doing harm to others.

A useful way of understanding trauma and its impact on human beings is to recognize that trauma is analogous to a computer virus. It fundamentally disrupts the human attachment system in a wide variety of ways, and that disruption can sabotage healthy functioning.

Like computer viruses, traumatic experiences affect human systems unpredictably, are contagious, and spread through our interpersonal networks. In a computer, a viral infection may slow down the system or may disable it entirely. Similarly, the disruption caused by trauma can wreak havoc on many of the "applications" we use to adapt to the world, applications such as learning, emotional management, memory, the capacity for empathy, and moral judgment. Depending on the nature and characteristics of the virus, it may interrupt specific applications or disrupt the entire functioning of the system.

A computer virus infection may be immediately evident or it may be timed to go off at some time in the future like a delayed detonation. The effects of trauma and disrupted attachment can likewise be transferred silently and insidiously intergenerationally, and the burgeoning field of epigenetics informs us that these effects may even be carried in our genome [18]. And like a computer with a virus, an infected human can pass this infection on to other people in the form of interpersonal violence, thereby infecting the operating systems of countless other individuals.

Since healthy brain development is based on healthy attachment, having loving, caring, supportive, and structured experiences with caregivers in early life is like loading good antivirus software as soon as you buy a new computer. Most of us are born with all the necessary hardware in place for our brains to develop in a healthy and successful fashion. Like a firewall, a loving family cannot prevent all possible intrusive damage to a young person, but it is a good start. But just as a loving, stable family provides a good firewall for the child, families that are unstable, violent, or unavailable to sufficiently protect the child from harm leave the child vulnerable to the viral impact of trauma and adversity.

A virus can impact different computers differently based on a number of factors. Some computers have superior antivirus software that limits the adverse impact of the virus. Similarly, different people may have very different reactions to the same level of adversity based on a variety of factors, such as genetics, family history, level of support, level of understanding, or sense of self-efficacy.

Organizational Culture: The Organizational Operating System

Like computers and people, organizations also have operating systems. While computers have a program and humans have attachment, organizations have networks of social relationships as their operating systems. The operating system, how people relate to each other in an organization, is embedded within the organizational culture. Organizational culture arises spontaneously whenever groups of people come together for any length of time and focus on tasks long enough to create common traditions, rites, and history. It is binding in that it determines how people enter the organization, survive within it, and learn to solve problems. There are close and interactive relationships between individual identity and organizational identity, as we will learn in future chapters. The organizational culture has both conscious and unconscious components, and both elements get transmitted to new organizational members. Organizational culture determines strategies, goals, modes of operation, and the ways in which values are actually practiced [19].

Changing Operating Systems: Developmentally Grounded and Trauma-Informed

Using our computer analogy, the usual level of focus for treatment is at the level of "application software," which determines how people change cognitions, change behavior, and manage emotions. But for people to heal from chronic and repetitive traumatic experience, this level of change is often not enough. They may need to change at a deeper level. This means changing their operating system, what is generally referred to as "character" or "personality," while building a new capacity to attach to others. Those kinds of change are possible but usually require a significant investment of time and resources.

This is why research over the last few decades pertaining to the impact of trauma and disrupted attachment offers a different paradigm for defining what we mean by "treatment." Particularly in the more complex cases that populate our mental health, substance abuse, child welfare, and criminal justice systems, treatment as usual is not enough. These clients will need trauma-specific treatment approaches to resolve the post-traumatic symptoms. But these too, although necessary, are not sufficient. This is why we emphasize that not only must our systems become trauma-informed but they must also be developmentally grounded—grounded in all the knowledge we now have about the complex unfolding of development and what goes wrong when attachment is disrupted. Providing trauma-specific, integrative, and trauma-informed care that is developmentally grounded means changing the operating system for treatment itself.

The Impossibility of Engineering Human Service Delivery Change

Embedded in the history of virtually all human service delivery systems are many debates about how services should be delivered, what constitutes help, and how each institution should be structured and managed. Many attempts have been made and are being made to alter this situation, but unfortunately, most organizational change methods are based on the idea of "social engineering," which assumes a cascading intention from the top to the bottom of a hierarchy as leaders tell everyone else what to do, and they do it.

Unfortunately, according to organizational change research, 70% of these change efforts fail. So dramatic is the failure of past methodology that organizational development investigators have declared that *social engineering as a context is obsolete"* (p. 13) [20]. They reason that organizations are not machines but rather living systems and cannot be predictably engineered, and that *"living systems isn't a metaphor for how human institutions operate. It's the way it is"* (p. 7) [20].

Why Sanctuary? Why Now?: A Public Health Approach

Nobody's Coming

As a result of the destructive parallel processes we have discussed in *Destroying Sanctuary*, many people who work every day at trying to improve the lives of others are themselves drowning in crises. While speaking to an audience of educators and social service workers in Philadelphia, Geoffrey Canada, the change agent who has created the Harlem's Children Zone, urged us to address our problems locally because if we are waiting for someone in higher authority to come and solve the problems of Philadelphia's families, he warned, "nobody's coming."

His remarks rang true. If those of us in the helping professions wait for some imagined future time when our work is finally appreciated by the larger culture, when emotional labor is valued as a vital part of individual and cultural health, when the problems of health care delivery are remedied, and when the haves in our society recognize that a ruined world will be ruined for their children's children, just as it will be ruined for everyone else, we might wait forever. As we wait, even more knowledge will have uselessly slipped away and more lives will have been needlessly wasted. The bottom line is that we are going to have to fix our organizations ourselves. And we are going to have to do it with the resources we already have because "nobody's coming," and even if they are, they are probably bringing us more regulations and paperwork, not more resources.

Change may not be as impossible as it seems if we take our cues from the examples of recovery provided by individual clients who have been exposed to repetitive adversity and toxic stress since childhood. It is clear that people can change their life trajectory after overwhelming events. In fact, one of the useful definitions of what makes something traumatic is that it *does* inevitably change your life. The challenge after such an event is finding a pathway away from that traumatic event that leads to better rather than worse outcomes.

Shifting to Developmentally Grounded, Trauma-Informed Systems

The current operating system for the human service delivery system that we described in *Destroying Sanctuary* is outdated, mechanistic, and inappropriate to human health and well-being. This helps to explain why there are so many chronic clashes between our organizations and the individuals who comprise them. In order to adequately address the needs of the traumatized clients who fill the ranks of our human service delivery system, we need a new operating system, what is referred to here as a "developmentally grounded, trauma-informed" operating system for human service delivery organizations. Like attachment in humans, social relationships serve as the basis for organizational culture or organizational operating systems.

Our experimental laboratory for creating developmentally grounded, trauma-informed system change is the human service delivery system because we have a deep understanding of the dynamics of that system [21]. Within our health, mental health, and social service system reside the most vulnerable and injured members of our population. If we can figure out how to help them to heal, then the lessons we learn are probably applicable to all of us. If we can figure out how to help our organizations to function in a healthier, life-supporting way, then those lessons should likewise be applicable to all of our social sectors. We call that realistic and achievable system the "Sanctuary Model." In the original Sanctuary programs, the clients taught the staff what kind of environment they needed to heal from the multiple misfortunes that had beset them. This work inspires our belief that we can change and improve our systems of care in spite of all that has happened to social services in recent years.

The Good News: Most Human Dysfunction Is Preventable

It's truly amazing what happens when we stop blaming people and instead empathize with them and share with each other the scientific information we have now about how disrupted attachment, exposure to adversity and toxic stress, and trauma and allostatic load affect people, all people. It becomes far easier for us to open up to the possibility that although what has happened wasn't our fault, it is now our responsibility to prevent further injury and to create the opportunity for our existing injuries to heal.

Given the number of people in America and around the world who have experienced intergenerational trauma and exposure to significant adversity, the outlook for healing can seem pretty dismal. Results from the landmark Adverse Childhood Experiences Study and the subsequent incorporation of that study into states' health survey data indicate that a majority of Americans have been exposed to childhood adversity—in the wealthiest country in the world [22–24]. The result is millions of people in every walk of life whose lives have become trauma-organized.

We can now connect the costly individual and social problems that confront us. Child maltreatment, school failure, delinquency and crime, family failure, most mental illness, substance abuse, homelessness, domestic violence, community violence, poor job performance, and many chronic health problems are all related to childhood adversity. That means that these are problems that we can prevent. Knowing what we know now, it is entirely possible to *imagine* a future in which these multiple chronic, relentless, and seemingly insoluble problems of humanity have been eliminated. It is our choice. But prevention means taking a public health approach to the effects of stress, particularly to the forms of stress that accompany exposure to any kind of violence.

The idea of "universal precautions" is a public health idea that recognizes that everyone is a potential carrier of infections, so before every healthcare intervention, it's important to wash your hands. Likewise, everyone is a potential carrier of the germ of violence, so there are important things to know and ways to behave that apply to everyone [25]. We will see that this is the way we use the Sanctuary Commitments—as universal precautions that everyone in an organization must employ to prevent the emergence of violence.

Imagination is not enough. Individual change is not enough. Humanity has reached a crisis point, a critical choice point. Can we use the rapidly accumulating scientific knowledge about the real causes of human-inflicted suffering before we self-destruct? This is the key choice that every individual trauma survivor at some point in his or her life confronts. That is the choice point at which we have all arrived.

We do not have the time to wait for individual change. Destruction always requires less energy, less creativity, and less collective action than creation. We need to find *systemic* methods of creating the tipping point in favor of fulfilling the vision that has always been a subtext of human thought, not a utopian vision of heavenly promise but a realistic vision of adequate human problem-solving. True prevention means that we have to address change at the level of culture, not just at the individual level. There are, of course, many levels of culture change that are possible: global, national, regional, local, organizational, familial. Our work focuses on organizational change at the level of organizational culture.

The Sanctuary Model: A Parallel Process of Recovery

Addressing the theoretical and practical complexity necessary for organizational change is where the Sanctuary Model comes in. The Sanctuary Model is not a trauma-specific intervention. It functions underneath all the other

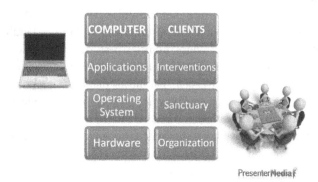

PresenterMedia

Figure 1.10 Sanctuary: a new operating system for organizations.

things that go on in a treatment program, all the approaches, kinds of therapy, techniques, and practices, as long as those are compatible with the Sanctuary Model's operating system (Figure 1.10). It is designed to change the operating system of the organization, that is, the organizational culture. It integrates long-established but often forgotten good organizational practice with the newer sciences of attachment, trauma, and interpersonal neuroscience.

The Sanctuary Model is designed to create the context within which groups of people in an organization are encouraged and supported to make what are sometimes radical shifts in the very foundations of the way they think, what they feel, how they communicate, and how they practice. The current challenge for everyone in human services is to consider how we unwittingly, and often in the name of science, erect barriers to recovery that prevent self-organizing change in the individual life of clients and in our organizations as well. We must wrestle with the fact that our diagnostic categories often shame clients from the moment they enter care. Our rigid hierarchies frequently prevent participation and innovation when what we actually need are staff members who can exercise almost constant creativity in order not to be drawn into traumatic replays of previous negative life experiences in the lives of the clients we serve.

Confronted with the reality that our systems of care are alive, that they are continually developing, AND that they are currently trauma-organized, it is clear that a model of intervention must (1) be easily understood by all staff and clients, (2) be adaptable to a variety of settings, (3) stress the need for empowerment of all organizational members and improved integration of services, and (4) stress the need for constant creativity and imagination.

The explicit assumption of the Sanctuary Model is that most of the clients who present to human service delivery organizations have been exposed to significant adversity, chronic stress, and frequently overwhelming trauma. Despite this exposure, they have the capacity to heal from these injuries and change the trajectories of their lives, but they frequently need help to do so. Most importantly, they cannot heal within the context of traumatizing or traumatized organizations that may actually create more instead of less pathology. The goal of the Sanctuary Model is to facilitate the development of an organizational culture that can contain, manage, and help transform the terrible life experiences that have molded, and often deformed, the clients in care. But no one person can change an organizational culture, at least not for the better. Living systems are comprised of living people who tend to support what they help to create and who fail to support change efforts that exclude them.

We believe that parallel process can work to our benefit. If organizations, and the staff who work in them, can become healthier, they will have a more positive impact on the clients who come to them seeking help. Although many organizations may be trauma-organized at this point, they can choose to respond differently. They can choose to become truly trauma-informed. The ability to respond to chronic stress and collective trauma is significantly improved if a group of people can pull together and move in the same direction. But to achieve unified action on a consistent basis, people have to be on the same page. This means they have to share a body of knowledge and a system of values and then commit to holding each other accountable for those values. Getting on the same page, despite the diversity of experiences, education, culture, ethnicity, gender identity, sexual orientation, and age in every setting, requires universal training in psychobiology, trauma theory, therapeutic relationships, individual, group, and organizational dynamics, cultural competence, and attachment theory. But it also'means that we need processes that allow for "knowledge creation," the formation of new ideas, as well as ongoing collaborative conversations about how to systematically apply that new knowledge.

Our method for accomplishing these complex tasks is the Sanctuary Model, an evidence-supported plan, process, and method for creating trauma-informed, developmentally grounded, democratic, nonviolent cultures that are far better equipped to engage in the innovative treatment planning and implementation that are necessary to adequately respond to the extremely complex and deeply embedded injuries that our clients have sustained. Our imagined goal is that we help to create a parallel process of recovery for everyone simultaneously: clients, families, staff, organizations—and maybe even our society.

Chapter Summaries

In Chapter 2 we will begin to outline our vision of health for individuals and for organizations as a way of introducing the basic elements of the Sanctuary

Model. Beginning with Chapter 3, we elaborate on the Sanctuary Commitments, chapter-by-chapter, as a way of putting some flesh on the bones of what we mean by organizational culture. Just as we started this book with a vision, every chapter begins with a vision of that particular Sanctuary Commitment being fulfilled within an organization and a story that illustrates that commitment in some way. We then describe what we mean by that particular commitment, the special relevance that the commitment has for trauma-informed practice, and the implications for leadership, and we end each chapter with the current Sanctuary Toolkit elements relevant to that commitment.

Chapter 3 begins with the Commitment to Growth and Change, in which we explore the concept of "traumatic reenactment" in some detail, since we see rescripting reenactment as the key to change. Chapter 4 covers the Commitment to Democracy, which necessitates an exploration of what we mean by the word "democracy" in the Sanctuary Model and why democracy is essential to healthy organizational functioning. Chapter 5 explores the idea and the practice of the Commitment to Nonviolence, including what safety means, how violence emerges in a group, and how we can protect what we have called "social immunity." The focus of Chapter 6 is on the Commitment to Emotional Intelligence, which details some of what we consider to be essential in operating an organization that respects those who do the difficult "emotional labor" that is the hallmark of working in human service delivery environments. Chapter 7 describes the Commitment to Social Learning and all that goes into creating a living-learning environment. Chapter 8 explores what we mean by a Commitment to Open Communication, with an emphasis on organizational transparency and both recognizing and responding to collective disturbances. Chapter 9 stresses the Commitment to Social Responsibility and all that the term means, including the weighing of individual versus group needs and the pursuit of just organizations. The book ends with our lessons learned and concluding remarks in Chapter 10. We hope that by the end of this book we will have equipped you with a different and more empowering way to think about how you are going to help change your own organizational culture in an effort that we hope will change the larger social culture that connects us all.

Chapter 2

Turning Imagination into Reality: A Vision of Health

SUMMARY: *In Chapter 1, we asked you to use your imagination to envision a better world. Now we want you to use your powers of imagination as we describe what we think of as healthy people and healthy organizations. We will begin to provide you with a framework for how to move from imagination to reality by describing the key Sanctuary Model concepts and the implementation process we have used to help hundreds of organizations become healthier, more productive, trauma-informed, and developmentally grounded.*

"Healthy" and "Normal"

We see strong parallels between the relationships that create healthy attachment in children and the relationships that create healthy functioning in organizations. Similarly, the relationships between leaders in an organization and those working in the organization parallel our original parent-child relationships. We are fully aware that staff people are not children and should not be treated like children, but in reality it is quite common for familial relationships to be played out in the workplace and good leaders embody many of the same qualities of good parents.

In our society, there appears to be a reluctance to define what health is. By "health," we don't mean "normal." The word "normal" means conforming to an average. Our experience tells us that for the most part, there is an increasing level of divergence between what is considered normal and what is actually healthy. The World Health Organization (WHO) defines health as *"a state of complete physical, mental and social well-being and not merely the absence of disease or infirmity"* (p. 100) [26]. Another useful definition is *"a state of optimal regulation and adaptive functioning of body, mind and relationships"* that depends on the integration of these functions (p. A1–35) [27]. The Center for the Developing Child at Harvard University has defined health as *"more than merely the absence of disease—it is an evolving human resource that helps children and adults adapt to the challenges of everyday life, resist infections, cope with*

Universals	Individual	Organization	Sanctuary Commitment
The Inevitability of Change	Integrated physical, psychological, social and moral development; ability to move through loss and anticipate future	Purpose and mission	Growth & Change
Managing Power	Manage personal power without abuse	Participatory and democratic	Democracy
Envisioning Safety	Safety and security	Safety and security	Nonviolence
Emotional Intelligence	Full range of emotional expression; able to manage emotions	Emotionally well regulated	Emotional Intelligence
Learning All the Time	Love learning and adaptable	Real-world classrooms; adaptive	Social Learning
The Constancy of Communication	Communicate constantly, openly, honestly	Transparency; respect process and feedback	Open Communication
Justice and the Common Good	Responsible for self and others; fair and concerned with social justice	Encourage individual and social responsibility; just and concerned with social justice	Social Responsibility

Figure 2.1 Signs of health.

adversity, feel a sense of personal well-being, and interact with their surroundings in ways that promote successful development" (p. 2) [28]. These definitions include many determinants of health in the social and economic environment, including social status, social support networks, education, working conditions, and healthy child development. It is now recognized that nations with the most positive indicators of population health, such as longer life expectancy and lower infant mortality, typically have higher levels of wealth and lower levels of income inequality [28–30].

In the following section, we will describe some of what characterizes health in individuals and, in parallel, in organizations as a way of introducing the Sanctuary Commitments that are the foundation of the Sanctuary Model. The Sanctuary Commitments form the value system to which any organization that aspires to become trauma-informed must subscribe. Figure 2.1 summarizes what we define as healthy for individuals and for organizations and the Sanctuary Commitment that is relevant for maintaining health.

The Inevitability of Change

Healthy People Adapt to Changing Conditions

The entire course of child development is one of constant adaptation and change aimed at the unfolding of individual human potential and the continuation of the species. Within the caring scope of his or her earliest attachment, the child will have the first experience of loss and all of the emotional pain that accompanies loss for human beings. Every new developmental experience means learning something new and giving up something old. This constant adaptation to changing conditions is one of humanity's most difficult and enduring challenges. A child is constantly undergoing a process of "transformation," and although that's a nice word, usually associated with the beautiful unfolding of a butterfly, rarely do we look at it from the point of view of the challenges that confront the caterpillar.

These transformations are both psychological and physical as the brain goes through major periods of reorganization in the transition from infancy to toddler, from toddler to school-age child, from school-age child to adolescent, from adolescent to adult. As the organizational theorist Russell Ackoff humorously noted about adults, *"The only thing harder than starting something new is stopping something old"* (p. 17) [31].

Over the course of childhood, each child learns to cope with loss and adapt to change. In the interaction with loving caregivers, the grieving child will be comforted, the feelings that typically accompany loss, sadness, anger, helplessness, and despair, will be recognized, respected, and supported, and the child will be comforted. Family members will encourage the child to use the human perspective on time as part of that comfort, helping the child envision a future, recover from the loss, let go, and move on in time. In this process the child will learn how to adapt, roll with life's inequities, anticipate consequences, and look forward to what the future holds.

Healthy Organizations Have a Purpose and Can Adapt

A healthy organization begins with a strong sense of mission and purpose. There needs to be a sense that the organizational mission matters and contributes something to the greater good so that members feel they are part of something bigger than themselves. Even in businesses where the primary goal is to make a profit, there needs to be a sense that the organization's efforts make a contribution to the well-being of the greater society. If purpose and direction are lacking, it becomes easy for an organization to lose its way and make ethical compromises.

In addition to having a purposeful mission, a healthy organization has some sense of vision. There is a clear understanding about what the organization does and who it serves, but there is also a strong sense of what it can and should become. There is always something new to strive for, something more its members can learn. A healthy organization has a strong future orientation and a drive to learn, change, and grow.

Leaders in such an organization are willing to change if the strategies they are using are not yielding the desired results. They are clear about what they are in business to accomplish, and they are willing to make the adjustments needed to achieve desired goals and become the best they can be and help others do the same.

A healthy organization realizes that change is constant and that the organization must adapt to meet the demands of a changing world. This is particularly true in human services, where our mission is targeted at helping clients make meaningful changes in their lives. In a healthy organization there is a fundamental understanding that all change entails some level of risk, and leaders must be willing to tolerate and accept a reasonable level of risk. At the same time, a healthy organization realizes that change is difficult and that all change is accompanied by loss. When we ask members to change, they are likely to feel unsettled, threatened, and uncomfortable. Healthy organizations acknowledge these feelings but push for change nonetheless.

Commitment to Growth and Change (Chapter 3)

People who seek help from our social institutions do so because they need to change. In Sanctuary, we recognize that our primary goal is to bring about change. We fully recognize, however, that all change involves loss and that neither individuals nor organizations are comfortable addressing the issue of loss.

The human ability to predict, and therefore avoid danger, is an evolutionary adaptation that has served us well in the past. However, life seems to be constantly presenting us with paradoxical choices and at a certain difficult-to-define point, our search for stability and predictability becomes itself pathological and maladaptive. When a situation demands change, we must engage powerful forces and allow new information into our systems, but these are inherently destabilizing and unpredictable.

An organization that chooses to adopt the Sanctuary Model makes a *Commitment to Growth and Change* because as individuals and as organizations we must find ways to manage the anxiety associated with change while allowing, encouraging, and even propelling change. This means that as a whole system we must constantly juggle the forces of stability and change, risk and reward, creativity and unpredictability.

Managing Power

Healthy People Value Diversity and Participation

Our children will have to survive in a world of increasing diversity, not homogeneity, as we become a globally connected species. Therefore, parents must teach their children the skills necessary to survive and thrive in an interconnected and networked world. Children must learn to listen to other people, integrate ideas and concepts, negotiate and compromise, and learn to recognize that there is no single absolute truth in any situation, but only the shared process of seeking truth. Children growing up in modern Western societies are constantly being influenced by many different people, and those influences continue throughout adulthood. Acquisition of such complex skills begins in early childhood as the parents listen to the child's input and respect the child's point of view while still asserting their own. Parents teach their children that there are limits to one's individual strivings in interaction with others and that power is to be used, not abused.

The parent-child relationship provides the first experiences with mutual respect and power differentials that the child will encounter throughout his or her life. These experiences lay the groundwork for all subsequent authority relationships, including authority with oneself and authority with others. If the parents are very authoritarian, then children are likely to imitate command and control strategies in social interactions with others as they mature. If the parents are more democratic and participatory, while still exercising appropriate parental authority, then these are the traits children will model their behavior on later in life.

Healthy Organizations Are Democratic

In a healthy organization, decisions are made with as much input as possible from the parties that will be affected by the decision. To achieve this, leaders must be willing to share power, listen deeply, and incorporate feedback into the planning process. Empirically evaluating results and feeding that information back into the system is the basic practice of science. It is time for human service delivery organizations to function in a more scientific, results-oriented manner. To do this, all members need to feel that their opinions matter and that their participation in decision making, monitoring, and evaluating progress is important and useful.

In a healthy organization, leaders understand that not all members will feel the same degree of comfort with sharing ideas and participating in key organizational processes. Issues of race, gender identity, sexual orientation, age, education, role, and experience may influence the ways people express themselves. Special efforts and invitations will sometimes need to be made to marginalized groups in order to ensure full involvement. Healthy organizations recognize that the best decisions emerge out of complex, diverse participatory processes that engage people's creativity and capacity for innovation. Creating a climate that encourages and supports such emergence is a requirement of good leadership. Healthy organizations, like healthy parents, promote and support leaders who can balance power and responsibility and who are able to discern when to gather more input and when to make a decision.

The subject of power—who has it, who doesn't, and how it is used and abused—comes up for open discussion in healthy organizations. Good leaders guard against the tendency to exert overbearing control when problems arise instead of seeking out consensus-building approaches.

Commitment to Democracy (Chapter 4)

There are a number of reasons why in Sanctuary we insist on the embrace of democratic processes. Democracy is the most successful method of nonviolence that groups of people have ever evolved. Even groups as large as nations do not engage in armed combat against each other when they are practicing democracy [32]. Democracy is designed to minimize the abusive use of power and level the command hierarchy that so easily emerges in groups of people who are under stress [33]. When we use the word "democracy" in Sanctuary terms, we do not mean the simple act of voting; instead, we mean an attitude, an underlying organizational philosophy, what others have termed "deep democracy" or "strong democracy."

In a Sanctuary organization making the *Commitment to Democracy*, a number of people with different backgrounds, training experiences, knowledge bases, and roles are brought together with a common goal to help the people in their care. The complex problems presented to them require complex solutions that are more likely to emerge in participatory, respectful, and responsible environments. In the Sanctuary Model we see the leveling of hierarchy as a critical component to creating and sustaining a healthy environment that allows an organization to share common goals and methods for reaching those goals.

Envisioning Safety

Healthy People Are Safe and Secure

Every child needs the sense of safety and security provided by a stable, secure mothering relationship to use as the scaffolding for further neuroregulatory development. In the early days of life, mothering will largely focus on attending to the child's physical safety, but over the course of development a child's safety needs change. The child's sense of psychological safety is beginning to form at birth once the physical separation between mother and child has occurred. At that point, the child begins the long process of developing his or her own separate identity and self-functions including self-esteem, self-confidence, self-discipline, and self-control, all of which promote psychological safety.

Human babies begin interacting socially as soon as they are born. They are imitating others within the first hour of birth [34]. Beginning with a trusting relationship with his or her mother and then in interaction with other family members, the young child will begin to develop a sense of what it means to be socially safe and the skills necessary to promote and sustain interpersonal relationships. This basic sense of safety and security predicts outcomes far into the future, including how capable the person is going to be in protecting his or her own children. When people feel safe within themselves and safe with others, they do not engage in violence— any kind of violence.

Children must also learn what is right and wrong by the definitions of their culture, as well as learn how to make moral decisions for themselves in the complex situations that will inevitably occur over time. As soon as the mother begins to teach the child what to do and not do, say and not say, the child's early sense of moral safety is being laid down. As research has shown, the roots of morality are innate, based in our fundamental relational neurobiology and developed over time in the context of social relationships [35].

Healthy Organizations Are Safe

Healthy organizations are inherently safe places in which to live, work, and do business. This does not mean that bad things never happen. But when a high premium is placed on safety by everyone in the environment, efforts are made to align policies, procedures, practices, and systems to ensure the well-being of all stakeholders. Organizational leaders make efforts to build trusting relationships with staff by supporting staff's best efforts, helping them acquire new skills and competencies, being honest and direct, and cultivating a sense of mission and community. The focus on safety is not limited to physical safety but includes psychological, social, and moral safety as well. People feel safe to say what is on their minds, be who they are, and trust that others have their best interests at heart. High levels of trust ensure that members will identify threats, problems, and conflicts before they erupt into violence.

In a healthy organization, leaders are aware of their own vulnerabilities and challenges. They use power to advance the organization's mission, not their own personal agenda, and they never abuse the power that is conferred upon them. Breaches in safety are taken seriously and become part of an open dialogue in an effort to guarantee that safety is restored. Innovation is abundant, and members are willing to take reasonable risks because it is safe to do so. Change is likely to be seen as an opportunity rather than a threat in a safe organization.

Commitment to Nonviolence (Chapter 5)

A *Commitment to Nonviolence* is a necessary part of a Sanctuary organization. We live in a divided, violent world, and as a species we are increasingly ill-adapted to survive while our continued existence threatens the survival of every other species on the planet. We have not yet truly come to terms with our primeval, biologically based inclinations to retaliate whenever we are injured. We now know a great deal about the nature and structure of violence, enough to conclude that progress in humankind has been made through the gradual development of the ability to manage power effectively without violence. Human setbacks and failures occur when we do not.

As the World Health Organization has made clear, violence is preventable and should be viewed as a major public health concern [36]. In the Sanctuary Model, when we refer to violence we mean all types of violence—physical, psychological, social, and moral; self-directed, interpersonal, and collective forms of violence. Figure 2.2 illustrates the relational, interactive nature of all forms of violence.

Similarly, in the Sanctuary Model we recognize that safety does not lie solely in the physical domain. For human beings to truly feel safe, they must be physically, psychologically, socially, and morally safe. This requires a dedication to creating nonviolent environments that define violence and nonviolence very broadly and see the pursuit of consistent nonviolence as essential to human survival.

The simple fact is that we can no longer allow the primitive origins of our biologically based systems to determine our present and future actions. We can no longer continue to do what often feels very natural. Helping individual victims and perpetrators of violence to heal provides us with the human laboratories for organizational healing; likewise, learning how to heal within the context of our groups lays the groundwork for social healing. It's all about parallel processes, the parallel processes of recovery that require a Commitment to Nonviolence.

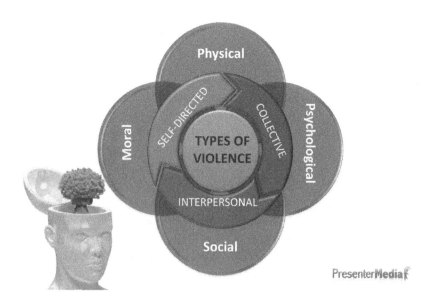

Figure 2.2 Types of violence.

Emotional Intelligence

Healthy People Can Manage Their Emotions

Before we have thought processes, we have emotions. Hard-wired into our brains and bodies, emotions provide us with the first information that we have about the world, what to avoid and what to approach, what to like and not like, what to fear and not fear, what we need to survive. Initially, babies only have emotional on-off switches. Screaming one moment, gurgling with pleasure the next, it takes many years for human beings to learn to cope with emotional arousal. Ultimately, we must learn enough emotional control so that we can thrive in our culture while not being so emotionally controlled that it interferes with the capacity to establish and maintain relationships. By the time we are adults, we need to be able to consistently self-manage our emotional states.

The infant and early childhood relationship with mother provides the early context for emotional management. The child's mother must fine-tune a balance between tolerance of emotion, support, and limit-setting, a sequence that varies from child to child and across different ages. Children must depend on caregivers in the first months and years of life to help them manage overwhelming emotions, particularly those aroused by threats such as fear, anger, and shame, all of which are a natural accompaniment of learning about the world. Over time, the brain weaves together the elements of experience into a cohesive whole. When all goes well, the mother begins the process that other adults continue, helping the child to interact in a stable and secure way with his or her environment, using emotions to provide a basis for valuing what is worthy and unworthy in the world, ultimately informing but not dominating thought and action.

Healthy Organizations Are Emotionally Well Regulated

A healthy organization is able to contain and manage the difficult and distressing emotions of the people who comprise the organization. Fear, anger, anxiety, grief, shame, and frustration are unavoidable feelings in all of our work lives. In human services, these feelings can be exacerbated by our interactions with clients who may have extreme difficulties in managing their emotions. A healthy organization accepts that distressing emotions are inevitable and creates the space and time for people to be able to talk about, and recover from, the challenges that trigger such emotions.

Because of the organization's future orientation and the understanding that all change is accompanied by loss, a healthy organization not only makes it possible for people to discuss these feelings, it makes such conversations mandatory. Leaders in healthy organizations consistently model emotional intelligence and encourage healthy expression of emotions. Leaders understand and appreciate the impact of emotional labor on caregivers and provide the support necessary to be successful. Feelings are contagious, and if there are no avenues for the healthy expression of emotions, feelings will be expressed in ways that can reduce productivity and destroy morale. A healthy organization is one in which emotions are recognized, discussed, and managed while ensuring that the organization's mission remains in clear sight at all times. In an emotionally intelligent workplace, there is a general recognition that stress and unmanaged conflict can easily dominate a work environment unless there are adequate conflict management resources. A healthy organization is emotionally intelligent and encourages its members to be emotionally intelligent as well.

Commitment to Emotional Intelligence (Chapter 6)

Conscious awareness and rational thought are only fragments of what is happening within the individual and the organization at any point in time. Imagine that you are in a very large room and you have no idea how large the room actually is because it is dark and all you have is a small flashlight. When you turn on the flashlight and the light picks out an object ahead of you, that point of light is all you can see. The spot of light represents our consciousness and the room, which may actually be of infinite dimensions, represents the rest of reality, most of which remains a mystery, shrouded in darkness.

We all come into the world with a biologically based emotional system that becomes attuned to others throughout the course of our early attachment experiences and through which we evaluate our experience. In Sanctuary, the *Commitment to Emotional Intelligence* establishes the critical goal of constantly working together to make that which is unconscious conscious and to manage emotions that threaten to overwhelm our capacity to think while integrating emotional information into our decision making. The clients in our care often enter our service environments engaging in destructive behaviors that affect themselves and others, but their feelings, their behaviors, and the motivation behind these are largely unknown to them. We must help them become known to themselves and to us. To do this as staff, we must become known to each other and ourselves. We must always be curious about what behavior *means*.

Learning All the Time

Healthy People Love Learning and Are Able to Adapt to Changing Conditions

A great leap forward occurred when mammals evolved from earlier forms of life because mammals have the capacity to learn. As we have evolved, humans have become increasingly complex, instinctive forces have become less dominant, and learned experience has assumed a greater influence on behavior. We have the longest period of helplessness of any species and take the longest time to develop into our adult form. This prolonged period of immaturity is necessary because of the complexity of our brain development.

Human babies are utterly helpless at birth because most of the "wiring" of the brain occurs after birth. We come into the world with twice as many neurons (brain cells) as we will ultimately have. Eliminating half of these brain cells is a natural process called "pruning" that occurs in early childhood. Genetics determines that this process of pruning occurs, but the actual shape that the brain takes, what connects to what, and the strength of each connection are determined by what is going on in the young child's environment [37].

Beginning at birth, caregivers must help children learn about the world around them and how to be safe in that world, balancing learning and risk and altering the boundaries of that risk as children experiment with the world and learn from those experiments. The experiences children have must match each child's capacity to cope as his or her coping skills expand over time. In order for children's cognitive abilities to unfold, they must be protected from being overwhelmed by emotions they are not yet prepared to deal with, yet their emotional system must be stimulated enough to provoke learning.

Healthy Organizations Are Real-World Classrooms

A healthy organization is a learning organization, one that learns from its successes and failures and grasps the notion that all of its staff and clients are both students and teachers. In a healthy organization, we are all capable of using our experiences to both learn and instruct. To really become a learning organization, there must be a willingness to not only tolerate but also embrace dissent and hear different ideas and points of view. In such an organization leaders are not only willing to listen to dissenting voices, but they actually seek out and invite disagreement and multiple points of view.

In a healthy organization, there is a willingness to continually hold what we do up against what we believe and to work tirelessly to close gaps between the two. Additionally, such organizations continually assess what staff and clients need and take necessary steps to meet those needs. Similarly, there is a willingness and openness to learn from others outside of the organization and integrate best practices into the organization's practice repertoire.

Commitment to Social Learning (Chapter 7)

As living organisms, we are designed to *learn* from our mistakes in order to get increasingly better at making choices that help and do not harm the whole. It is therefore vital that we constantly create for each other *learning opportunities* that reduce the likelihood of recurrent mistakes and that increase the likelihood of growth, innovation, and maturation.

However, important as it is to constantly learn from our mistakes, learning consumes energy, and it is in our best interest, as living beings with limited life spans, to make as few mistakes as possible. We can reduce the odds of making mistakes by drawing on the knowledge, experience, and wisdom of a diverse group of other people.

In Sanctuary we describe methods to create safety between and among people, sufficient safety to allow us to take risks that are necessary for change to happen; to learn from the mistakes that inevitably follow at least some of those risks; and to reduce the harm to the whole, whether that whole is the body of an individual, the social body of the organization, the natural environment, or the world as a whole. We do not provide easy solutions because there are none. There is no how-to cookbook for Sanctuary. We are attempting to create organizations that can successfully learn from experience and creatively apply those lessons to the needs of the future.

The Constancy of Communication

Healthy Human Beings Communicate Constantly, Verbally and Nonverbally

The ability to communicate with others is innate. As we mentioned earlier, babies begin initiating imitative behavior not long after birth as the mirror neuron system in the brain is activated by other people [38]. Initially, communication is dominated by emotion, gesture, bodily responses and sensations, images, sounds, and smells. The brain develops from the bottom up; circuits build on circuits. So, a baby's attention to sounds and babbling speech, listening to words and the way they are being said, is laying the groundwork for the development of language skills, reading and writing, and adult communication skills.

The mother is the first great communicator for the child. In what has been described as the "serve and return" relationship between the infant and mother, the baby is learning the rudiments, the basic building blocks of communication [39]. This flow of information back and forth must be both open and bounded. Communication flow is necessary for safety, emotional management, and learning, but the child must be neither overloaded with emotional or cognitive information that he or she is not yet prepared to understand nor ignored. The child must learn how to communicate, when to communicate, how much to communicate, and who to communicate to, and all of that will vary over time, with different people, and under differing circumstances. With his or her growing ability to put feelings into words and not just behavior, the child learns the meaning of healthy relational communication.

Healthy Organizations Encourage Conversation and Feedback

Healthy organizations create opportunities for people to talk to each other, resolve conflicts, share ideas, solve problems, and set goals. In a healthy organization important information is shared in a timely and useful way, and members are willing to seek out answers when they are confused or unclear. Information exchange is abundant and occurs up, down, and sideways in the organization. There is a healthy respect for boundaries, but boundaries are not used as an excuse for secrecy. Leaders in such organizations model good communication skills and encourage efforts to embed good communication practices in the structure of the organization.

In healthy organizations there is recognition that keeping communication channels open is always challenging. The discoveries we made as children about how easily a message can become garbled as it is transmitted one-by-one through a group are just as relevant to adult workplaces, complicated even further by the elimination of nonverbal information via email and texting. In healthy organizations, people recognize that "actions speak more loudly than words" since words only account for a part of communication; therefore, everyone is expected to be responsible for their nonverbal as well as their verbal forms of expression.

In living systems, healthy organizational function is dependent upon the maintenance of feedback loops. There is also a general awareness that "elephants in the room" take up too much space and, therefore, that the availability of conflict management resources is an important priority.

Commitment to Open Communication (Chapter 8)

To create and sustain the right conditions for positive group processes, a *Commitment to Open Communication*—nonviolent communication—is essential. People must feel safe to discuss conflict-laden topics so that the group can clear out the elephants in the room. Everyone must learn how to promote dialogue over discussion, and find shared meaning, if they are to achieve complex reasoning and problem solving. Communication has to *flow* because an organization is a living network of constant communication that keeps all of its members engaged and healthy. In Sanctuary, we are particularly reminded about the importance of open communication when we discover how dangerous secrets can be and how much more able people are to make good decisions when they have the accurate information they need.

Justice and the Common Good

Healthy People Are Socially Responsible and Care about Social Justice

All social species come into the world equipped with the basic notion of reciprocity, also known as "tit-for-tat" or "do unto others as they do onto you" [40]. First in interaction with the mother, and then soon with other family members, the child has his or her first experience with fair play. In these interactive relationships the child begins to develop what ultimately will be a sense of justice and the basis for how just relationships are to be conducted. The child must learn how to put aside his or her own strivings and the satisfaction of his or her own needs in the service of "the other." Originally the other is mother, but then as the world expands for the child, the other includes other family members, playmates, teachers, colleagues, and the larger community. If the child has experienced justice, then he or she will develop a concern with personal justice, social justice, and concern for the common good.

Healthy Organizations Encourage Individual and Social Responsibility

In a healthy organization, there is awareness that achieving its mission means that all members must behave in a socially responsible fashion. All members must be expected to do their best at all times, meet their responsibilities, and help others do the same. There must be an understanding that no matter how capable people may be, they all need help from time to time. In a healthy organization, expectations are clear and members are required to meet expectations and ask for help when they are struggling. There is a clear ethical climate that guides issues such as responsibility, accountability, communication, regulation, equity, trust, and the common good. When members pull up short, leaders and colleagues must be willing to identify the problem and provide the support needed to help them. In a healthy organization, lowering expectations is never an option. Healthy organizations recognize that each member is a part of a larger whole and therefore has a responsibility to work toward social justice and the common good.

Commitment to Social Responsibility (Chapter 9)

Living means making choices all the time, and the choices we make determine whether we help or harm the whole. Through the choices we make today, we are determining the course of the future in our individual lives and in our organizations. Because it is so difficult to see the whole, we are largely unaware of the total impact of our choices as we make them. We make most of these choices in small ways that appear inconsequential until they accumulate and geometrically compound over time. In our houses of government, on Wall Street, in our businesses, schools, and homes, we are deciding every day who is going to live a life of pleasure and who is going to suffer. We are deciding whether or not the human species, and all living things, are going to survive or perish. In our social service programs, we are making choices that are either going to further the healing of the people in our care or not. But we remain largely unaware of *how* we are making these choices or what kind of future we are actively creating.

The search for justice, and what justice means, is as old as humanity and has itself a developmental history that moves from blood vengeance, to state retribution, toward concepts that now revolve around restorative justice. It is essential that as individuals, organizations, and entire societies we wrestle with this very difficult issue and fully understand the interaction between individual responsibility and social responsibility. We must make a *Commitment to Social Responsibility*. Laws, conceptual frameworks, and our responses to injustice must change as we become better informed about the true sources of human behavior and misbehavior. Organizations adopting the Sanctuary Model must be committed to furthering the common good in the interest of both individual and collective justice.

The Sanctuary Model: Transforming Vision into Reality

The Sanctuary Model is built upon what we call the "Four Pillars" of Sanctuary: Trauma Theory, the Sanctuary Commitments, S.E.L.F., and the Sanctuary Toolkit (Figure 2.3).

Trauma Theory provides the scientific underpinning for the Sanctuary Model. The Sanctuary Commitments provide the anchoring values and are tied directly to developmentally grounded, trauma-informed treatment goals as well as the overall health of the organizational culture. S.E.L.F. is a simple and easy-to-use conceptual framework that provides a "compass" allowing everyone to navigate the challenges of complex interventions, while the Sanctuary Toolkit offers practical, grounded tasks that support implementation. "Creating Sanctuary" refers to the shared experience of creating and maintaining physical, psychological, social, and moral safety within a social environment—any

Figure 2.3 The four pillars of Sanctuary.

social environment—and thus reducing systemic violence and counteracting the destructive parallel processes that we described in Chapter 1.

Trauma Theory

The study of trauma gives us a lens into the workings of people under extreme conditions, but we are learning much about the entire stress continuum and the extent to which stress, particularly repetitive and toxic stressful conditions, can impact normal development. Along with the expanding field of interpersonal neuroscience, this knowledge is leading to the recognition that most of our behavior is determined by previous experiences that may have occurred even before we were born. We are learning how limited our freedom really is at a neurological base. As it turns out, what we call "free will" is not nearly as free as we would like to believe [41]. At the same time, we are learning how much our social milieu can influence the brain, now known to be more malleable and "plastic" than was once assumed, and how important belief, faith, meaning, and purpose are to changing the brain [42].

In the Sanctuary Model, everyone in an organization needs to have a clear understanding about how the impact of toxic stress and trauma has affected the clients we work with as well as the staff doing the difficult work. It is also vital that everyone recognizes that stress causes us to revert to old habits that we may have overcome in the past. Learning about the psychobiology of stress, toxic stress, and trauma is liberating for people. It gives us explanatory reasons for some of the puzzling behaviors we engage in and the feelings that can come to dominate us.

Our expanding understanding about the impact of disrupted attachment, toxic stress, adversity, and trauma represents the possibility of being able to base helping and caregiving work on outcomes, a concept that has only rarely been expected from social service and mental health organizations. Embedded in the notion of services that truly understand the complex biopsychosocial impact of traumatic experience is the underlying premise that all people can change, even if only slightly, and that if change is not occurring, maybe it is because the service provided is not adequately matching their needs—which means that *we* need to do something different.

The Sanctuary Commitments

The Seven Sanctuary Commitments represent the guiding principles for implementation of the Sanctuary Model (Figure 2.4). They embody beliefs about human conduct that are common to human rights cultures around the world, regardless of gender, ethnicity, religious belief, or location on earth. As the basic structural elements of the Sanctuary operating system, each commitment supports trauma recovery goals for clients, staff, and the organization as a whole.

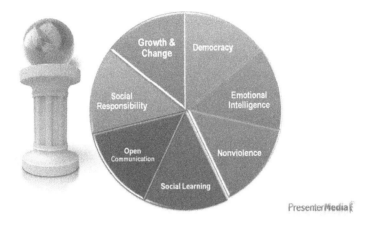

Figure 2.4 Sanctuary Commitments piechart.

The Sanctuary Commitments work together as a cohesive whole, not as independent functions. The visual image we use to illustrate that harmony looks like Figure 2.4.

In Chapter 1 we discussed the impact of trauma and toxic stress on organizations, staff, and clients. Figure 2.5 illustrates how the Sanctuary Commitments are the remedy to the impact of trauma.

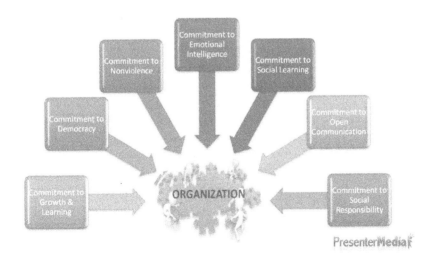

Figure 2.5 Sanctuary Commitments: a developmentally grounded, trauma-informed system.

For a complex organization to function, it needs the right number of principles that guide short-term, everyday conduct as well as long-term strategy. Too many rules and a system becomes rigid, inflexible, and even paralyzed. Too few and it becomes overly individualistic and chaotic. The Sanctuary Commitments structure the norms, values, and moral climate of the organization that together determine the organizational culture. Many people fail to realize that we are communicating what we believe in every moment by what we do and don't do, what we say and don't say, what we reward and what we punish. The Sanctuary Commitments offer a way to be clear about what we believe and consistent in what we do and say. This moral consistency is vital in the face of the profound cruelty that so many of our clients have experienced at the hands of other people.

The *moral climate* in an organization includes the individual's perceptions of how others in the system typically address moral issues, and this helps to determine how each individual addresses those issues as long as he or she remains in the organization. To a great degree, the organization's moral climate reflects the values of those who lead the operation, although an organization can have more than one climate. A moral climate emerges in an organization in the way leaders transmit expectations about the way employees are to treat each other and their clients, as well as the ways in which social responsibility is to be exercised [43].

The challenge in the Sanctuary Model is to establish and maintain a value-based system, even in the face of what are extraordinary ethical dilemmas, the kinds of dilemmas that human service delivery professionals encounter every day. What is fair? To whom? How do I keep my patient safe when only my patient has the power to keep herself safe? What is the best way to empower people without putting them at risk? What is my responsibility and what is not my responsibility in this particular situation? When do my interventions promote recovery and when do they inhibit or discourage recovery? How do I manage a coworker whom I think is mistreating a client? How can my patients trust me if I have to lie to them all the time about what I really think they need, or if I have to lie to keep them in the hospital, or if I have to lie to their insurance company in order to get them care? If a person is suffering from an injury that is a result of a social, fixable problem, what is my role in preventing further injury to this person and to others? When safety is a priority, how can I choose between the safety of my client and the safety of my colleagues? If I am committed to nonviolence, does that mean I should not defend myself? Or respond violently to violent provocation? Does it mean that we are adequately preparing people who must go back to a violent family or community?

There are all sorts of tensions that exist within any meaningful value system. Does the *Commitment to Open Communication* mean that I should break confidentiality to a client or to a colleague, and if so, under what conditions? If the

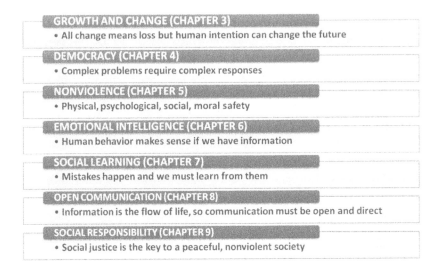

GROWTH AND CHANGE (CHAPTER 3)
- All change means loss but human intention can change the future

DEMOCRACY (CHAPTER 4)
- Complex problems require complex responses

NONVIOLENCE (CHAPTER 5)
- Physical, psychological, social, moral safety

EMOTIONAL INTELLIGENCE (CHAPTER 6)
- Human behavior makes sense if we have information

SOCIAL LEARNING (CHAPTER 7)
- Mistakes happen and we must learn from them

OPEN COMMUNICATION (CHAPTER 8)
- Information is the flow of life, so communication must be open and direct

SOCIAL RESPONSIBILITY (CHAPTER 9)
- Social justice is the key to a peaceful, nonviolent society

Figure 2.6 Sanctuary Commitments summarized.

only way to get someone reimbursed for services is to reveal their personal information, is that the right thing to do? Does the *Commitment to Democracy* mean that I have to get everyone's input even if it means that I have less time to spend with the clients? Is it okay to lie if it protects someone? Does the *Commitment to Nonviolence* mean that I shouldn't reprimand the staff member who cursed at a client? Does the *Commitment to Social Responsibility* mean that I have to work when we are short-staffed, even when it takes me away from my own family? The objectives of the Sanctuary Commitments are trauma-informed and apply to clients, staff, and the organization as a whole. But we know that there will inevitably be conflicts, unintended consequences, and unforeseeable circumstances that will need to be resolved each day in each program. We need organizational processes that provide us with enough structure to be able to move, without so much rigidity that innovative solutions to complex problems never are allowed to emerge.

We have structured the rest of this volume around a deeper exploration of the Sanctuary Commitments, what they mean, how they are central to becoming trauma-informed, and some of the practical steps we take to implement those commitments. Figure 2.6 offers a shorthand visual summary of the Sanctuary Commitments.

Leadership Commitment

For the organizational climate to be ethically consistent, the Sanctuary Commitments need to be embraced by the Board of Directors and senior leadership and conveyed throughout the organization, through middle management, to the direct care staff and ultimately to the clients. The Sanctuary Commitments apply to everyone. If the organizational leaders do not get on board, efforts to change may not be effective. If the middle managers do not get on board, efforts to change may not be effective. If the direct and indirect care staff do not get on board, efforts to change may not be effective.

What do we mean by getting on board? At first, many organizational leaders hear a review of the Sanctuary Commitments and believe that those commitments already constitute their organizational culture. In many cases, this is at least partially true. It is only when leaders engage in a different kind of dialogue with other members of their organizational community that they find out how divergent people's views are on what these commitments mean and how to make them real in everyday interactions. When these dialogues begin, we inevitably discover the gaps between the kind of organization we want to work in, or think we work in, and the one we actually do work in. When confronted with these gaps, we need to be humble enough to acknowledge them, wise enough to figure out what we need to do to change, and brave enough to make the necessary changes. Experience has taught that courageous leadership is critical to system change; without it, substantial change is unlikely to occur. The view from the top of the organization is almost always more pleasant than the view from the bottom.

This change process, however, can be frightening for people in leadership positions and they rightfully perceive significant risk in opening themselves up to criticism, in leveling hierarchies and sharing legitimate power. The gains are substantial, but a leader finds that out only after learning how to tolerate the anxiety and uncertainty that inevitably accompany real change. It should also be noted that change does not occur just because a leader wants it to occur. Leaders may be willing to share power with others, but this does not necessarily mean that others are always willing to assume power and the responsibility that comes with it. Although staff and clients may indicate that they want a greater voice, creating the conditions in which others have a greater voice is not always welcomed. It is easy to stay in or slide back to a familiar and comfortable arrangement.

Learning how to be an effective democratic leader necessitates a sharp, often steep, and sometimes painful learning curve. Crisis-driven organizations sacrifice communication networks, feedback loops, participatory decision making, and complex problem solving under the pressures of chronic stress. In doing so, they lose healthy democratic processes and shift to an increasingly hierarchical, top-down control structure that discourages creativity, innovation, and risk-taking. This results in an inability to manage complexity. The cure for this situation is more democracy. This requires leadership buy-in and immersion in the change process, an increase in transparency, and deliberate restructuring to ensure greater participation and involvement.

S.E.L.F.: A Compass for the Recovery Process

S.E.L.F. is an acronym that represents the four interactive key aspects of recovery from bad experiences. S.E.L.F. provides a nonlinear, cognitive behavioral, therapeutic approach for facilitating movement, regardless of whether we are talking about individual clients, families, staff problems, or whole organizational dilemmas (Figure 2.7). It is a crucial concept in the Sanctuary Model and will be revisited repeatedly in the chapters on the Sanctuary Commitments. We can best describe the nonlinear aspects of S.E.L.F. using a visual image:

S.E.L.F. is a compass that allows us to explore all four key domains of healing:

- *Safety:* attaining physical, psychological, social, and moral safety in self, relationships, and the environment.
- *Emotional management:* identifying levels of various emotions and modulating emotion in response to memories, persons, and events.
- *Loss:* feeling grief and dealing with personal losses while recognizing that all change involves loss.
- *Future:* trying out new roles, ways of relating and behaving as a "survivor" to ensure personal, professional, and organizational safety, to find meaning, to make more viable life choices, and to help others.

While using S.E.L.F., the clients, their families, and staff are able to embrace a shared nontechnical language that is neither blaming nor judgmental. It allows them all to see the larger recovery process in perspective. The accessible language demystifies what sometimes is seen as confusing and even insulting clinical or psychological terminology that can confound clients and staff while still focusing on the aspects of problematic adjustment that pose the greatest challenges.

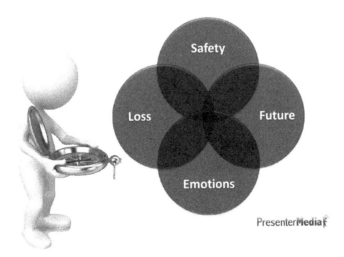

Figure 2.7 S.E.L.F.—a nonlinear tool.

When faced with the complex problems that are typical of the children, adults, and families that we serve, it is easy for helpers to lose their way, to focus on what is easiest to understand and manage, rather than what may be the underlying stumbling block to progress. Similarly, our clients are most likely to pay attention to whatever problems are causing the least pain for them in the immediate present, even though from a helper's point of view, what they are doing or not doing is causing them great suffering.

As a result, it is easy for staff and clients to get stuck on safety issues. When someone is doing something that is obviously leading to dangerous behavior, it is hard *not* to focus entirely on that danger. But as we all find out sooner or later, an exclusive focus on safety often leads us nowhere and keeps us spinning in circles. So, S.E.L.F. helps us to get out of the maze of confusing symptoms. That's what we mean by saying that it is a kind of compass. Using these four apparently simple concepts that actually are like the cardinal points of a compass, helpers and clients can rapidly organize problems into categories of "safety," "emotions," "loss," and "future," which naturally leads to a more complex treatment or service plan. S.E.L.F. has the added value of conveying to both parties that it is actually possible to do something to change what has previously seemed like an overwhelming mess. It divides the chaos of people's lives into more manageable bits without losing the complexity of the challenges.

But we don't just apply S.E.L.F. to the clients. In parallel, these compass points represent the problems that arise within the treatment or service setting between staff and clients, among members of staff, and between staff and administration. Applied to such issues as change management, staff splitting, poor morale, rule infraction, administrative withdrawal and helplessness, and misguided leadership, S.E.L.F. can also assist a stressed organization to conceptualize its own present dilemma and move into a better future through a course of complex decision making and conflict resolution. To do so, an organization must envision the Future it wants to reach, wrestle with the inevitable barriers to change that are related to Loss, and develop skills to manage the individual and interpersonal Emotions and inevitable conflicts surrounding change while calculating what the present and potential Safety issues are in making change but also in *not* making change.

The bottom line is that S.E.L.F. is an exceedingly powerful tool for pushing the envelope of change. It is nonlinear because it is not about stages, but rather about constant movement. Whenever we get stuck in one domain, we simply move to another domain and go from there. If we cannot get movement by focusing on safety, then we move the focus to imagining how the future would be different if the safety issues were not in play. If the underlying reason for a lack of change is fear of loss, then it is important to determine what emotions are aroused that are too painful to deal with and what skills we can help develop to manage those emotions. Only in doing so can we help people become safe enough to work through the loss. If a person has trouble with "anger management," is it really about anger or is the problem that the experience of shame carries with it such a sense of danger that anger is much safer? If so, can we think about what the person would have to give up in order not to act violently when shame is aroused and to imagine a future without shame or violence? If our organizational safety is threatened by funding changes, then what could the future look like if we are to become safer, what would we have to give up, and what feelings would we have to manage in order to arrive at that future?

This is why we organize virtually everything around S.E.L.F. When we first encounter a person or a problem, we learn to think about the four key points of our compass: What are the safety issues? What are the emotions that are barriers to change or that can facilitate change? What will have to be given up? What is the vision? Where are we trying to go? In the Sanctuary Model we use S.E.L.F. as a cognitive tool for many different tasks. We use S.E.L.F. Treatment Planning for assessment and planning. Our psychoeducational materials are organized around S.E.L.F. Red Flag Reviews represent one method we use for problem solving, and the method is organized around S.E.L.F., allowing us to deal more effectively with problem situations as they emerge. S.E.L.F. allows us to evaluate progress in the moment and over time in a way that is easily understood by children as young as five years of age. In Team Meetings it allows people with various degrees of experience and education to get on the same page. It helps us stay on track, keeps our focus, and provides a shared language and meaning system for everyone. It also helps us see the parallels between what the clients have experienced and what is going on with the staff and the organization. In doing so, we are able to see the interactive and interdependent nature of our shared lives.

Sanctuary Education and Training

At this point in the development of services that help people to heal and recover from the terrible circumstances that so many children and young people are exposed to, human service delivery professionals must often make significant change. Someday, when knowledge about interpersonal neuroscience has been fully integrated into advanced learning environments, trauma-informed care will become just the way things are done. But for the foreseeable future, most professionals must unlearn beliefs, ideas, and practices that they may have embraced for decades while learning new methods based on some dramatic changes in the theoretical underpinnings for how we understand human behavior. Making such dramatic changes in mental models—commonly called a "paradigm shift"—is demanding and difficult at the best of times and even more so when our systems of care are bending and breaking under the impact of a failing economy.

In human services, we bring people together in an array of settings because we recognize that group genius, when it arises, is far more effective in solving complex problems than individual effort alone. Beside economic cost savings, that's why we have inpatient units, group homes, residential treatment programs, classrooms, and community collaborations. But for groups to be effective, it is vital that all the members of a group get on the same page and have a shared theoretical framework to deal with complex problems. Theory needs to be taught, applied to practice, supervised, and reinforced. Interpersonal conflict will inevitably occur, but if there are shared values, it is more likely that people will find effective methods to manage and resolve those conflicts. But the theory and practice must be relevant and accessible to people who represent a wide variety of backgrounds, education, and experience.

We have developed an implementation process to facilitate group change. The Sanctuary Model offers a structured methodology to help groups create change processes by taking advantages of learning experiences without having to reinvent everything for themselves.

Sanctuary Implementation

The Sanctuary Institute is a collaborative effort of ANDRUS and Dr. Sandra L. Bloom. The objective of the Sanctuary Institute is to help organizations implement the Sanctuary Model. The implementation process begins with a five-day intensive training experience. Each organization sends teams of five to eight people from various levels of the organization, who come together to learn from our faculty (who are colleagues from other organizations implementing Sanctuary) and each other. Together teams begin to create a shared vision of the kind of organization they want to create. Each team will eventually become the Sanctuary Steering Committee for their organization. This initial training experience usually involves several organizations, and generally these organizations are very different in terms of size, scope, region, and mission.

This diversity helps to provide a rich learning experience for the participants about the neuroscience of attachment and trauma, the reasoning behind the Sanctuary Commitments, the application of this knowledge to systems using the notion of parallel process, ideas for preventing vicarious trauma and burnout, practical steps for integrating this knowledge into practice, and a shared plan for moving ahead.

The Sanctuary Steering Committee is instructed to go back to their organization and create a Sanctuary Core Team, a larger multidisciplinary team that expands its reach into the entire organization. It is this Core Team that will be the activators of the entire system. The Core Team should have representatives from every level of the organization to ensure that every voice is heard. It is vital that key organizational leaders become actively involved in the process of change and participate in this Core Team.

The Core Team is armed with a *Sanctuary Direct Care Staff Training Manual*, a *Sanctuary Indirect Staff Training Manual*, a *Sanctuary Implementation Manual*, several psychoeducational curricula, and ongoing consultation and technical assistance from Sanctuary faculty members to guide them through the process of Sanctuary Implementation that extends over three years and leads to Sanctuary Certification.

The Sanctuary Toolkit

The Sanctuary Toolkit comprises a range of practical skills that enable individuals and organizations to develop new habits and deal more effectively with difficult situations, build community, develop a deeper understanding of the effects of adversity and trauma, and build a common language. Throughout the chapters that follow, we will show how the various tools in the Sanctuary Toolkit are integrated into practice.

Sanctuary Certification

Sanctuary® is a registered trademark, and the right to use the Sanctuary name is contingent on engagement in our certified training program and an agreement to participate in an ongoing, peer-reviewed certification process. The Sanctuary Certification process is designed to promote, sustain, and strengthen an organization's commitment to the maintenance of a developmentally grounded, trauma-informed culture for all stakeholders. Certification is a symbol that an organization provides a higher level of care, a trauma-informed environment for consumers, and a better environment for staff who provide care. This process affirms an ongoing commitment to ensure fidelity to the Sanctuary Model and meet the standard of providing a safe, secure, and developmentally appropriate environment in which clients and staff will recover and thrive.

Agencies that meet the standards can expect to experience:

- redefinition of what safety means for everyone in the community;
- less violence, including physical, psychological, social, and moral forms of violence as well as self-directed, interpersonal, and collective violence;
- systemic understanding of the complex biopsychosocial and developmental impacts of trauma, abuse, and exposure to adversity, particularly when it occurs in childhood;
- understanding of the role that attachment and disrupted attachment experiences play in the lives of our clients and staff;
- better emotional management in clients and staff;
- less victim-blaming; fewer punitive and judgmental responses;
- clearer, more consistent boundaries, higher expectations, clearer understanding of rights and responsibilities;

- better understanding of group dynamics;
- earlier identification and confrontation of perpetrators' behavior;
- better ability to articulate goals, create strategies for change, and justify the need for a holistic approach;
- understanding of reenactment behavior and resistance to change;
- better, more open and direct communication;
- increased ability to deal with issues of loss and change;
- more democratic environment at all levels;
- diversity of representation, voice, and perspective;
- more scientific approach to methods and outcomes;
- fewer critical incidents and fewer sentinel events;
- fewer staff injuries and lowered workmen's compensation claims;
- less absenteeism;
- lower rates of staff and management turnover;
- increased job satisfaction and staff morale;
- better outcomes for clients, staff, and organization.

When an organization becomes a Certified Sanctuary Organization, there is an agreement that each organization will maintain the practice of a trauma-informed environment in accordance with the tenets of Sanctuary, utilize the S.E.L.F. framework for Sanctuary practice, maintain Sanctuary training and trauma-informed clinical treatment, and routinely recertify its staff and the organization. Certified Sanctuary organizations also agree to follow and maintain the certification standards postcertification between surveys.

Sanctuary Network

As of May 2012 the Sanctuary Institute had trained over 250 organizations worldwide. These organizations are part of our Sanctuary Network. The Sanctuary Network is a community of organizations helping each other to improve services. The Sanctuary Network sponsors an annual conference that features innovations in practice. The Network also disseminates new materials to its members and holds regular webinars and other opportunities for members to share and learn.

Results of the Sanctuary Process

In these days of evidence-based practice, it is important to recognize that practice-based evidence is what gives us our first inkling of what to test, that is, what methods may work when put to the test of rigorous scientific methodology. The Sanctuary Model evolved out of 20 years of practice among dozens of professionals in an unlocked, open therapeutic milieu, without seclusion or restraint, that has been well documented [2, 25, 44–49]. In Chapter 5, we tell the story of Dr. Lyndra Bills' transformation of a state hospital inpatient unit for the chronically mentally ill in the 1990s. Dr. Maggie Bennington-Davis and her colleague, Tim Murphy, led their staff in transforming an acute care unit in Salem, Oregon, in the early twentieth century with remarkable results, including a 97% decrease in the use of seclusion and a 100% decrease in restraint despite a 39.8% increase in annual admissions. Similar to the experience of Dr. Bills and her staff, the Oregon team experienced fewer staff injuries, improved staff morale, and lowered staff turnover, while patient satisfaction radically improved.

These were the kinds of practice-based evidence that gave rise to a controlled, randomized trial of the implementation of the Sanctuary Model in children's residential settings, a research project developed by the Jewish Board of Family and Children's Services in New York. To summarize the results of this study, from baseline to six months there were five significant changes in staff attitudes and perceptions among those who received the Sanctuary Model training that appeared to be leading to changes in the children: *Support*: how much children help and support each other; how supportive staff is toward the children; *Spontaneity*: how much the program encourages the open expression of feelings by children and staff; *Autonomy*: how self-sufficient and independent staff perceive that the children are in making their own decisions; *Personal Problem Orientation*: the extent to which children seek to understand their feelings and personal problems; *Safety*: the extent to which staff feel they can challenge their peers and supervisors, can express opinions in staff meetings, will not be blamed for problems, and have clear guidelines for dealing with children who are aggressive. Changes in the children were just beginning to unfold as the study was drawing to a close, but even given the short time frame, there was a significant decrease in incendiary communication and increased tension management among the children, as well as trends toward decreased verbal aggression and increased internal locus of control by the children in treatment [50].

In a quasi-experimental study, residential programs for children using the Sanctuary Model showed a positive change in organizational culture while comparable programs not using the Sanctuary model did not, supporting its positive impact on the culture of the workplace [51].

The first seven child-serving facilities that participated in the Sanctuary Institute were evaluated for changes in their rates of restraints and holds. Three programs exhibited over an 80% decrease in the number of restraints, two had over a 40% drop, one exhibited a 13% decrease, and one had a 6% drop. A subsequent three-year study of child organizations using the Sanctuary Model showed an average of 52% reductions in physical restraints after the first year of implementation [52]. Within the first six years of implementation in the Andrus residential and day programs, there was a 90% decrease in critical incidents [53].

Working with schools is part of the Sanctuary Institute focus. In one school for emotionally disturbed children that has become certified in the Sanctuary Model, after two years of implementation 64% of the students achieved realistic or ambitious rates of reading improvement. In addition, 99% of the children were promoted to the next grade. With regard to hospitalizations, a 41% reduction in the number of children requiring inpatient psychiatric hospitalization and a 25% reduction in days children spent in inpatient hospitalization was recorded. The same school enjoyed a 56% placement rate in public and private school programs once the students graduated [54].

As part of the Pennsylvania Department of Public Welfare's (DPW) efforts to reduce and eliminate restraints in children's treatment settings, DPW entered into a partnership with the Sanctuary Institute to bring the Sanctuary Model to Pennsylvania in 2007. The University of Pittsburgh worked with the DPW, the Sanctuary Institute, and 30 participating provider residential sites to conduct an open evaluation of the implementation of the model. Annual surveys were conducted from 2008 to 2010. The evaluation of the implementation of the Sanctuary Model in residential facilities found that implementation was associated with a number of positive outcomes: lower staff stress and higher staff morale, increased feelings of job competence and proficiency, and a greater investment in the individuals they served. The implementation of the Sanctuary Model was also significantly associated with an improved organizational culture and climate and a substantial decrease in the reported use of restraints at many sites [55].

Additionally, an analysis of service utilization from 2007 to 2009 of children discharged from Sanctuary Model residential treatment facilities (RTFs) versus other RTFs was conducted by Community Care Behavioral Health (CCBH). It demonstrated that although both groups had a similar average (mean) length of stay in 2007, by 2009 Sanctuary Model RTF providers had a substantially shorter length of stay and a somewhat greater decrease in median length of stay; a substantial increase in the percentage of discharged youth who received outpatient services in the three months following discharge; and a lower increase in the percentage of children readmitted to RTFs in the 90 days following discharge [56]. As the authors of the report wrote, *"the implementation of the Sanctuary Model in residential facilities in Pennsylvania appears to have had a positive impact, with the greatest benefits being seen by residents and staff of those sites who were most successful in implementing the full Sanctuary Model. These positive outcomes occurred at a time of uncertainty and programmatic and staffing change in many facilities, which speaks to the dedication of all involved in the implementation of Sanctuary. At the same time, the variation observed in implementation does suggest an opportunity to consider strategies to support future implementation efforts, as well as the need for providing continued support to sites that have implemented Sanctuary to ensure sustained positive outcomes"* (p. 7) [55].

As of the beginning of 2011, the Sanctuary Model was considered to be an "evidence-supported" practice by the National Child Traumatic Stress Network and a "promising practice" according to the California Evidence-Based Clearinghouse. Continuing evaluation projects are underway. We now have a significant amount of experience in watching the Sanctuary process unfold in many different kinds of organizations. What we see is that adopting a trauma-informed organizational paradigm causes organizational members to think and act more effectively than attempts to influence individual behavior alone. We attribute this to the power of group influence. Changes in thinking lead to changes in habits and therefore to changes in habitual routines. The S.E.L.F. framework changes how people use language, the Sanctuary Commitments delineate how best to sustain interpersonal relationships, and the Sanctuary Toolkit improves the way we all practice. These changes create a sense of possibility and hope in our organizations, which in turn inspires hope in those who come to us for help. Changing behavior then changes the entire organization, as demonstrated in reduced turnover, improved morale, improved communication, and decreased incidents of violence. Changing the organizational behavior then changes client outcomes, resulting in the development of safety skills, radically improved emotional management, a greater readiness to participate in trauma-specific treatment approaches, improved social skills and relationships, more satisfactory academic or job performance, and improved decision making and judgment. So now, let's dive into what this process of change looks like and how it works.

Chapter 3

Growth and Change: Isn't This the Whole Point?

"Men's courses will foreshadow certain ends, to which, if persevered in, they must lead" said Scrooge. "But if the course be departed from, the ends will change. Say it is thus with what you show me."

Scrooge speaking to the Ghost of Christmas Future
A Christmas Carol, Charles Dickens

SUMMARY: *We begin this chapter as we will each chapter with a vision of what things might look like if we all truly embraced the Sanctuary Commitments in our personal and organizational lives. After describing a vision of growth and change, we spend time explaining the key barrier to change, which is reenactment, meaning the compulsive tendency to repeat patterns of the past. Understanding and working with reenactment is the key to individual and group change. Unless we really understand reenactment, true trauma-informed care will remain illusory. We will explore the normal context in which our tendency to reenact the past occurs, and what happens to us as a result of disrupted attachment and traumatic experience. The underlying resistance to change that we see in individuals and institutions, and therefore the likelihood of repetition, is a result of resistance to loss. So, we also look at the organizational tendency to reenact past failed strategies and then explore some of the implications of growth and change for leadership. We end this chapter by offering some strategies for facilitating growth and change in caregiving organizations in the section on the Sanctuary Toolkit.*

A Vision of Growth and Change

- Together with our clients we set clear and achievable goals for change, and everything we do is oriented around whether or not we are achieving those goals.
- We use a vision of a better future to motivate us to achieve those goals.
- We all understand how readily we create habit patterns and how rapidly those patterns become automatic and often unknown to us.

- We recognize that habits, once formed, are very hard to change and that stress makes changing habits even more difficult.
- We recognize that when people resist change, it is because they are resisting what they are going to lose in order to change, and in honoring their losses, we help them to move.
- We recognize that the past always has a grip on us, that reenactment is a powerful force, because rather than lose whatever we already have, we are likely to repeat the past, even if it brings us more pain.
- Because we recognize the connections between past, present, and future, we are able to recognize repetitive patterns and are not tempted to help someone repeat a painful past.
- We have become adept at understanding what behavior means and skillful at helping other people to change problematic habits.
- We have learned that one of the best ways to break out of unsuccessful patterns is by using play, creative expression, and laughter.
- We grapple together with the tragic nature of human existence instead of always looking for someone or something to blame.
- We acknowledge that we cannot force change in others; we can only facilitate needed changes. But we cannot facilitate change in others without first making changes in ourselves, and when our clients are not making the agreed-upon changes, we need to change.

What Do We Mean by Growth and Change?

A Boy Named Peter

Peter's early years were spent in a violent, chaotic home, and by the time he arrived at Andrus for residential treatment he was thirteen, had already been kicked out of school, had unsuccessfully been through several treatment programs, and appeared to be on a straight line to jail. Diagnosed with conduct disorder and attention deficit hyperactivity disorder (ADHD), he was a big, strong child, particularly aggressive with male staff. According to his history, he had a close relationship with his mother, who had a series of live-in and sometimes violent or rejecting boyfriends when he was growing up. He didn't have contact with his father, but memories of physical abuse at the hands of his father continued to haunt him. He had cared deeply for his elderly grandfather, who had died when Peter was nine.

In the early days of his stay, he got into many conflicts with staff members who tried to set limits on his behavior. It became clear that he was quite good at being scary and aggressive. It also became clear that the staff were not going to beat him at that game by responding to his aggression with more aggression. Nonetheless, common assessments were "He just needs more discipline" and "He needs to know who is boss."

The child-care staff, the teachers in the school, Peter's clinician, and the manager of the cottage where Peter resided were all becoming increasingly afraid of him. At the time, Andrus had begun using the Sanctuary principles, and this meant that the staff members involved with Peter were beginning to question themselves about repetitive and problematic behavior by looking at the course of his history and the patterns of Peter's behavior over time.

A turning point came in a team meeting when they shifted their conversation about Peter's bad behavior and began to speculate about what he could be trying to tell them by responding to any kind of even momentary closeness with violence. In questioning their own responses to the boy, they observed that there was a noticeable difference between his interactions with male and female staff members. He seemed more relaxed with females, even protective at times. With male staff members, particularly those who tended to be rigid and demanding, his aggression was easily triggered. One of the female staff members shared a conversation she had with Peter about his grandfather and how much he missed him and the things they used to do together. The rest of the team was surprised to hear that he had ever been close to anyone.

Someone else on the team, a new young staff member, who did not look much older than Peter, had noticed something about the boy that no one else had recognized. When Peter was engaged in a task, he was quite focused and did not need a great deal of supervision. Work seemed to be good for him, but it couldn't be work assigned as punishment; instead, it needed to be tasks that could draw upon what the team was surprised to recognize: his latent and apparently natural helpfulness.

This led to some creative changes in feeling and action toward Peter among the adults around him. There was one moment that really stood out. Late in the winter there was a severe snowstorm, and Peter was enlisted to help the Maintenance Department shovel snow. He worked for hours clearing paths and helping staff members dig out their cars. He was a huge asset. This storm was a breakthrough for Peter and for the staff, and gradually Peter began to talk a little more openly about the pain inside him, particularly the unresolved grief over the death of his grandfather that he had never shared with anyone.

Several weeks after the storm, Brian, the Chief Operating Officer at Andrus, hosted a lunch for the Maintenance Department to thank them for their amazing effort during the storm. They had put in long hours and worked like bulls. The Maintenance Department foreman, who had also been trained in Sanctuary, had the presence of mind to invite their honorary maintenance man, Peter, to the luncheon. He sat with a room full of men, ate pizza, listened to their stories, and shared some stories of his own. During the storm and during lunch he was not Peter, the tough, violent guy or Peter the bully. He suddenly was a positive force, someone who was reliable, hardworking, and helpful. He became Peter, one of the good guys. After that, he willingly took on a host of jobs, each with increasing responsibility, and got more and more positive feedback. By the time he left Andrus, he had developed positive and trusting relationships with the staff, felt good about himself, and had enjoyed several months of significant growth and success.

On some level, the staff had changed their "script" for Peter because they had to do so. He was big and a little frightening, and the staff needed to find a way to work with him that did not constantly put them in harm's way. But whether it was accidental, purposeful, or just self-preservation, the staff helped change this boy's life script and provided a wonderful opportunity for him to be something other than the brute he had learned to be. The loss of his grandfather, added to a series of experiences with violent or dismissive men, had kept Peter confused about his identity as a male, stuck in time, unable to grow. When the adults around him were able to see his potential, when they could light a tiny match of hope for change, Peter was able to do what he needed to do to begin to heal. In changing the interactional script, Peter and his treatment team were also altering his path toward a different possible future.

Starting with the Future

We start this description of the Sanctuary Commitments with the *Commitment to Growth and Change* because that is the whole point of delivering services: growth and change, even if that change is small. Peter's story illustrates how simple it can be if we keep our own focus and have a coherent way to think about what we are all experiencing with each other. It is important to remember that if our work is not committed to growth and change, then it's not worth doing. But in pursuing this commitment, clients, staff members, and whole organizations have to grapple with two key concepts: envisioning and moving toward a different future and dealing with the loss that accompanies any kind of change, as well as the losses they have already experienced in the past.

There have been countless times that we have seen children, adults, and families grow in our care. In almost every case we can point to a series of events in which someone, despite all the evidence suggesting that this was a mistake, widened his or her field of vision to see who the person could be rather than who the person wanted us to believe he or she was. The clients we struggle with the most are those who are so injured that they simply will not let us help to change the script.

Our growing sense is that we need to be able to take more rather than fewer risks with these children, adults, and families. But doing so can be threatening, particularly when staff members do not feel safe in their positions, with each other, and when the organization itself is under constant stress and struggling for survival. In reminiscing about the last few years at Andrus, Brian describes how important it is to have some guiding framework, especially when the going gets rough.

Over the last decade there has been struggle after struggle after struggle: the retirement of our long time CEO, the loss of several long-time staff people, loss of family members, two mergers with organizations with completely different programs and cultures, the stepping down of our long-time Board Chair, a series of anonymous allegations launched by a disgruntled former employee. At times it has felt like we could not catch our breath. As we have moved through all of this change, loss, upset, and pain, I have been thankful that we found Sanctuary about two years before it all started. We are fond of saying that Sanctuary does not mean that bad things will never happen. In fact, bad things always happen, because they are as much a part of the human experience as joy, happiness, and success. When you are moving through all of this, it is good to be reminded that we do not have to move through it alone; we can lean on each other. It is good to know that no matter what is happening, we can refer back to the commitments and what we know about how people, even administrators, react and manage when under stress. Sanctuary has kept us on the straight and narrow, because it has become our touchstone. When things go bad, it is easy to think that it's all bad. It's easy to lose hope and direction. But we can't afford to do that because we have to be in the business of promoting hope for our hurting clients.

Hope and Saying Goodbye to the Past

One of our senior faculty members, David McCorkle, has frequently reminded us that we have to be the "hopekeepers" for our clients. But to be the hopekeepers, we have to model the possibility of change in ourselves. We need to recommit to the youthful idealism that told us that we are here to help people and communities change and grow. What we need to come to grips with is that before we can help others change and grow, we have to be willing and able to change and grow ourselves. If leaders are committed to personal growth and change, we will inspire growth and change in our organization, our colleagues, and our clients. By making changes in our own lives, by being a little braver, a little kinder, a little more compassionate, a little more curious, a little less complacent, we can inspire others to do the same. When we do that, we never quite know where it will lead. In his book *The Systems Bible*, John Gall writes that when it comes to trying to change a system, *"you can't change everything, and you can't change only one thing"* (p. 155) [57]. When we make a change in the way we do things, there will be corresponding change, even a little change, in those around us. In Chapter 1 we discussed parallel process, and it is with the Commitment to Growth and Change that we can begin to put parallel process to good use in our organizations.

Ken Hardy, family therapist and lecturer, tells people that he is in the "hope manufacturing business" [58]. Hope is at a premium for our clients, and many days it is at a premium for those of us who do this work as well. As Paul Hawkin, entrepreneur and environmental activist, pointed out in his 2009 commencement address at the University of Portland, *"Hope only makes sense when it doesn't make sense to be hopeful"* [59]. If our clients were brimming with hope and confidence, they would not need us or our services and they would most assuredly be doing other things with their time and energy. Our clients rely on us to muster up some hope for them. They need powerful people in their lives to help them discover that they too have power. We need to find some reservoir of hope every day whether we are at the top of the organizational hierarchy or at the bottom. That's what we must do together, in a community, in a Sanctuary.

The "F" in S.E.L.F. stands for future as a constant reminder to us that the ball is rolling along a timeline in only one direction and we can either roll with it or against it. By applying pressure from various angles we can alter its course to some extent, but the future remains undetermined; it is all a matter of choice. Many factors will determine how that future unfolds, and what has happened in the past may affect the future. But we still have choice.

At the same time, it is very common in our line of work to hear someone complain that his or her client, boss, direct supervisees, parent, child, or partner is "resistant to change," meaning that they keep doing the same thing over and over. But we infrequently ask "why?" What happened to this person that causes him or her to remain stuck in a past that is no longer working? Why, even in the face of disastrous circumstances, do we have such a difficult time changing our thoughts, feelings, and behavior even when we want to make those changes? The "L" in S.E.L.F. stands for loss, and as in Peter's story, it is essential in every case to understand the issues of loss and to remember that *all* change involves loss.

As human beings, our difficulties in managing loss keep us stuck in quicksand, slowly sinking, and the more we struggle, the deeper we sink. We are social creatures, who need to attach to other people from conception to death. To extricate us from the mire of the past, other people have to throw us a line and pull. At first, they will have to do all the pulling because we have no solid ground to stand on. Once we can get a safe hold on solid ground, we can begin the climb to get out, and think back on how we got ourselves into that mire in the first place and learn from our mistakes. Then we can deliberately decide where we want to go as we roll into the future.

In exploring what we mean by the *Commitment to Growth and Change*, we are going to plunge into some speculation about why human beings so frequently make very bad choices, choices that often lead to the brink of destruction. We hope to begin answering some critical questions: Why do we have such a problem with loss? When we are perfectly capable of seeing patterns and changing them, why do we so often not do so? Why is it so difficult for us to make the changes in our lives that we need to make? Why do we keep repeating or, as it is called, "reenacting" past traumatic events?

The answers to these questions can be found in our basic humanity. Understanding what happens to us when we do not get what we need from the people around us is the key to understanding compulsive repetition. After we put some basic concepts on the table, we can go back to Peter's story and understand how he got into so many traps and how people helped him get out. So, let's start at the beginning, with babies.

It All Starts with Being a Baby: Attachment and Development

It all starts with being a baby, a helpless, partially formed being, entirely dependent on the care of others for basic survival. Even before we are born, the physical attachment we have with our birth mothers provides us with what we need to live. Before everything else, we attach, defined as any behavior designed to get children into a close, protective relationship with their attachment figures whenever they experience anxiety [60]. After we are born, attachment relationships provide the scaffolding upon which all physical, psychological, social, and moral development occurs. We learn good habits that can serve us throughout our lives. We learn to communicate with others, first through signaling what we want and need nonverbally and then with words, in the context of safe attachment. In the serve-and-return interactions between mother and baby, the brain is constantly creating new pathways, expanding the integration of the developing brain circuitry. Through repetitive, safe interactions we learn how to be in the world.

Before We Have Words

For the first months of life, children do not have a brain that allows them to use words to communicate. But as anyone who has spent time around a child knows, children are very good at communicating their feelings and needs in other ways. Long before they have any verbal abilities, newborns recognize the rhythm, pitch, and other nonverbal components of their own mother and her native language. The brain system known as the "mirror neuron system" is activated within minutes after birth, and the newborn begins the long process of signaling other people what he or she needs from them. Mirror neurons in the infant brain are formed by the interactions between self and other [38].

Later in life, we use the same brain cells to understand the mental states of other people. We use the same cells to build a sense of self. Through early attachment interactions we learn how to begin managing our emotions, how to make sense of the world around us, what we are supposed to be and do in relation to other people, what is right and what is wrong. Vast amounts of information are conveyed to the baby by the way the mother holds him or her, the tone of her voice, the feel of her body, the look in her eyes, and her responses to the baby's early actions.

As soon as they can move, babies use "signals"—actions, gestures, or signs—to communicate with another person. Good parents quickly become adept at understanding and responding to the signals of their infant and toddler, even if no one else can understand. And humans are the great imitators; in less than an hour after birth, infants are already imitating other humans [34]. "Emotional contagion," which occurs between people within a fraction of a second, is the tendency to automatically mimic and synchronize facial expressions, sounds, postures, and movements with those of another person and, consequently, to feel the same feelings [61]. The research on the mirror neuron system has shown that our brain produces a full simulation of the experience of pain in another person, not as a private experience but as a shared one. This shared experience then forms the basis of empathy and compassion.

So, within the attachment relationship experienced over a significant length of time, children learn how to communicate with other persons and how to understand the communications of others. Once the capacity for verbal expression develops, the socially engaged child begins the long process of integrating verbal and nonverbal information into a holistic understanding of the world, learning gradually what things are, how they work, whether or not they have feelings, who they belong to, and so forth. But the earlier form of communication through signaling never goes away. It remains as the substrate for all communication and becomes the only way we can communicate once again when life overwhelms us. According to a great deal of anthropological, anatomic, and evolutionary research, the nonverbal signaling layer of communication survives under the surface of all human beings and human cultures because nonverbally representing our thoughts, feelings, and experiences forms the core of an ancient root culture that is uniquely human [62].

Are the signals we give to other people always deliberate, intentional, and conscious? No, they are not. The nonverbal signals we give to others become largely unconscious and habitual and may even contradict our verbal communications. When we recognize that each of us individually and collectively as a species have highly developed communication skills that predate our acquisition of words, we can see that we are signaling all kinds of information to each other through our actions all the time. And we may be completely oblivious to what this nonverbal part of us is saying to another person. In this way, we can express ourselves in great detail without having any awareness that this is what we are doing.

Habits

A "habit" is a recurrent, often unconscious pattern of behavior that is acquired through repetition. We are designed to form habits. Consciousness requires a high level of energy, and the brain is always looking for patterns that can become automatic routines, controlled by older parts of the brain and therefore using less energy. Habit is part of what makes us efficient as a species, but it is also why it is so hard to change established habits. We develop and maintain efficiency by repeating any strategy that has worked for us in the past, meaning any strategy that has helped us to survive.

Habits are mental shortcuts that go a long way toward determining what we feel and how we behave in a wide variety of situations. Habits and skills reside in our minds as implicit memories and involve different parts of the brain than memories of facts or explicit memories. Habits allow us to automatically do a lot of things that would otherwise require our full attention. This means that instead of having to pay attention to the same things in our environment repeatedly, we can instead direct our attention to what is immediately most important to us since we only can pay attention to one thing at a time [42].

When you think about it, most of your life revolves around reenacting habitual behavior. If every day, all day, everything you did was experienced as novel, as if you were doing even the simplest things for the first time, life would be very different and exceedingly tedious. One of the reasons new drivers have more accidents than experienced drivers is that they have not yet developed habits, so everything they do is novel. They don't react well to the unanticipated because they are so focused on basic functions.

Habit formation follows a predictable sequence: cue, routine, reward. The brain pays attention to cues that indicate a pattern to use that will conserve energy. Once a cue is perceived, the brain responds automatically and the cue leads to a routine that can be physical, mental, or emotional. Then there is the reward that reinforces the notion that this is a sequence worth maintaining. Once established, this sequence comprises a habit that can be cued by anything that sets up a train of associations to that habitual behavioral pattern.

If you learned how to drive when you were a teenager, then when you get into a car five, six, or seven decades later, the sequence of behaviors—sitting behind the wheel, putting your key in the ignition, putting your foot on the brake, and so on—will happen automatically. If you spent years driving with a backseat driver, then you may also experience heightened anxiety along with the automatic sequence of behaviors. The bottom line is that the contexts of experience trigger habitual responses automatically, far beyond the reach of a person's rational mind. The more this cue–behavioral sequence–reward response occurs, the more deeply embedded and automatic (*unconscious*) the behavioral sequence is for the person. At this point, the basal ganglia in the deep and very old part of the brain has taken over and the conscious brain stops working. The sequence has become a habit [42]. Stress makes the habit even more invulnerable to change by propelling us to do the same thing over and over whether it works or not [63].

Every time we develop a new habit, the brain reorganizes itself. Changing habitual behavioral patterns therefore means changing the brain. Habits can be changed, that is, the brain can learn new things, but the old pattern of activity remains dormant and can be easily activated by a stimulus from the person's earlier experiences and assert itself automatically, particularly under stress [59]. Anyone who has ever tried to quit smoking or stop eating favorite foods has experienced this. The reason is that habits create "neurological cravings"—a powerful need to complete the entire habit loop. This is how we can get "addicted" to just about anything—from a physiologically addictive substance to behaviors like compulsively checking our email. Cue–routine–reward: that's all it takes.

Change, Attachment, and Loss

This difficulty in altering habits is probably due to the fact that we are not built for rapid change. As mammals, we are better equipped to adapt to changing conditions than dinosaurs were. As humans, we are better built for change than, say, dodo birds. But even so, we still aren't very good at it. We are built for slow, gradual alterations in our physical and social environments. For most of our evolutionary history, repeating the past was a good idea. It was better to keep on doing whatever helped you to survive today because it was likely to help you survive tomorrow as well. There wasn't much need to change rapidly unless there was real and present danger, and even when there was, the habits of fight-flight-freeze would kick in to help you to survive.

Our modern world has brought with it an ever-increasing *rate* of change even though we are not terribly good at adapting to the pace of change we have created. We are a bit like an adolescent learning to drive a very fast, powerful car. With a lot of luck, we won't crash and kill ourselves and anybody else. But the faster we go and the less practice we have, the greater the risk. Meanwhile, the biologically based response to threat hasn't changed, so we respond to any number of things as if they were threats, even though our immediate survival is not at stake. Think of the way you feel when someone cuts you off in traffic or jumps a line you are in, or when your child defies you. At the same time, we find it very difficult to respond to threats that are not immediate and therefore do not set off the alarm response, even though those threats may mean long-term danger or even extinction: escalating divisions of wealth, widespread poverty, loss of industrial jobs, environmental toxins, climate change.

Change is so difficult because change inevitably involves loss. Healthy humans are inherently social creatures and can attach to anyone and anything. That being the case, the pain of loss does not end when we grow out of infancy; it just becomes distributed among many more relationships with animate and inanimate objects. To do something new, you have to stop doing the old thing to which you have formed an attachment.

The emotions that accompany any loss of attachment are distressing: anxiety, pain, frustration, confusion, disorientation. The more important the attachment

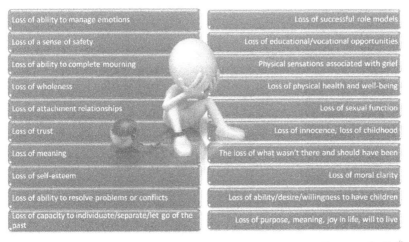

PresenterMedia

Figure 3.1 Losses associated with childhood adversity.

and the more permanent the loss, the more these feelings are not just distressing but rather overwhelming. In the state of acute grief, we are unable to cognitively function. Without an opportunity to share this state of loss with anyone else, the grief can remain as a living presence as the ghosts of the past haunt the present. The losses associated with exposure to childhood adversity may be tangible or intangible losses, often compounded over time (Figure 3.1) [64, 65].

Sending Out Signals

As Iacoboni has pointed out, *"the initial automatic mirroring of the facial expressions of babies triggers a whole cascade of other automatic simulative brain responses that reenact interactions between mother and baby in real life"* (pp. 128–129) [38]. Because of the amazing human mirror system, we have been signaling to other members of our social group for as long as human beings have existed, and our social group has responded to us through the development of largely nonverbal rituals to help each of us, and the community as a whole, to move through life passages [66].

The emotions associated with loss are so overwhelming that we cannot move on in life unless we *do* something, take some form of action. Thinking and feeling are usually not sufficient. Historically, rituals have been a central part of group life. Even today, if you visit a Native American community, much of their time, energy, and devotion will be spent in preparing for and performing their traditional dances. All of our modern Western transitional rituals—graduations, bachelor

:ties, bridal showers, baby showers, retirement parties—are designed to help :ople let go of one state and move to something entirely new.

Likewise, we have always dealt with overwhelming experiences by creating rituals in which individual and group healing takes place as a group ceremony, usually accompanied by deliberately changing our physiology through music, dance, sleep deprivation, pain, fasting, and the use of mind-altering substances. Historically, group ceremonies have often required a reenactment of initial and pathogenic trauma paired with a reenactment of great myths of the tribe; afterward, the injured person is reintegrated into the group and expected to help heal others.

Tragic experiences of loss in particular require social responses for healing to occur. Memorials, funerals, and burials all embody various ritual passages to deal with the tragic aspect of human existence, the uncontrollable nature of loss. The grieving persons signal their loss by doing things like crying, tearing their hair out, dressing themselves and their houses all in black, retreating from normal activities, burning the loved one's possessions, and carrying out many other actions that vary from culture to culture and across time. Other people respond by specifying a time-honored pathway for remembering what is gone, gradually letting go of one attachment in order to move into a future that holds new attachments.

So far, so good. We can understand why we have such a strong tendency to repeat the past: we form strong attachments; we signal what we need to those to whom we are attached first with nonverbal signals and then with words; based on the patterns of how we maintain attachments, we learn to deal with the world through habits that we readily form; and when we are overwhelmed by the loss of attachment, we turn to other people for help in guiding us through a culturally established passage between the past, the present, and the future.

These very natural facets of human experience drive our tendency to repeat the past. We have all experienced this sequence as a part of normal human existence. But what happens when the attachment is not completely lost but is disrupted? What happens when those disruptions occur again and again? What happens if the loss of attachment is not recognized by other people, or occurs at an early age, or is so traumatic that no one can think about it, much less talk about it? Understanding the normative human experiences we have just described forms a bridge between understanding healthy growth and change and the compulsive repetition of the past known as "traumatic reenactment."

The Commitment to Growth and Change and Trauma-Informed Practice

Traumatic Reenactment

People who are traumatized appear to lose all or some of the capacity to choose courses of action. Their behavior, particularly problematic behavior, is often repetitive, even when it is self-destructive. Sigmund Freud called this puzzling phenomenon the "repetition compulsion" and defined it as *"an ungovernable process originating in the unconscious"* (p. 78) [67]. He went on to describe the ways in which the person deliberately places himself in distressing situations, which then automatically creates a repetition of old experiences, while the person remains oblivious to the patterns that are related to the past but instead feels as though it is all happening for the first time, in the moment.

As early as 1889, it was recognized that traumatized people are likely to respond to reminders of the past by automatically engaging in physical actions or sequences of actions that were formerly relevant but are no longer appropriate to the present time and place. Pierre Janet, a contemporary of Freud, noted that *"traumatized patients are continuing the action, or rather the attempt at action, which began when the thing happened and they exhaust themselves in these everlasting recommencements"* (p.4) [68].

"Traumatic reenactment" is the term we use to describe the lingering behavioral enactment and automatic repetition of the traumatic past. It is unconscious in that the person engaged in the reenactment usually makes no connection between present circumstances and past events. Such behavior has puzzled many people working in the field of traumatic stress because it appears so counterintuitive at first glance. Why would anyone, having survived great danger, place themselves in situations where they reexperience it over and over?

There have been a number of possible explanations for this common occurrence. It has been proposed that sometimes people are trying to master the experience and at other times they seem to be seeking punishment for real or imagined crimes. Some people may become addicted to the state of arousal, and others may induce pain to facilitate the avoidance of memories [69].

In addition to these possible explanations, there are circumstances directly related to the states we achieve when we are very frightened, especially when our lives are threatened, that also seem to play an important role in the development of this seemingly self-destructive behavior: disrupted attachment, fear conditioning, state-dependent learning, addiction to trauma, the loss of language, failed enactment schemas, and self-fulfilling prophecies. We will explore these one by one and then put it all together in an integrated theory about why we repeat the past.

Disrupted Attachment

Because attachment is so vital to our survival, any disruption of attachment from birth to death triggers feelings of protest, anger, anxiety, fear, and, if the disruption is permanent, despair. These disruptions then interfere with the unfolding of healthy development in ways that are unique to each individual but that are at the heart of most physical, psychological, social, and moral dysfunctions. As one traumatized child put it, *"there is a hole in my heart."* Disrupted attachment creates a hole that we cannot fill by ourselves. But whatever the case, when we are overwhelmed, we turn to other people for help. We signal our distress because when we are trapped in the quicksand of grief, we cannot get out by ourselves. But if you have experienced disrupted attachment—if the people who were supposed to respond to your distress did not do so—then you cannot directly ask for help. Instead you must request help in indirect ways often by doing things that the rest of us call "symptoms."

Fear Conditioning

A pattern of behavior that has been learned when we have been very frightened tends to become deeply embedded in our minds. This is called "fear conditioning." Once fear conditioning has occurred, it is very difficult, if not impossible, to undo it. This kind of emotional memory is likely to function completely outside of our conscious awareness and is stored in parallel with more cognitive memories about the events so that we do not even recognize that we are responding to something because it reminds us of something very frightening in the past. We call these things "triggers." Generally, what we call a trigger is a cue for some behavioral sequence that originated in the context of something very frightening or even life-threatening. The reward is a temporary relief from the fear. It is easy to see how this could set up a vicious cycle for someone who has been frightened so that the behavioral sequence easily becomes detached from any meaningful response in the present but instead is stimulated by any arousal of fear or threat. In other words, it becomes a habit.

State-Dependent Learning

State-dependent learning is part of this picture as well. It occurs when what is learned in one state of mind, or under the influence of a particular drug, appears to be lost and forgotten until the person once again enters that state of mind. When the event is recalled, or triggered by some association, the cognitive memories may be recalled in parallel with the emotional memories, not as a recognized memory but as a state of being, sensations in the body, feeling states that the person may not consciously even connect to the cognitive memories of something from the past. The state of awareness the person is in then may trigger or cue the habit [70,71].

The Addictive Potential of Arousal

Complicating things further may be the role of substances that our own bodies produce known as "endogenous opioids." These powerful chemicals, which are similar to morphine and heroin, are an essential part of both the attachment system and the stress response. Under conditions of repetitive stress and as a result of the repeated release of these endogenous or internal opioids, the person may develop what is called "stress-induced analgesia." In this way, people may become "addicted to trauma," putting themselves in conditions of otherwise avoidable danger because they unknowingly seek the relief they will get from the effects of the opioids, even though it is only temporary relief [72]. This biologically based response may be part of what keeps the habit in place, part of the reward experience in the cue–routine–reward sequence.

Loss of Language—Speechless Terror

This situation is complicated even further by the nature of traumatic memories. Conscious recall of our experience is called "declarative memory" or "explicit memory," and traumatic experience appears to interfere with this part of the human memory system, the ability to capture the experience in words or symbols. Instead, the person experiences "speechless terror," encoding the information from the experience in nonverbal somatosensory form, not in words. But it is words that provide us with the context of experience: when the event happened, who was there, what we did, where we were. Whatever has not been put into words cannot be properly categorized and contained as a "past" event. The context of the experience is separated or "dissociated" from the experience itself [73]. The dissociated content of the traumatic experience(s) then forms the elements of the experience that is reenacted through behavior and in relationships with other people. In this way, the past haunts the present.

Failed Enactment

When we are confronted with a threat to our survival, our minds form action plans for surviving, our muscles respond, and we take action. This happens automatically and instantaneously and is not under conscious control. It is part of the basic mammalian survival response that we all have. But when the trauma actually occurs and we get hurt, or someone else does, our action plan was a failure because it did not prevent the trauma. This often arouses feelings of significant guilt and shame in the survivor. One of the early pioneers in studying the impact of trauma, Robert Lifton, called this "failed enactment" and defined it as *"some beginning, abortive image forms toward enactment in a more positive way that is never possible to achieve . . . a schema for enactment that is never completed"* that continues to press for enactment and ends up being reenacted in current relationships (p. 9) [74]. Usually, neither the person involved nor the people around him or her make any connection between odd behavior in the present and the past history of trauma. Researchers now are taking advantage of this phenomenon by using things like Virtual Reality as treatment approaches so that the person can recall the experiences in a vivid way but this time can alter the outcome [75]. We found that psychodramatic approaches had a similar and powerful positive impact, but they are frequently no longer available in treatment settings because of funding cutbacks.

Self-Fulfilling Prophecies

Once repetitive patterns are in play, what keeps them there? Why don't people just "get over it" and change? Another key to understanding this complex phenomenon is a specific form of habitual patterns called "self-fulfilling prophecies."

A self-fulfilling prophecy is a false definition of a situation that evokes a new behavior that makes the original false conception come true [76]. Self-fulfilling prophecies represent a basic mechanism behind reenactment behavior. For example, research has demonstrated that teachers who communicate low expectations to students by paying them less attention, smiling less often, maintaining less eye contact, calling on them less often, providing fewer cues, criticizing them more and praising them less, providing them with less feedback, and demanding less from them elicit lower performance regardless of the actual abilities of the students [77].

Similarly, managers can communicate low expectations of clients or employees by doing or not doing the same things: paying attention to someone only when he or she does something wrong, failing to praise, failing to give any feedback at all, and failing to provide the information the person needs to learn how to do the job well. Self-fulfilling prophecies can be mutual and take on a life of their own.

Foreshortened Sense of the Future

Complicating this situation further, and connecting to difficulties with growth and change, is a central issue with imagining the future, an activity that should precede action. It is well established that trauma survivors often have a "foreshortened sense of the future," meaning that they have difficulties in anticipating the consequences of behavior. People who have trouble with this often function on the basis of maximizing pleasure and minimizing pain in the immediate present without apparent thought to where that style of coping is leading them. There is some research showing that a part of the brain called the "hippocampus" may be involved in imagining future events, and since we know that the hippocampus can be damaged by psychological trauma, this may be an underlying cause, not only for many of the memory and learning problems associated with trauma, but for the foreshortened sense of future as well [78].

Putting It All Together in Peter's Story

Combine these very human and natural processes together, and what we end up with is traumatic reenactment (Figure 3.2). In this way, the past comes to

Figure 3.2 What drives traumatic reenactment?

haunt the present outside of a person's conscious awareness and without the person's willing consent. Our "will" isn't nearly as "free" as our social and legal systems would have us believe [15]. Children and adults who have experienced substantial adversity and trauma are highly likely to reenact their terrible experiences in new and apparently unrelated contexts because like everyone else, they have formed habits of responding to the events of their own experience. Unfortunately, because they have been helpless to prevent these fear-provoking, horrifying, and shaming experiences, the behavioral sequence that is automatically repeated can produce dire results, often creating self-fulfilling prophecies. In this way, traumatic reenactment becomes relational as the person's signals are misread by those around him or her and are often responded to in ways that directly counter what the traumatized person requires in order to change.

If we use this understanding, we are able to look at Peter's problem from a new perspective. In his case, the initial cause of his developmental problems was multiple experiences of disrupted attachment throughout his early childhood because of the violence in his mother's life and the effect that violence had on their relationship. She loved him, but when she was hurt herself, either physically or psychologically, she was not available to him. Before he had any words, he had multiple experiences of terror in his daily life (*speechless terror*), feelings that were overwhelming and intolerable. On many occasions, even as a very little boy, he tried to protect her, only to be tossed aside by men big and stronger than him (*failed enactment*). He learned that other people could not be relied upon, and he developed the habit of protecting himself by doing things that would keep people away (*self-fulfilling prophecies*). He watched what the males in his life did when threatened, and he learned to use his fists to ward off all kinds of distressing emotions whenever he was frightened (*fear conditioning*). Frightening other people felt better than being frightened himself, and whenever he experienced any kind of threat, he would automatically enter a state over which he had no control. In this state his belligerence would increase, his anger and sense of power would rise, and he would become aggressive (*state-dependent learning*). When he could start a fight or bully someone less powerful than himself, he felt especially good, so that whenever he felt the pain of loss or shame, it felt good just to provoke a fight (*addiction to trauma*), and when he got hit, it didn't even hurt (*stress-induced analgesia*). This behavior had become so habitual that he could not imagine relating to people in any other way (*foreshortened future*). Peter was trapped and alone in a vicious cycle of reenactment.

The death of his grandfather was both a crisis and an opportunity. This relationship had been one island of relational health with a male in his life, a man whom he could identify with in order to help him figure out what it means to be a man. Within that relationship, his aggressive habits were suspended and he had the opportunity to experience and learn entirely different ways of viewing himself and others. The "good" Peter who emerged after the snowstorm was there all along, but the loss of his grandfather had left that part of him stranded in the quicksand of grief. He desperately needed other people to see the potential for good in him and throw him a rope to pull him out of the mire. That is exactly what the staff at the treatment program did: they gave him an opportunity to make some different choices, and he did so. They viewed his symptoms as signals, as cries for help., They responded, threw him a rope, and Peter was able to climb out and set himself on a different future pathway.

Will Peter be able to stay on that pathway? We hope so. But whether he does so or repeats the past is not entirely in his hands. He has both challenges and strengths. The challenges include habits of a lifetime, even a young lifetime, and habits are hard to break. The more deeply wired the brain has become, the harder it is to change habits, a very good reason why treating injured people as early as possible makes a great deal of sense. Change in adults, even older adults, is certainly possible. You can, in fact, teach old dogs new tricks [65]. It does, however, require more repetitions, and young as he still is, Peter will require many positive experiences with trusting adults before he changes the basic wiring of his brain.

Another challenge is the addictive and contagious nature of violence that he has already experienced and that is now also wired into his brain. This leaves him vulnerable to a return to past habits when he is confronted by threat in the future. The seductive temptation of exerting power and control over others that Peter has seen modeled in his early life, particularly in response to feelings of anxiety, helplessness, shame, and loss, leaves Peter vulnerable to interpersonal violence in his own adult relationships at home, at school, and at work. He also is a traumatized child, and we know that a past history of trauma can resurface as ugly problems that reside in the body, in emotions, in haunting memories, and in behavior sometimes decades after the events have occurred.

But Peter also has significant strengths. Although he has a disrupted attachment with his mother, he did have an attachment and has had the opportunity to drink from the cup of human kindness. His mother wasn't perfect, but she did love him and still does. It is impossible to emphasize how important that preverbal maternal love, care, and attention are for the development of body, brain, and basic trust. His relationship to his grandfather and all it meant to him is a significant strength that opens up the possibility and hope that he can be like his grandfather, who was a hard-working, kind, compassionate man. The obviousness of the signals he gives, the ways in which he draws attention to his pain, are also, ironically, a source of strength because he demands that other people respond to him and engage with him. And now he has had a positive experience in a treatment program of moving along an entirely different, and therefore less predictable, pathway.

But one positive experience is not usually enough to change a person's life trajectory. Peter is probably going to need experiences with many people that mimic what happened at Andrus if he is going to break the deeply entrenched habits he has developed. We use him as an example to illustrate how important it is for anyone in a position to help other people to have or develop expertise in reading the cries for help that are embedded in all behavioral symptoms. And make no mistake about it—change is what intervention of any sort is all about. If, as helpers, we have not changed the trajectory our clients are on, then we have not done our job effectively. So, let's take a moment and consider how the *Commitment to Growth and Change* is applied to whole organizations.

Organizational Commitment to Growth and Change

Since organizations are comprised entirely of living human beings, the same forces that help determine Peter's behavior affect everyone's behavior. We readily create habits that help us become efficient, we are constantly signaling our distress to others around us, and those signals readily create self-fulfilling prophecies that help us feel good or not so good about ourselves and others. Every staff member has a history of relational experiences that is likely to include exposure to sustained adversity and to trauma. Organizations as a whole, along with everyone who is a stakeholder in the organizations, experience multiple losses and sometimes trauma.

Individuals who have been hurt are extremely attentive to threat. They scan the environment constantly looking for signals that they are at risk or unsafe. As a result, they often have difficulty focusing on many other activities in front of them, such as learning math, reading a book, or having fun. The attention to threat impedes growth and the ability to live a well-rounded life.

The same thing happens to staff members who are charged with the task of helping clients to recover from their injuries. Because many of these clients pose significant safety risks, they may hurt themselves as well as others and often thwart our efforts to engage them in activities that promote growth. We end up focused exclusively on the threat and, as a result, our field of vision narrows. The program becomes all about physical safety and all of our programs, interventions, and conversations focus on how to make sure that no one gets hurt rather than make sure that everyone grows, changes, and learns. As our field of vision narrows, so does our sense of what is possible. In that space, there is little choice but to reenact the patterns that people have always been used in dealing with the client. We do not explore what is possible, but instead stick with what appears to be safe.

Traumatic reenactment is a powerful force, not only in the lives of our clients but in our treatment, service delivery, and educational programs as well. Clients come to us with a long history of injury, disrupted attachments, rejection, and failure. Once in our setting, their behavior sets the stage for this familiar pattern to repeat itself with us. The client engages in dangerous or aggressive behavior and prompts the treatment staff to respond in an all too familiar way. In most instances, our staff responds to the behavior by doing things like punishing it, isolating the client, or removing privileges. In acute care settings the responses may be even more dramatic, such as calling in police S.W.A.T. teams, using stun guns, intimidating people with police dogs, forcing medications, and, of course, seclusion and restraint. The program becomes riveted on the threat caused by the behavior, and the primary task becomes reducing or eliminating the threat.

The *Commitment to Growth and Change* requires us to have a basic understanding of what is behind reenactment behavior, what it looks like, and what to do to change the script that is being delivered to us, regardless of whether we are talking about our clients, our colleagues, or the entire organization. A significant contributor to creating a social learning environment and fulfilling the *Commitment to Growth and Change* is being able to recognize patterns of reenactment as they may manifest in self-fulfilling prophecies. The objective is to intervene before they occur and to identify patterns of traumatic reenactment that trap staff members and clients in repetitive cycles of adversity.

In order to successfully rescript reenactment, we need to be constantly creative and innovative, and that is much more likely to happen if staff members do not have to function as isolated individuals, but instead are always backed up by a team of people they trust. The interesting thing about this is that since we are so influenced by social expectations, when those expectations are changed, we change as well, as we described happened to Peter. The loops that reinforce positive rather than negative behavior have been called "virtuous cycles" [79]. This is usually a matter of expecting the best of people instead of the worst; we tend to live up or down to social expectations.

Recognizing Reenactment

It is sometimes difficult for staff and teams to recognize when they are caught in a reenactment, and although reenactment is not the only reason clients do not make the gains they hope they will make, it is a major impediment. It is crucial that providers recognize when this is happening and adjust as quickly as possible. The key questions we have to ask in helping people change their scripts are: Is anything we are doing helping this person to change? In what ways? If not, are we caught in the other person's reenactment scenario? If so, how do we change that script to produce a different outcome?

When we honestly and searchingly ask those key questions that focus on reenactment, we find that we ourselves are often the biggest barriers to change. We chide our clients for their reluctance to make change while at the same time we keep doing the same thing over and over, even though it is clearly not working. In doing so, our clients' cries for help often go unheeded. Instead, we label and judge the pain and devise coercive or punitive measures to deal with it, but we fail to recognize the signal the person is sending to us and his or her cries for help [46].

Too often we respond to these cries for help by engaging in a reenactment with the client; as a result, the "help" we offer only repeats past experiences. Our helping organizations are often entrenched in repeating habits that have become automatic, accepted, and unchallenged. As we meet the client's problem behavior with the age-old responses—coercion, rejection, isolation, reprimand, punishment—the established pattern of reenactment is repeated and the groove, already worn into the brain and psyche of the client, is dug deeper and deeper. As time passes, these patterns become so commonplace that it grows progressively easier to fall into the ruts. When this happens, the team seems unable to do anything other than focus on the threat presented by the client. It becomes easy to meet the ongoing scary behavior displayed by the client with more and more restriction, isolation, and containment.

Since reenactment is an unconscious process, identifying its invisible hand in the service delivery process is challenging. Paying ongoing attention to the Sanctuary Commitments and using the Sanctuary Toolkit, especially Red Flag Reviews, are the best ways to avoid this trap, and once in the trap, are our best hope of finding our way out. If we remain unflinchingly committed to growth and change, then we will not accept that we are trapped with our clients in a loop of reliving and reexperiencing the past. If we are not getting the change we say we are committed to, then we will need to change what we are doing. "Things change when we change things" has become somewhat of a mantra in our work, and it is a constant reminder that we do have the power to change and we need to be willing to exercise that power.

Rescripting Reenactment

What we need to be able to do with our most troubled and most injured clients is alter our field of vision and be open to the possibility that the last thing we think of, the goofiest or most outlandish idea, might actually be the thing that will make a difference. Changing reenactment scenarios requires innovation. Why would the goofiest idea be the one that sparks change? It seems to us that it is the one that is least expected, and as such is the one that is most likely to break the pattern the client has found him- or herself in for years. It is this intervention that, oddly enough, focuses more on what the client could be rather than what he or she has always been (Figure 3.3).

Dr. Maggie Bennington-Davis, now the Chief Medical and Operating Officer for Cascadia Behavioral Healthcare in Portland, Oregon, shared one of her experiences with a staff that was adopting the Sanctuary principles for an acute care inpatient unit.

> *We had to admit a middle-aged, chronically mentally ill man named Tom to our acute care inpatient unit. The staff members were dreading his admission because he had been in the hospital many times before. Each time he was hospitalized, a staff member had been injured by his violent conduct. At this point we had already had some Sanctuary training and were meeting regularly*

Figure 3.3 Rescripting requires innovation.

to figure out how to apply the principles, particularly the Commi
Nonviolence, to our program. I knew the nursing staff had met to dis
they were going to handle him, but I was at another meeting and di.
the outcome when I returned to the unit and watched a scene unfold. While
I watched, three of my nursing staff members advanced toward his room, where
he was poised for attack, barricaded behind his bed. One of the staff members
held a sedative-filled hypodermic to administer if he had to, another held his
medication and a cup of water, and the third was clearly there for "muscle." All
three entered his room and then, to the surprise of Tom and me, they broke
out in a rather loud rendition of "God Bless America." Their unpredictability
launched an unpredicted response in Tom—he stood up, relaxed, and put out
his hand for his medication. The ice was broken, everyone laughed, and Tom
had a brief and uneventful stay in the hospital.

Unfortunately, people who work in social service and mental health programs are often afraid to take necessary risks because the bureaucracies we all
function in are also riveted on the risks and attend almost exclusively to threat
rather than opportunity. Rules and regulations are all directed at avoiding the
possibility that something can go wrong. The fundamental problem is that
something is bound to go wrong. How can it not? We serve people who have
significant difficulties and have sometimes been unmanageable in their home,
school, and community; that is precisely why they were sent to us. There is no
magic about treatment or any kind of social intervention. We cannot suddenly
wave a wand and make people better. No, staff members must struggle with the
same challenges that everyone else already has, and there are bound to be risks.
We try to minimize those risks, but if we are going to bring about change, we
will need to try something that hasn't been tried before, and when we do, there
is *always* a risk that it will fail. But in the current climate, we end up spending
the bulk of our time avoiding risk rather than seeking recovery. So, the important questions that we should be asking are "What is the greatest threat?" and
"How do we move from simply managing risk to supporting growth, change,
and recovery?"

Brian shared another story of a challenging teenager and how the staff broke
away from the compulsive reenactment of his pain.

We were treating a teenager who was very aggressive and explosive. In previous
months, we had tried to manage his aggressive behavior by placing the child on
one-to-one care and thereby frequently isolating him from his peers, whom he
routinely threatened and hit. None of these interventions had put a dent in the
problem behavior; in fact, it was getting worse. It became clear to everyone that
dealing with this behavior simply by trying to contain and manage it was not
working. But when we are exposed to behavior that scares us, we do not always
respond in ways that advance the work. In this boy's case, we finally provided a

different response. The team knew that he loved to cook and often liked to help out with such projects. The opportunities for helping out were becoming quite limited, because most staff did not want this boy in the kitchen, where there was access to flames, knives, forks, glass, and other dangerous implements. So, the one thing we knew he liked we took away.

Upon reviewing the case, the team decided that it was worth taking a risk, and so we set up a program with the child in which every day he would leave school early (he was pretty tapped out academically by the afternoon anyway) and then return to the cottage to bake cookies, cakes, and pies with one of the staff. When his cottage mates returned from school, they had fresh-baked snacks every day. The former scourge of the cottage was now a hero, much loved and appreciated by his cottage mates for his culinary efforts. The response was not the standard response for this boy. The script in which he hurt others and was therefore feared and reviled was completely different. He now served others and was appreciated and thanked for his efforts and kindness. We broke out of his reenactment, and that allowed him the opportunity to experience an entirely different way of relating to others.

Implications for Growth and Change Leadership

It is much easier for us to talk about the changes our clients need to make than to institute the changes we need to make to create the conditions for the desired change to occur. It is easy to blame clients or staff who are stuck, referring to them as "resistant," "avoidant," or "hostile," while never really exploring how we might change *our* approach and potentially yield a different result. As an administrator, Brian had a remarkable experience over the past 18 months as he attempted to make change happen in his own organization.

I have talked a lot over the years about the idea that if we want clients to change we have to change first, but sadly, I did not really walk the talk. I was often frustrated that I had managers who did not push their direct reports. I was comfortable complaining about this situation, but I was doing very little to change it. I was more comfortable whining about how others were not doing what was needed, how they were not changing. But I discovered that I was complaining that the people who reported to me were not willing to do things that in fact I was not willing to do either. I made excuses, saying that I had to pace the change, manage things incrementally, avoid major disruptions. All of this kept me stuck, comfortable in my own discomfort.

One day I realized that I was the problem. I cannot explain how or why it finally hit me, but it did. Looking back, I think that as my role has changed in the organization over the years, I have continued to hold on to familiar ways of operating, comfortable habits. I enjoyed being the chief problem solver, and the way I did my job maintained that familiar role for me. I was not changing my method of operating as my responsibilities expanded. For a long time people had told me, as the Chief Operating Officer, that I need to be more of a cheerleader, more positive and enthusiastic. I used to respond by saying, "That's not really who I am; I am really, not that way. I am kind of a curmudgeon."

But I started thinking, "I am really not that way today, but could I become that way? If I was a little less inhibited, a little braver, a little more willing to fail, could I be that way?" Saying "That's not really who I am" is essentially saying "I can't change." I know I cannot change all at once, but I can change a little at a time, and maybe I can become that person I am not today. After all, we usually do not accept it when one of our clients says, "Hey, I am just explosive...I get mad, I hit people, that's just me." Or when a staff member says, "I'm just kind of lazy; I don't like working very hard. It's just my way," we don't generally say, "Great, we'll learn to live with that." But when it comes to senior managers making a change, it is pretty easy to say, "I am fine—you change."

The truth is, if the only thing I can really change is me, then I'd better be ready to change. Since I came to this realization and started making the necessary changes in myself, everything has begun to change. I have taken great pains to be as respectful as possible and as compassionate as possible, and I occasionally fall short of that goal. Nonetheless, the direction has been unflinching, unwavering and relentless. I have taken some lumps, but we have assembled a team that I believe can really do the hard stuff and work together. It is difficult to admit that I was the problem, but I was. It is nice to report that I think I may also be the solution. The take-away for me was that the mantra "The change begins with me" was really true. Change in our organization has cascaded since this initial revelation. Now something new and exciting happens every day.

Be the Change You Want to See

If we could change ourselves, the tendencies in the world would also change. As a man changes his own nature, so does the attitude of the world change towards him. This is the divine mystery supreme. A wonderful thing it is and the source of our happiness. We need not wait to see what others do. (p. 241)

M. Gandhi, *The Collected Works of M. K. Gandhi*, The Publications Division, New Delhi, India, Volume 13, Chapter 153

We lay out this challenge with a little (actually a lot of) reluctance because both of us can point to many times when we have not volunteered when we had to take on the status quo. What we are suggesting is that the things that keep *us* from changing situations may be the very things that keep our clients from making hard changes in their lives. When all is said and done, we are not that different from each other. We just have more or less to protect. We all have our own habits and ways of operating that we are reluctant to change.

It is not uncommon for us to feel powerless and ineffective when working with very challenging clients, but what would happen if we all chose to smile and say something nice to a client or a coworker, even when we are not really "feeling it?" We often convince ourselves that it does not matter, but it does. And it matters more when we are in a supervisory or leadership position. To paraphrase Gandhi, we have to be the change that we want to see. It starts with us.

Leadership and the Emerging Future in Complex Organizations

It has been pointed out in dozens of management books that one of the main roles of leaders is to inspire people to move toward a different vision of the future than they would hold on their own. The future is actually where leaders must begin, just as we began this book and these chapters with a vision of possibility. Without that imagined lamp directing us into the future, we all are stumbling in the dark, bumping into each other and usually going off in the wrong direction.

The world of organizational leadership has become increasingly challenging and complex; there is a growing recognition that leaders cannot predict and control the organization's future simply because the future is so unpredictable and complicated. This is essentially why top-down, hierarchical control is giving way to a different way of doing things. Once we recognize that the future is constantly *emerging* from the vast, interconnected nature of all the forces within and playing upon an organization, it becomes clear that a different kind of leadership is required. It has to be leadership that helps organizations to adapt more rapidly and with less stress than ever before.

The Sanctuary Model process is designed to help effective leaders recognize the importance of promoting interactions between and among people rather than trying to control those interactions. The Sanctuary Model itself has emerged out of the complex interactions of many people over several decades. As Sandy recalls,

> I began working with Andrus in 2000. They asked me to come in and consult with them because the knowledge about trauma was just then receiving attention and they wanted to be on the cutting edge. But at the time, I had no clear idea what to tell them to do. I knew what we had learned in treating adults in a specific place at a particular time, but I wasn't sure what they should do. I did believe, however, that if I created the right conditions, something new and different would emerge. I also knew that the organizational commitment to the welfare of children in their care was very high. So, I had Brian organize a team of about two dozen people representing most of the layers of the organization. We met together two days a month for a year. It was a huge commitment of time and resources for a small organization. It was an enriching experience for

*me and I think for everyone who participated. But what emerged out of it—
the Sanctuary Institute—was completely unexpected and unplanned. If I had
tried to control the outcome, I do not think that there would have been room
to grow. Believing in the self-organizing property in groups and organizations
requires us to tolerate a high level of uncertainty and provide support without
always being in control. It is an entirely different kind of leadership than what
we are accustomed to think about as leadership.*

Adaptive Versus Technical Problems

In human service delivery, we have a historical burden to carry in that there
is a long-standing belief that in our line of work we are dealing with technical problems. A client carries a diagnosis, and that means we give him or
her a medication or a specific behavioral plan and the client should respond.
Technical problems generally lend themselves to cookbook kinds of solutions
such as "Ten Easy Steps to Put Your Backyard Grill Together" or "The Proper
Procedures for Filing XYZ Form."

But in reality, the problems we are dealing with are generally adaptive problems, problems that have never been solved before. We may have solved a problem like this before but not this one. This is a different client. This is a different
day, a different year. The people involved in delivering the new response are
different. There are always different variables that make this problem different
from the last one. Every story is a different story; every reenactment is a different reenactment (Figure 3.4).

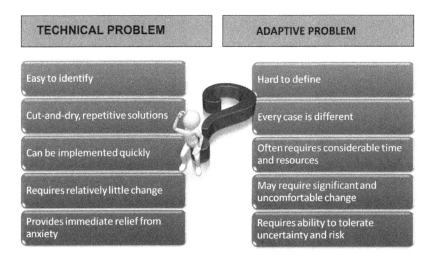

Figure 3.4 What kind of problem is it?

Because our work is so complex and the outcomes are so uncertain, we yearn for technical problems; as a result, we often treat adaptive problems as if they are technical problems. Point systems and standard operating procedures on how to handle a specific crisis might help us feel better, but they cannot replace a good discussion between a group of caring and committed people.

In order to reach good solutions to adaptive problems, the group leader needs to be able to contain the group's anxiety enough to allow it to do its work while encouraging everyone to participate and provide input. The leader may maintain ultimate authority for decision making, but allowing for and benefiting from the experiences and wisdom of the team will serve to improve the decision-making process.

Organizational leaders play a key role in managing the emotional world of the organization. If we are reactive, anxious, scared, hopeless, and helpless, others will likely follow suit. The ability of managers to regulate their own emotional world is crucial. When we become overwhelmed, we may be more likely to jump in and try to fix a problem without knowing all the facts, not because we necessarily know the answers, but because we just want to feel that we are doing something to better manage our emotions. Conversely, we are also susceptible to withdrawal when we feel overwhelmed. Just like workers who may behave too aggressively or too passively in the face of a challenge, leaders can behave the same way. As Brian recalls,

> What I think the last few years have been about for me has been a constant and steady push to the future. Because I fundamentally want people to like me and want to have good relationships with the people I work with, I have tried to bring some people who grew up in an old system— ours or the system of an agency we merged with— along in the new direction. But over time, some people's idea of the future is a return to the past or a desire to hold on to the past. But the quest has been to build a team that shares my vision for the future. Although my vision is fuzzy sometimes, I know that we need to keep our feet moving and that I can't do it by myself.
>
> I used to talk about the process of change as being akin to rolling a very large rock. I have a house in Pennsylvania, and overall, it is a pretty rocky state. I have dug some large rocks up out of my yard and have attempted to move them across the yard. Because none of these rocks are perfectly round, they do not roll straight, and when you try to roll them they take some rather circuitous routes. But I have found that the key to rolling a rock is to keep it moving, even if it starts to go off course a little; you try to adjust it as you roll it because you can't adjust when it is just sitting there.
>
> When you are trying to change things, big things, heavy things, like culture, you need to keep the rocks rolling and you need people with you who do not say things like "It's too heavy," "It has always been there," "Let's just work around

it," "It's not round enough; it will fall on my toe," or "It's not really a rock." You need people who share your vision of a rock-free yard who will roll it with you, even when it rolls a little off course. At times, I do lose my way and abdicate responsibility because I lose sight of the future, or the "rock" gets too heavy. But I am starting to get some people around me who will help me roll this thing. I know we are going to get somewhere.

Sanctuary Toolkit for Growth and Change

So, now you are armed with some understanding of why it is so difficult for clients, staff, leaders, and organizations to change, even when change is the primary reason for their existence. It's important to always keep your eye on the ball or on that awkwardly shaped rock that is rolling ahead into the future. In the following sections, we discuss some of the methods we use in the Sanctuary Implementation Process to help organizations identify and contend with the forces that keep them and their clients stuck in the past.

The Reenactment Triangle

All clients and staff need to be taught the concepts associated with traumatic reenactment. If they do not understand what is going on, how will they be able to pull themselves and each other out of these repetitive patterns?

The Reenactment Triangle is a useful tool for staff and for clients. We teach it to staff members in orientation, teach it to clients in our psychoeducational groups, and use it on a regular basis (Figure 3.5). Originally known as the Karpman Drama Triangle, traumatic reenactment can be seen in the shifting roles that clients and staff assume in the "rescuer-victim-persecutor" triangle." First described in the 1960s by a transactional analysis therapist named Stephen Karpman, it started as a bunch of doodles that Karpman was drawing while contemplating basketball and football plays [80]. It turned out to be a powerful tool in understanding some of the more perplexing aspects of human behavior. Karpman described three dramatic roles that people act out in daily life that are common, unsatisfactory, repetitive, and largely unconscious and that are related to events in the past rather than in the present.

If you are stuck in playing any of these roles, you and the other person are destined to play all three of the roles, and unless you can put a stop to it, you will be playing those three roles endlessly. Playing any of these roles represents the *lack* of change even though one role is exchanged for another. A key notion here is that it is impossible to rescue someone from something that has already happened, and that is what reenactment is about. We are not saying that when a child is drowning in a pool, there is something wrong with rescuing him and chiding the other kid who pushed him in. But if the near-drowning incident occurred 10

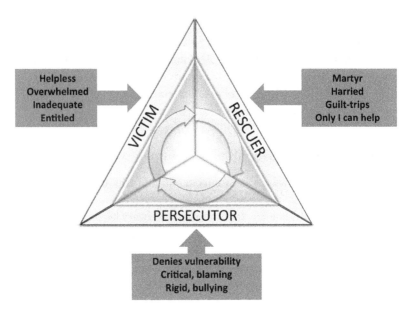

Figure 3.5 Reenactment triangle.

or 20 years ago, no matter how hard you try, you cannot undo the past that the other person is still stuck in. Your job is to figure out how to free the person from being stuck in the past, how to get yourself and the other person off the triangle; everyone else's job is to figure out how to make that happen as well.

Red Flag and Green Flag Reviews

In reality, the clients in our care who have made the greatest strides are the ones who someone or everyone took a risk on and decided that their future did not need to be a repetition of their past. Someone realized that the riskiest thing of all was to play it safe and continue to do what was not working, never had worked, and never would work. When a team member or a client recognizes that something is wrong, a problem is occurring in the community, or there is no progress, it is his or her responsibility in the Sanctuary Model to call a "Red Flag Review."

A Red Flag Meeting is a team meeting called to respond to any critical incident or concern. Some examples include elopements, a rise in physical holds, an incident of aggression, an injury to a client or staff member, a complaint from a client, a breakdown in communication, an unrelenting staff conflict, an unexpected and unannounced change, sudden implementation of a bad policy—basically any circumstance that is likely to require the combined brain-power of the entire community.

The purpose of a Red Flag Review is to respond to a problem before it becomes a bigger problem with a collective voice, to learn as much as possible as a mechanism of social learning, and to formulate a plan that will prevent the problem from escalating or spreading. It requires us to talk directly to each other rather than using intermediaries, and it requires us to treat everyone involved with honesty, integrity, and respect. A Red Flag Review is a good time to reestablish boundaries and make accountability and responsibility agreements among the people represented at the Review.

Red Flag Meetings can be called by anyone in the community to discuss an issue facing the community—and we mean anyone. Red Flag Meetings are truly becoming embedded in the culture when a child or adult in a treatment setting can call one, or when people who are perceived as having little formal power call one to discuss a problem. Red Flag Reviews are most effective when they include everyone involved in the critical issue, are structured, are focused on the patterns of reenactments, and involve planning, a written plan, and a review process.

A Green Flag Review is called for the same purpose as a Red Flag Review—social learning to further growth and change. But the purpose is different in that Green Flag Reviews focus on a notable success or achievement and how it was obtained. After all, success is what we want more of, so we need to start paying as much attention to what works as to what fails. This represents a significant shift for human service delivery environments since we tend to take for granted the things that go well, the superior efforts of the staff, and only pay attention when there is a problem.

The "L" in S.E.L.F.: Assessing Organizational Loss

Assessing losses that the organization has experienced is a good way to prepare the way for the *Commitment to Growth and Change*. Organizations resist honoring their own losses. This is especially true if the losses are connected to incidents that also evoke shame. When bad things happen, lawyers representing the best interests of the organization often bar any discussion of the events. But unfortunately, they never come back later and say that it is now acceptable to discuss what happened. As a result, losses experienced years and even decades earlier may continue to exert a profound effect on organizational function. One of the important parts of the implementation process is to help organizations look at the issue of loss in the organization and open up conversation about past unresolved issues [81].

When initiating a process to review and eventually shelve old losses, it is useful to use a S.E.L.F. framework to help the organization recognize the intimate, interactive, and cyclical nature of keeping oneself safe and managing distressing emotions, particularly emotions surrounding loss, while always keeping in mind a positive vision of the future. Similarly, using S.E.L.F. as a regular part of any psychoeducational environment brings the issue of loss into regular and routine usage [82].

People working in this field have a responsibility to be aware of their own issues of trauma and loss and the ways in which these issues may become activated in the present. It is vital that people in the organization, working at every level, become aware of their own individual vulnerability in attending to issues of trauma and loss from their own personal and professional past and the ways in which these issues may become activated again in the present.

Knowledge about normal and traumatic bereavement, and the more normative losses that accompany change, should become part of routine activity and part of the orientation program for new staff and clients. In team meetings and management meetings, issues surrounding losses, both those that are tangible and those that are symbolic, need to be a part of every clinical and management conversation. Organizational leaders should communicate with peers about how they have dealt with issues of loss, trauma, and bereavement in their institutions and learn from the things they did well, the mistakes that were made, and the learning that they experienced.

We have a good example of how that can be done. One of the programs in an agency we trained was faced with closure several years after they began the Sanctuary Implementation process. Two months after it was learned that the program was closing, the facility director asked the members if they wanted to continue the Sanctuary implementation process. Everyone realized what being slated for closure meant: within several months there would no longer be any clients, senior staff would be reassigned, and those who were less senior would likely lose their jobs. For some, that meant the possibility of losing a job they had had for a decade or more and the benefits that went with it. The mood was somber and depressing. Many staff members were in shock, some in denial, and most were angry and hurt.

> *The members decided that they would continue three things: they would continue the Sanctuary module training for those who needed to make up particular modules; they would take charge of the history of the center that was closing; and they would continue to support each other. The education staff opened their vocational software usually used to teach residents how to apply for a job in order to help staff members who might be facing layoffs so that they could become better prepared for the job market. As time went on, the staff decided that trying to teach the modules to an ever-decreasing workforce didn't make sense. Instead, they switched their focus to retraining staff members who would ultimately be placed at other locations within the agency.*
>
> *The staff felt very strongly that there should be some record of what it meant to work in the program. The resulting effort was impressive. A committee was formed to locate every staff member who had ever worked in the program from*

its inception over four decades before. Hundreds of names and addresses were compiled in a list, including those who had passed away, retired, and transferred. Artifacts, photos, videos, media stories, or other remembrances and recollections were gathered and displayed on huge bulletin boards. A date was chosen for a gathering of all who could attend at a local restaurant to reminisce and remember. The Core Team recognized that having this celebration was a way to deal with their loss and also to help people better prepare for the future. As one Core Team member said, "We need Sanctuary for each other more now than ever before." The celebration was planned in the recognition that people needed a way to say good-bye, to tell others that they mattered and would be missed, and to do all that in an emotionally intelligent and safe way. The members of the staff who remain have been instrumental in reviving the use of the Sanctuary tools in other programs within the agency.

The degree of "social offensiveness" of a loss can determine how much an event impacts a group [83]. Incidents of sexual abuse, suicides, homicides, and criminal behavior are all social offenses and may be even more difficult for people to talk about; therefore, they become undiscussable. If an event occurs that causes people or subgroups to be physically dislocated, there will be real and symbolic losses that may not seem important but that become symbols of grief to those who focus on the loss of tangible things like parking spots, office space, or privacy. The greater the helplessness about change, the more difficult adjustment is likely to be. To the extent possible, it is a good idea to help people exert as much control as possible over the changes that occur.

The "F" in S.E.L.F. Is for Future: Scenario Planning and Managing from the Future

We may not be able to see into or predict the future but we can imagine many different futures, and that helps us to evaluate what we are doing now against the possibility of achieving a future we would like to achieve. In the world of business this is often called "scenario planning," where diverse groups of people bring their individual intelligence to bear on many possible futures [84].

This is the meaning of the "F" in S.E.L.F.; it is about using our imagination to "manage from the future." It is really the future that is the source of magnetic energy, and we each must have a compelling enough vision of a future possibility that we are drawn toward it. So, stand in the future and look backward from that imagined place. Decide what you have to do today (tomorrow, next week, next month) to get to that future, and then make a plan and follow it. Also consider what you will need to give up and make note of that as well. *"Managing from the future can shift how people see the world. They come to believe that they are playing in a larger context that has revolutionary potential"* (p. 245) [20].

In the Sanctuary Model, the "L" for loss and the "F" for future are inevitably linked. Whenever you feel that change is not occurring, in yourself, a client, a colleague, a significant other, or the program as a whole, ask the key question: "Am I (we) getting caught in a reenactment?" and give an honest answer. In the educational process, people will begin to recognize their own and other people's repetitive patterns, and this recognition is the gateway to change.

Teach people to imagine various possible outcomes and deliberately shift group processes to look down different possible avenues of interaction and response to potential futures. Two questions are of particular value: "What happens if nothing we do works?" and "What happens if we are successful?"

As we discussed earlier, the Commitment to Growth and Change is at the heart of the work that we do. If we are not creating the conditions for change and not seeing change in our clients, we are not doing the job we are supposed to be doing. In the next chapter, we will discuss the *Commitment to Democracy*. The kind of change we hope to see in our clients, staff, and organizations can only be achieved when people experience themselves as valuable, powerful and influential.

Chapter 4

Commitment to Democracy

> However successful institutions may be in coming close to it, democracy itself—like justice, equality, and liberty—remains a critical standard against which all institutions may be measured.
>
> C. Douglas Lummis, *Radical Democracy* (pp. 22–23) [85]

SUMMARY: *After discussing our vision for a democratic workplace, we tell a story that illustrates the sometimes simple changes that can help a leader make progress in a more participatory direction. We then go on to explain the four key reasons why democratic practice is a platform for trauma-informed care and the elements of the Sanctuary Toolkit that serve to support this commitment.*

A Vision of Democracy

- The skills that are necessary for democratic participation—expressing oneself, deeply listening to others, conflict management, compromise, self-control, self-discipline, self-respect, and respect for others—are taught and modeled in the organization.
- Clients and staff expect to have a say in their homes, schools, workplaces, and communities and view participation as a responsibility, not just a right.
- Diversity of opinion is actively sought because it is of benefit to the individual and to the group.
- Abuse of power rarely happens, in part because the social norm no longer tolerates it and in part because the system of checks and balances on the misuse of power is kept in good working order.
- Work teams have a much greater ability to solve very complex problems by learning the skills necessary for innovation, stability, group process, and integration of multiple points of view.

- Democratic processes are guarded carefully because everyone understands how easily participatory processes can become hierarchical, controlling, and finally abusive.
- Democratic leaders who know how to implement healthy group processes and who are able to creatively synthesize multiple viewpoints are treasured, while people are automatically suspicious of, and know how to manage, authoritarian leadership.
- Leaders lead through moral authority and by creating a positive vision for the future.
- All stakeholders are empowered to create healthy, sustainable, effective, profitable, and contributing workplaces.

What Do We Mean by Democracy?

The Case of the Open-Toed Shoes

We thought we would begin this chapter with another story from Andrus, this time at the organizational level. The "Case of the Open-Toed Shoes" illustrates how easy it is for us to overlook democratic processes and end up with a variety of complications that can distract us from our primary goal of trying to help people. At the same time, it demonstrates that in the Sanctuary Model, when we talk about "democracy," we refer to the everyday processes of hearing from everyone who will be involved in the decisions that affect their lives. We are not talking about a representative democracy used in running a government.

This event happened in 2002, before we had created the Sanctuary Institute or had even clearly articulated the importance of democratic practice. One afternoon a child care worker was injured at work. She was walking into the classroom and someone slammed the door, and it hit her foot. She happened to be wearing flip-flops (not the best footwear), and the impact of the door tore the nail off her big toe. This was messy, painful, and, in the mind of her managers, preventable. In their next leadership meeting Brian, the Chief Operating Officer, raised the issue and suggested that people needed to dress more appropriately for the job at hand. Flip-flops are really not the best footwear for working with kids, not to mention the fact that "This is not a beach, so why are people dressing so informally in the first place?" The conversation went on, and the leaders knocked around the pros and cons of footwear and what is acceptable and what should be restricted.

At the time the leadership group consisted of four men, and as Brian recalls, "four men with enough fashion sense to fill a thimble." After an animated discussion, they decided that there would be no more flip-flops worn at work. But then they decided to take the decision one step further and prohibit open-toed shoes entirely. If we step back and look at the magnitude of the problem, what we see is that the total number of serious toe injuries that had been sustained by the entire Andrus staff over the course of at least 20 years was one: the one mangled toe from the previous week. The management response was not addressing a rash of toe-related injuries. It was *one*. As Brian admits now, he was responding to a completely separate issue: he had become concerned about an increasing lack of professionalism, which was being manifested in the way people were dressing for work. So, he took this opportunity to get up on his soap box and rant about footwear and the threat it posed to the health, well-being, and safety of the entire institution.

Once the management team had made the decision, Brian went to his computer and sent out an e-mail announcing the new prohibition on open-toed shoes. Within the hour he got over a dozen responses from women indicating that they thought he was an idiot—not in so many words, but that was basically the meaning behind the messages that prohibiting open-toed shoes was really dopey. Being a reasonable man, it was clear to Brian that he had made a mistake. He didn't think he was mistaken about the fact that people were not dressing appropriately for work, but he did begin to think that maybe he hadn't addressed the issue properly.

At that point he was tempted to do one of two things, both of which would have been easier and less time-consuming, at least in the short run, than what he did do. He could have just changed his position, since it was wrong; alternatively, he could have simply exerted his authority and made the prohibition on that type of shoe wear a hard-and-fast rule. But he decided to do something else. He wrote back to all the people who had objected and said, *"I got your note and appreciate your feedback. My concern was that someone got hurt while wearing flip-flops at work, and flip-flops seem to be questionable footwear. While I am willing to accept that a ban on open-toed shoes might be an excessive response, I would like the group of you to get together and propose some alternative position that will ensure safety and professionalism. Until I get a counterproposal, let's stick with the 'no open-toed shoes policy.'"*

In the next three or four days, Brian stopped about 10 women with open-toed shoes and asked, *"Didn't you get my e-mail on the shoe thing?"* Usually they answered, *"Yeah, but it was stupid."* He repeated what he had said in his follow-up e-mail: *"Make me a counteroffer; don't just blow it off."* Meanwhile, the rumor mill was churning away. The female staff were indignant. *"Does he expect us to go out and get all new shoes on the salaries we make?"*

A few days later, presumably after people had gotten together, talked, and come up with what they thought would be an acceptable solution, Brian got a call from one of the teachers at the school, who asked if he could meet with several of them to discuss the issue. He happily agreed and showed up after school. They explained to him that almost every woman's shoe was open-toed. Brian admitted that in the past week he had noticed that for the first time. Everyone agreed that clearly flip-flops are not appropriate work attire, nor are shoes with heels more than two inches high: they are neither safe nor appropriate for working with troubled and often aggressive children. They asked Brian if it would be okay if everyone agreed that staff members should not wear those items to work, but that regular open-toed shoes would be okay. He said, *"Sure, that sounds fair; let's go with that."*

As Brian recalls, *"I am quite sure that at the end of the day many of these folks still thought I was a jerk, and maybe I was. My intention was to be clear that democracy is not the absence of rules, but the active engagement in making the rules. My decision to outlaw open-toed shoes was a bad one. But just ignoring it was not the way to go either. The way to go was to set a community standard we could all agree to, live with, and commit to. I think this is a pretty good tale of how to make democracy work. It was a clunky start but a good outcome."*

Deep Democracy and the Sanctuary Model

The *Commitment to Democracy* is the commitment that seems to be the most challenging for many organizations. That is largely because there is so much confusion about what democracy actually is. We use the definition that democracy scholar John Gastil uses when he describes it as *"the ideal of a cohesive community of people living and working together and finding fair, nonviolent ways to reconcile conflicts"* (p. 5) [86]. Unfortunately, when people hear the word "democracy" as applied to an organization, their automatic reaction is, "You mean everybody gets to vote on everything?" No, that's not what we mean. Voting is one practice associated with democracy, but it is not the only practice. However, that captures a fundamental problem. Democracy today too often refers to *behavior* rather than to the more fundamental *awareness* that is necessary if abuses of power are to be checked. Power without awareness is likely to lead to abuse. Every day we see clients who come seeking services as a result of their own experiences with abusive parents, abusive colleagues, and abusive systems. When the word "democracy" is used, people usually focus on the behavior of voting and majority rule. But this behavior alone can lead to the tyranny of the majority instead of the integration of various points of view that is so necessary for complex problem solving.

That's why we prefer to use the term "deep democracy" because it requires a change in awareness, not just behavior. We recognize that all people, and their ideas and feelings, are necessary in moment-to-moment interactions and institutional practices. This suggests that all of the information carried within these various voices, points of view, and frameworks is needed to understand the complete process of any system and to create the opportunity for the *emergence* of new and creative ideas. Deep democracy is an attitude that focuses on the awareness of voices that are both central and marginal. Deep democracy is the practice associated with a worldview that recognizes the basic ecological fact that everything is interconnected, that all life is a complex and interdependent web [87].

But participatory, deeply democratic processes must be experienced and the skills required must be learned. It is evident that in the United States we talk a great deal more about democracy than it is truly practiced. Few people have actually grown up in democratic homes, attended democratic schools, or have had the opportunity to work in democratic workplaces led by democratic leaders. Organizations and the people that manage and lead them are likely to have no more expertise in creating and sustaining participatory environments than the people they are leading, so the learning must be universal and experimental. We are all still discovering, individually and collectively, what democracy actually means, but as one educator aptly put it democracy represents

> "a moral commitment to the common good, and community, that transcends both individual self-interest and emotionalism and exposes the tendency for more powerful individuals and groups to manipulate and cajole the rest of us." (p. 17) [88]

Although globalization and global democratic movements may be changing that situation in the business community a little bit at a time, the social service and mental health delivery systems remain fundamentally hierarchical, intensely bureaucratic, and frequently authoritarian. There is a strong tendency within organizations to gravitate toward hierarchical modes of structuring themselves, even in organizations that claim to be democratic, largely because of expedience.

Hierarchies create a top-down structure. Sending orders down through the chain of command can appear to be less time-consuming, and it can work better when there is technical and repetitive work to be done [89]. In the short term, as we mentioned in our opening story, it is easier to either give way to the loudest voice or assert one's authority and ignore dissenting voices. Practicing democratically is more time-consuming, at least at first while organizational members are learning how to participate. Encouraging free speech can feel as threatening to managers as finding one's voice may be for direct care staff. Encouraging free speech is so threatening, in fact, that court decisions pertaining to freedom of speech have revealed a general assumption *"that conflict and dissent are always bad and no good can come from them; a concept that flies in the face of modern thought on organizational conflict and free speech"* (p. 260) [90]. As a manager himself, Brian can speak about the challenges involved in bucking this authoritarian tendency in organizations, particularly those that remain haunted by their own authoritarian roots:

> *A major hazard of having power is that people often do not tell you the truth. This is not malicious or mean-spirited, it is simply self-preservation. I have*

found that the story of the Emperor's New Clothes captures a reality that is a very real threat to healthy organizational functioning. If you are in a position of leadership, it is not uncommon for people around you to say nothing or to agree with you and tell you that you are brilliant, regardless of what you actually do or say. To be effective as a leader, you need people to tell you that you are naked, inadequate, stupid, out of control, or whatever when you are. You need to trust that people can be honest with you, but to make this possible, you need to make sure that, at every turn, you are willing to listen to contrary points of view. We need to remain open-minded and accepting of opposing points of view, or they will stop coming, even when we most need them. The larger the organization, the more difficult it is to establish a participatory work environment. Since trust is crucial, how do we come to trust people whom we have little or no contact with? It is particularly challenging to make this shift in an organization that has historically had a more autocratic style, because under stress we tend to revert back to our habitual ways of operating.

Learning the skills required for participatory democracy is a particularly important component of any culture that hopes to be trauma-informed for four fundamental reasons that we will explore further in this chapter: (1) democracy is a method for minimizing the abusive use of power; (2) democratic practice is necessary for the fulfillment of the other Sanctuary commitments—to nonviolence, emotional intelligence, social learning, open communication, social responsibility, and growth and change; (3) democratic practice encourages and supports the complex and creative problem solving necessary to address the difficult and perplexing dilemmas that confront today's human service organizations; (4) democratic practice serves as an antidote to traumatic experience. But before we explore all these issues, let's focus for a moment on what we mean by "workplace democracy."

What Is Workplace Democracy?

Surely one of the great ironies of the modern world is that democracy, imperfect as it is in the political realm, seldom extends to the workplace. In fact, most U.S. citizens do not even question the fact that they are required to "check their voice at the door" of the shop or office.

Professor George Cheney,
"Democracy in the Workplace," Journal of Applied Communication Research
(pp. 167–168) [91]

There is, as yet, no universally accepted version of what a workplace committed to democracy actually looks like, although examples of various workplaces that use participatory methods crop up throughout the business literature. Very little, however, has been written about the application of workplace participatory practices in the human services domain. In the Sanctuary Model, our objective is that each organization will take on the responsibility of defining for itself a participatory structure that best serves the needs of the clients, the staff, and the organization, including structures that ensure fair and just resolution when conflicting needs emerge. A group is thought to be democratic when there is equally distributed decision-making power; an inclusive membership committed to democracy; healthy relationships among its members; and a democratic method of deliberation.

In 1976, a famous article in an economics journal discussed the various levels of employee participation that needed to be considered in any discussion of a more democratic workplace. Just because you think you have a democratic workplace doesn't mean that in practice it actually exists. When assessing just how democratic your organization is, ask yourself these questions: (1) How much influence do employees actually exert in decision making? (There may be a suggestions box, but suggestions are not implemented.) (2) What are the issues over which employee control is strictly limited? (Committees may exist, but they are not allowed to discuss compensation or organizational structure.) (3) What level of the organization's hierarchy can employees influence? (Committee minutes are shared, but top management often retains an autocratic, top-down mode of directing policy and work.) [92].

When you answer these questions honestly, you get a good idea of the challenges involved in the *Commitment to Democracy*. Time is always a constraint, so with every decision it is important to consider who needs to participate. Not everyone needs to participate in every decision. Such a policy could paralyze the decision-making process and end in disaster. A democratic group strives to include those people who are *profoundly* affected by its decisions, invite those *significantly* affected, and at least consider the views of those *marginally* affected [86].

Why Create a Democratic Workplace?

So, if it is difficult, why do it? What is the case for organizational democracy? When tasks are technical, repetitive, and have a low demand for innovation, then the practice of organizational democracy may be both impractical and self-defeating. But in situations that call for constant adaptability to changing conditions, where flexibility in dealing with novel situations is an everyday occurrence, and where morale and creative thought play significant roles in determining success, then the more egalitarian and decentralized the management style, the better.

In fact, *"Democracy becomes a functional necessity whenever a social system is competing for survival under conditions of chronic change"* (p. 169) [93].

Democratic practices allow and encourage greater and more diverse inputs from organization members, and the shift to a trauma-informed approach to all consumers of human services requires a flexibility and a problem-solving capacity that must be central to organizational function.

What is perhaps the most shocking realization in the human service delivery environment is the lack of recognition that providing services to very injured people, services that help them to recover function and change their outcomes, demands constant innovation and creativity on the part of the helper. Likewise, organizational survival in chronically stressful economic and social times necessitates constant innovation and creativity on the part of managers. The social service world is characterized by constant change, regardless of whether we look at provision of services to the mentally ill, the homeless, child protective services, juvenile justice programs, educating the young, or any other human service delivery system. The practice of democracy is crucial to the generation of innovation and creativity.

Many national reports have focused on the present workforce crisis that will affect human service delivery far into the future [12]. This is not surprising given that we are frequently financially compelled to hire the wrong people for the job. It is well established in the business world that the more talented, educated, and committed the workforce, the more valuable the democratic process is likely to be to the organization's competitive position [94]. Although salaries are low and the work is potentially dangerous, the work demands an enormous amount of creative thought and imagination. If organizational managers do not grapple with our current and future workforce needs, we will be left with a workforce that is poorly prepared and unable to contend with the complex problems presented by reenactment.

Employees who feel secure only when they are told exactly what to do may find the demands of democratic participation very anxiety-provoking. They are more likely to resist greater involvement on the part of other staff and clients, seeing all such change as threatening and dangerous. When democratic practices are successfully introduced in the Sanctuary Model they may seek employment elsewhere, sometimes only after putting up significant resistance. Thus, employee turnover may be temporarily increased until the workforce is stabilized. On the other hand, the most apparently resistant staff members may become the strongest advocates as they see different outcomes in clients, leaders, colleagues, and the organization as a whole.

When democratic participatory environments are truly established, they are more likely to promote an increase in employee loyalty and an increase in the capacity to deal with the complex problems of injured children and adults (Figure 4.1).

Holding on to democratic process under conditions of stress and threat can be particularly challenging, especially in a mental health environment where

- More communication
- More interaction
- More coordination
- Greater information richness
- Greater commitment
- More analysis of results
- Richer conflict
- Innovation, creativity

PresenterMedia

Figure 4.1 Democratic workplaces.

individual and group safety may be at stake. Sandy recalls that even on the small scale of an inpatient unit for adults, protecting liberty can be challenging and time-consuming but always instructive.

> We can offer a concrete example of the suspension of liberty under conditions of threat and then the reclaiming of democratic conditions once again. When we had an inpatient psychiatric unit for traumatized adults, we did not use seclusion or restraint and had a voluntary open-door policy so that people could come and go as they pleased, as long as they cooperated with the program and demonstrated responsible behavior. We treasured that open door as a symbol of respect, personal liberty, and human rights. But occasionally, and only very occasionally, there would be someone on the unit who could not or would not respect the level of responsibility that liberty involves. On such occasions, we would have to lock the door of the community. We would make it clear to everyone why this was necessary and then, over the course of the next few days, the entire community, patients and staff, would engage in a process of figuring out how to re-create an environment that would allow us to reopen the door and get back to normal. This process typically occurred through repeated community meetings during which everyone could have their say. The result was that other members of the community would have to take responsibility for helping whoever it was that was having difficulties with the responsibility that liberty necessitates. The process also emphasized for the wandering or elopement-prone individuals that they had to be responsible members of the

community if everyone was to benefit and that if they needed help to do so, help was available to them.

It should be noted that the suspension of democratic processes in the short term is done to protect democratic principles in the long term. The goal is to become more democratic. Too often organizations suspend democratic processes to restore safety or reduce anxiety, and this becomes the new order. We tell ourselves that this is better and safer, and we never return to a more democratic way of functioning. This is the beginning of how our organizations become trauma-organized. It happens with good intentions, but it is insidious and subtle. Thomas Jefferson is said to have declared that "eternal vigilance is the price of liberty," and we have found that to be true.

Democracy and Minimizing the Abusive Use of Power

Democracy is a critique of centralized power of every sort—charismatic, bureaucratic, class, military, corporate, party, union, technocratic. By definition it is the antithesis to all such powers.

C. D. Lummis, *Radical Democracy* (p. 25) [85]

As a method of governing, democracy was created or, perhaps more accurately, is being created in order to minimize the abuse of power. Throughout history, it has been clearly demonstrated that the concentration of power in the hands of the few, when the few have little or no accountability to the many, is a prescription for despotism. At the same time, the human desire for freedom of action, thought, and speech has drawn increasing numbers of people into the struggle for human rights. The vast tyrannies of the twentieth century were unmatched in their capacity to create destruction and the possibility of total annihilation. But never before have so many people around the world been aware of each other's existence and chosen to honor the desire for basic human rights.

So, what is "power?" Everybody wants to be powerful; after all, what is the choice other than being powerless? But power can be expressed in ways that create and in ways that destroy. Figure 4.2 highlights the complicated nature of power. None of these factors are good or bad in themselves. It all depends on the context of the situation and the intentions of the people employing the use of power. But these many expressions of power simply point out that power can be exercised in very obvious or more subtle ways. And all versions of power can become abusive.

Students of democracy recognize that democracy is an effective method of nonviolence largely because it does minimize abusive use of power, creating a complicated system of checks and balances that prevents any one person or faction from becoming so powerful that they can overwhelm the rest. In studying

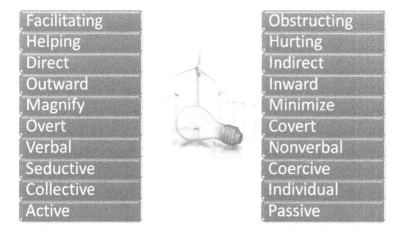

Facilitating	Obstructing
Helping	Hurting
Direct	Indirect
Outward	Inward
Magnify	Minimize
Overt	Covert
Verbal	Nonverbal
Seductive	Coercive
Collective	Individual
Active	Passive

PresenterMedia

Figure 4.2 The complicated nature of power.

countries around the world, it has become clear that the more democratic two nations are, the less likely it is that war or lesser violence between them will occur. The more democratic a nation is, the less severe its overall foreign violence; the less likely it will have domestic collective violence; and the less likely it is to kill its own people [95]. Our experience tells us that what is true for countries is also true for organizations; the more democratic they are, the less violence there is likely to be.

Democracy and the Interdependence of Commitments

Practicing deep democracy is a fundamental commitment of the Sanctuary Model that enables the fulfillment of the other six commitments. Without democratic participation, fulfilling the other commitments becomes impossible. The Sanctuary Commitments, all of them together, are designed to provide the bedrock, the common shared background, the dance floor for the ballet of diversity that is required if we are to achieve environments that are creative and innovative enough to undo the damage wrought by childhood adversity and trauma. Every organization that embraces the Sanctuary Model will look different, characterized by the diversity of its own composition, its own mission, goals, and culture, but beneath the differences lie significant similarities of approach. In Table 4.1 we contrast the broad definitional differences that separate democratic from nondemocratic environments.

Table 4.1 The Sanctuary Commitments and democratic environments

Sanctuary Commitment	Democratic	Nondemocratic
GROWTH AND CHANGE	• Shared values and mission, walk the talk • Tolerance of uncertainty, moving toward a better future	• Values not supported in behavior, not mission-driven • Fear-based responses to uncertainty; controlling, top-down behavior
NONVIOLENCE	• Nonviolence actively practiced in word and deed; interpersonal respect • Clear boundaries that are respected	• Coercion, force, violence, and bullying accepted and encouraged • Boundary violations
EMOTIONAL INTELLIGENCE	• Moderating response to stress/threat • Balance between competition and cooperation • Mutual respect	• Escalation of fear; stress under threat • Intense competition encouraged, no reward for collaboration • Respect for power, not people
SOCIAL LEARNING	• Complex decision making • Tolerance of difference • Flexibility	• Simplistic decisions • Intolerance of differences • Rigidity
OPEN COMMUNICATION	• Wide communication network, all-inclusive • Feedback and error correction • Freedom of speech • Open communication • Dissent welcomed • Methods to resolve conflicts	• Communication largely top-down, little communication bottom-up • Broken feedback loops • Undiscussable topics • Secrecy • Suppression of dissent • No methods to reduce conflict; dog-eat-dog atmosphere or conflict suppressed and denied
DEMOCRACY	• Diversity • Checks and balances • Leadership as stewardship • Leveled hierarchy • Control through social norms • Active debate and dialogue	• Discrimination and favoritism • Few checks and balances • Bullying leadership • Strict command hierarchy • Emphasis on obedience to rules • Little participation or dialogue

Table 4.1 (Continued)

Sanctuary Commitment	Democratic	Nondemocratic
SOCIAL RESPONSIBILITY	• Civic responsibility	• Responsibility only to authority figures
	• Responsible authority	• Self-interest primary concern
	• Commitment to the well-being of the whole	• Fragmentation, silos
	• Mutual accountability	• Upward accountability only
	• Fairness	• Little concern about fair play
	• Social justice	• Little concern for social justice
	• Clear, fair rules	• Differential enforcement, favoritism

The Sanctuary Commitments Provide Checks and Balances

When the Sanctuary Commitments become the value system of the organization that is endorsed and practiced by everyone, they provide a complex and interactive system of checks and balances that minimizes the abusive use of power. Let's explore what this means.

To create participatory environments, people must feel safe; therefore, the *Commitment to Nonviolence* is essential to democracy, and the *Commitment to Democracy* provides support for environments of nonviolence. But at the same time, the *Commitment to Nonviolence,* with its expanded emphasis on all forms of violence—physical, psychological, social, and moral—puts a check on the veiled violence that can become the typical modus operandi for leaders of what pass as democratic environments. In Sanctuary, if you verbally or socially abuse your colleagues, you are engaging in violence. This is one thing that is fundamentally wrong with the present discourse in our larger culture. In Sanctuary, everyone must participate, but each person must figure out how to do that nonviolently.

Likewise, in order to engage in participatory environments, each individual must develop self-awareness and learn to manage distress in ways sufficient to allow engagement in conflict that does not rise to the level of violence; hence, the *Commitment to Emotional Intelligence* is indispensable. It is not difficult for a whole group to come to a decision that appears democratic but is emotionally dimwitted when we pause to examine where the consequences of the decision are likely to lead. In this case, the *Commitment to Growth and Change* and the *Commitment to Emotional Intelligence* serve as a check on the *Commitment to Democracy.*

Democratic environments will survive only if the group has the ability to engage in learning, that is, to accumulate wisdom as a result of acquiring knowledge secondary to conflict that is at the heart of the *Commitment to Social Learning*. But for that learning to occur within conflict-laden situations, there must be a *Commitment to Democracy* so that the learning thoroughly engages all involved parties. It must be nonviolent and thus must guarantee the *Commitment to Nonviolence*. There should be clear goals for what we are learning, what we need to unlearn, and where we want to go; the *Commitment to Growth and Change* prevents us from wasting our time learning things we don't need to know.

Free speech is a fundamental requirement of democracy and can only occur in an organization that values open communication and transparency. All staff members need to have a basic understanding of organizational functioning if they are going to participate effectively in decision making and thereby fulfill the *Commitment to Democracy*. Therefore, the *Commitment to Social Learning* and the *Commitment to Open Communication* support each other, while the *Commitment to Nonviolence* helps to check the emergence of violence that can occur whenever there is conflict. *The Commitment to Emotional Intelligence* then requires us to think about how we communicate with each other and communicate new learning in a way that promotes continuing emotional management and provides a check on the more violent and out-of-control expressions of emotion.

Democracy requires individual accountability and responsibility for the welfare of the whole and the furtherance of justice in the service of the common good, which is where the *Commitment to Social Responsibility* finds its place. Harmonizing individual rights and social responsibilities in a democratic environment is a rigorous and never-ending balancing act that often gets neglected, particularly if an organization is failing to comply with the *Commitment to Open Communication* and the *Commitment to Nonviolence*. To ensure that the *Commitment to Democracy* does not lead to an attitude whereby everyone is only out to satisfy their own interests, the *Commitment to Social Responsibility* and the *Commitment to Emotional Intelligence* are essential. Democratic environments require a willingness to grapple with the living presence of loss and constant change while recognizing that those of us who participate today are paving the way for those who will come after us. This makes the *Commitment to Growth and Change* a critical component of a democratic environment and a buffer against destroying the future because we only attend to the concerns of the present.

Balancing the Sanctuary Commitments is a constant juggling act. If you drop any of the balls, they all tend to fall; and yet, using all of them all of the time is conflict-laden and challenging. However, it is in the process of juggling competing demands that we become better able to deal with the tests presented to us by complexity.

Democracy and Emergent Solutions to Complex Problems

Although we believe in the moral importance of creating democratic, participatory workplaces, another reason why the *Commitment to Democracy* is such
an important component of the Sanctuary Model is a practical consideration.
The most convincing reason for establishing democratic processes in human
service delivery systems is the need to ensure that there are complex responses
to the complex problems presented by virtually every client who walks through
our agency doors. All of us are smarter than any one of us.

Our systems of care are living systems, not machines, and they cannot be
effectively managed using a mechanical approach that is more suitable for ser-
vicing a car than a group of people. One of the key concepts differentiating
living systems from machines is that new and more complex things emerge
from groups of simpler parts. You, as you, *emerge* from the interactive effect of
trillions of cells in your body. If we look at your individual cells, we can't explain
you. Groups of people are capable of creating emergent solutions to problems
that no single individual could solve.

Under the right circumstances, groups are remarkably intelligent and are
often smarter than the smartest people in them. Groups do not need to be dominated by exceptionally intelligent people in order to be smart. Even if most
of the people within a group are not especially well informed or rational, the
group can still reach a collectively wise decision [96]. That's why democratic
processes are critical for dealing with the problems of our clients. Although
democratic processes do not guarantee it, they still stand the best chance of
promoting *emergent* solutions.

Our teams need to be constantly innovative, self-managing, imaginative,
and unpredictable if they are to successfully outmaneuver each client's reenactment and help the client to change problematic habits. And as we discussed
earlier, this is not a technical problem, but one that requires constant adaptation to new clients, new situations, and new combinations of staff—all in the
context of what are frequently reconfigured organizations. We contend that
democratic practice is the only method that can help small and large groups
of people deliver complex solutions to complex problems, solutions that are
new and creative and that emerge out of an interconnected, diverse, democratic
group of persons who are then willing to implement and follow through with
what they have decided. People support what they have a hand in creating, and
if they haven't been part of creating the solution, they may just go on being part
of the problem.

Managers need to manage in a different way as well because the main role of
the leader is to create the improvisational space within which creative responses
are more likely to occur. Such democratic leaders do not run the show, but they
are actively involved in the creative process. It is their responsibility to carve out

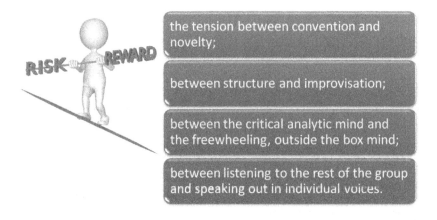

the tension between convention and novelty;

between structure and improvisation;

between the critical analytic mind and the freewheeling, outside the box mind;

between listening to the rest of the group and speaking out in individual voices.

PresenterMedia

Figure 4.3 Group flow: when many tensions are in balance.

and protect the physical, psychological, and social space that allows what has been called "group flow" to occur when groups of people feel a sense of competence and control, a loss of self-consciousness, and an absorption in a task so complete that they lose track of time [97] (Figure 4.3).

We had a good example of this in the work we did developing the original Sanctuary Institute training. We assembled a team of staff members whom we thought could work together and develop an interesting product. We assigned one of the staff, Sarah Yanosy, the leadership role in the group, and we asked Sarah to assemble a team she thought she would be able to work with and who would be able to work together. Although Sandy and/or Brian might have been the more obvious choices to lead the group, we assumed the roles of just two of the participants in the group. Although Brian was just another group member, he did ensure that the group had the resources necessary to do their work. He allowed people to carve out the time to meet and work outside of these meetings (although in reality, most of the group members did most of this work on their own time). He also allocated resources to hire a curriculum writer to work with the group. Sandy was able to give up enough control to allow this group of relative novices to pull apart her life's work and transform it into something very different.

We met every week for almost a year and did a considerable amount of work in between sessions. These meetings and this process were extraordinary. There were countless terrific ideas, a good deal of heated debate, and more than our fair share of laughs. Good ideas were made better and bad or marginal ideas died on the vine. While it is likely that there were some hard feelings at different points, it seemed that whatever conflict we had was focused on the task and never was personalized. Many of us who were involved in this process describe it as one of the more creative, rewarding, and exciting projects we ever participated in. Something magical happened in this process, and the result far exceeded what any of us had anticipated. Additionally, the result far exceeded anything that any one of us could have accomplished on our own.

In complex organizations where large numbers of people must engage regularly in interrelated, complicated, ever-changing, and demanding work, context is everything, and if that context is not a participatory one, morale will inevitably decline and productivity will decrease. Individuals who are innovative and creative and who will thrive only in a democratic environment will leave; as a result, the organization will not be able to respond adequately to the needs of traumatized people with complex problems. Democratic processes are an extremely important component of creating trauma-informed systems of care.

The Commitment to Democracy and Trauma-Informed Practice

Jonathan Shay is a psychiatrist who has spent his career working with Vietnam War veterans and has published extensively on combat trauma, ancient and modern [98, 99]. As a scholar of ancient Greek literature, he has reported on the ways in which posttraumatic stress disorder interferes with the ability to participate actively in democratic processes.

> *Over a period of years I have observed that unhealed combat trauma disables the basic social and cognitive capacities required for democratic participation: being able to show up at an appointed time and place, possibly in a crowd of strangers; being able to experience words as trustworthy; seeing the possibility of persuasion, negotiation, compromise, concession; seeing the possibility of winning without killing, of losing without dying; seeing the future as real and meaningful. (p. 1) [100]*

In many years of working with survivors of community violence, childhood adversity, and all forms of interpersonal violence, particularly those that are chronic and repetitive, we have observed a similar phenomenon. The chronic hyperarousal, irritability, short-temperedness, increased fear of unknown people and places, emotional volatility, and excessive need for control so typical of chronic exposure to stress compel people to think and act in ways that make democratic leadership and participation extremely difficult, if not impossible.

Democracy As a Cultural Antidote to Trauma

With a large proportion of the U.S. population experiencing chronic stress and exposure to violence, this does not bode well for the future of democracy unless we have institutions that can counteract this effect. The Sanctuary

Commitments, particularly the *Commitment to Democracy*, provide an anchoring framework for the requirements and challenges of counteracting the effects of violence by creating nonviolent, participatory environments. We see democratic participatory processes as providing cultural antidotes to the havoc that repetitive adversity wreaks on the social self; this is particularly important in programs for children, who are still in the process of developing social and cognitive skills.

The greater the involvement of the clients in creating more democratic environments, the more likely they are to have experiences throughout any typical day that are directly counter to many of the habits they have already developed. The constant repetition of alternative ways of living and working with each other lays the groundwork for changing habits in a normal, educational, and social context rather than focusing on pathology and punishment for infractions. To participate, be esteemed by others, and get recognition in a democratic environment, we have to develop skills that are in direct opposition to the skill set a client has often had to acquire to survive the rigors of a violent upbringing. Figure 4.4 illustrates what we mean by democracy as an antidote to trauma.

The Importance of Involving Families

Family members have to deal with the problems of their loved ones and then with the challenges encountered when they have to interface with a service environment. This can be overwhelming, and their reactions to these problems may sabotage service delivery. So, part of practicing democratically means engaging

Figure 4.4 Democracy as an antidote to trauma.

all stakeholders in ongoing collaborative processes. Dennis McCarville, former Chief Executive Officer of UtaHalee-Cooper Village, a residential program in Omaha, Nebraska, recounted this story about including families in the process of change.

> *I attribute several significant changes in the organization to Sanctuary implementation. I feel that the experience of the training and implementation has changed my outlook and has opened me up in a different way. Since we began implementation, we have totally remade our family programming. I believe this is a direct outgrowth of the Commitment to Democracy. After returning from the Sanctuary Institute training, I was reading a book written by the parent of a child who was in care. She spoke about her experiences and the feeling that parents had no voice and no power in their children's out-of-home care. I was moved by her remarks and called her. We spoke, and I eventually hired her to come in and train our staff on how to engage parents. We are now looking at ways to get parents involved in Quality Assurance, other standing committees, and the Board of Directors. The Commitment to Democracy and the Commitment to Social Responsibility changed the way I responded to the book I read and the conversation I had with this mother. And that response totally changed the way we are engaging the families in the work.*

Implications for Democratic Leadership

Democratic leadership has been described as behavior that influences people in a manner consistent with and conducive to basic democratic principles and processes, such as self-determination, inclusiveness, equal participation, and deliberation [101]. Democratic leadership is easily contrasted with authoritarian leadership styles and laissez-faire or free-rein styles (Table 4.2).

Deliberation is at the heart of democracy; therefore, high-quality deliberation requires effective democratic leadership [101]. Democratic leadership aids the deliberative process through constructive participation, facilitation, and the maintenance of healthy relationships within a positive emotional setting [86]. Constructive participation means defining, analyzing, and solving group problems through deliberation. This means that problems must be carefully analyzed so that all relevant information and perspectives are put on the table for consideration. Possible solutions must be generated and assessed through creative reflection and critical evaluation. Careful listening and the respectful acknowledgment of others' views can help move the discussion forward. A particularly important form of listening, sometimes called "discernment," consists of carefully listening to group members' ideas and values, then tentatively attempting to identify the "public voice" or the solution that best represents the group's collective interests.

Table 4.2 Leadership styles

Democratic	Authoritarian	Laissez-faire
• Share understanding of the problem with team members	• Solve problem or make decisions sometimes with, sometimes without, consultation with others	• Are hands-off and allow employees to make the decisions
• Distribute responsibility and empower other members	• Expect team members to provide information, not to generate alternative solutions	• Are good at delegation of responsibility
• Facilitate a deliberative, participatory process	• May or may not tell team members what the problem is in getting information from them	• Tend to avoid conflict
• Aid the group in its deliberations	• Work "by the book," ensuring that staff follow procedures exactly	• Wait for a solution to a problem to emerge on its own
• Help the group reach a consensus	• Impose strict and systematic, sometimes punitive, discipline	• Are flexible and can be influenced
• Do not use position to influence the group	• Are empowered via the office they hold: position power	• Minimize personal influence
• Willing to implement the group solution	• Favor individual over group decisions	• Are best in situations where employees are organized, competent, and need little oversight
• Exercise discernment and self-awareness	• May hold power through personal charisma	• Expect to be liked for leaving people on their own
• Determine the "how," not the "what"	• Tell others what to do	• Let others figure it out
• Are relationally transparent	• Expect unquestioning obedience	• Minimize relationship
• Hold the mission and guiding values as the central concern	• May be guided by the mission or may be dominated by self-interest	• Believe in mission internally and assume same for everyone else

Organizational managers who are naturally inclined toward participatory practices may find the transition to more democratic environments relatively easy, a confirmation of deeply held and long-standing beliefs. Managers who have adopted more autocratic styles, however, may find the demands of facilitating participatory structures to be exceedingly anxiety-provoking because of the fundamental redistribution of power and authority. It's important to recognize, however, that becoming more democratic does not mean abdicating responsibility for decision making. When programs begin adopting the Sanctuary Model, people in leadership positions may not act when they need to act simply because they think they are "being democratic." Becoming more democratic means that leaders will not abuse power. But it also means they will use power appropriately to witness, inspire, clarify, and facilitate. Relatively few people have had experience working in participatory environments, so it is likely that managers will underestimate the time and training that are necessary to support and encourage democratic practices, as described in Figure 4.5.

Moving Away from Authoritarianism

We live with the delusion that we are all experts in democracy when in reality we are complete novices. When moving from a system that has been very authoritarian, it is better to gradually open up participation, keeping the goal of a more participatory organization as the aim, moving in careful and planned steps to get there. A sudden or forced transition is likely to raise so much anxiety throughout the organization that something will happen to sabotage all progress in a participatory direction. Managers may pull back too quickly, leaving a vacuum in the authority structure that employees are not yet ready to fill. Since nature abhors a vacuum, this vacuum may rapidly be filled with problems that the most resistant and skeptical members of the organizational community have predicted. Then the "failure" of democracy becomes a self-fulfilling prophecy.

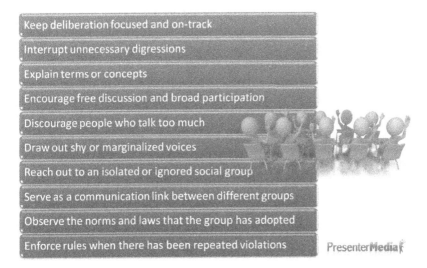

Figure 4.5 Guidelines for facilitating democratic groups.

Earlier we discussed reenactment as an impediment to change. These forces are always at play in the organization and will seek to maintain the status quo. An unfortunate result is that those organizations that could and should benefit the most from the democratic process are exactly those that will have the most difficulty in implementing it. As one authority has pointed out:

> *[It] is a common finding that resistant managers will undermine the transition to democratic process by subtly limiting the information available to decision-making teams, by holding them to unrealistic expectations, by failing to provide necessary resources, or by abandoning them as they attempt to work through their new tasks and responsibilities.... The challenges of moving from bureaucratic structure to democratic process are formidable enough to discourage even those managers who are convinced of the potential benefits. In fact, managers often become disillusioned with democratic process as transition obstacles and difficulties begin to emerge in earnest. Rather than work persistently through the inevitable complaints, anxieties, and performance glitches, they retreat to watered-down, half-hearted versions of their original objectives. The potential benefits are never realized (though many of the costs are), the hierarchy reasserts itself, and employees end up more cynical about management's integrity and competence than before the experiment began.* (p. 92) [94]

Moving Out of Chaos

Likewise, moving from a very disorganized and chaotic organization to a democratic organization will not happen overnight and needs to be a careful, planned, structured change. Our faculty members help organizations plan and pace this change to ensure that change occurs at a manageable rate. Organizations that are chaotic may have experienced leaders who have leaned too much in the direction of the laissez-faire style of leadership, the virtual opposite of the authoritarian leadership style.

In such a case, there may need to be a greater exercise of central authority in order to get the situation under control. Without such a progression, the introduction of the Sanctuary Model may flounder because there is too little leadership rather than too much. Like everything else, creating a more democratic culture is all in the timing.

And even when an organization has succeeded in becoming more democratic, that does not give license for a free-for-all, anything-goes attitude. Decision making needs to happen within the framework of the Sanctuary Commitments. Therefore, all change needs to be safe, nonviolent, nonsecretive, knowledge-building, emotionally intelligent, socially responsible, and mission-driven. Janie Hogue is the manager at Rose Rock Center, a substance abuse facility for women in Vinita, Oklahoma, and the first Sanctuary Certified agency. As Janie observed:

> *We function more democratically than we once did. Staff make more decisions and are accountable for those decisions. This is still a work in progress and probably always will be. Staff still look to leadership too often to solve problems. In recent months, budget cuts have reduced the number of middle managers, and I have discovered that some managers were masking their struggles with conflict by claiming to be democratic. Leaders have to be willing to make tough decisions guided by the Sanctuary Commitments.*

Fitting the Leadership Style to the Situation

Organizational leaders who are committed to democratic participation discourage authoritarian structures but are not hands-off. They teach the skills necessary for responsible, more democratic participatory structures. But in real-life situations that confront human service professionals all the time, it is best to have a flexible range of responses to a wide variety of situations. After assessing their own leadership style, managers and supervisors should make efforts to develop different styles of leadership to match different situations. Some of the circumstances surrounding such a decision are noted in Figure 4.6.

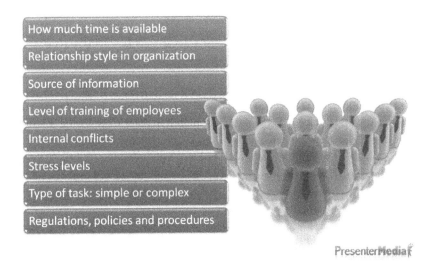

How much time is available

Relationship style in organization

Source of information

Level of training of employees

Internal conflicts

Stress levels

Type of task: simple or complex

Regulations, policies and procedures

PresenterMedia

Figure 4.6 Forces that determine leadership styles.

There is no role for either petty tyrants or bullies in the human services environment. However, there is no one best leadership style for decision making, leading, and motivating. The "situational approach" offers leaders the most useful framework for leadership. Leadership styles can vary, depending on basically two factors: the *quality of the decision,* meaning the extent to which the decision will affect important group processes, and *acceptance of the decision,* or the degree of commitment of employees needed for its implementation. This theory suggests that when the decision will affect few members of the group and little commitment from others is required, the leader should use an autocratic style and just make a decision. But when the decision is likely to affect many people and can only be implemented if employees support the decision and carry out the implementation, leaders should use a participative style [102].

Determining whether to move more authoritatively, or more democratically, or just let things emerge on their own is a balancing act for managers. It's really a matter of constantly balancing different and often competing needs because that is what complex problems demand. Leaders need to be aware that the stress of their jobs may cause them to misjudge circumstances and, at times, select a leadership style that is inappropriate to the situation.

Effective leaders know how to match styles to situations and get things done. Ineffective leaders do not. Ineffective leaders are likely to employ only one dominant style and use that style in all situations. They are therefore ineffective in addressing the real complexities of the modern work environment. Although there may be innate qualities that foster leadership, all leaders need on-the-job experiential training; we learn by doing.

Sanctuary Toolkit for Democracy

The Core Team

After the Sanctuary Five-Day Training, the Sanctuary Steering Committee is instructed to go back to their organization and create a Core Team, a larger multidisciplinary team that expands its reach into the entire organization.

The Core Team should have representatives from every level of the organization to ensure that every voice is heard. It is vital that all key organizational leaders become actively involved in the process of change and participate in the Core Team.

The Core Team can be comprised of several dozen people who may constitute the entire staff of smaller organizations. However, in larger organizations, the Core Team will by necessity be a representative body. This requires a team composition that is diverse along every dimension that comprises the organization: age, race, gender identity, sexual orientation, ethnicity, religion, profession, class, education, status, and experience. The responsibility of Core Team members is to actively represent and communicate with their constituents and to become trainers and Sanctuary leaders for the entire organization. The Core Team develops team guidelines and expectations of involvement for individual team members, as well as a meeting schedule, and decides on safety rules for the constructive operation of the team itself.

The Core Team is ultimately responsible for the development of an implementation process aimed at including the entire organization in the change process. The ultimate goal is to take meaningful steps to improve the organization's culture and engage as many staff members as possible in that process. As discussions begin in the Core Team, participating staff begin to make small but significant changes. Members take risks with each other and try new methods of engagement and conflict resolution. They feed these innovations and their results back into the process discussions. The Core Team must always maintain a balance between process and product. It is not enough to talk about how they will change things. They must also make actual changes in the way they do business. The Core Team therefore not only plans together how best to share what they are learning with the larger organization, but also plans how to train all agency personnel and clients in the Sanctuary principles, how to integrate the Sanctuary Toolkit into the day-to-day operation of the organization, and how to evaluate how these initiatives are taking hold in the organization.

Through the implementation steps of the Sanctuary Model, staff members engage in prolonged dialogue that serves to reveal the major strengths, vulnerabilities, and conflicts within the organization. By looking at shared assumptions, goals, and existing practices, staff members from various levels of the organization are required to share in an analysis of their own structure and functioning, often asking themselves and each other provocative questions that have never been overtly considered before. As this happens, the development of more democratic, participatory processes begins to emerge. These processes are critical because they are most likely to lend themselves to the solution of very complex problems while improving staff morale, providing checks and balances to abuses of power, and opening up the community to new sources of information.

The Community Meeting

The easiest and least expensive method for promoting democracy and nonviolence is by having regular Community Meetings. Since its origins in post–World War II England and Scotland, the Community Meeting has been a central concept of the therapeutic community (TC), a spatial expression of the democratic process that is central to the democratic TC [103–106].

In traditional democratic TCs, the Community Meeting is where much of the psychotherapeutic work of the community actually occurs. When the TC concepts were adapted for shorter-term settings and became "therapeutic milieus," the Community Meeting became the critical time when staff and clients gathered together to discuss issues affecting everyone. Over time, however, and as a result of the wide-ranging organizational stresses that we described in *Destroying Sanctuary*, the knowledge base about how to run Community Meetings and their basic functions in a milieu setting have been largely lost. As a consequence, many staff members currently working in therapeutic settings are afraid to bring groups of clients together and have never experienced the power of one of the simplest methods of creating and maintaining a nonviolent environment.

But the Community Meeting isn't just a therapeutic tool for clients who are in treatment settings. It's an interesting fact that although most workplaces in the for-profit and nonprofit worlds are dependent on collective effort, rarely is any attention paid to how a collection of independent individuals becomes a group. To be effective, a group must be capable of thinking and acting together in the service of a shared goal, rather than thinking and acting as separate individuals. We just assume that when it works, it works and when it doesn't it's because we don't have the right combination of individuals. It may be true that the right people aren't in the room or the problem may be that we don't have the right process, a process that honors the transition from "me" to "we." That's what makes starting a meeting, any meeting, with some version of a Community Meeting necessary if you want groups of people to pull together in the service of a larger goal. Community Meetings are actually as ancient as human beings. Gathering in a circle to meet each other eye-to-eye has been the basic structure of human groups for as long as human groups have existed. Circling up, circling the wagons, and the sacred hoop all represent this vital form of interactive connection and interdependence.

The regular use of Community Meetings is necessary for the practice of nonviolence and for deep democracy. A Community Meeting is a deliberate, repetitive transition ritual intended to psychologically move people from some activity that they have been doing into a new group psychological space preparing the way for collective thought and action. In the form and content of the meeting, people nonverbally and overtly pressure each other to conform to community norms and expectations. For all members of any group, this provides a predictable bridge that directly and indirectly reinforces community norms. Rules are made and administered by authority figures and are likely to be broken. Norms emerge out of a group, and most people are influenced by group norms. The Community Meeting is *not* a therapy group, although therapeutic things are likely to happen during it, and for the purposes of the Sanctuary Model it is meant to be brief and meaningful in a way that does not interfere with the logistics of the meeting or the day ahead.

The Community Meeting gives everyone a voice and offers a safe and nonthreatening environment in which people can begin finding words to express feelings on a regular basis. It conveys to the community that emotional intelligence is important while at the same time recognizing that feelings are "no big deal" because everyone in the community can watch feelings, even distressing feelings, come and go, wax and wane even over the course of a 15-minute meeting. The leveling of hierarchy that is expressed by the equal participation in the process signals to everyone in the community that "we are in this together" and reinforces the *Commitment to Social Responsibility*. At the same time, the importance of relationship always remains in the forefront. Once the skill and safety of the Community Meeting are established, the meeting becomes a natural and spontaneous process that any member of the community can use when trouble is brewing, tension is rising, or an untoward event has occurred. In this way, the Community Meeting becomes an extremely effective tool for creating and sustaining an atmosphere of nonviolence.

For Community Meetings to be most effective, they must include all members of the community having the meeting, and the meeting itself must embody the Seven Commitments of the Sanctuary Model and therefore must enact the group norms on a regular basis. As people become accustomed to the form, they can actively demonstrate concern for others, interpersonal safety, open communication, a sense of social responsibility, a willingness to learn and to listen, and a shared commitment to the well-being of the whole group. The physical space of the meeting, and the opportunity for everyone to have a voice, represent the practice of democracy in its most basic form (Figure 4.7).

Figure 4.7 Community Meeting.

Team Meetings

Team Meetings are at the heart of most meaningful work in human service environments. The problems that we routinely encounter are so complex that no one person can grasp all of the details and implications in order to create a workable plan to help. As we have said before, *"no one of us is as smart as all of us,"* and our emphasis on the importance of Team Meetings exemplifies this. The terrible irony about Team Meetings is that they are the first thing to go when demands for productivity increase. And yet, they are the most powerful tool we have.

Preventing mental health and other social service workers from collaborating with each other, particularly in residential settings, or in situations where caregiving is distributed among a number of different providers, makes as much sense as telling a radiologist that he or she cannot use special machinery or that a surgeon can have no scalpels. From our observations, the decrease in Team Meetings, or at least of *meaningful* Team Meetings, has almost paralyzed our systems of care and has made providing integrated care virtually impossible.

Routine Team Meetings are one of the times when the *Commitment to Democracy* can be actively practiced. A Team Meeting is an active, focused meeting where every member feels comfortable talking and listening, is engaged and contributes, shares insights, generates new ideas, and builds trust. It provides the opportunity for all members of a team to see and affirm that they are, in fact, members of a team and to recognize that to be a team, their work together must be coordinated. A Team Meeting is the time to address client issues, gather ideas for working with individual clients or with the entire community, and discuss new initiatives to improve the activities or events on the horizon. It is an open forum for addressing staff concerns. It provides the time for the critical work of integration that is missing in so many service environments. Every individual may be doing a great job, but if staff members do not take the time to integrate their work with what everyone else is doing, the result can be chaos instead of effective intervention.

The Sanctuary Toolkit, S.E.L.F., and the Sanctuary Commitments play an important role in Team Meetings. First, we encourage all teams to begin their meetings with a Community Meeting. It is crucial for staff to be aware of their emotions and the powerful role they can play in team planning and decision making. At Team Meetings in a Sanctuary program, leaders and members must remain cognizant of S.E.L.F. and be willing to address issues that compromise safety, become comfortable with the expression of emotion, grapple with both tangible and intangible loss, and keep an eye on the overall goal of their work together, that is, what they want the future outcome to be (Figure 4.8). At the same time, team members need to be willing to acknowledge coworkers' efforts to honor the Sanctuary Commitments and address times when they have pulled up short and let their team down. It is crucial that Team Meetings consistently reinforce the shared Sanctuary concepts and language.

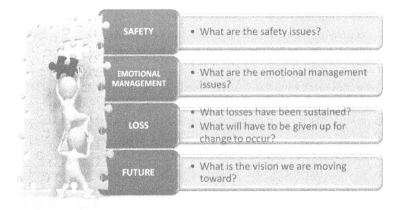

PresenterMedia

Figure 4.8 Team Meetings.

Team Meetings should have a clear agenda, preferably one that is available to everyone in advance, and have a predictable time and place where they are held. Everyone on the staff should have the opportunity to put items on the agenda. Each organization will need to define what it means by a "team" so that the group is neither too small to have a diversity of opinion nor so large that nothing can be accomplished if everyone is to have input. There should be a designated facilitator for the meeting who raises important topics, encourages meaningful input from everyone, ensures that all members of the meeting feel safe and respected, and summarizes key points and decisions. Minutes should be kept, particularly of the key points and outcomes of discussions, so that the group does not lose the thread of continuity over time. Follow-up on the outcomes of the previous meeting should occur at every subsequent meeting.

Establishing democratic practices in an organization is crucial to becoming trauma informed. When we are confronted with challenges and problems, the answer always lies in expanding democratic processes, not contracting them. Any suspension of democratic processes should be temporary and should focus on teaching members the skills needed to behave more democratically. The *Commitment to Democracy* and the *Commitment to Nonviolence*, the subject of our next chapter, are inextricably linked.

S.A.F.E. Level System

As our community of practice has grown, exemplified by the development of the Sanctuary Network, we have gained from the innovations of our programs. One example of this kind of innovation is in the Green Chimney's level system. A level system is a structured set of steps that indicate the person's progress in treatment, usually tied to a treatment plan and increasing levels of privileges.

Green Chimneys is a residential program, school, and community service provider for children and their families in Brewster, New York, and one of the Sanctuary Certified Programs. Green Chimneys had a long history of animal-assisted therapy before they began Sanctuary Implementation, and they used the Sanctuary Model to further enhance their services.

Highly structured programs usually have some kind of level system that is often more focused on punishing people for their indiscretions than rewarding them for therapeutic gains. In the process of Sanctuary Implementation, a multidisciplinary and diverse team from the Green Chimneys community that included representatives from several departments, students, residents, and family members decided that they needed to change their level system.

The purpose of this team was to design and implement a unified trauma-informed level system across the agency programs utilizing the framework of the Sanctuary Model for Organizational Change. The team believed that a unified level system would promote the use of a shared language among all members of the community when referring to treatment goals, behavioral expectations, rewards, consequences, and transitions. A shared language, within the Sanctuary Commitments framework, provided common grounds for a democratic discussion and created a strong philosophical base on which the delivery of effective treatment became a community effort in order to accomplish the Green Chimneys' mission of maximizing children's potential.

What the team developed was a behavior and growth level system defined by four levels that reflect increased independence and responsibility. The acronym S.A.F.E. is used to define each level as follows: Striver, Achiever, Forward, Exemplar. Each level encompasses a set of behavioral expectations that reflect the ability of the child to be a safe member of the community and indicates progress on individual treatment goals by the use of a behavior modification system.

Chapter 5

Commitment to Nonviolence

We¹ have learned through the grim realities of life and history that hate and violence solve nothing. Violence begets violence; hate begets hate; and toughness begets toughness. It is all a descending spiral, and the end is destruction— for everybody.

Reverend Martin Luther King [107]

SUMMARY: *In this chapter, after offering our vision of what the Commitment to Nonviolence might yield, we describe what we mean by "nonviolence" and what Sanctuary looks like as a "safety culture." We discuss how violence emerges in groups and how important it is for all of us to keep our social immune system healthy. We highlight some of the implications that the Commitment to Nonviolence has for leaders. Most of the children, adults, and families we see have been victims of violence in some form; therefore, a shared Commitment to Nonviolence is an essential element of a developmentally grounded, trauma-informed culture. We conclude by summarizing the essential tools that we use in the Sanctuary Model to embed this commitment in organizations.*

A Vision of Nonviolence

- It is universally recognized that all forms of violence—interpersonal, self-directed, and collective—are interconnected and interdependent and that physical violence erupts when there is a violation of moral, social, or psychological safety.
- Violence is no longer perceived as acceptable or welcome, but is always perceived as a form of socioemotional injury that is contagious.
- Coercive forms of intervention in institutions are rarely, if ever, used. When they are used, they are seen as a negative outcome and are always debriefed. As a result, there are few injuries to staff or clients.
- People who harm the well-being of others and of the community are perceived as having injuries—treatable injuries, but injuries nonetheless.

- Punitive forms of response to misbehavior and socioemotional injuries are seen as useless, inherently violent, and retaliatory in nature and thus become a breeding ground for escalating retaliatory violence.
- Clients are never hit, disrespected, neglected, or abused. Staff members recognize that their personal safety is directly tied to their ability to treat those who receive services with respect and dignity.
- Bullying behavior is addressed whenever it emerges in the organization, regardless of who is engaging in this behavior.
- Leaders understand that they need to treat the staff with respect and dignity.
- Since safety is valued, violence is seen as stupid, even boring, and everyone learns to manage conflict productively.

What Do We Mean by Nonviolence?

Tranforming Violence into Nonviolence—Lyndra's Story

It was 1993 and Dr. Lyndra Bills was a young psychiatrist just out of her residency. She had trained with Dr. Lou Tinnin, one of the early pioneers in applying trauma theory to people with a wide variety of psychiatric problems. Being a cowgirl and accustomed to wrestling cows, she decided to take a challenging job in a rural state hospital for the chronically mentally ill. In retrospect, accepting this job was either very brave or extremely foolhardy because the hospital was an exceedingly violent place. Even before she started, Lyndra knew about the violence between patients and between patients and staff, and the violence that patients inflicted on themselves, but that only served to convince her that there had to be a great deal of unresolved trauma in the backgrounds of these patients that had never been addressed. She decided to see what she could do to reverse the situation and turn a violent, chaotic, and frightened group of people into a working community using her knowledge about the impact of trauma and the systematic use of the therapeutic milieu that was then just being articulated as the Sanctuary Model [108, 109].

Lyndra's first few moments of her first day on the job, however, made her reevaluate her decision. "*As I opened the door, I looked down a long, dimly lit, drab hallway. The sound of women's screams filled the air and as I stared, halted in my progress for a moment, a chair flew across the hallway and crashed to the floor, and then a large woman, presumably a patient, came up behind a staff member and began to pound the nurse on the head*" (p. 350) [109]. As Lyndra interacted with the patients and staff, the causes for the astonishing level of interpersonal assault became clear. The staff had been instructed not to talk with the patients, and they retreated behind the Plexiglas wall of the nursing station whenever they could. They had been told that their job was to observe, record, and report, not interact, a bit like what zookeepers did before zoos realized that animals have feelings too. There was no therapeutic program for the patients because these patients were not considered safe enough to do anything except sit around, eat, and watch television. There was no clear idea of therapeutic progress: what it would look like, how it could happen, who would be involved. Violent interactions were normative behavior, with over 100 reported incidents a month and hundreds more that were unreported. A significant amount of this violence was directed at the staff, but the frequency of extreme self-harming behavior was also alarmingly high. Lyndra was struck by the ingenuity of the patients in finding ways to hurt themselves.

> *Everyone abhorred the violence but felt helpless to do anything to stop it, nor were there any real efforts made to understand the factors that may have provoked the violence. It was as if Violence was an active entity that ran the unit. The patients routinely lashed out violently at each other, sometimes provoked by an insult or a despised behavior, other times provoked by what appeared to be nothing. The patients were frequently and unremittingly violent towards staff, who resorted to the use of seclusion and restraint as their only defense against serious harm. Even in those early days it was apparent to me that the patients were engaged in some kind of bizarre reenactment behavior that was satisfied only by the use of strait jackets and solitary confinement.* (p. 352) [109]

And Lyndra was not immune to the effects of the violent culture. She was hit in the head, thrown down steps, and repeatedly threatened. She had trouble sleeping, was plagued by nightmares, and, like the patients and the other staff, became hypervigilant herself. The cost of this violence was high for everyone. The patients were terrified of mingling with each other and were discouraged from talking to the staff. Work time was lost as a result of being bitten, hit, splashed with hot coffee, and kicked. In one month alone, 75 hours of employee time were lost due to injury. The patients were also frequently injured by each other or themselves, and visits to the local emergency room were common.

Lyndra began reviewing each chart and learning about each patient and what had happened to her. There were 24 women on the unit. As she reviewed their charts, she was not surprised to find in many of their backgrounds brutal stories of sexual abuse, incest, domestic violence, childhood physical abuse, emotional abuse, and neglect. One-quarter of them had been hospitalized for periods ranging from 6 months to 4 years, and another one-quarter had been in the hospital for more than 10 years. The charts were voluminous; one patient's chart alone required two shopping carts to haul the paperwork onto the unit for Lyndra's review. The average age of the patients was 38. Fifty percent of the patients had a high school diploma or equivalency and two had master's degrees. Three-quarters of them were diagnosed with schizophrenia, and all were considered to be "chronically mentally ill" and "untreatable."

Undeterred, Lyndra began meeting with each patient individually and in a short time had rediagnosed 60% of those carrying a diagnosis of schizophrenia. As she had suspected, of these patients, 50% met criteria for posttraumatic stress disorder or a dissociative disorder. Lyndra also began meeting regularly with the staff, teaching them what she had learned about psychiatric symptoms, self-harming behavior, violence, dissociation, and trauma, as well as teaching them about the principles of a therapeutic milieu.

Bloom and her colleagues had just started writing about their experiences in an acute care psychiatric setting for adults, and she drew on their guidelines to start making significant changes [6]. Once she had oriented herself to her patients' histories, Lyndra decided that it was time to work on building a nonviolent community. She started that change with very simple strategies.

I began my intervention by freely vocalizing the way I felt about the violence on the unit. I directed the staff to begin daily community meetings that would engage all of the patients in face-to-face encounters with each other, the staff, and myself. At these meetings I spoke about the devastating effect that the unit violence was having on all of us. I shared my own experience and feelings about the conditions and urged other staff members to do the same. Using violence as the central focus, I gradually trained the staff and the patients in the basic rules of the therapeutic milieu: the patients should be responsible for much of their own treatment; the running of the unit should be more democratic than authoritarian; patients are capable of helping each other; treatment is to be voluntary whenever possible and restraint kept to a minimum; psychological methods of treatment are seen as preferable to physical methods of control; the community itself, and all the individuals who constitute it, are expected to be the most powerful influence on treatment. These concepts were largely new to the staff and certainly new to the patients. I remained convinced that much could be done if we were jointly able to change the existing norms of the institution. In my analysis of the situation, I had come to recognize that violence was not only condoned but encouraged by the normative structure of the unit and by the lack of an alternative model. And I was going to guarantee that there was, in fact, an alternative option. (p. 358) [109]

Lyndra knew from her own experience and from what she had begun to learn about the Sanctuary Model that progress in treatment can only be expected if safety has been established—physical, psychological, social, and moral safety. And that could only happen through an effort that involved the whole community. She educated the staff in the Sanctuary Model and wrote a beginning set of unit rules that were extremely explicit about the insistence on nonviolence. She never wavered in iterating nonviolence as the goal they were moving toward. She and the staff, frequently accompanied by the patient who had been involved, reviewed every episode of violence in detail. They looked at the pattern of what had happened, how that pattern could have been altered, and alternative methods for coping with the same emotional arousal the next time. This provided an opportunity to learn about how violent episodes evolve, not independently within each person, as had been assumed, but within the context of interpersonal relationships in which violence was easily triggered by each individual's psychological vulnerabilities.

Reviewing every episode was an education for the staff and the patients.

Gradually, with repeated debriefings after every episode of seclusion and restraint, both the patients and the staff began to recognize what events in the environment tended to trigger these episodes and how these triggers related to unresolved traumatic experiences from the past. Over the course of a few months they began to see how much harm they were doing to each other while at the same time learning that violence was not inevitable, that they could individually contribute to making their seemingly impossible situation better and together they began to envision an end to violence. As the violent episodes began to be contextualized and understood, it became possible for the staff and patient community to begin to experiment with other kinds of interventions that preceded and often prevented the violent outburst. (p. 360) [109]

Lyndra also had to serve as the interface between the staff and the administration, who, oddly enough, were not entirely happy with the positive changes that were occurring on this ward. She saw that the staff did not feel that they had sufficient administrative support, and their lack of safety had a direct effect on the patients and the whole community. She was forced to look at the values that the administration was conveying to the nursing staff and the patients, and found that she had to advocate and mount moral arguments about care in order to get her patients the services they needed.

Under this new and simple strategy that demanded no increase in existing resources, the incidence of violence plummeted. After three months violence started to decrease, and six months after that, in October 1994, there were no incidents of seclusion or restraint for the first time in the long history of this institution. As Lyndra expected, many of the patients who had been considered untreatable responded to a more intensive, trauma-based therapeutic milieu. The ward had become a nonviolent community, and many of the therapeutic interactions were carried on from patient to patient. When the violence was reduced, more individual and group therapies were initiated. Lyndra left her position about a year after her arrival but kept in touch with staff members for several years. Within two years, one patient had died of medical causes, but only two of the original patients remained in the hospital. The rest had been discharged and were coping reasonably well in the community without readmission. One patient, with a dissociative disorder and a master's degree, had been on two-to-one supervision—meaning two staff members within arm's reach of her for 24 hours a day—when Lyndra arrived because of her astonishing level of self-harming behavior. She had done so well that she was released from the hospital and, at least for the next three years of Lyndra's follow-up, had not harmed herself, been suicidal, or been rehospitalized.

What Do We Mean by Nonviolence?

When Lyndra took this job and decided to change things, she had a deep moral commitment to stop the violence around her. In doing so, she became part of a struggle to understand the concept of "nonviolence" that has existed for a very long time. Many of the people who command the most respect, and even awe, in our culture are those who have actively practiced nonviolence: Jesus, Buddha, Gandhi, Martin Luther King, the Dalai Lama.

But the very awe that these men evoke can be off-putting to average people who minimize their own nonviolent practice in the face of these mighty figures. That's why it is so useful to tell a story about a young woman, a cowgirl from Texas, who wanted to work in a better place. Lyndra wasn't a magician or a spiritual guru. She was, however, firmly *committed* to doing something to stop people from being harmed. Nonviolence is not just about being nonviolent today. It means choosing to put aside our very natural inclination to retaliate when we are hurt and instead to actively respond nonviolently to circumstances that would otherwise provoke violence. To truly make *a Commitment to Nonviolence* means objecting to violence in principle, not just in today's practice, even though we may have the reason, means, courage, and physical and emotional strength to be violent.

The practice of nonviolence is rooted in every major religion: Judaism, Christianity, Islam, Buddhism, Hinduism. The practice of nonviolence is a significant part of the founding of the United States and has been a consistent narrative throughout our history. As the writer Ira Chernus has said, "*The nonviolence tradition runs quietly, like an underground stream, through U.S. history. Its effects have been less visible than the tradition of war and violence. But its effects may someday prove to be more lasting*" (p. xi) [110]. In fact, Chernus continues, the heritage of nonviolence in the United States is a world heritage with roots in the religion of the Quakers and the Anabaptist Protestants, leading the world to a new idea: "*that society can be permanently improved when people band together in organized groups to work actively and nonviolently for social change*" (p. x) [110].

Nonviolent social and political movements emerged first among the Quakers in colonial North America, so it is not a coincidence that the Sanctuary Model traces its roots to the Moral Treatment of the mentally ill, introduced by the Quakers in England and then in the United States in the last part of the eigh-

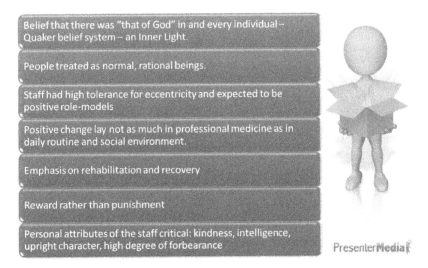

Belief that there was "that of God" in and every individual – Quaker belief system – an Inner Light.

People treated as normal, rational beings.

Staff had high tolerance for eccentricity and expected to be positive role-models

Positive change lay not as much in professional medicine as in daily routine and social environment.

Emphasis on rehabilitation and recovery

Reward rather than punishment

Personal attributes of the staff critical: kindness, intelligence, upright character, high degree of forbearance

PresenterMedia

Figure 5.1 Principles of moral treatment.

teenth century and the first quarter of the nineteenth century, with astonishingly good results (Figures 5.1 and 5.2).

The hospital where Lyndra went to work had originally been a part of the movement for Moral Treatment, but by the mid-twentieth century the principles

Five-Year Period	Patients Admitted	Patients Discharged	
		Recovered	Improved
1833-37	300	211 (70%)	39 (8.3%)
1838-42	434	324 (75%)	14 (3%)
1843-47	742	474 (64%)	34 (5%)
1848-52	791	485 (61%)	37 (5%)

PresenterMedia

Figure 5.2 Moral treatment results.

for creating nonviolent therapeutic communities had eroded and hospitals like this had become violent, coercive, punitive places. Like democracy, upon which nonviolence is so critically dependent, maintaining a nonviolent community requires clear values and constant vigilance.

Types of Nonviolent Commitment

People who have studied nonviolence have differentiated between two fundamental kinds of nonviolence. One has been called "tactical nonviolence." This refers to the prohibition of physical violence alone, even though there may be antagonism and a strong desire to coerce the other party into another way of thinking or doing. The second fundamental form of nonviolence is Satyagraha (SOT-yah-GRAH-hah), or Gandhian nonviolence, characterized by a prohibition of both physical and psychological violence, a refusal to retaliate, active caring toward the opponent, and the intention to convert the opponent to the practice of nonviolence. Gandhi called this the *"nonviolence of the strong"* (p. ix) [110].

The Sanctuary *Commitment to Nonviolence* is unconditional and is based both on principle and on practical humanitarian considerations. This was the form of nonviolence that led to the overthrow of British rule in India, that ended racial segregation in the United States, that propelled the Velvet Revolution in what is now the Czech Republic, and that guided South Africa to end apartheid [111].

It is this second fundamental form of nonviolence that is most endorsed in the Sanctuary Model. Our intention is not just to reduce coercive practices in mental health settings, but to create environments that are safe for everyone, including staff, clients, and families. This means helping people who have been exposed to violence, and who have often learned to use violence as a way of getting their needs met, to have a conversion experience. They have been affected by abusive, often violent forms of influencing others. We want them to discover that there is another way of being in the world, another way of influencing others that leads to positive, often transformative change. That is exactly what Lyndra set about doing: converting the entire program to the unconditional practice of nonviolence.

As history has shown, practicing nonviolence has never been easy. People often hear the word "nonviolence" and assume it to mean passivity. When Lyndra first began talking about nonviolence, it seemed like a crazy idea to the repeatedly brutalized staff and the disorganized, wounded patients. But the reality, as the historical examples above illustrate, requires intense and disciplined leadership action, not passivity, in the face of violence. Retaliating when we are provoked is the simplest, most direct course of action, particularly if we have more power than the person or persons provoking us. Retaliation comes to us quite naturally. Behaving in a counterintuitive fashion, and asking others to do the same, requires determination, inner strength, commitment, faith, and courage. That is precisely why Gandhi called it the "nonviolence of the strong."

Sanctuary as a Safety Culture

The concept of "sanctuary" refers to the strong emphasis we place on the active and conscious development of a sense of safety within any environment [2]. In other organizational settings it has been referred to as the creation of a "safety culture" or a "safety climate," described as "*the product of individual and group values, attitudes, perceptions, competencies, and the patterns of behaviors that determine the commitments to and the style and proficiency of, an organization's health and safety management. . . . characterized by communications founded on mutual trust, by shared perceptions of the importance of safety*" (p. 1124) [112].

In order to create a Sanctuary safety culture, we need to define what we mean by safety, how violence emerges within a group, and how to create and sustain social immunity to the incursion of violence. Safety, however, is not easy to define. In providing healing environments, we found that to adequately describe safety in the community context, we had to understand four levels of safety simultaneously and dynamically: moral safety, social safety, psychological safety, and physical safety (Figure 5.3). In defining each realm of safety,

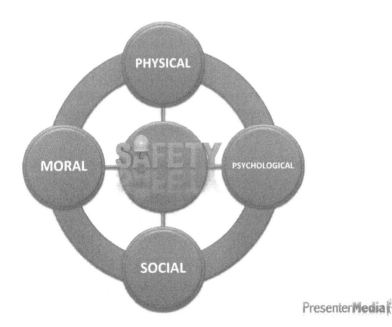

Figure 5.3 Sanctuary as a safety culture.

we identify what practices need to be eliminated from our settings and what we need to do in order to ensure that kind of safety.

Moral Safety

We start with moral safety because it is at the heart of all other safety issues. Creating a morally safe helping environment is probably more challenging today than it has ever been. In *Destroying Sanctuary* we discussed the concept of "moral distress" at great length. In brief, moral distress is *"the pain or anguish affecting the mind, body or relationships in response to a situation in which the person is aware of a moral problem, acknowledges moral responsibility, and makes a moral judgment about the correct action; yet, as a result of real or perceived constraints, participates in perceived moral wrongdoing"* (p. 5) [113].

Moral distress occurs in situations where you know what the right thing to do is, but doing it is thwarted by constraints.

Brian recently had an experience with a staff member that illustrates the exceedingly challenging moral dilemmas we are all faced with when we know what our clients need but cannot afford to give it to them:

> *I recently had a conversation with one of the clinicians at our mental health division, which, like all services of its kind serving the public sector, has been struggling to stay afloat financially. We discussed the productivity targets for the program, and she indicated that she felt they were too high and that they prevented her from doing quality work. She described her clients' extensive needs and indicated that she could not meet all of those needs in the time allotted. I told her that I did not disagree with her assessment, but in reality there was a reimbursement structure that confines us in many ways. I indicated that I appreciated the struggle she had but pointed out that we're all working with the same constraints. I asked her if she thought she was helping the kids she worked with at all. She said she was but they needed so much more. I suggested she take solace in the fact that she was helping kids make changes they need to make and not discount the work she was doing because she could do more. It was a useful conversation because we both were on the same page, we both wanted the best for the children, and we both experienced the terrible sense of moral distress that we simply cannot keep the organizational financially safe without making decisions that may adversely affect people's care. It was one of the first times that we agreed on the challenges that we face in the work we do. In the past I would have gotten defensive, angry with her for making me feel bad, and impatient with her for not understanding the bind we are in. But I realized that she wasn't whining; she was trying to tell someone about her moral distress, and the only way I could create a morally safe interaction was to share in that distress with her. I think she knows that I will do whatever I can to relieve her distress, and she knows that the problems that exist are beyond my immediate control, so that she will make the most out of what she can do for the children.*

Social service and mental health providers experience moral distress when they must act in a way that contradicts their personal beliefs and values. There is a sense of being morally responsible but unable to change what is happening [114]. It has been shown that moral distress is a result of reactions originating in the need to act in ways that contradict our beliefs or the inability to act in ways that are consistent with our beliefs. Depending on who we are, we can have many reactions to moral distress that actually cause more problems than they solve. Instead of directly confronting Brian with her concerns, this staff member could have just acted out by refusing to continue seeing the client, who had been assigned to her, or by seeing the client and not billing for him, or by lying about services she was delivering to the client, or any number of possible outcomes, all of which would have become a form of violence directed at the client, herself, or the organization.

When Lyndra entered the violent hospital, she did not believe that she could immediately change the level of physical violence. She knew that the only way to stop people from being physically violent is to throw them in a cage, chain them to the wall, force sedating drugs on them, or terrify them into tempo- rary submission, but all these actions increase the likelihood of more violence because they deprive human beings of basic human rights. She felt moral out- rage and saw the violence as a challenge to moral integrity, to the basic right of every human being to be safe from harm. She saw, moreover, that to bring about such a change, she would have to address the issue on those grounds: that the violence was morally wrong and that all of them— her as the leader, the staff, and the patients—were together going to reclaim the environment because it was the right thing to do.

A morally safe environment is one in which you are able to do your work with a sense of integrity because your sense of what is right is supported by the institution in which you work and the people who directly supervise you. Of course, what is right is likely to be perceived differently depending on who you are, your experience, and your position in the hierarchy of the organi- zation. Different people have different moral responsibilities that can seem contradictory.

There also may be significant differences in how people perceive fairness in the way they are treated or the way resources are distributed. An administrator at a Sanctuary-trained agency recalls a situation that illustrates this. A grateful donor gave a new van to the cottage where his child had received excellent care. But when the staff members of the other cottages saw the van and learned that it was for the use of only one cottage, rumors grew about the favoritism that the administration was showing to this cottage. All of the cottages needed new vans and if only one cottage got it, this was clearly a sign that the administra- tion cared more about that cottage and the people who ran it. After one of the administrators worked through his own frustration about the rumors, he called a staff meeting and informed the staff about what had happened, the priorities of the donor, and how the decision had been made. *"We could have refused to accept the gift unless he bought a new van for all of the cottages, but that wasn't going to happen. He had one van to purchase, and he wanted it to go to the cottage and staff he knew. We decided to accept the gift, and we will work on getting new vans for all of the cottages in the future."*

The administrators were irritated that they had to explain the situation, that there was so little trust from the staff. On the other hand, people who have less power in an organization use such opportunities to question the nature of moral safety in their organization. When leaders rise to the occasion and conduct themselves in a way that reassures the staff, this conveys the message that moral safety matters, that staff too are expected to be guided by a clear value system.

All individuals bring to the workplace their own set of values, which they try to live up to. Until we actually get to know each other and work with each other, we have no way of knowing whether there is alignment between the values of the individual and those that the organization endorses. Our ideas about fairness, honesty, compassion, and tolerance are dependent on our status, our experience, and our family backgrounds. Creating the proper alignment in an organization takes ongoing communication, learning, and growth.

So, like the rest of what we describe as Sanctuary, discovering moral safety is a process that is constantly unfolding. It requires all of us to be willing to ask questions, raise concerns, and work together to find definitions we can all agree on. It is an attempt to reduce the hypocrisy that is present, both explicitly and implicitly, in our social systems. A good place to start is where Lyndra did, connecting the lack of moral safety to the lack of physical safety. People may argue about how to treat clients or how much information to communicate to staff, but few people can argue that educational, health delivery, mental health care, and social service settings should be safe places for the administrators, the staff, and the clients.

One of the first things Lyndra did to reclaim her environment was to immediately start treating people as people. When she arrived, the staff and the patients had been dehumanized. To be morally safe, we must honestly look at the ways in which our bureaucratic structures, which are created for greater efficiency in handling large numbers of people, can inadvertently dehumanize the very people the organization is supposed to serve. The greater the distance between those who make policies and those who have to live with the policies, the easier it is to create policies and enforce procedures that cause people to suffer more, not less.

In Lyndra's story, the people who ran the institution were insufficiently concerned about the violence their staff members were enduring. They were not subjected to it themselves, so they could distance themselves and just categorize the staff injuries as an inevitable part of the job. In doing so, the organizational managers were treating the staff members as less human than themselves. Likewise, the staff so treated felt justified in their inhumane treatment of the patients, who were living like animals in a cage, deprived of social contact, isolated, and abandoned. This is an example of how readily institutions may develop destructive parallel processes.

When someone is being deliberately abusive, cruel, or violent, it is relatively easy to recognize violations of moral safety. When there is frank corruption, as when high administrative salaries or expense accounts rob the organization of resources that should go to the clients, that corruption may eventually come to light. Organizational policies and procedures, as well as external laws, are designed to capture and respond to the worse violations, so at least there is a remedy, even if it occurs after these violations have already occurred.

But what happens when people in the organization are dishonest, hypocritical, discriminatory, or simply ignorant? Who decides what is morally safe? We say dishonest things to avoid hurting people's feelings. We say that we care about the staff and emphasize how important it is for them to take care of themselves, and then we ask them to work 12-hour shifts with no breaks and add on overtime pressures. We deplore favoritism when the staff has clients who get special treatment, but we do not confront the same behavior when a manager gives a staff member special treatment. We say that we practice in a nondiscriminatory manner, yet we have no people of color in key positions, or do not promote women as rapidly as we do men, or do not even hire people who are openly gay. Our emphasis on moral safety means that each one of us as individuals must develop what are called "moral competencies" [115] (Figure 5.4).

Being morally safe means having a system of values that are consistent, that guide behavior, and that are founded on a deep respect for each other and all living things. Moral safety is outlined in the Universal Declaration of Human Rights of 1948, which recognizes that *"the inherent dignity and the equal and inalienable*

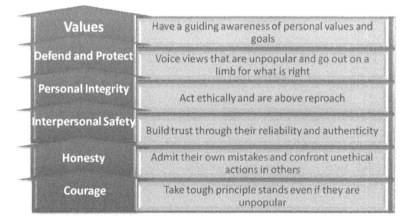

Figure 5.4 Examples of moral competencies.

rights of all members of the human family is the foundation of freedom, justice and peace in the world; that disregard and contempt for human rights have resulted in barbarous acts which have outraged the conscience of mankind," and which looks toward *"the advent of a world in which human beings shall enjoy freedom of speech and belief and freedom from fear and want has been proclaimed as the highest aspiration of the common people"* [116]. In 1990, the Convention on the Rights of the Child became the first legally binding instrument to incorporate a full range of human rights for children—political, civil, social, cultural, and economic, stating that *"children have the right: to be protected from physical and mental violence, degrading punishment, injury, neglect and abuse; to be protected from work that places them in danger, from drug abuse, sexual violence, trafficking, and other forms of exploitation; to health, education, medical care, and a decent standard of living; to express their opinions, form organizations, and participate in them"* [117]*.

Moral safety is about being able to look yourself in the mirror without shame or guilt, and that is not always easy to do. The Sanctuary Model requires us to remember the multiple ways in which we demonstrate our values: in what we do and don't do, in what we say and don't say, in what we reward and what we punish, in who we protect and who we fail to protect, in what we admit and do not admit to ourselves and others, in what we stand up for and what intimidates us into silence, in what we deliver on and what we don't. Being in a morally safe environment means being free from all forms of violence: physical, psychological, social, and moral (Figure 5.5).

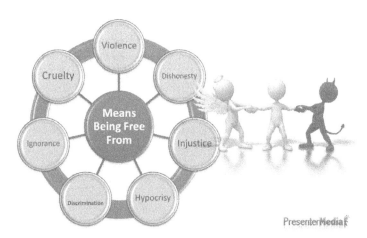

Figure 5.5 Moral safety means being free from...

---

* As of October, 2012, the United States is the only country in the world, aside from Somalia, that has not yet ratified the United Nations Convention on the Rights of the Child.

A morally safe environment engages in an ongoing struggle with the issues of honesty and integrity and what those concepts mean in different situations among different people. Creating a morally safe environment means that we must take a self-evaluative look at our basic assumptions, our training, our rationalizations, our beliefs, and our practice. We must look at our own issues with authority and become willing to participate in, not just manage, the relational web that forms the structure of our workplaces. Moral safety requires us to ask some important questions about what we are doing and why we are doing it (Figure 5.6).

These can be tough and embarrassing questions with answers that are, at times, difficult to swallow, particularly for managers who feel morally responsible for what happens in their organization. In an era of managed care, which is rationed care, a morally safe environment demands that we be honest with our clients about our limitations, about our increasing inability to provide them with what we may know they need, while continuing to offer them hope for the future and encouragement to pursue the struggle toward recovery, even when they cannot get the support they need and deserve. Moral safety permits and encourages us and our clients to behave and model specific values (Figure 5.7).

Social Safety

Social safety emerges from the values that we share and put into action in group settings. Workplaces are, by their very nature, social environments, and social

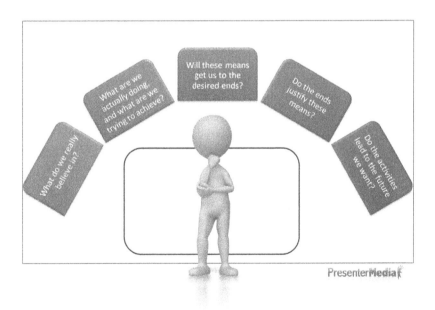

Figure 5.6 Questioning moral safety.

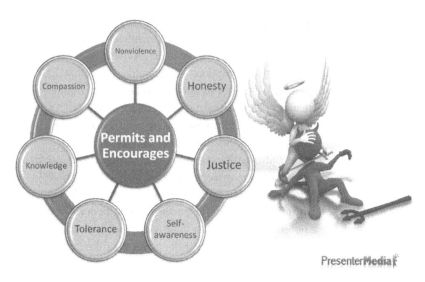

Figure 5.7 Moral safety permits and encourages…

safety describes the sense of feeling safe with other people and in one's community while having the ability to make and sustain healthy relationships. How many of us have ever felt truly safe in a social setting, a setting in which we felt secure, cared for, trusted, free to express our deepest thoughts and feelings without censure, unafraid of being abandoned or misjudged, unfettered by the constant pressure of interpersonal competition and yet stimulated to be thoughtful, solve problems, be creative, and be spontaneous? Yet this is the kind of setting that human beings need to maximize their emotional and intellectual functioning in an integrated way. In Lyndra's story, one of the first things she did was exercise her authority as a leader in a new way. At her first Community Meeting, she brought the entire community together over the protests of staff and patients, apologized for the abysmal conditions, and rallied everyone in the community to reclaim the environment for nonviolence. In doing so, she was setting a new value for the entire community.

Our social environments provide us, as inevitably flawed beings, with a very necessary "reality confrontation." As we re-create the relational patterns we learned as children within a social context, we have the opportunity to change those patterns so that we can be safer with other people. It's easy to see, then, how placing someone who is already injured in a highly dysfunctional organization that unconsciously repeats destructive relational patterns could be a major barrier to healing. It's also easy to see why an individual approach is simply insufficient.

Environments that are not socially safe are often described as "hostile work-places" where there is constant and unresolved interpersonal conflict that may become overtly abusive [118]. People in such places feel unsupported and are largely unsupervised so that boundary violations are common among clients, between clients and staff, and between staff. Gossip and rumors are the main source of information flow. There is a lack of empathy for each other and, in some cases, overt evidence of long-standing grudges, hatred, and bigotry (Figure 5.8).

A socially safe environment is one that is free from abusive relationships of all kinds. People are not isolated, but instead are connected to each other in a network of support. Emotion is successfully managed, boundaries are safe, and the level of emotional intelligence is high. The past can be looked at, dealt with, and finally left behind. There is tolerance for diverse opinions, beliefs, and values, but what ties everyone together is a shared belief in the importance of being safe. There is tolerance for individual eccentricities as long as they do not harm others. Boundaries are clear and firm, but flexible. There is a high level of awareness in a socially safe environment about group dynamics and the likelihood of getting caught in reenactments with other people, as well as a willingness to learn how to get out of these tough situations without harm. People can work productively and creatively toward a shared goal.

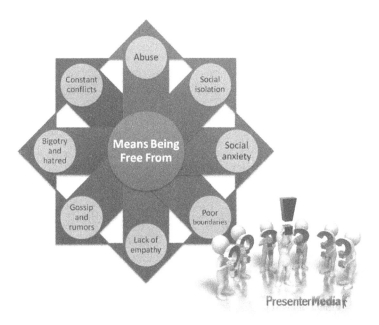

Figure 5.8 Social safety means being free from...

In the course of the Sanctuary Implementation process, organizations must evaluate their own level of social safety over time and move toward enhanced safety and support for everyone in the organization, from the top administrators to the direct and indirect care staff, to the clients and their families. Environments that are safe are characterized by more interaction, less interpersonal conflict, safer and more secure boundaries, honest and direct communication, tolerance and compassion, and good conflict resolution resources (Figure 5.9).

Psychological Safety

"Psychological safety" refers to the ability to be safe with oneself, to rely on one's own identity, to rely on one's ability to protect oneself against any destructive impulses originating from within oneself or from other people, and to keep oneself out of harm's way. The loss of the ability to protect oneself is one of the most shattering losses that can occur as a result of traumatic experience, and it manifests as an inability to protect one's boundaries from violation by other people. Another loss is the loss of a sense of self-efficacy, the basic sense of experiencing oneself as being able to relate to the world on one's own terms without abusing power and without being abused by it.

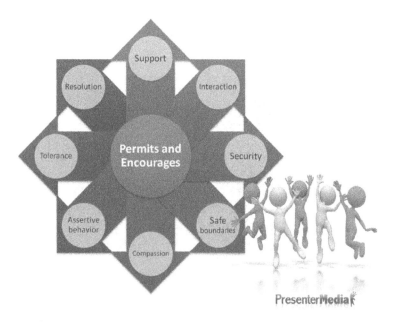

Figure 5.9 Social safety permits and encourages…

In the hospital where Lyndra worked, there was no psychological safety at first for anyone. She began educating and supervising the staff by working with and comprehending the problems of every individual patient. She understood that there was an intimate connection between what had happened to the patients and both the self-harming behavior and the violence they inflicted on other people. In doing all that she did, Lyndra rehumanized every person on that unit. She treated them with the respect and concern that every human being deserves, and as a result, they all began living up to her expectations, even the patients with the most disabling symptoms. She also understood and sympathized with the incredible stresses on the staff and made herself one of them, affirming their individual strengths and weaknesses but finding ways for them to be effective as a team. As the staff saw that her approaches were decreasing the violence, they began to change their expectations of the clients and of each other as well. In this way, the norms that were initially Lyndra's individual norms became shared group norms.

What are common threats to psychological safety? Unfortunately, they happen all too frequently in the workplace: things like sarcasm, lecturing, put-downs, outbursts, public humiliation, negative tone of voice or body language, inconsistency, unfairness, rigidity, favoritism, endless rules and regulations, infantilizing treatment, blaming, and shaming. We are all vulnerable to these kinds of behaviors from others, but people who have been psychologically unsafe while growing up are particularly vulnerable to profound reinjury by psychological torments and to adopting behaviors that have been inflicted on them in the past, the kinds of problems we illustrate in Figure 5.10.

An environment that is psychologically safe encourages self-protection, attention, and focus, self-knowledge, self-efficacy, self-esteem, self-empowerment, self-control, self-discipline, consistency, initiative, curiosity, achievement, humor, creativity, and spirituality. A sense of personal safety is achieved as individuals learn how to effectively protect themselves from violations of their personal and psychological space (Figure 5.11).

Physical Safety

Physical safety is the easiest aspect of a safety culture to describe, largely because it relies on tangible and concrete factors that can be easily evaluated and measured. Physical safety is usually what people think of when describing the sense of being safe. Psychiatry has always recognized the importance of physical safety. Locked doors, bars on the windows, straitjackets, seclusion and restraints, drugs, physical threat, and force have all been used, and misused, in the service of physical safety. Unfortunately, as Lyndra's story illustrates, an exclusive focus on the maintenance of physical safety within institutions tends

Figure 5.10 Psychological safety means being free from…

to result in the creation of environments that are more like prisons than therapeutic spaces and that are inevitably violent.

We have discovered that our refusal to tolerate safety breaches at the moral, social, and psychological levels constitutes our best defense against any breach in physical safety [2]. Physical safety alone does not constitute a safe environment

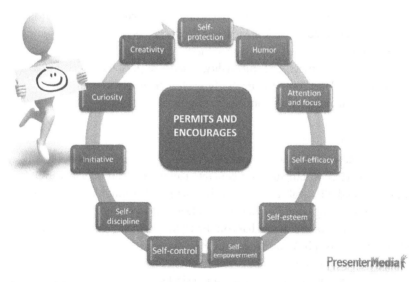

Figure 5.11 Psychological safety permits and encourages…

for growth. In fact, physical safety is unattainable if there are gaps in moral, social, and psychological safety. Breaches in physical safety generally do not occur until other forms of safety have already been violated. Clients resort to physical violence because they cannot trust that their needs will be met without this behavior. Given their histories, they can be exquisitely sensitive to any real or perceived threat in the environment.

Historically, we have tended to address breaches in physical safety by imposing more controls and employing interventions that constrain or coerce the perpetrator. The use of seclusion or restraint is a typical example. Such interventions serve to make people feel less respected and less powerful. As a result, we unwittingly undermine social, emotional, and moral safety and increase the likelihood of future violence. If we are ever going to make our environments less violent and much safer, we need to respond to incidents of physical violence by traveling upstream and addressing the root causes of violence. Subtle micro-aggressions and slights create a fertile environment for the emergence of physical violence.

A physically safe environment is free from threats of violence, regardless of whether they come from the self or from others (Figure 5.12). Being physically safe also means that basic needs for food and shelter are satisfied. Hungry people are not safe. Homeless people are not safe. Families that are being plowed under by debt are not safe. Organizations that cannot pay their bills are not safe. But safety at one level can be misinterpreted at another. A parent whose children are starving may steal to supply the basic necessities of life. An executive in an organization may spend money for something that looks like an unnecessary expense to staff members, such as a special dinner or a golf tournament, because the staff members are not in a position to understand the perilous financial status of the organization and that fund-raising is a necessary activity.

At the same time, there are things we can do to protect our physical safety in order to keep ourselves from harm by not engaging in violent conduct, by caring for basic needs including responsibly managing money, by having safe and reliable social and sexual relationships, and by being aware of dangers and refusing to take unnecessary risks (Figure 5.13).

Putting It All Together: Sanctuary Safety Culture

Safety is a complex concept. Too many people treat it as if it were simple by focusing just on physical safety and responding to danger by invoking physical responses, such as more security, stronger doors, more locks, guns, cameras, more police, and more restrictive laws. Such responses may be necessary in the short term, but they are never sufficient. Unfortunately, as demonstrated in Lyndra's program, increasing levels of physical safety measures can actually have the opposite effect of the intended result by reducing individual and group

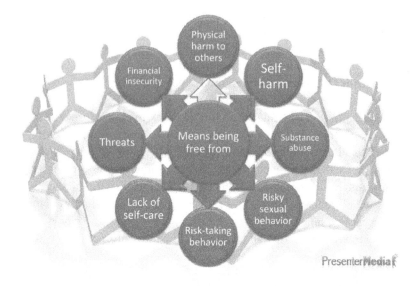

Figure 5.12 Physical safety means being free from...

responsibility for the emergence of violence. A focus on physical safety often results in ignoring the importance of the other kinds of safety we have explored here.

Unfortunately, when physical violence erupts in a community, the kneejerk response is to punish, coerce, contain, or expel the perpetrator. Lyndra's staff

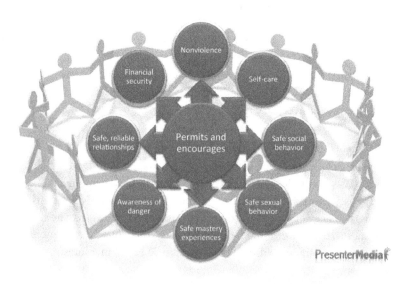

Figure 5.13 Physical safety permits and encourages...

and patients had been involved in this vicious cycle for years before she arrived and had not found a way out of it. It was simply assumed and accepted that such responses were effective, and despite the high level of violence, this was an unquestioned assumption. Punitive responses may make the people in control feel better for a while because they provide a satisfying sense of evening the score. But often those very responses are actually setting up an inevitable reenactment, which leads to more violence and further breaches in moral, social, and psychological safety.

Johnny, one of the children at Andrus, ran off the campus after a physical confrontation with another child. A busy street runs in front of the campus, so the staff members taking care of Johnny were reasonably worried about the potential danger involved. But Johnny was upset and refused to come back with the staff member who followed him. The worker tried for over a half hour to coax him back, but to no avail. Finally, the worker called the supervisor and said, "I think I can get him to come with me if I offer him some ice cream. Would that be okay?" The supervisor, who had no better solution to the problem, approved the plan. The worker asked the child if he wanted to go for ice cream, and Johnny readily agreed. The two of them got ice cream and then sat and talked about what happened.

We are sure that there are people reading this right now and thinking that this was a crazy response. Why would we reward negative behavior with ice cream? Won't the kid just do it again the next time to get more ice cream? For the last several decades, we have been taught that this is the way to think about what motivates people. Many mental health and social service programs continue to struggle with the idea that punishment works when decades of research show that it is mostly ineffective and often does more harm than good [119]. What if, for all these years, we have been entirely wrong in our assumptions? What if our behavioral approaches have been completely off-base and, instead of changing behavior, we have instead been repeatedly trapped in other people's reenactments? If our behavioral plans are not trauma-informed, this is probably the reason for a lack of change in our clients. We may be inadvertently helping them *not* to change.

In this case, Johnny did not leave the campus without permission after that experience, and his aggressive incidents decreased. How do we explain that? We believe it happened because this intervention was totally off the script for this boy and not at all what he had come to expect. No one had ever responded to his negative behavior—what we now think of as his cries for help—with a trip to the ice cream parlor. This boy was in distress and was expressing it in the only way he knew how. When we did not answer his signal with a punitive response, but instead responded to his distress and did something caring, he *felt* cared for and the conversation over ice cream made him feel valued and heard. He felt safe at all levels. This was enough to prompt some beginning change in this boy.

The *Commitment to Nonviolence* requires us to think outside the boxes we are in about how to respond to violent cues. That's what the staff did with Johnny and that's what Lyndra did with the patients on her unit when she began treating them not as animals but as people (an approach that is also effective with animals!). It's all about breaking the reenactment and rescripting the story. And that means "repeopling" the story and looking at the part everyone is playing in inadvertently helping the person who has become violent to repeat the violence. In high-functioning programs, staff members are able to move upstream and identify what might be happening that is compromising safety at other levels and is now erupting in the form of physical violence. In this way, they learn together how moral safety and social safety form the essential stable base for psychological and physical safety.

It is, however, far easier to externalize and blame other people when violence erupts. It is very difficult, after you have been assaulted by a client, to ask, "What might I have done to elicit that response?" or "What is happening in the treatment setting right now that is provoking this reaction?" But in the Sanctuary Model, that is exactly what we expect people to do, because violence *emerges* within the context of groups.

Violence Emerges within Groups

In the Sanctuary Model, we challenge groups to think in an entirely different way about violence. Typically when violence occurs, individual and community energy is expended on chasing down the violent person and finding some way to punish him or her for the violence. In the Sanctuary Model, we start with the assumption that violence is a group phenomenon and that when violence has occurred, the entire group has failed to prevent it, not just the individuals immediately involved. We see the violent person as the weak link in a complex web of interaction that culminates in violence after a cascade of previous, apparently nonviolent events has occurred, creating another vicious cycle.

The greater the proportion of people in any community who have been exposed to violence, the more violent the community may become. Rarely is an episode of violence in a community a singular and unconnected event. Violent episodes always have a history, but that history is not always immediately evident. Violence is relational. It may take a great deal of probing and investigation to figure out the cause-and-effect relationships, but they do exist.

Here's an example of the kinds of things that can easily occur in an organizational setting. Unless we ask the question "What happened?" and instead just make assumptions about who is and isn't wrong, we never get to the heart of the matter.

Upon receiving his paycheck, a staff member working as a childcare worker in a residential cottage saw that his pay was not what it should be: a whole week's pay was missing. Like most people, he lived on a tight budget, from pay-check to paycheck, and if this error was not corrected, he would not be able to pay his bills. Obviously upset, he immediately asked someone else to cover for him with a difficult child he had promised to read to so that he could go to the finance office. When he arrived, the person he needed to talk to told him rather abruptly to come back later. She was under a great deal of pressure to get budgetary figures completed for that afternoon's meeting of the Board of Directors at the urgent request of the CEO. Apparently there was a shortfall, and the Finance Chair of the Board was pressuring the CEO to explain the problem. The childcare worker, of course, knew nothing about the executive-level strains, nor would it have necessarily mattered to him if he did know. Knowing the details would not pay his bills, but a little explanation from the finance employee might have at least helped him to manage his anxiety, and together they could have come up with a plan for meeting later in the day. As it was, the finance person's inadequate, albeit understandable, response left the childcare worker steaming with anger and frustration. He went back to the cot-tage, and when the child he was assigned to complained to him that he hadn't been there to read to her as he had promised, he snapped at her. She said noth-ing immediately and silently retreated to her room. The childcare worker who had been shortchanged finished his shift and went home, still angry. During the next several hours, the child picked a fight with several other children, refused to clean up after dinner, and finally escalated her defiant behavior until she completely lost control, hit another staff member in the eye, and ended up being restrained.

As you can see, when the story is completely laid out, it is difficult to find someone to blame. This is all part of the day-to-day strain of any workplace. Everyone could have done better, but no one really intended harm. What sets human services organizations somewhat apart from other workplaces is that we must deal with people who are extremely vulnerable and often volatile, so the stakes may be much higher. Only if we take the time to map out all of the cause-and-effect relationships do we see what started this cascade of events. Unfortunately, without a safe structure to analyze the cascade, bad feelings are not contained, we learn nothing, and the most vulnerable members of the interactive chain, the child and the child-care worker, are blamed entirely for what has happened. It is this lack of learning that easily, readily, and frequently leads to chronic collective disturbances, which we will review in our discussion of open communication in Chapter 8.

Getting the whole story and looking for repetitive patterns represents a major shift for organizations and for the persons who work there. The idea that what we do or fail to do sets the stage for violence is difficult to understand. At the same time, it is incredibly empowering. It suggests that what we do really matters and that we have the power to change these dynamics if we change the way we approach our clients and each other. Helping organizations to understand that violence is more than just physical violence and that it is perpetrated not only by clients, but by staff as well, is essential. The bureaucracy can be violent, board members can be violent, leaders can be violent, middle managers can be violent, and staff can be violent. We are just a little more sophisticated about how we perpetrate violence. Organizations that begin to implement Sanctuary start by understanding this cascade of violence and seeking ways to interrupt it (Figure 5.14).

The only real buffer against overwhelming stress and the combined impact of violence is nonviolent, trustworthy social support. The insufficient social support that is so characteristic of today's human service delivery system has left all of our programs vulnerable to the impact of systemic violence. The *Commitment to Nonviolence* has proven to be very challenging to operationalize in organizations, even those committed to caring for the wounded. We have been committed to the use of violence, punishment, and coercion for so long that we often do not even identify violence as violence. We use other terms, like "treatment" or "behavior management" or "consequences," to disguise our real motivation. When people, even young children, are violent toward us, we want to get even. It is easy for those of us with more power to impose our will on those with less power. We believe we know what is best for the other person, and if this is unclear to a client or a staff member, a little pain might be just enough to get them to change their mind. If a little pain does not lead to enlightenment, perhaps a little more pain will do the trick.

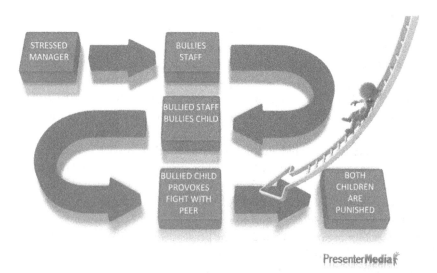

PresenterMedia

Figure 5.14 A cascade of violence.

Physical violence is a cry for help that, translated, says, *"I am in pain and no one is listening to me. I am not being respected. I am not being heard."* Instead of asking the fundamental question *"What's happened to you?"* we leap to an assumption and ask *"What's wrong with you?"* Frequently, the answer to the second question is that you are out of control, selfish, undisciplined, bad, or crazy. Our response then is to exert control, show you who is boss, punish the behavior. If we stick with *"What's happened to you?"* then the responses are different. *"What happened that made you feel disrespected or unheard?"* What *might have been going on in the program or the lives of staff members that may have contributed to that feeling?* [6]

If we can illuminate the whole cascade of violence, what we see is illustrated in Figure 5.14, a flow of events that often begins as a result of stress. The purpose of such an exploration is not to fix blame but to understand how the effects we have on each other spread. The manager in this example certainly did not intend for anyone to get hurt, but his bullying behavior precipitated a cascade of events that ended in violence. And yet, no one—not the manager, the staff members, or the children—saw the ways in which these events were connected and therefore ccould learn nothing about preventing violence. In an events analysis that is part of a Red Flag Review, everyone in the situation is responsible for identifying the part he or she played in the development of a violent event and learning how to do things differently the next time. In this way, the *Commitment to Nonviolence* turns into a practical method for eliminating violence.

Social Immunity

When we shift our focus away from individual outbursts of violence and instead look at all episodes of any kind of violence as a breach of our social defenses that involves everyone in the group, we begin thinking in a different way about the entire issue. Every episode of violence then becomes the means whereby we learn how to prevent the violence from emerging the next time. This means that new strategies for analyzing problems must become available to the group. If every act of violence is recognized as a problem for and of the entire community, then every act of violence must be resolved by the individuals involved *and* by the group.

A useful way to think about this interaction between the individual and the group is through the metaphor of our own immune system. We are each surrounded by potentially harmful bacteria and viruses all the time, and yet we usually stay well. What keeps our immune system healthy? As long as you are healthy, your immune system is steadily working to keep infectious agents away from your vital organs, and as a result, you don't get sick. But if you are overtired, stressed, depleted, or if the infectious agent is overwhelmingly powerful, then your defenses are breached and you get sick. Once the immune system is vulnerable, all kinds of things can snowball.

The social body is vulnerable in a similar way, and we call a group's ability to protect itself "social immunity." We define social immunity as the social body's ability to recognize and respond to threats to its well-being. We used the metaphor of the computer earlier, so think of such a threat as a computer virus. If you have adequate virus protection software, then it automatically senses when your computer is threatened and reacts to that threat. Similarly, whenever such a threat enters a relatively healthy social body, complex social activities are set in motion to defend and protect the social body against the emergence of violence (Figure 5.15). Someone senses the emotions of an escalating conflict, brings the parties together, grievances are aired, apologies are made, and restitution is accomplished. We view a physical infection as an exception to the rule of health. Similarly, in healthy organizations, violence is the exception to the rule of peace that typically governs a social species. Everyone who works and lives in a community is part of the "firewall," and whenever there is a breach in that firewall, violence is likely to break through.

But when we are in a poor state of social health, when there are unconscious interpersonal conflicts, when there are secrets, when there is a great deal of stress, the usual defenses of the social body are breached. It is at these times that violence is most likely to emerge. Instead of finding someone to blame, we can then ask, *"How and why has our social immunity failed? How did the violent impulses that exist as potential acts within all of us all the time suddenly emerge?"*

We recognize that the best protection against violence is a shared *Commitment to Nonviolence*. But to fulfill that commitment, everyone in the community must respond to every episode of violence as a breach of community norms.

Figure 5.15 Protecting the social immune system.

And we also recognize that the best method for nonviolence is democracy. So, when the social immune system becomes compromised, often due to repeated and overwhelming stress and trauma, potential solutions must include everyone if they are to be effective. Democratic processes help strengthen the social immune system, and when democratic processes are eroded, our social immunity is inevitably compromised.

Lyndra used democratic processes to turn her violent environment into a peaceful therapeutic environment. She was a naturally democratic leader and recognized that she alone was utterly helpless against the enormity of the problems she encountered. If she was going to change things, everyone would have to be involved. Every single time a violent incident occurred, Lyndra, the staff, and the patients spent time as a group figuring out how and why it happened. As they began to see the patterns, they were able to enhance the strength of their social immune system, ultimately enabling them to prevent violence from even emerging.

Protecting social immunity means that there must be universal training so that everyone in the system is on the same page. Conflict management resources must be available and accessible, and everyone in the system must be expected to utilize those resources as acts of socially responsible behavior. Social norms of nonviolence must be accepted, endorsed, and supported, and the emergence of violent incidents must be understood as signs of collective, not just individual, disturbance. In the Sanctuary Model, Red Flag Reviews are our method for routinely responding to any rupture in our social immunity.

Unsafe behavior must be identified, confronted, and given clear and consistent responses by the entire community, but if we are not to make things worse, then these responses must be designed to instruct and correct, and they must be fair from the point of view of the people involved. Otherwise, people who are being punished feel unjustly treated and the impetus for violence and retaliation escalates. In the Sanctuary Model, individuals are still accountable for what they do and don't do. However, there is a general awareness that violence emerges in the context of the group and that some individuals are most easily triggered by what is going on in the group. This means that we cannot fool ourselves into believing that we have solved the problem just because we have created some consequences for the perpetrators If we view violence as a contagious agent that can be spread physically, psychologically, socially, or morally, then we can begin to think about what keeps us safe from "infection." When we start thinking this way, it becomes easier to define our individual responsibility for keeping our social immunity intact, since every one of us is a potential carrier. One of the most important barriers against the emergence of violence in any group, and therefore a vital component of our social immune system, is interpersonal trust.

The Importance of Trust

In the stories we have presented in this chapter, the key element that helped create or restore social immunity was interpersonal trust—reliance on the integrity, strength, dependability, and safety of another person. Lyndra described many actions she took that were directed at establishing trusting relationships with the staff and the patients. The staff member who took Johnny for ice cream was creating a relationship of trust between himself and the boy and between the boy and the institution. His supervisor was demonstrating his trust in the child-care worker to approve his plan. In the example of the staff member and his paycheck, he felt that his trust was betrayed when he was shortchanged and he reacted to that betrayal as we often do, immediately and without thinking of the consequences.

Trust is the basis of all social relationships and is a vital component of the social immune system in any environment. Trust at the organizational level has long been recognized as an essential quality of successful organizational relationships over time, but this topic has become even more important in an era when change happens rapidly and the time available to create trusting relationships is often very short while being no less essential [120]. As one business consultant has written, *"All work place practices and changes should be evaluated by a simple criterion: do they convey and create trust, or do they signify distrust, and destroy trust and respect among people?"* (p. 62) [120].

Since building and sustaining trust is such an important aspect of developing social immunity to the emergence of violence, previous breaches of trust between management and staff, members of staff, and staff and clients must be addressed in a constructive way that provides community members with opportunities to restore relationships and reestablish trust. That's when saying you are sorry really matters.

Restoring Broken Trust: The Usefulness of Apology

One of the first things that Lyndra did when she decided to get the entire community together was to stand on a chair in the community room, with all the patients and staff around her, and offer an apology for the violent conditions that everyone had been living with. Now, she was not responsible for any of it and she had nothing to personally apologize for, but she intuitively recognized that as a physician, she represented Authority in the eyes of everyone else and Authority had clearly failed them all repeatedly. Sometimes, the only way to repair a relationship and reestablish the sense of trust that has been breached is to apologize. Apparently, strong norms of politeness govern our interactions, and when these norms are violated, retaliation often occurs [121, 122]. Apologizing or explaining things before the person gets upset is more of a deterrent to hostility and retaliation than giving the same information after the person is already upset [123] (Figure 5.16).

Mean what you say and show remorse

Give a little time for a cool-down

Don't wait too long

Explain any mitigating factors but don't make excuses for yourself

Learn from mistakes

Express desire to rebuild trust

Don't do the same thing again

PresenterMedia

Figure 5.16 Make apologies count.

Now let's look at why the *Commitment to Nonviolence* is absolutely essential if we are to create and sustain trauma-informed systems of care.

The Commitment to Nonviolence and Trauma-Informed Practice

Identifying Violence: The Real Diabolos

The *Commitment to Nonviolence* is essential for trauma-informed systems of care simply because VIOLENCE IS THE PROBLEM!! Regardless of what component of the social service or educational system you are working in, you are inevitably working with clients who have experienced terrible injuries in their lives, and most of the injuries will have occurred through violent action on the part of other people. Some of these injuries have been physical, some have even occurred before they were born, but most of them have been psychological, social, and moral. These past injuries have left these clients very susceptible to the impact of violence, and have compromised their psychological immune system as well as their physical immune system. The more experiences they have had, the more vulnerable they have become. A small "germ" of violence therefore can make them very sick and put them, and everyone in contact with them, at great risk.

Violence is a self-replicating virus that propels its own reproduction, taking advantage of innate capacities in the human species, the most social of all animals. When, as a species, we were weak and helpless against the overwhelming power of nature, our puny forms of violence posed no real threat to anything but our individual or family group existence. But we are not weak and puny anymore. Our intellectual and creative powers have far outstripped our emotional and moral development. Now we have the power to destroy all life on earth, but it remains an open question whether or not we have sufficient emotional and moral intelligence to prevent such destruction. As a species we are profoundly fragmented, still very much at the mercy of biological urges and social norms that perpetuate violence. It is the continuing immersion in violence that is at the root of this fragmentation. As a result of scientific advances in understanding the impact of exposure to trauma, adversity, toxic stress, and disrupted attachment, we now know much more about how violence becomes self-perpetuating at the physiological, psychological, social, and spiritual levels.

Violence *is* the demonic presence that haunts human existence. One word for the Devil is "Diabolos," the divider, the splitter-into-fragments [124]. The Devil is not some supernatural creature with horns. Violence is the devil walking among us. Once we become violent, once we do intentional harm to others in all of the ways we can do harm, physically, emotionally, socially, economically, and spiritually, we identify with the perpetrator, the Devil, and we become like what we most oppose, we lose our moral integrity, our spiritual center. The longer we walk down that road, the more damage we do or fail to prevent, the harder it is to admit to any of it.

For those of us who work in the human service delivery system and have had fewer experiences of adversity, it is easy to miss how subtle and nuanced this work is and how small acts of disrespect, seemingly insignificant failures in empathy and compassion, can set clients off and drive them to violence. For those of us doing this work who have suffered a great deal of adversity, it is difficult to identify and admit that we are vulnerable to the regular breaches in psychological, social, and moral safety we experience at the hands of our clients and our supervisors, and how these breaches impact our own behavior and the choices we make.

Making a *Commitment to Nonviolence* is not for the faint of heart. Because violence comes so naturally to us, living and working nonviolently takes tremendous discipline, self-reflection, and group support. We live in a culture that is fundamentally fear-based. Fear makes us do crazy things, and in trying to manage our fear we often create even more terrifying conditions.

Implications for Nonviolent Leadership

If you are in a leadership position in an organization, taking on the burden of leading Sanctuary implementation requires endless self-reflection, largely because you are going to be the model that everyone in the organization looks to for the *Commitment to Nonviolence*. With great power comes great responsibility, and before wading into the organizational change process, it would be worthwhile to spend some time on the personal discovery and change process that comes with being a leader in a Sanctuary organization. The process will require you to engage in continual reevaluation of your beliefs, values, assumptions, and behavior throughout Sanctuary implementation. We need to be willing to be the change we want to see in our organizations. If we can practice nonviolence, our organizations will become less violent and the people we serve will be more likely to get better or at least not be reinjured.

It is always shocking to find out just how powerful leaders are in an organization. If you are in a leadership position, it is troubling to discover that people assign great meaning to your throwaway remarks and may easily misinterpret a quick glance or a long sigh. It is difficult to remember that even though some event might mean very little to the leader, it can be quite meaningful to someone else in the organization.

So, a basic first step in making the organization safer is for leaders to take greater responsibility for what they do to compromise overall feelings of safety, even when they do not intend to do so. Leaders must not minimize the importance of their role and the power they have in the organization. Remember that intentions are not the same thing as consequences. Neither of us can think of a time when we really intended to hurt someone we worked with, but we can think of many times when we have in fact hurt someone. The fact that we didn't intend to hurt them doesn't help it hurt any less.

Sanctuary requires getting people on the same page. But this means that for some period of time we will *not* be on the same page. Large groups of people do not change all at once. The process is slow, challenging, and painful. In fact, when organizations begin to engage in Sanctuary implementation, things often get worse before they get better because the usual way of doing things is discarded and the system is therefore out of equilibrium. Dissonance increases in the organization, with some people trying to return to the way things have always been, helpful or not, and other people moving in a new direction. It is crucial that leaders keep moving forward and maintain a consistent message about where they hope to go.

The tricky part is that leaders must deal with what they perceive as the stubborn resistance to positive change by modeling the nonviolence they are hoping to see everyone adopt. Too often the momentary chaos that results from organizational dissonance causes leaders to abandon the change process prematurely or, even worse, resort to violence in an effort to ensure that everyone behaves more nonviolently. Brian uses an example from his own experience as a father about how important being a role model really is:

Many years ago when my daughter Katie was still in diapers, I stood her up on the changing table to change her. She was about 20 months old, and as I changed her, she playfully took her two little hands and wacked me on both ears. Cute. The force of this rang my bell. I reached behind her, swatted her on the behind, and said, "Don't hit!" I still remember the perplexed look on her face.

The moral of this story, of course, is that our actions need to square with our words. Although we may want to retaliate against a staff person who coerces or humiliates a client, violence is violence, and when leaders behave violently the process is set back, not advanced. Violence is contagious, traveling through a family, an organization, or a community. Leaders cannot behave in a violent fashion with staff and then fool themselves into believing that such actions have no impact on the clients they serve.

Trust needs to be built and cultivated, and its survival is always precarious. We get busy, we break a promise, and then when we realize it, we might assume it is not a big deal. We don't take the time to repair the problem. The breach lives on and drifts through the organization, attaching itself to other such breaches. Over time, these breaches of trust become *The Story* of the organization for old and new staff alike. Brian shares an example in the following story.

Recently, we were faced with a challenging situation in one of our programs. We were discussing whether or not to inform the parents of the children about what was going on. Some were concerned that the information would create unnecessary upset, while others felt that we needed to be completely candid with the parents and then let the chips fall where they may. I was in the second group. As the conversation progressed I said, speaking as a parent, "You need to be truthful; you obviously care more about your enrollment than you care about my kid's safety." The program coordinator seemed pretty deflated after the conversation. At first, I assumed it was because she was facing some tough phone calls that evening. But as I thought about it, I wondered if she had taken my statement, which I intended to be a devil's advocate position, as a commentary on her integrity. The next day, I called her to check in and I asked her about the comment. She said that she did feel terrible about what I had said, and she had taken it as a comment on her integrity. I apologized for my remark and clarified what I had intended. She felt better; the exchange not only cleared the air but improved our relationship.

Sanctuary Toolkit for Nonviolence

Safety Assessment as the "S" in S.E.L.F.

In Chapter 1 we briefly described S.E.L.F., the nonlinear compass tool that we use in many different ways to orient ourselves and each other to appropriate interventions and treatment responses. The ongoing assessment of where we are in terms of safety, both individually and collectively, represents the "S" component of S.E.L.F., and change often begins with a safety assessment. To make effective use of the tool, however, it is vitally important to understand that when we refer to safety in the Sanctuary Model, we mean an assessment of physical, psychological, social, and moral forms of safety. Figure 5.17 outlines the attributes of a nonviolent community [125].

Orienting New Staff around Nonviolence

We encourage organizations that are adopting the Sanctuary Model to get new staff members off on the right foot from the very beginning. That means incorporating the Sanctuary Model from the very first contact that a prospective employee has, through the interview process and in materials that are distributed even before the interview process begins. Once new employees are hired, they should be expected to read about and be able to answer questions about the Sanctuary Model as part of the orientation process. The orientation process should include preparing new employees to respond to provocation with nonviolent action and nonverbal communication [126]. Additionally, they shoud be helped to expand their definition of violence and avoid breaches in moral, social, and psychological safety. Ideally, and especially for direct care workers who will have to confront violent provocation on a regular basis, role plays are probably the best way to teach new employees alternative means of responding nonviolently without retaliation.

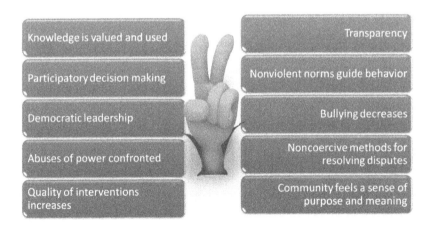

PresenterMedia

Figure 5.17 Attributes of a nonviolent community.

Safety Plans

A Safety Plan is a list of simple activities that a person can choose to do when he or she feels overwhelmed in order to avoid engaging in the unsafe, out-of-control, or toxic behavior he or she is accustomed to resorting to under stress and, instead, use an activity that is safe, effective, and self-soothing. The items in a Safety Plan should be simple things that people can do anytime, anywhere without embarrassment. In the Sanctuary Model, everyone has a Safety Plan so that having one and using it becomes a social norm, not simply an instruction pointed at a client. It is a form of universal precautions like washing one's hands. Staff members often carry their Safety Plan on the back of their ID badges, always there, always conveniently accessed. A Safety Plan is a relational tool. One of the first things we do when violence has emerged is to ask whether or not people used their Safety Plan, whether it worked, and if not, how the plan needs to be altered to be more effective.

Universal Training in Trauma Theory

One of the early, often introductory steps in the Sanctuary Model is teaching everyone in the organization about the psychobiology of trauma: what it looks like, the vulnerabilities that clients are contending with, and the challenges their experiences present to any helping environment. Developing an understanding of the impact of disrupted attachment, trauma, stress, and adversity on neurodevelopment begins to lay the groundwork for approaching clients with a different level of compassion, understanding, and empathy. Teaching trauma theory is integrated into our entire training and education process. In our implementation, the Core Team is responsible for training everyone, using the manuals, slides, and handouts we have designed to make it as easy and straightforward as possible.

We are hoping that readers will come away from this chapter with a different definition of violence and a different understanding of how physical violence can emerge in a community. We are confident that when you take this information on board, you will be motivated to change the way you respond to violence. We now move on to the *Commitment to Emotional Intelligence*. In order to effectively practice nonviolence, we need to effectively manage our emotions.

Chapter 6

Commitment to Emotional Intelligence

Emotions are among the primary determinants of behavior at work...and profoundly influence both the social climate and the productivity of companies and organizations.

R. Pekrun and M. Frese (p. 153) [127]

SUMMARY: *After offering a vision of what emotionally intelligent organizations look like, we use Sanctuary in the Kitchen as a way of showing that improvement in our level of emotional intelligence is not just an academic concern that you read about in books. Instead, the Commitment to Emotional Intelligence can be, and should be, practiced anywhere and everywhere. In this chapter, we focus on the elements of emotional intelligence that are vital to understanding and practicing the Sanctuary Model: emotional labor, managing conflict, and the implications of this commitment for trauma-informed care and for leadership. We close this chapter with more examples of the Sanctuary Toolkit especially relevant to the Commitment to Emotional Intelligence.*

A Vision of Emotional Intelligence

- Emotions are an important component of thought, and it is universally understood that our emotions help us to value what is important in life when rational thought alone may betray us.
- Emotions are always considered as a part of solving problems, individually and collectively.
- Clients and staff are encouraged not to control or suppress their emotions, but rather to manage all of their emotions, and are actively taught skills for doing so.
- Our organizations are safe, secure, reliable, playful, loving, and compassionate because we understand that people are better able to learn to manage their emotions in such environments.

- Change and conflict are not avoided in an effort to avoid the emotions associated with such events.
- Everyone learns ways in which their emotions can be manipulated by others and are therefore able to adequately protect themselves.
- Everyone who has experienced disrupted attachment is helped to heal through helping, safe, meaningful relationships.
- Clients and staff are helped individually and collectively to manage distressful emotions without resorting to violence.
- When powerful emotions erupt into violence, it is viewed as a problem involving the whole group and a problem the whole group must solve.
- The work of emotional labor is understood, honored, and valued.
- Leaders understand that a key part of their job is to recognize, contain, and manage emotions in their organizations.

What Do We Mean by Emotional Intelligence?

Sanctuary in the Kitchen

Lutheran Settlement House–Jane Addams Place is a homeless shelter in West Philadelphia that serves women and their children. Nine members of the leadership team attended the Sanctuary Institute in July 2008. After returning, they set about using the Sanctuary Model to create Sanctuary, one room at a time, supported and encouraged by their Sanctuary facilitator, Joe Foderaro, one of the original founders of the Sanctuary programs, and led by the Chief Cook, Sherrice Jones.

The kitchen is the heart of any home, but as with most institutional kitchens, the strict rules and regulations in a commercial kitchen can make eating there feel impersonal. The rules are created to maintain safe food handling, but the result is that the homeless women often do not feel in charge of the most basic maternal function: feeding their own children. Many arguments, some that can even become violent, can break out in a shelter. On the surface these arguments seem to be about food, but they are really about dependency, frustration, loss, and shame. So, at Jane Addams, the kitchen staff set about creating Sanctuary in the Kitchen and thereby making the kitchen the secure heart of their facility.

They started with the kitchen because complaints about the kitchen were common. The kitchen staff often became the brunt of the complicated feelings that all the women bring "to the table," and naturally it was difficult for the staff to avoid responding defensively. The staff had to figure out how to abide by the regulations mandated for shelter kitchens while still making mealtime a safe and satisfying event for everyone. They decided that the best way to start was to try to apply the Sanctuary Commitments to every aspect of their work, with special emphasis on the *Commitment to Emotional Intelligence*.

The kitchen staff took on this project wholeheartedly. Some of the staff had previously been homeless themselves, so they were able to empathize with the families. They started with meaningful conversations that they had never had as a whole staff about the clients and their needs, particularly as these related to food. The Chief Cook, who had attended the Sanctuary Institute Five-Day, worked to make sure that everyone would be safe while having these conversations as they opened up sensitive topics that they had never talked about together. At the same time, she began teaching the other members of her team about the Sanctuary Commitments and how important it was for them to be constantly building community, because their population was changing frequently. Everyone agreed on the importance of food and food preparation in anyone's home. They recognized that food provides comfort and that the kitchen and dining room are where community is created naturally.

The staff also recognized that the children in the shelter are an important part of the community and that their opinions need to be valued and considered because, as we all know, food is really important to kids. The staff emphasized the importance of never denying children food, particularly breakfast, since children do not always get breakfast at school. They felt that their likes and dislikes should be respected as much as possible. They discussed all of the special memories that everyone has about food and the fact that adults and children have favorite foods. As Sherrice Jones said, *"We understand people's emotional connections to food and to the kitchen. We challenge everyone who walks through our doors to remember and share memories related to food. We use this knowledge to make our kitchen and food special. We think about the food we serve, the manner in which we serve it, and making meals as special as possible"* (personal communication).

The staff started seeking input from the residents and then used those suggestions in meal planning. The kitchen team recognized that the process had to begin as soon as a family was admitted to the shelter, so meeting with the kitchen staff became a part of the basic orientation to the program, allowing the kitchen staff to establish a relationship with residents and their children. That way, the residents were able to share their own ideas right away about what would be comforting for them as well as information about their nutritional needs. It also gave the staff an opportunity to begin orienting the family to the rules and regulations that are a part of any shelter environment. Then, rather than responding punitively when a rule was violated, the staff could get off on the right foot with the family, helping them understand the kitchen regulations as safety issues and explaining what they meant. This orientation also provided an opportunity to define safety as a critical social norm for the community while simultaneously demonstrating sensitivity to the way human beings routinely manage emotions with the help of food. The staff also discussed the importance of food preparation during holidays and how difficult it was to have to spend the holidays in a shelter while everyone else had a home to go to.

The kitchen staff realized that there were also some rules they needed to create for each other because of the tensions that arise when a group of women are charged with preparing three meals a day, in limited space and with diminishing resources, for a large group of people. In reviewing the recurrent interpersonal difficulties they encountered, they realized that sometimes they did not set clear boundaries. By delaying responding to a child's or adult's request by saying "Can you please wait a minute?" or "I will get back to you later" when it was clear that the answer had to be "no," they realized that they were sending confusing messages to the clients. But it was also clear that in order to create a respectful environment, both children and adults had to understand the "no" by having the reasons behind it explained to them.

In their conversations together, staff members also were able to focus on their own sensitivity to the frequent critical comments they received, comments that were difficult to listen to when they were trying hard to keep people fed and happy. But demonstrating the *Commitment to Emotional Intelligence*, they realized that the derogatory comments and criticism were often not about them or the food, but rather were reactions related to the adversity, frustration, and helplessness the client was feeling at the time about his or her current or former life that the client couldn't yet talk about in any other way. So, they made another internal rule: they would guide and support each other in helping to calm down whenever someone's emotions were triggered. They agreed upon a code phrase—"just don't take it personally"—that they could easily use with each other, and they agreed they would each use their own Safety Plan.

As these meaningful conversations unfolded and emotional intelligence increased within the kitchen staff, they were able to confront some other underlying problems, one of which was that they often competed with each other instead of working as an integrated team, particularly when they were under stress. They discussed their individual strengths and weaknesses, and how much better their work day would be if they could remember to compliment each other, rather than getting frustrated and putting each other down.

The Sanctuary in the Kitchen implementation made the whole shelter a more peaceful, responsive, and helpful environment for very vulnerable women and children. The kitchen staff and the other staff members realized that it was important to make more of an effort to integrate the kitchen staff into the larger community since they were part of the team. Members of the kitchen staff were recruited to occasionally run the S.E.L.F. psychoeducation groups. The skills and input of the kitchen staff came to be seen as invaluable to the rest of the shelter staff. The administration even found a way to use some funds to expand food selection and get some new and desperately needed kitchen equipment.

Even after implementation of Sanctuary in the Kitchen, however, complaints concerning the kitchen and the food did not disappear. Given human nature, that would be impossible. But the staff learned that when inevitable complaints bubbled up, there were specific things they could do within a broader, safety-driven, emotionally intelligent framework to address them. They also developed a way to use the complaints to push for growth and change. In 2009, the Sanctuary Institute awarded Sherrice Jones, the Chief Cook, our Sanctuary Network award for her creative use of the Sanctuary Commitments.

Emotional Intelligence Defined

This story about emotional intelligence in the kitchen demonstrates that this kind of intelligence is not about education or status. Emotional intelligence is a valuable asset to an organization and can be found in anybody, regardless of whether he or she has an academic degree. But let's look a bit more closely at what we mean by emotional intelligence (Figure 6.1).

We can't talk about emotional intelligence without also talking about the brain and the body. Emotions aren't just psychological. Every emotion we experience triggers a complex series of changes in our bodies that provide feedback to the brain about what we are feeling. That's why when people talk about feelings, they often use physical metaphors to express them. "I had a lump in my

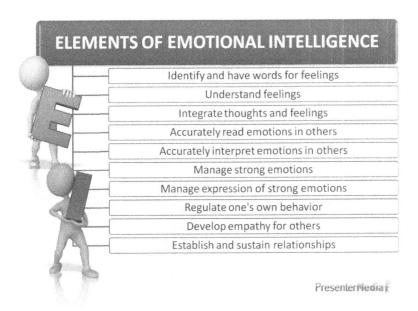

Figure 6.1 Elements of emotional intelligence.

throat," "my stomach was tied up in knots," and "my heart was breaking" are just a few of the thousands of expressions that every language has for this connection between body, brain, and emotions. The brain builds from the bottom up in the context of the attachment relationship between mother and child. Although we are born with basic emotional equipment, it takes a long period of time and loving and supportive attachment relationships for our brains to get wired properly. As research has shown, "*early experiences determine whether a child's developing brain architecture provides a strong or weak foundation for all future learning, behavior, and health*" (p. 3)[128].

The core features of emotional development unfold over time, enabling us to develop the emotional intelligence we need to interact effectively with other people [128, 129]. Emotional intelligence is a basic requirement for people who work in human service delivery of any kind because managing all that is going on in the body and brain while reacting to other people is challenging work, work that is best described as "emotional labor."

Emotional Labor

For the kitchen staff at Jane Addams Place, cooking a large amount of food in a short period of time was hard enough. But when workers are criticized for what they have just done, it is very difficult not to lash out at whoever is doing the criticizing. It takes work, a very special kind of work, to "not take it personally," and to maintain empathy and resist the desire to retaliate when hurt, while still responding to the other person. That's what we mean by emotional labor.

The concept of "emotional labor" was first developed by the organizational sociologist Arlie Hochschild. She talked about the ways in which people who are service employees have to manipulate their own feelings and the expression of those feelings as part of the job requirement. She pointed out that in this respect, employees are required to control and use their own emotions in order to influence the emotional state of others [130]. In the human service field, emotional labor happens when you have to induce feelings you may not have or suppress feelings that you do have. It is the everyday work of virtually every helping encounter in every service environment. It sets the stage for positive helping relationships, but it also helps us understand what can go radically wrong in an encounter as well.

Expressing appropriate emotions when face-to-face and voice-to-voice with a client who may be enraged, attacking, frustrated, shamed, sad, or grief-stricken is emotionally demanding. When someone is very upset and you are with that person, you feel their feelings AND you feel your own responses to their feelings. That's because emotions are contagious. Emotional contagion is

"[t]he tendency to automatically mimic and synchronize facial expressions, vocalizations, postures, and movements with those of another person and, consequently, to converge emotionally"(p. 81) [61].

We respond to another person's emotional state within one-twentieth of a second, and our own physiology is automatically changed while our bodies become synchronized with the emotional state of the other person.

Now if the same thing happens but you too are already upset, then your contact with the other person is likely to rapidly increase your distress. It's biology at work here. Because we are a social species, dependent for our survival on other people from the time we are born, evolution designed us to resonate with the emotions of others. It is lifesaving for a mother to react to the cry of her child. Our children are totally vulnerable. Emotional resonance exists to help our species survive, and the mirror neuron system in the brain, present at the time of birth, is the brain system that fosters this resonance. Likewise, a lack of emotional resonance during critical developmental periods is extremely damaging to the child's emotional and perhaps physical health.

Watch an emotionally intelligent worker manage a difficult situation and you will realize that you are watching an artistic performance. Keeping your voice down and containing your own normal threat responses, and not emotionally escalating on the inside, even when a child or adult is cursing you, spitting at you, or threatening you with bodily harm requires a level of self-control and emotional management that is, well...amazing. And yet that is what human service workers are called upon to do almost every minute of every day. We have worked with remarkably talented staff members who were able to stay engaged and supportive with a client who was extremely volatile by drawing on a well of positive emotions to see themselves and the client through. Like an actor who may draw on a life experience to convey a powerful emotion to an audience, direct care staff need to draw on this well of empathy and unconditional positive regard to avoid getting caught in the client's orbit. It is incredibly difficult work, and people who do not do this kind of work routinely have no true concept of how challenging it is, day after day.

One of the problems with support staff at places like Jane Addams and most other social service organizations is that many staff members have not been professionally trained to do the kind of emotional labor that requires constant adaptive changes to different people, situations, and experiences. They were hired because they know how to cook, fix things, manage a general ledger, or perform some other task vital to the welfare of the organization. But what people discover in the workplace is that all staff members need to develop emotionally intelligent strategies to deal with each other as well as with the other people in the organization, which is exactly what the Jane Addams staff discussed. Remember the example we used in Chapter 5 on the *Commitment to Nonviolence* about the staff member who didn't get the right pay in his paycheck? If the finance person had used a more emotionally intelligent strategy to address his needs, the whole problematic outcome that ended up causing problems for a number of people might never have happened.

Similarly, one of the difficulties for people in professional roles, such as doctors, nurses, therapists, and other service professionals, is that emotional labor, and what it takes to do it, has never been adequately addressed as a skill that is essential to perform the work. Instead, it goes unmentioned, a part of the job, always glaringly obvious when that labor is done poorly, but usually under appreciated in the day-to-day work. Little effort is put into preparing the service professional for doing this emotional labor, nor is it even labeled as such. When that is the case, we do not systematically screen for emotional intelligence and the capacity to perform emotional labor in interviewing or hiring practices. That is a *big* mistake.

The need to perform emotional labor is a basic requirement for managers as well as for frontline workers. And interestingly, this can pose an enormous challenge for people who are promoted to management positions. Within social services and mental health organizations, there is no universal requirement for anything that resembles management training. Chief Executive Officers and Chief Financial Officers may have had training in their background if the organization is large and especially if they came up through the ranks of some other business sector. They are also more likely to have an MBA or some administrative degree that at least academically qualifies them for the job of managing other people. But the key middle managers who actually set in motion the routines that guide daily interactions with staff, children, and families usually are promoted from within the organization or at least from within the social service, education, and social service professions. The training these professionals typically receive consists of whatever they experienced while being managed by other people in similar circumstances, beginning, of course, with their own parents.

Contrast this with an organization like Starbucks, where even a newly hired high school dropout working as a barista in the first year will spend at least 50 hours in Starbucks' classrooms, and dozens more at home with Starbucks' workbooks and talking to the assigned Starbucks mentor or the Container Store, where employees receive more than 185 hours of training in their first year alone. They are taught to recognize what to do when confronted with an angry coworker or an overwhelmed customer, and they rehearse routines for calming shoppers or defusing a confrontation [42].

In an emotionally intelligent environment, people recognize that one of the most important organizational goals is the containment and management of emotions that exist within everyone. Without sufficient emotional management skills training, the more stressful the work, the more likely we are to emotionally "leak." On a physical level, the body's muscles can only work so long without giving out. It's the same for the emotional "muscles," and because the emotional muscles are being used to maintain relationships, when those muscles give out, somebody is likely to get hurt. If there was more general sensitivity to how challenging the work is, then our organizations would build in periods of respite from emotional labor that are just as necessary as respite from physical labor.

Human service organizations need to maintain a balance between understanding just how hard it is to do this work and making the commitment to consistently do it well. It is easy to waffle back and forth between thoughtlessly and callously expecting staff to just do what they need to do, and do it with a smile on their face, and seeing the job as simply impossible and lowering our standards of care. Worse yet is thinking that anybody can do this work, that it is just a form of baby sitting. Our clients need staff members who consistently do the almost impossible, and managers need to figure out what staff need from them in order to consistently deliver on that promise.

An organization that has made a *Commitment to Emotional Intelligence* needs to look closely at job categories, performance evaluations, and commensurate pay scales, while funding systems need to address the underlying bias against considering the importance of emotional intelligence and emotional labor in caring for very troubled children and adults. We also need to develop criteria for determining how to evaluate employees based on their ability to truly care *for* and *about* the people in their care.

How Do Organizations Manage Emotions? Emotionally Intelligent Teamwork

The Jane Addams Place example offers a look at how an organization learns to manage troubling emotional conflicts. The kitchen staff identified the repetitive problems they were having. Then, rather than addressing them as problems of the individual, they worked together to figure out what the problems meant. They looked at the patterns that lay beneath the discontent with the shelter's food and kitchen staff. This is an example of the normal problem-solving, decision-making, and conflict resolution methods that must exist for any group of people to operate effectively. The more complex the work demands, the greater the necessity for collaboration and integration and therefore the more important it is to engage in emotionally intelligent teamwork.

For a team to function properly, there must be a certain level of trust among team members, who must all share in the establishment of satisfactory group norms that are sufficiently structured to allow group members to tolerate the anxiety of uncertainty among people working on a task long enough for creative solutions to problems to emerge. This requires norms that promote balanced and integrated decision making so that all essential points of view are synthesized and the staff can contain and resolve the inevitable conflicts that arise between members of a group.

When the Sanctuary Steering Committee for Jane Addams Place, which included Cook Jones, returned from the training, they were able to initiate new ideas about teamwork that everyone could understand and embrace. Knowing that there was something they could do that would make a difference, and that they could do it together, helped to build trust and confidence. Together the kitchen team was able to share the challenges of working with people who were often overwhelmed by past traumas and present dilemmas. When an organization is functioning well on an emotional level, it is able to serve as a container for the enormous emotional labor that is an irreplaceable component of helping people to heal.

Conflict Management in Organizations

But no matter how well an organization helps its members manage emotions, conflict is bound to emerge. If members of the team share similar goals, have a basis for mutual concern and trust, and are committed to similar values, they are able to engage in healthy task-related conflict. This occurs when a diverse team feels safe and confident enough in dealing with each other to disagree and to exercise emotional intelligence in doing so. When the tasks of the work are complex and call for creativity, dissenting views and some conflict about how to perform those tasks lead to better outcomes [131, 132]. Research has shown that groups that report task-related conflict are able to make better decisions than those that do not [133–137].

For a group to be emotionally intelligent, it is extremely important to have a diversity of perspectives that emerge from people of different ages, genders, races, educational levels, disciplines, sexual orientations, and experience working together [138]. Diversity encourages multiple viewpoints that are so important for innovation, makes it more unlikely that groupthink will dominate the group, and makes the emergence of group genius more likely. But the greater the diversity, the more people will have to spend some time and energy establishing shared goals, mutual respect, and shared values in order to have the kind of productive conflict that leads to collective learning experiences. Failing to do the groundwork on team development can cause the group to easily drift into interpersonal conflict. Even under the best circumstances, any conflict evokes emotion. In the heat of a conflict, interpersonal difficulties can arise.

When they started on their Sanctuary project, the kitchen staff at Jane Addams Place were plagued with chronic conflict, and they decided, in an emotionally intelligent way, to do something about it by creating more trust, setting clear boundaries from the beginning, not getting defensive when conflicts arose, and working constructively to resolve problems. In Sanctuary, conflict will never be eliminated—that would be neither healthy, nor possible—but good conflict *management* is entirely possible. There must be a shared framework and an environment of safety and trust so that when breaches of trust occur, they can be repaired.

If reparative efforts are not made, however, then what begins as task-related conflict can lead to misunderstanding, miscommunication, and increased interpersonal conflict that then sabotage good decisions. The bottom line in an organization is that you want less interpersonal conflict and more task-related conflict. This means that organizational leaders will have to make a strong effort to foster the skills of good conflict management (Figure 6.2).

Joanne Dixon, Director of Clinical Services at the Pace School in Pittsburgh, Pennsylvania shared a story about using emotional intelligence in a school to simultaneously reduce conflict and support the treatment of children.

In a recent meeting of administrative and supervisory staff, I was struck by the example of emotional intelligence in action on several levels. The meeting was about difficult treatment issues with challenging kids. After discussion and planning focused on helping the students, someone suggested that we also talk about how staff were feeling and what supports they needed. That conversation felt just as important to those in the room as the one about the students: that is, that everyone's feelings had value. The caring culture at Pace continues to impress me. In my experience, this is not typical of other schools or mental health settings. I was further impressed because I know that the supervisors were themselves working very hard under difficult circumstances at the time, yet they were able to consider others' feelings and plan helpful strategies to facilitate understanding while still needing to regulate their own emotions.

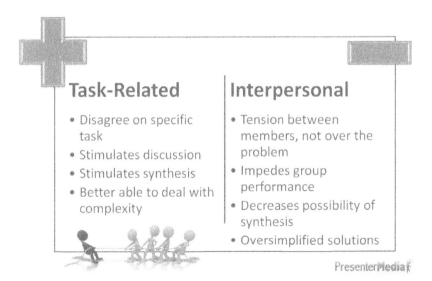

Figure 6.2 Types of conflict.

An Emotionally Intelligent Approach to Trauma-Informed Practice

Emotional Dysregulation

Emotional dysregulation is central to most of the problems plaguing the people who seek help in all of our social service organizations. When children have not had the safety and security of a healthy attachment relationship and feelings are not well managed, distress overwhelms them. When this happens, the integration of emotions and cognition does not occur as it should. Recent scientific advances have shown how the interrelated development of feelings and thoughts relies on the emergence, maturation, and interconnection of complex neural circuits in multiple areas of the brain [128].

"Alexithymia" is a word used to describe the inability to define feelings. The term was first used to describe Holocaust survivors, but it is now recognized as a common characteristic of traumatized people, particularly those exposed to repetitive adversity [139]. We have all had the experience of feeling something so intense that "there are no words for it," and for many people these experiences are associated with joy and wonder, experiences like falling in love or watching one's child being born. And we all know what it is like to be unsure, at any moment in time, what we are feeling while at the same time showing what we feel to others through our nonverbal communication.

In a place like the Jane Addams shelter, all of the clients are trauma survivors. Not only are they homeless, but the backgrounds of the mothers and many of the children are filled with experiences of childhood physical abuse, sexual abuse, domestic violence, sexual assault, exposure to community violence, neglect, substance abuse, and the stresses that accompany living in extreme poverty such as chronic hunger. For this reason, staff sensitivity to the effects of trauma on the emotions, thoughts, and behavior of their clients is essential if they are to provide adequate services.

It's important to remind ourselves that a substantial proportion of people who work in human services are themselves trauma survivors. That's both good news and bad news. On the one hand, it increases the likelihood that that they will have a special empathic regard and understanding of what the people they serve have been through. On the other hand, a previous history of trauma exposure can increase their vulnerability, particularly if they have not worked through their own issues and developed the skills they need to increase their emotional intelligence. Emotional intelligence requires each of us to know what our own emotional triggers are and to recognize the physiological symptoms that warn us that we are about to be "emotionally hijacked." As Dan Goleman explains, "*Emotional explosions are neural hijackings...that occur in an instant, triggering this reaction crucial moments before the neocortex, the thinking brain, has had a chance to glimpse fully what is happening to decide if it is a good idea*" (p. 14)[140]. To prevent themselves from being emotionally hijacked, the kitchen staff at Jane Addams Place made a commitment to each other to respond in healthier, more modulated ways to the difficult issues clients bring from their past. In this way, they could prevent their own problems from adversely impacting the relationships they were developing with the clients in the present.

Each of us must develop emotional management skills so that if our emotions areare triggered, we recognize it and know how to minimize the interpersonal damage that we can do. And we need to be in collective environments where we help each other instead of judging and criticizing each other. That's why the Sanctuary Toolkit items such as Community Meetings, Safety Plans, and Red Flag Reviews are so important.

Symptoms as Coping Skills

As we discussed earlier, exposure to trauma causes a lack of integration of behavior, emotion, sensation, or awareness. Survivors of trauma and adversity do the best they can do to adapt to difficult circumstances, but over time those adaptations can cause significant problems.

For all of us in human service delivery organizations, that means understanding that the things we call "symptoms" or "behavioral problems" are the best solutions our clients have been able to come up with to help them manage unendurable feelings that accompany the lack of integrated experience. They may be drinking or drugging themselves, involving themselves in all kinds of high-risk behavior, losing control, or hurting themselves (Figure 6.3). Whatever they are doing, it is, or at least originally was, a useful coping skill that, over time and with overuse, became maladaptive and then became a habit. It also means that their ability to cope with distress using any other strategies probably halted whenever they began using that problematic coping behavior.

That's why otherwise successful adults can end up behaving like very young children when they are overwhelmed by emotion. They haven't yet learned any other way to deal with their feelings, especially the bad feelings. Up to this point, other people in their lives may have viewed their problems as a crutch, automatically implying a derogatory judgment. But do you know anyone who has ever used crutches who didn't need them?

If someone needs to use crutches, then it is likely that if you suddenly pull the crutches out from under them, they will fall over. So, it's not likely that clients will stop doing whatever they are doing just because they are told to do so. From their point of view, their behavior is helping them fend off something worse. They have to prepare themselves to "walk" without their crutches, to try out their weak legs and risk falling and having to get up and try again. To do that, they have to trust us when we say that we will catch them if they fall. Lack

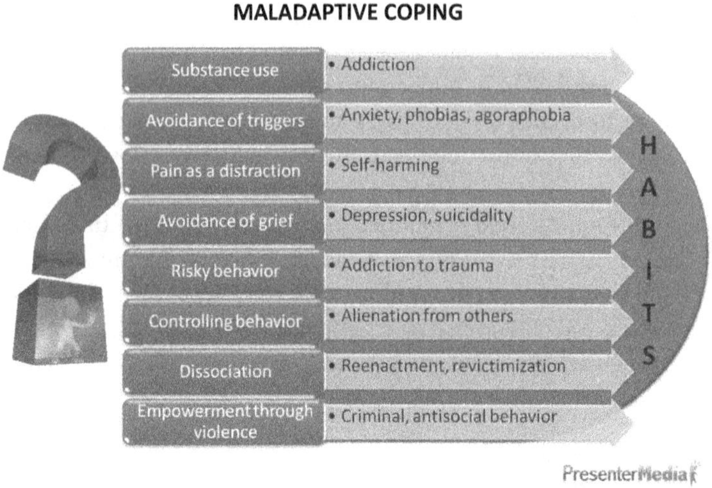

MALADAPTIVE COPING

Substance use	• Addiction
Avoidance of triggers	• Anxiety, phobias, agoraphobia
Pain as a distraction	• Self-harming
Avoidance of grief	• Depression, suicidality
Risky behavior	• Addiction to trauma
Controlling behavior	• Alienation from others
Dissociation	• Reenactment, revictimization
Empowerment through violence	• Criminal, antisocial behavior

HABITS

PresenterMedia

Figure 6.3 Adaptive coping becomes maladaptive.

of trust can be the reason it takes people so long to use the help that's available to them. In the past, other people couldn't be trusted, so they had to learn to trust only themselves, whether they had bad judgment or not. To trust someone else after that experience can be very scary.

Similarly, in an organization, there may be a whole range of behaviors, procedures, and interventions that are employed to help staff or the organization cope with the overwhelming stress of working with distressed clients. Rigid point systems, seclusion, restraint, ejection, and other coercive practices may be used to allow caregivers to manage the fears and frustrations associated with this very difficult, emotionally demanding work. Helping staff members to throw away their own crutches is no less challenging and takes a great deal of time and effort, as well as the development of trusting relationships. Providing the staff with new trauma-informed tools and practices is crucial to helping them move away from practices that serve to reinjure the clients they are charged with helping. But staff members can initially feel crippled by the withdrawal of the tools they already know how to use.

Boundaries

A common trauma-related issue that crops up in service delivery environments is boundary problems. People who have been exposed to abuse, neglect, and violence have had their interpersonal boundaries violated. When people violate our boundaries, we usually feel angry, frustrated, or scared. If you have had to contend with this problem repeatedly, then you may never have learned how to create, maintain, or protect normal interpersonal boundaries, and that can lead to a wide variety of problems.

Punishing people for not knowing how to do this will not help them learn. One of the unique things about service delivery environments is that we get the opportunity to experiment with what will help other persons discover what they need to learn. We can set up systems that improve the odds that they will, in fact, learn (creating responses that make sense for each individual person); then, if they are not learning, we can work to figure out why that is the case (more about that when we get to the *Commitment to Social Learning*). An emotionally intelligent environment is an educational environment where people are always learning from their mistakes, and the system is built so that the opportunities to learn are infinite.

That is not to say that anything goes. We all need limits; we all need boundaries. We need to know where we leave off and another person begins. We need to know how we affect other people. We need to be responsible about the fact that emotions are contagious. To be successful in the world, it's important to be able to exercise self-control and self-discipline, to know what you can and cannot deal with, and to know when you have had enough or you will lose control over your own emotions. The kitchen staff at Jane Addams Place realized that they needed to set clear rules and convey those rules up front. They worked on setting boundaries in an emotionally intelligent way that would not be punitive or disrespectful but would be clear, fair, and consistent.

Hurt People Hurt People

The people who seek services from us are not always loving and charming to others. Exposure to pain, suffering, prolonged abuse, and betrayal may ultimately improve their character, but it's usually not the first thing that happens. Human beings are programmed for reciprocity, so when they have been hurt, they want to get even with someone. It's really very simple: "hurt people hurt other people." That's not exactly rocket science; we have all experienced the urge for revenge since we were toddlers. Nonetheless, we still want to believe that we can divide the human race neatly into the good guys and the bad guys, and if we can effectively make that division and lock up all the bad guys, the rest of us will be safe. If only it were that simple. It's not.

Violence creates an endless cycle of violence and if we cannot even the score directly with the people who hurt us, maybe because they are bigger, stronger, scarier, out of reach, or dead, we will get even with somebody else. And that somebody else is likely to be a completely innocent person. And so it goes, on and on, until somebody decides to break the cycle and stop the retaliation. If we want to understand why someone is doing something he shouldn't or not doing something he should, then we need to ask why. The answer will virtually always have something to do with the inability to manage some kind of emotional experience. In reality, people are doing the best they can with what they've got, and when we recognize that and honor the coping skills embedded in the problematic behavior, it can help move the conversation in another direction.

The people who do human service work often have the same tendency to retaliate when they are hurt, shamed, or disrespected. We can be easily activated by the clients we work with. We work with hurt and angry children and adults in our settings and their emotions are easily triggered. Something in the present reminds them of something from the past that was very distressing, and they end up experiencing the same overwhelming feelings as they did then. When their emotions are triggered, they can lose the ability to successfully manage emotions and become quickly overwhelmed.

In Chapter 3 we discussed traumatic reenactment. It is very easy to get caught in a reenactment with our clients in which we continue to repeat the past with them over and over again. It takes a great deal of self-awareness and help from the extended team to avoid being drawn into these dramas repeatedly. Ensuring that there are practices in the organization that help staff members get in touch with their own feelings and recognize the feelings of clients and coworkers is essential in figuring out the pattern of reenactment, in developing healthy staff, and in creating emotionally intelligent organizations.

The staff at Jane Addams Place discovered why emotional intelligence is so important. It is important for helpers to manage themselves and, when this fails, to have coworkers who will step in and support them in this process. Training of staff needs to focus on this process, and Team Meetings and 'supervision should focus on reviewing how important it is for staff members to help each other.

If You Can't Stand the Heat, Get Out of the Kitchen

Not everybody should do human service work. It's difficult and emotionally demanding. You won't get hired to program a computer if you don't know how to do computer programming. You won't get hired as an airplane pilot if you don't know how to fly a plane. Human service delivery organizations need to be able to hire people who possess the emotional intelligence necessary to understand how human beings operate.

But there are many times when we have to hire people because they are available without evaluating their ability to do the emotionally demanding work of care giving. The human service professions are high-risk professions—psychologically as well as physically. But at the same time, for the most part, members of these professions are grossly underpaid. So, if you have to hire someone a bit short in the emotional intelligence area, then be aware of it. Develop training programs and tighten up supervision.

Also, do not think that an advanced degree or years of experience will ensure emotional intelligence. Emotional intelligence is a specific kind of intelligence, and it generally is not cultivated in a classroom, but rather in life situations and in relationships. Fortunately, emotional intelligence skills can be taught. Human service delivery organizations should therefore identify the problems associated with emotional intelligence, teach the skills necessary, and monitor the progress. This is one of the places where everyone's participation is important. If persons important to the organization are not teachable, then move them to a position where they can do the least harm to other people. Help them discover the helpful things they can do and allow them to make a contribution.

Be Curious, Be a Scientist

Those of us with a reasonable level of emotional intelligence are likely to have acquired the skills necessary to manage distress in early childhood. We often forget what it is like to be overwhelmed by relatively uncomplicated situations. If so, when confronted with a child, adolescent, or adult who is not behaving in an age-appropriate manner, we are likely to get angry, frustrated, or judgmental, particularly if we are in a position of power over the other person. We expect people to control their emotions, and we don't like it when they don't.

Instituting developmentally grounded, trauma-informed care means getting less angry and more curious. Human behavior actually does make sense if you know enough about what has happened. If the other person doesn't make sense to you, it's because you don't yet have enough information, so get it. Ask. Probe. Look for the gaps in the person's story. Listen deeply until you get the whole story. What's not being said? Where is there an inconsistency between the feelings being expressed verbally and those demonstrated nonverbally? What might explain why this person is doing or saying these odd things?

Unfortunately, there is not enough science in the work we do. Science isn't just about biology, chemistry, and physics. It's about an attitude toward knowledge and truth. The word "science" comes from the Latin word *scientia,* meaning knowledge. The essence of science is experimentation. When faced with a problem, develop a hypothesis and test it. Do not follow the dictum that is the modus operandi in too many institutions, *"If it isn't working, do more of the same thing."* If it doesn't work, then do something different.

The Best Medicine Is Laughter

Trauma makes people feel bad, really bad. The antidote to feeling bad is feeling good, and the fastest way to get there is to laugh. It has been shown that positive emotions are all-around better for you and for the workplace. People are more productive when they feel good about themselves, other people, and the place where they work. So, generate laughter and goodwill wherever and whenever you can. Smile, play jokes (as long as they are not at anyone's expense), introduce novelty into the work. An emotionally intelligent environment is a playful environment. Sure, trauma is serious, but life is ridiculous at times, and laughter is good for your body, your relationships, and your soul. Although nobody talks about it very much, it may be that laughter and humor, even if it sometimes is a kind of gallows humor, is probably what keeps many people in our professions coming to work day after day. Sandy recalls one such occasion:

> *Our program was in a psychiatric hospital that had a strong psychoanalytic tradition. Our program was entirely focused on treating trauma, so all of our 26 patients had terribly traumatic backgrounds. We were having a particularly difficult week as a staff. I don't remember why; I just remember that was the case. At the time, our unit looked out on an enclosed courtyard on the ground floor. We came out of yet another long, tedious meeting and noticed that several of our nursing staff members were looking out the window onto the courtyard, laughing hysterically. Naturally, we all rushed to the window, and what did we see but all of our patients out in the courtyard, perfectly still, in various formations and body postures, holding bedpans and other miscellaneous vessels containing water that they had tinted yellow with food coloring and that they were pouring from one vessel to another. They had created a living sculpture for us that they had titled "Ur-In-Analysis."*

It is pretty clear by now that emotional intelligence throughout the organization is important to the well-being of the workplace environment as a whole and to individual members as well. Studies have shown that a person's tendency to experience positive emotions and moods is associated with increases in work performance as measured by things like more positive supervisory evaluations, higher income, enhanced negotiating ability, and performing acts for the benefit of the organization [141].

Not surprisingly, feeling good improves performance, cooperation, and a sense of fairness. It also reduces interpersonal conflict [142, 143]. It doesn't seem to matter what aspect of organizational function is studied and reviewed—decision making, creativity, prosocial behavior, staff morale, staff turnover, absenteeism, negotiation, conflict resolution, or team behavior; a positive emotional climate makes a difference: *"the evidence is overwhelming that experiencing and expressing positive emotions and moods tends to enhance performance at individual, group and organizational levels* (p. 51)[143].

The Sanctuary Model is designed to be an approach to a whole culture that increases the emotional intelligence of everyone. As emotional intelligence in the organization improves, the organization is better able to achieve its mission, meet the needs of its clients, manage and contain the difficult emotions of clients, and assist them in making the needed changes in their lives. Sometimes positive emotional contagion starts at the top of the leadership hierarchy, but sometimes its source is in the primary workers, the people in the trenches and on the ground.

Implications for Emotionally Intelligent Leadership

Leadership positions carry their own burden of emotional labor. We have both had the pleasure and pain of being leaders in an organization and have experienced the constant challenge of absorbing the frustrations, grief, and struggles of staff and clients. As Brian recounts,

> *Some months ago I was in our school. I was just stopping by on the way to my office and ended up in the middle of a dustup with a child who was really struggling. I got punched, bit, and kicked, and the worst part was that I had all this stuff in my office that I had to get done and now I was held hostage by this little boy. After about an hour with him, someone came in and relieved me. I opened the door to the room where I had been sequestered for the previous hour and I said to myself, "smile." I walked down the hall with a smile on my face and said "hello" to everyone I saw in the hall, and by the time I reached the exit I actually felt better. My effort to be positive was not only good modeling, it made me feel better, because I got positive feedback. As I am writing this, I am mindful that I am kind of a wimp. This was only an hour of my day—a frustrating hour, but an hour. I am always mindful that as I exit the building at ten o'clock in the morning, everyone else has five more hours in front of them.*

Emotional intelligence is a critical component of leadership. Both positive and negative emotions are contagious, and leaders have extra "contagion power." Whenever there are uncertain situations, members of a group look to the leaders' emotional responses. When leaders are optimistic, group members' positive moods are increased and group performance improves. But when leaders display negative emotions, group members' negativity and frustration increase, which decreases group performance [144]. These effects are particularly important during times of crisis or any negative organizational events, so leaders who engage in emotional labor by displaying positive emotions, even more positive than those they are feeling, will increase their subordinates' feelings of confidence and optimism, even in the face of stress.

If emotion is contagious, then leaders must deeply express the emotions they want their workgroup to feel; they can't just put on a "surface act." Surface acting is stressful for leaders, and faking it just doesn't work. Emotionally intelligent people pick it up and distrust what is happening. This, of course, is part of the reason that periods of crisis are so exhausting to anyone in a position of leadership. The emotional labor of containing everyone's emotions, which is a fundamental component of leadership, is enormous.

It is also useful to remember, whether we acknowledge it or not, that staff members worry about how they are viewed by leaders and are fearful of saying or doing the wrong thing in their presence. If leaders are poorly regulated, staff members will be more reluctant to speak their mind or share their point of view out of fear of retaliation or embarrassment. If a leader is seen as hot-headed or reactive, it will stifle the participation of staff in problem identification and problem solving and reduce the organization's ability to function democratically and solve complex problems.

Middle managers often have special challenges because they are just that, in the middle, and therefore have to contain emotions coming up and down the hierarchy in an organization. Managers who have a low level of control but a high level of responsibility will feel greater stress than workers on the frontline when performing emotional labor. Managers who must act tough even when they don't feel that way and do not believe in the way they are handling a situation will experience heightened levels of stress. At the same time, leaders who have high personal control and who use emotional labor to express positive emotions that are consistent with their own identity will experience an increased sense of well-being and fulfillment [144]. Leaders who have been described as facilitative or transformational in style have been shown to help subordinates overcome the mood-damaging effects of stress in the workplace and increase work performance [145].

Sanctuary Toolkit

Psychoeducation: The "E" in S.E.L.F.—Basic Skills for Emotional Intelligence

The Sanctuary Model is designed to be an approach to a whole culture that increases the emotional IQ of everyone and the organization as a whole. In our society we have some distorted ideas about human nature, and often our explanations for what motivates people are simplistic ("punish 'em...that'll teach 'em") because we tend to attribute to people much more conscious intent and free will than actually exist. We are certainly capable of making informed choices, but our emotional states always, wholly or partially, have an impact on those choices, usually outside of our conscious awareness.

Because people who have experienced trauma frequently have problems managing emotions, it is crucial that our treatment environments understand and appreciate these difficulties and provide constant opportunities for clients to learn emotional management skills. Using S.E.L.F. helps guarantee that we won't miss issues of emotional intelligence and emotional management in our work with our clients, each other, and the organization as a whole. There is not necessarily any connection between formal education and emotional intelligence, so every environment has to start out with the ABCs of emotion—for everyone.

The "E"-based psycho educational lessons are designed to make sure that all members of an organization share a common and simple language about emotions so that the emotional component of every discussion is never overlooked.

The ability to assign simple names to our basic emotions, to recognize how each emotion affects our bodies, and to begin to learn how we can control our own emotional states must be taught to everyone in an effort to create an emotionally intelligent environment with a shared language.

The following is a brief summary of three simple lessons.

How am I Feeling?

At first, we are not looking for nuances of blended feelings, but instead limit them to mad, sad, glad, scared, and shamed. We have found that these five are the major feelings that must be identified for people to develop emotional management skills. Over time and with the expansion of emotional intelligence, we can incorporate many more words for feelings and the blending of feelings. But in the beginning, the process needs to be simple and five words are sufficient to help people begin the process. We originally used these concepts with adults who had been maltreated as children, but the simplicity of the ideas has made them useful for children as well. Remember, talking about what we feel is the dominant way that we are able to exercise self-control and not just act on the emotion. To reduce "acting-out" behavior, then, it is essential that we all are able to label what we are feeling and not just automatically act on it. We also try to "depathologize" the issue of emotional management.

Volume Control

People who have been traumatized often lose their capacity to "modulate arousal" and therefore cannot manage the overpowering emotional responses they may have to events that are in reality not very threatening. This is called "chronic hyperarousal" and represents a change in the central nervous system over which the person has little control. People to whom this has happened tend to become irritable with very little provocation, stay irritable longer than they otherwise would, and may accelerate rapidly to out-of-control rage. We call this a loss of "volume control," meaning that they have lost their ability to modulate the emotional volume and are left with only an on-off switch. We all lose our volume control whenever we are under stress. We are emotional creatures, and therefore we are all vulnerable to disordered integration of thoughts and feelings under stress. Remember, the issue is not *"What's wrong with you?"* It's *"What happened to you?"* [6]. If the overwhelming events started in childhood, then the person may never have developed much volume control in the first place. The person has to learn the basic connections between his or her body, mind, feelings, behavior, and environment.

Words for Boundaries

Again, whenever we can, we make the process simple, so we use simple terms for learning about how to create, maintain, and protect boundaries (Figure 6.4).

If you have not learned these five basic boundary operations as a child, then you have no clue about what normal boundaries are, how to protect your own, or how to protect those of other people.

Screening for Emotional Intelligence

Agencies that are implementing the Sanctuary Model are encouraged to develop an employment screening tool to better assess the ability of their employees to truly care *for* and *about* the people in their care. Managers who are interviewing and hiring people must recognize the importance of emotional intelligence in our work and ask specific questions about how the candidate has handled emotionally challenging issues in the past.

Managing Conflict

The *Commitment to Emotional Intelligence* is both an individual and a group responsibility. One of the greatest challenges, and a sure sign of successful implementation of Sanctuary, is a team's ability to safely raise, tolerate, and work through conflict as a means to growth and change. Because stressed environments tend to promote unsafe quarreling or conflict avoidance, differences tend to go unresolved. The ongoing strength and effectiveness of the Core Team, therefore, requires the ability to effectively master the challenges associated with unresolved conflict.

During the implementation process of the Sanctuary Model, there are several carefully planned conflict management retreats. All teams experience conflict because of differences in perspectives, feelings, status, or power. We recognize that conflict can lead to newer insights and growth. If not handled

LEARNING TO PROTECT BOUNDARIES

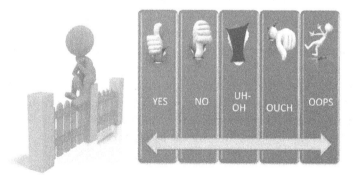

PresenterMedia

Figure 6.4 Boundaries.

well, however, conflict can also lead to destructive outcomes for individuals and teams exposed to chronic stress or trauma.

Indirect Care Staff Training

Everyone in an organization is connected to everyone else. There is no one in an organization who should be exempted from Sanctuary training. If you want to have an emotionally intelligent, nonviolent, democratic, transparent, socially responsible organization, then you have to train everyone. However, we do recognize that different people performing different functions need to focus on different parts of the Sanctuary Model.

Dr. Maggie Bennington-Davis, whom we referred to in Chapter 3, described some experiences she has had in her position as the Chief Medical and Operating Officer of Cascadia Behavioral Health in Oregon. Like so many other social service agencies that provide services for public clients, Cascadia has had a rough time surviving in the difficult economic environment of the last decade. As Maggie says, *"Cascadia has been to hell and back, so there has been a ton of evidence of what happens during such a time."* Here she offers some examples of what it looks like when a whole organization is committed to being emotionally intelligent—not just emotional intelligence skill-building aimed at the direct care or clinical team, but development of emotional intelligence in the finance office.

> *I think the financial people in organizations like ours are usually overlooked. We are more likely to pay attention to the people providing direct care, but not to the people who comprise the infrastructure. But the infrastructure that involves MONEY in a nearly bankrupt organization is arguably the most stressed of all. I met with the people in payroll who knew we were close to the bone financially, and it was frequently touch-and-go whether we'd make payroll for our 800 employees. Those folks took the responsibility and worry about this on their own shoulders and lived in fear during payroll periods.*
>
> *As a result of this constant stress, the group began to fall apart. One man got surlier and surlier; a woman tried to take care of everyone else and felt offended and hurt when her ministrations weren't welcome; several reported going home, where they'd be uncommunicative or argumentative with their spouses and kids. They got nastier and nastier with each other, began having some absenteeism (especially around payroll time), and grew extremely disillusioned with Cascadia as an organization. Then we hired a new, excellent director who immediately recognized their stress-related symptoms, and she asked me to meet with the group. I did a basic educational half hour about stress and they began with arms folded and "grin and bear it" expressions, but within minutes of the basic educational presentation, some were in tears and all were engaged. They used the rest of the time telling their stories about*

what they were going through. We met again a couple of days later, and they strategized together about what they could do to cope with what we all knew would be ongoing stress. That department has done brilliantly well, certainly in terms of performance, and now they are a healthy, happy, customer-service-oriented group.

The same situation was going on with our billing group, which was coming apart in a similar way. They felt blamed and guilty for not bringing money in the door. As the organization unraveled, they had a harder and harder time doing their analyses, getting the billing cycle down to a short time, being assertive with payers (mostly state and county government), and in fact, things were getting progressively worse. A couple of the employees were having an especially hard time, and the way that played out was around one particularly dominant person who would often get pretty mean with others. He was the ostensible reason why I was asked to talk about workplace stress, not because of their performance. But once I was with them, I easily recognized the symptoms—dissociation, hypervigilance, rampant rumors, secrecy, very little emotional regulation. I used the same psycho educational approach with them, explaining the impact of stress on their emotions and work together. Like the other group, within a very short time, they felt understood and were relieved to have a different way of thinking about themselves and each other. I followed up with them three or four times, each time to refresh our thoughts about what was happening and why and to strategize. This group has come through and is performing amazingly well—unbelievably well, in fact. In some ways, their ability to get the billing cycle down to under 30 days in an agency like ours has made the difference for our survival.

To respond to this need to train both direct and indirect care staff, we created two different training schemes, one aimed at people who provide direct service to the clients and the other to indirect care staff, meaning all the people who support the infrastructure of the organization but who may have little direct contact with the clients.

Now that we have explored the *Commitment to Emotional Intelligence,* in Chapter 7 we will look at the closely related concept of social learning and the importance of creating learning organizations.

Chapter 7

Commitment to Social Learning

The Go for Greens project at Pace is an example of social learning. When me and my buddy first heard about it, I thought it was just about me and my ideas. He thought it was just about him and his ideas. Then we found out the whole school was involved. Through social learning you learn that you can't always put your own ideas first. When you listen to other people's thoughts and ideas, you always have a plan B or C or D. You might just find out that you can use different parts of different ideas to make something better than any of the ideas by themselves.

Student, Pace School, Pittsburgh, Pennsylvania

SUMMARY: *In this chapter on the Commitment to Social Learning we describe what we mean by a "living-learning" environment that is at the heart of any therapeutic community. Learning how to make better decisions and perform more creatively in teams, even under the impact of stress, is more important today than it has ever been. Our social environments are changing at a pace never seen before, and the pressure on organizations to adapt can feel overwhelming. To be successful, our service delivery organizations must get better at learning in different ways.*

A Vision of Social Learning

- Everyone—clients, staff, and leaders—is expected to learn and contribute to the learning of others all the time.
- Human service organizations know that in order to accomplish their mission of promoting growth and change in clients, they need to continuously learn how to do the work more effectively.
- Individuals and organizations learn from experience and make healthy adaptations to changing conditions.
- Preexisting knowledge is retained and integrated with new knowledge.

- We are able to identify recurring patterns and change the ones we do not want to keep.
- What we learn changes not only what we do but also the way we think about our work.
- We have reached consensus decisions to throw away ideas that are useless or harmful.
- Everyone participates in decision making and offers their ideas and feedback readily and consistently.
- Diversity of thought and opinion is valued and actively pursued in the organization.

What Do We Mean by Social Learning?

When we first met Sherrie Turner, she was working as the Sanctuary Facilitator at Glove House, a group home program for young people based in Elmira, New York. She told us a story about one of their clients that captures the essence of social learning and the Sanctuary Model and how it was used to facilitate the whole process of change and learning for this boy and his family.

At the time of this story, a boy we will call Tommy was 13 years old. He had been abandoned by his parents at a very young age after having been both severely neglected and physically abused by his father. He was admitted to Glove House after numerous failed foster care placements. He had no family other than grandparents who lived 1000 miles and several states away. His grandparents kept in touch with him regularly, although they were not sure if they could meet his needs, considering his long history of disruptive behaviors. He was diagnosed with reactive attachment disorder and was taking a number of medications.

Tommy was physically smaller than the rest of the residents. Nonetheless, he repeatedly goaded other male residents to physically assault him, and he refused to follow program rules. Fortunately, his peers refused to assault him, as the *Commitment to Nonviolence* had become firmly engrained in the program culture. Nevertheless, he accumulated countless hours of restrictions day after day. Because they had been using the knowledge gained about trauma and reenactment, the staff at Team Meetings were able to identify clear instances of traumatic reenactments in his behaviors and also were able to determine when male staff members were pulled into the reenactment.

The staff agreed to put a "do not restrain" classification on this boy, as he was physically small and was very skilled at manipulating the staff to play the role of persecutor. They recognized his basic scenario: he wanted to be punished—physically by men. The staff recognized this as a reenactment of his earlier experiences of abuse at the hands of his father.

Over the next year, through the S.E.L.F. Psychoeducational Groups, Tommy was educated about the psychobiology of trauma and reenactment. He made and repeatedly revised his Safety Plan. He participated in developing and revising his Treatment Plan. As he learned more about how the past had affected him, staff members were able to point out to him when he was beginning an abusive reenactment so that he could stop the evolving pattern before someone got hurt. He developed significant coping skills to maintain his own safety and the safety of the community by adopting the Sanctuary Commitments as his own value system.

Other residents also used the *Commitment to Social Responsibility* to help Tommy both inside the program, in the community, and in school. His progress was remarkable, and his grandparents decided that they wanted to petition for his custody. Predictably, as soon as they began the legal process, his reenactment behaviors escalated to a level that was almost unmanageable. The staff recognized that this was the typical regression to previously learned behavior that is not unusual when people are under significant stress, as Tommy was as he became increasingly anxious about moving in with his grandparents. His team members called a Red Flag Meeting with Tommy, his caseworker, other staff members he worked with, and his grandparents.

Tommy was very vocal about wanting to live with his grandparents, but he could not control his anxiety about the impending movement away from a safe environment where he had established his first trusting relationships with adults. A plan was made to move him into another program (at the same agency) while the interstate paperwork was finalized to mitigate the anxiety surrounding the impending loss and provide him and his grandparents with a more gradual transition. The staff members he had been working with held a goodbye ceremony for Tommy, and he moved into the new program.

His reenactment behaviors stopped and he successfully moved in with his grandparents, who were granted full custody. Two years later, he contacted the program to invite the staff to his adoption ceremony. Tommy and his grandparents reported a very successful adoption. He had been taken off all of his medications, was doing well in school, and still used his Safety Plan when his emotions were triggered.

Sanctuary as a Living-Learning Environment

Tommy's story beautifully demonstrates what can happen when a child who has been considered almost beyond help is challenged to learn and grow in an environment that has incorporated the *Commitment to Social Learning*. In the Sanctuary Model, this commitment represents a whole organizational vow to create a "living-learning" environment for clients, their families, and everyone who works in the setting. Maxwell Jones was one of the post–World War II founders of the democratic therapeutic community, first in the United Kingdom and then in the United States. It was clear to Jones and other founders of the therapeutic community movement that for such a living-learning environment to exist, certain preconditions were necessary, such as egalitarianism, permissiveness, openness, honesty, and trust [104, 146–148]. "Social learning" is the backdrop for all seven Sanctuary Commitments and has been defined as "*the little understood process of change which may result from the interpersonal interaction, when some conflict or crisis is analyzed in a group situation, using whatever psychodynamic skills are available*" (p. 70) [148].

In discussing a living-learning environment, Maxwell Jones was far ahead of his time. An extensive discussion of "learning organizations" as applied to other kinds of organizations did not really take off until the 1980s and 1990s as businesses began experiencing increasing pressure to compete in a technologically advanced, rapidly changing, globally connected environment. There is now a very active discussion in the business world about what is required to create a learning organization, one that adapts to changing conditions, that expects all employees to be learning all the time, and that values all staff members and includes everyone in the learning environment [79, 149–157].

Our organizational experience has shown that there are key aspects to becoming a learning organization in the human service delivery climate. We begin with a vision of what we want to become and then figure out what we need to learn to get there. We need to ask ourselves, "Are there things we are doing right now that square with that vision?" and if so, let's keep doing those things. But if there are bad habits we have picked up along the way, then let's agree to forget them.

The process of forgetting the things that we no longer need is called "unlearning." Unlearning is an important step in learning something new. Tommy's story makes it clear that change for him was a learning process, and although he had learned some very problematic interpersonal behaviors that had resulted in repeated failures for him, he *could* learn something new. But to help Tommy learn, the entire organization had to be on the same page and learn together how to help him rescript the future and, in doing so, save Tommy's life. This meant that they would have to *collectively* unlearn old patterns before they could learn new ones.

First Comes a Collective Vision

Everything we do should be grounded in our mission. So, our *Commitment to Social Learning* has to be mission-directed. There must be a clear articulation of what we're hoping to accomplish and then some clear way to measure whether or not the organization is achieving what it has set out to do. As we mentioned in Chapter 3 on the *Commitment to Growth and Change*, the mission of our organizations should be to promote growth and change in our clients and ourselves. If that is not happening, then we need to figure out what we must learn to create the context for change.

The Sanctuary Model is *not* about stabilization. Everybody can change, even if only a little bit, and change that is self-determined has to come about by learning something. We learn things in the context of relationship. So, in the context of our relationship with the clients, they can first learn that they are, in fact, capable of change.

Glove House had previously offered a very structured behavior management program, and the staff had little flexibility in dealing with a disruptive child. As they became more trauma-informed, the leaders and the staff came to recognize that if they were really going to help traumatized children, they would have to become more flexible and individualize treatment approaches. Before adopting the Sanctuary Model, the staff never could have agreed to a "no-restraint" policy, as they did for Tommy. By the time Tommy arrived, the leaders of the organization (all of whom attended one of the first Sanctuary Institute trainings) had already decided that the time had come for them to get better results with the children they were treating. They realized in retrospect that they had been getting caught in children's reenactments for years, and it wasn't helping anyone.

Through the Sanctuary Implementation process at Glove House, the staff had come to believe that all children in their care could change and that no child was hopeless. Despite the many setbacks Tommy had already experienced, and his awful history of trauma and disrupted attachment, the staff shared a vision of Tommy's ability to improve. With this belief in mind, they could start learning what they needed to know about Tommy to more effectively help him. This was not a new vision for Glove House, but a renewal of their originating mission. The program had been founded 40 years before by a man named Norman "Chuck" Jennings, a champion boxer, who believed that *"With a little love and kindness you can change a boy's life"* [158]. Trauma Theory and the Sanctuary Model gave that original vision new life.

What's Working and What's Not?

In the Sanctuary Model, we put a premium on learning all the time; that's our job. We encourage curiosity, which is at the heart of that fundamental question, *"What happened to you?"* We want leaders to be curious, staff to be curious, and clients to be curious; a key practice is to question everything. We are still in the very early stages of knowing what to do to alter the life trajectory of children and adults who have been exposed to significant adversity. So, this should be a time for great curiosity and experimentation to find out what strategy is most effective for which person. There are still so many questions to be asked and answered. This is a time for us to be excited about the possibilities rather than weighed down by the struggles.

When Tommy came to Glove House, everyone recognized that he was on a dead-end street after failing in every placement. As the pattern of Tommy's behavior began to unfold, the staff members were able to recognize the patterns and decide together what needed to change and how they could be the agents of that change. As they began to understand Tommy's history of abuse and how his behavior problems were actually a reenactment of physical abuse, they realized that their formerly rigid system of consequences was setting them up to reenact a punishment scheme with Tommy that was doing him no good at all. But to change that pattern, the staff had to unlearn many things that they had previously learned were the right things to do.

Before Learning, Unlearning

Mental models in the mental health and social service systems are deeply entrenched. Before we can learn from new experiences, we have to unlearn established patterns and routines. It is just as important to teach people how to forget, how to unlearn what they have been doing, sometimes for decades, as it is to teach new concepts. We find that this is one of the most difficult things to accomplish. Staff and leaders may have spent many years developing core competencies, like how to put someone in four-point restraints or the exact components of a point system or how to design a very structured and detailed behavioral plan, only to be told that they can no longer use those competencies or at least that they must use them in a new way. To bring about the system transformation involved in creating a trauma-informed culture, it is necessary to answer pressing questions about healing and recovery. This is not just about learning new things; it involves questioning the assumptions we have been making.

Organizational unlearning has been described as "*a change in collective cognition and routines that coordinate organizational change processes*" (p. 800) [159]. For unlearning to occur, a participatory process is needed that enables a group to decide what is important to remember and what it is safe to forget. There must be a structure that provides enough support for members of the group to tolerate uncertainty and welcome dissent. Then there must be feedback loops that tell the group if the new learning is actually happening.

This is exactly what Tommy needed the staff at Glove House to do. But before they could do this, with Tommy or any other client, they had to take a hard look at their policies and procedures, as well as the beliefs, values, and assumptions those policies were based on. It had been routine to restrain a child who was acting out. To help Tommy and other children like him, the staff had to unlearn their automatic routines and figure out what new response to use. But that is the only way to break out of a reenactment with a traumatized person. In order for the person to stop the automatic response, the staff member he or she is interacting with has to do something else *first*.

That couldn't be the action of just one staff member; a sudden change in restrictive policy by only a portion of the staff can lead to chaos. In that pause between unlearning and trying something new, the staff had to tolerate the anxiety of uncertainty. To do that, they had to know that the leaders had their back. The leaders also had to know that their own higher authority supported the change. The funding for Glove House to participate in the Sanctuary Institute had come from the Office of Children and Family Services for the State of New York. Some of the state public sector officials were participating in the Sanctuary Institute training because they also had to discover what had to be unlearned and what had to be learned to adequately address the needs of traumatized children, adults, and families.

Welcoming Discussion and Dissent

This process of learning and unlearning requires a great deal of discussion, disagreement, and high tolerance for dissent. As more people find that it is safe to speak up and participate, organizational learning improves, illustrating the indispensable connections between the *Commitment to Social Learning,* the *Commitment to Open Communication,* and the *Commitment to Democracy.* However, the increased diversity of opinions that begin to flow when people feel safe enough to truly engage with each other requires thoughtful and meaningful conversations and dialogue about tasks.

The disagreements that arise may come down to differences in individual strategies and opinions or may relate to deeper issues within the organization that lead to more open dissent. "Dissent" means expressing disagreement or giving voice to contradictory opinions about organizational practices and policies and can be triggered by some well-studied causes [159–161] (Figure 7.1). Topics that arouse dissent often make leaders nervous and readily become the undiscussables that get in the way of open communication, but the undiscussables must become discussables if the organization is to become healthy.

When Glove House first started to move away from a strict behavioral management program, there was a great deal of dissent among various staff members, some of whom had been there for quite some time. Because of staff concerns, Kevin Murphy, the Clinical Director at the time, wrote a brief essay answering the question "Is Sanctuary Too Soft on Kids?" As Kevin wrote, *"An important point to maintain is that recovery and healing cannot occur 'in a tornado', and as such routine, structure, and accountability are key components of an intelligent, treatment-based, social learning environment. Discipline, safe decision-making, and healthy relationships based on mutual respect are cornerstones of effective and sustainable growth and change"* (p. 2) [162].

Glove House then had to set up a process of having difficult conversations, tolerating dissent, and forming new ideas and opinions throughout the organization, which is what the Sanctuary implementation process allowed them to do. Creating environments that support direct and open dissent is important

Figure 7.1 Common causes of dissent.

for a number of reasons. Worker satisfaction is increased when employees feel that they can freely voice their opinions and be heard, and as people feel safe participating, there is an increase in commitment [160, 163]. Dissent from the majority opinion is actively solicited and encouraged in the Sanctuary Model in order to minimize groupthink, conformity, and the effects of group polarization. Dissent is also actively solicited because it makes everyone sharpen their own thinking in order to respond cogently, as Kevin's response to staff concerns illustrates. But most important perhaps, dissent provides corrective feedback within an organization that can avert disaster. Many studies have demonstrated that when disasters have occurred, the culture of the organization was one in which dissent was discouraged [12]. But to be useful, dissent must be direct; therefore, the conditions that promote dissent within an organizational culture must be conducive to free speech without retaliation.

Effective Decision Making

Along the road to change, many decisions will have to be made. In Tommy's case, the staff had to come together and make decisions that determined whether or not Tommy would actually get what he needed to change. In the process of implementing Sanctuary, they had to review how they had routinely made decisions in the past and what had to change. They had to learn new ways to make decisions that adhered to the *Commitment to Democracy* as well as the other commitments.

What defines good decision-making ability? To begin with, people *learn* to make effective decisions; the skill is not innate. Since making good decisions is

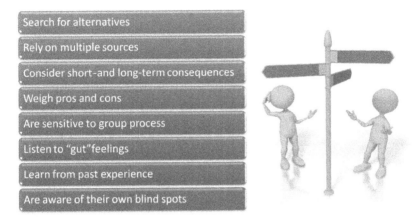

Search for alternatives

Rely on multiple sources

Consider short-and long-term consequences

Weigh pros and cons

Are sensitive to group process

Listen to "gut"feelings

Learn from past experience

Are aware of their own blind spots

PresenterMedia

Figure 7.2 Good decision makers.

a skill, it is possible to evaluate what goes into building that skill. The best decisions are likely to come out of a process rather than "just happening," which, unfortunately, are the kinds of decisions we are most likely to make under stress. Effective decision makers define as specifically as possible the decision that needs to be made and decide whether they are really the ones to make that decision. Faced with the need to make a decision, good decision makers share certain characteristics (Figure 7.2).

Decision Making in Groups

In the workplace, individual decisions must be made every day, but even these decisions must be made in the context of the group. What do we know, then, about the process of decision making when many factors must be taken into account, when many people must participate in the decision-making process, and when the decisions made may have significant and lasting consequences?

Making better decisions about the clients who seek services requires knowing more about each person and knowing that person from many different perspectives. The group, or the team, will provide the most well-rounded picture of the client. Clients evoke emotions in individual team members who are also experiencing challenges in their own lives. We know that decision making may be profoundly affected by emotions, so our shared emotional experience may play a significant role in the decisions we make [164] (Figure 7.3).

The hoped-for outcome of making a *Commitment to Social Learning* is that the organization and its members become capable of making better decisions by making them together. In Tommy's case the decision to not restrain him, but instead to teach him how to manage his own distress, was a key turning point

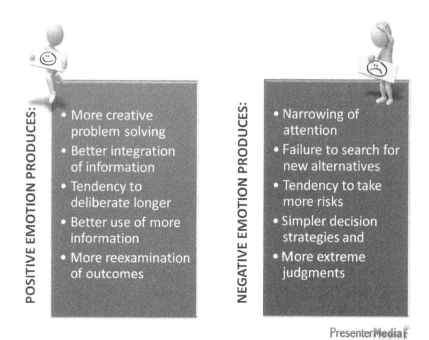

Figure 7.3 Emotions affect decisions.

for him and for the staff. As time went on, the team became more sophisticated in their decision-making ability so that when the opportune moment came, they were able to decide on a very complex strategy of transferring Tommy to a program upholding the same principles, so that he could transition from the attachments he had formed with staff members to a new attachment to his adoptive grandparents.

Decision Making Under Stress

When we are under stress, decision making can be compromised, because our biological system takes over, our thought processes become constricted and rigid, and every decision seems to be an urgent one. Attention narrows, we focus on whatever is threatening, and we become more cognitively rigid. This often results in what is called "premature closure"—making a decision before all the facts are in; that can lead to poor policy decisions with long-lasting and unintended consequences. What we can do is be aware of the impact of stress and do what is possible to reduce the number of stressors. For stressors that are not preventable, we can reduce the impact of the stress by curbing the long-term nature of the decisions we make under the influence of those stressors.

If we know that our thought processes are compromised under stressful conditions and if we still must make some decisions, on the spot, in the moment, then we must make sure that we keep our values in mind; adhere as much as possible to the policy of avoiding extreme, punitive, or draconian decisions; and establish a social norm that decisions made under stress can be revised when things calm down, that they are temporary solutions to immediate problems. We should be open to revising all of our decisions if new data suggest that a decision was flawed or if other conditions change, making a previous decision of questionable value.

These are essential practices for a program that is committed to social learning. Routinely, have people with the least experience and training are placed in the jobs that require the most engagement and flexibility. Tommy was expert at drawing staff members into situations requiring physical coercion. The staff members dealing with him had to learn how to avoid getting drawn in, and that kind of learning does not happen overnight. It is unfair to punish people for compromised decisions made in the heat of the moment when they are confronting potentially dangerous situations. However, overlooking or excusing poor decisions can lead eventually to corrupt and violent outcomes. In an environment of social learning, people are still held accountable for their decisions, but they are required to learn from their mistakes, to apologize to anyone who has been harmed by those mistakes, and to cease making the same mistakes. Tommy's Safety Plan had to be repeatedly revised, as did the Safety Plans of the staff members who had to deal with him.

Improving Decision Making

We can improve our individual and group decision making. One way to create improvement is to recognize that choosing how to make a decision should come before making the decision. There are four main methods for coming to a decision among a group of people: authority rules, majority rules, proportional outcomes, and consensus. In most organizations there is a mixture of decision-making methods, and each method has its strengths and weaknesses [86].

In an extreme emergency, it is very useful and frequently lifesaving when the person who knows the most steps in and makes a decision. "Authority rules" therefore is often the quickest and most efficient means of decision making. The downside is that the more often this decision-making method is used, the more it dumbs down everyone else. It also is the decision-making method most prone to the abusive use of power, and it places an unfair burden on both the leader and the led. This is true for situations of ever-increasing complexity, since one person is rarely able to know or imagine all of the potential outcomes in these situations and yet may be severely criticized if he or she makes what turns out to be a bad decision.

"Majority rules" means that power is distributed among a number of people. It provides a means of resolving disputes fairly when a group cannot come to a consensus. There is always a danger, however, in silencing the minority opinion, particularly when that minority voice becomes a permanent minority. When that happens, important information is eliminated and an entire group can become involved in systematic and repeated error. Bad feelings are often aroused when one subgroup's victory is another's defeat, and "discussions" can easily turn into hostile debates that go nowhere. Here again, majority rules may be a problematic method of decision making when the situation is complex, but second to having an authority figure alone making a decision, it is the most likely method that a group will use under conditions of stress.

The "proportional outcomes" method of decision making is a cross between majority rules and consensus decision making. In this method, decisions are designed to reflect the proportion of group members who hold different views. Compromise and concession occur to make sure that the minority group has some power as well as the majority. The danger with this method lies in the possibility that the group may split permanently into separate factions.

A good rule of thumb is that whenever possible, a group should be helped to come to a consensus about a decision or a problem. "Consensus decision making" is a method that stands the best chance of enhancing social learning because of the often arduous process of reaching a consensus. When people feel that they have been part of a decision-making process, they are much more likely to get behind the decision.

Consensus is not about unanimity. Consensus has been described as "a process of cooperation" in which a group carefully considers everyone's point of view and deals fully with every legitimate objection. In fact, if everyone agrees, either the decision was obvious or they weren't paying attention or they're not telling the truth. Consensus is based on principles that help a group to reach a consensus: that everyone agrees to search for a "common-ground solution"; that disagreement is seen as a positive force that helps the group avoid the dangerous pressures of conformity, groupthink, and the silencing of dissent; that everyone has an equal voice; and that at some point, people put aside their individual preferences for the sake of coming to a collective group decision.

In consensus decision making, even if they are not in full agreement with every aspect of the decision, all members agree to support it and believe that it represents good thinking, that it was made in good faith, and that it supports the organization's core values [165]. Consent does not necessarily mean total satisfaction, and that is part of the tricky process of reaching a consensus. Dissenters are obligated to air their views, but are also obligated to stand aside so that the group can come to a consensus. The process of reaching a consensus is more likely to draw out and integrate the insights of everyone in the group, but cooperation, not competition, is essential. It ensures that the minority opinion is not lost and is the surest safeguard against the abusive use of power.

However—and this is a big however—reaching a consensus is hard work, far harder than authoritarian solutions, at least in the short term. Consensus will fail if the group members lack sufficient experience, knowledge, patience, and discipline to tolerate the process of reaching a consensus, which is often fraught with anxiety and frustration. Achieving a consensus in a Team Meeting or a Leadership Meeting can be as simple as going around the table and asking everyone to have his or her say without interruption.

It is interesting that in human service settings, rarely is any time taken to acknowledge that a collection of individuals doesn't automatically become a group capable of collective thought and decision making. Without willing it to be so, we automatically experience collective emotions. If you want to create a learning organization, then it is essential to create processes that bring people together to think, feel, and arrive at decisions together and to evaluate and reevaluate the outcomes of those decisions so that learning can occur.

A somewhat chicken-or-egg situation currently exists in many human service settings. The reality of staff turnover makes consensus building more challenging. When new individuals enter a group, they can constrain the conversation and cause people to hold back. At the same time, we have found that organizations that have adopted the Sanctuary Model have experienced significant reductions in staff turnover, likely due in part to staff members feeling that they have a voice in decision making. The reduction in turnover then improves the organization's ability to learn.

Maintaining Feedback Loops

One of the keys to Tommy's successful treatment was that the staff members became more cohesive, in part because the Sanctuary Model gave them a shared meaning system that enabled them to understand Tommy in a different way. But progress didn't occur in a straight line. There were many setbacks along the way that provided direct feedback to the staff and to Tommy about what was working for him and what was not.

If we have found some intervention or practice to inspire positive change, we should ask ourselves, *"How can we do that again?" "How do we make sure that this practice becomes part of our regular practice?"* If our results are consistent with our intentions, then it is useful to figure out what we did to achieve the desired outcome. We should broadcast and replicate successful strategies. Repeating success and not repeating failures means that we have to be willing to learn and make sure that our feedback loops are working at every level. That may mean asking ourselves questions such as *"Where did our communication break down?"* and *"How can we mend that broken link?"*

If our results are inconsistent with our intentions, then we need to learn from our mistakes or shortcomings and make the necessary adjustments in our practice. If, however, we are not seeing the changes we are hoping for, then we should be asking ourselves, *"What do we understand about this client or this situation?" "What do we need to learn to move us in the right direction?"* Under the workaday stresses of our jobs, it is all too easy to lose sight of what we are in business to do. We can spend far too much time doing things right and never ask ourselves, "*Are we doing the right things?*" Brian has recently been practicing an experience in social learning.

> *In our mental health clinics we have had numerous discussions about productivity standards. The feedback we kept getting from some staff and managers is that our expectations were too high. Yet at the same time, there were a number of staff members who consistently exceeded expectations and delivered quality services to their clients. In the past, we had discounted the people who said we were setting impossible standards by just saying, "If it is impossible, how does she do it?" This approach had not done much to improve productivity or morale. So, not long ago, we sat down with our highest producers and asked them, "How do you do it?" We recorded their strategies and shared them with others in the division. We moved away from a process in which we basically told people that they weren't cutting it to teaching them how their colleagues, who were successful, were conducting their business. This learning process has done more to improve productivity than simply telling people to shape up.*

The goal of the *Commitment to Social Learning* is to create an ongoing learning organization that identifies opportunities and errors and seizes those opportunities, while self-correcting errors, as a routine and exciting part of the work of helping people to recover from the injuries they have sustained.

Thinking Outside of the Box

It is a sad and sometimes tragic irony that workplaces that demand enormous and constant creativity and spontaneous innovation on a moment-to-moment basis rarely teach their workers how to do that, nor is creativity or innovation usually even mentioned. In fact, conversations that focus on creative responses in the social service or mental health field are rare to nonexistent. At one point in writing *Destroying Sanctuary* and *Restoring Sanctuary*, we entered the terms "creativity" and "mental health system" in a university library search engine and six documents came up, none related to the need to be creative in the system. Put in "innovation" and you won't do a whole lot better. And yet, as we described in Chapter 3 on the *Commitment to Growth and Change*, the only way to effectively help clients stop reenacting a horrible past history and learn to live in a healthier way is to move creatively out of the position you are in with them and spontaneously deliver a different relational outcome. It's changing the problematic patterns of behavior that is important, not controlling behavior, although changing those problematic patterns does end up changing problem behavior. That requires thinking outside of the box, supporting innovation and creative problem solving, and being willing to tolerate the inevitable failures that precede success.

To effectively treat Tommy, the Glove House staff had to be creative; they had to think outside of the box. That meant being more open than they had ever been to the direct feedback they got from Tommy about what helped bring about positive change and what was simply replaying the old script. In every case like Tommy's there are always definite *wrong* answers. But it is less clear what the *right* answers are. Therefore, it is important for the organization, if it is to be a learning organization, to make it safe for people to think outside of the box. For an environment of creativity, innovation, and learning, there needs to be a diversity of opinions and ideas, and that means having a diverse group of people. Diversity is no guarantee of creativity, but it does increase the odds. The greater the diversity, the greater the number of possible options and combinations of ideas, and it is that generativity that can lead to actions that result in change.

The Benefits of Diversity

The dodo bird provides a good example of how isolated populations become extinct when new species are introduced; the process is called "genetic drift." It can happen to organizations when more and more energy is dedicated to tweaking the same old strategy that really doesn't change anything [20]. Diversity is no joke, and it is not to be taken lightly. It is what supports health in a gene pool, in a society, in an organization, and in an individual's life. In organizational life, diversity supports health by engendering the possibility of creative conflict. Up to a certain point, homogeneity induces trust that allows innovation to emerge, but the innovation will likely be incremental and not transformative. There must be a balance between unfamiliarity and novelty.

Managing and thriving in a diverse organization presents different challenges than working in a more homogeneous organization. There are many more layers of complexity that we need to think about and respond to. The concept of democracy is never easy to operationalize, but it becomes even more challenging when we factor in centuries of institutionalized experiences of racism, sexism, and homophobia. How do we ensure that all the voices in our organization are heard? When people fear to speak their mind, believing that this will not be welcomed and, in fact will be punished, how do you create the conditions necessary to begin to encourage real dialogue and participation?

When we talk about diversity in the Sanctuary Model, we do not just mean racial diversity, although given the context of institutionalized racism, racial discrimination is still prevalent and must be addressed in human service delivery organizations. People from different racial groups are likely to have had diverse experiences and diverse points of view, so taking into account the racial mix in order to promote group flow remains relevant. So too is diversity of age, religion, gender identity, sexual orientation, economic background, educational experience, class, geographical regions, and political inclination. Likewise, differences in thinking styles, affective styles, beliefs, and values can offer the diversity necessary to stimulate group innovation.

In an organization, there is a constant dance as groups of people establish the common ground for the sharing of ideas, feelings, hopes, and aspirations, create innovation together, and then disband in order to create new groups, infusing diversity into that process. As our organizations become more heterogeneous, the possibilities for really exciting ideas and innovation can dramatically increase, but not if this diversity of opinion and experience cannot be harnessed or harvested. Then it will always remain a potential strength. To become truly democratic, leadership needs to be able to create the possibility for people to say what is on their minds and in their hearts while finding ways to integrate that knowledge into a shared vision, goals, and practice.

Commitment to Social Learning and Trauma-Informed Practice

Learning How to Learn: Double Loop Learning and Reinventive Change

Creating trauma-informed organizations turns out to be a very big change. We are still in the early stages, but our growing knowledge about development and the impact of trauma and adversity is overturning many of our long-standing assumptions about what determines human problems, how to treat those problems, and what recovery we can expect. Particularly in mental health services, we have been tied to a diagnostic categorization system presented in a volume called the *Diagnostic and Statistical Manual* that is supposed to guide treatment. But many people who are working from a trauma-informed perspective find that system not only useless in guiding treatment, but at times actually harmful. Many mental health settings have come to depend on medication as the primary or only form of intervention that has value, but now the use of medications in many circumstances is being questioned, and we may find out that much of what we thought was useful and helpful is indeed harmful [166].

Learning under these circumstances means a different type of learning than we are accustomed to in human service systems. We are used to what is called "single loop learning" or "problem solving as usual." Single loop learning involves the detection and correction of error. We do something, look at the results, and then try to improve on what already exists. "Double loop learning," on the other hand, occurs when errors are detected and corrected in ways that involve questioning our basic assumptions and often changing the organization's underlying norms, policies, and objectives [167]. Learning about the ways in which disrupted attachment and traumatic stress evolve into a wide variety of problems and then figuring out what to do to more effectively address those problems requires double loop learning.

Organizations, and individuals for that matter, typically discourage or actively inhibit learning that calls into question their norms, objectives, and basic policies. We resist change, and we resist taking in new information that disturbs our basic mental models, the fundamental way we understand the world. And yet, this is exactly what we need to do. Our mental models are not working well for us or for our clients. We need to think outside the boxes we are in. We need to learn new "tricks," but we also need to change the assumptions we make that stifle learning.

Providing developmentally grounded, trauma-informed care means that our settings have to become more comfortable with double loop learning that enables us to discover new things about the other person, ourselves, and the organization as a whole. In our story about Tommy, the staff at Glove House mobilized curiosity instead of judgment and in doing so learned more about Tommy. What they learned challenged their existing belief systems. If they had simply made the usual assumptions about Tommy's intentions or motivations, then they would not have learned much. Tommy wouldn't have learned much either. And nothing would have happened except reenactment.

"Reinventive unlearning" is a term that has been recently used to describe radical. This requires fundamental changes in the existing beliefs and routines of an organization, that is triggered by high-level and rapid change, which compels us to move outside of familiar domains and envision what is coming and what is necessary for system transformation [159]. That term sums up what we are suggesting in this book. We need to unlearn much of what we have assumed to be truth and the behaviors that follow these presumed truths. We must reinvent ourselves and our organizations. For every individual and for every organization, that represents a process of discovery. Trauma survivors need approaches very different from the ones we have been accustomed to using. When we change our strategies, they change as well. Then they have the opportunity to reinvent themselves.

Retrieving Organizational Memory

Adopting the Sanctuary Model is in itself an act of retrieving organizational memory. It hearkens back to psychodynamics, the practice of the therapeutic community, social psychiatry, and the principles of Moral Treatment, but it updates all of these with our growing knowledge about the impact of trauma and what it takes to restore health to those who have been exposed to significant adversity.

In practical terms, to heal and move on, organizations must review the narrative of their own history and be willing to address the traumas that have occurred in the recent or distant past. All of the organizations we have consulted with have been startled to recognize the ways in which current functioning continues to be haunted by the unresolved past.

Retrieving split-off memories is a process, and it does not happen overnight. Part of being a learning organization is recursively visiting memories of how problems have been dealt with in the past, what has worked and not worked, and what was known that has been forgotten. Program leaders who may be decades older than the workers they are hiring must recognize that knowledge loss has been pervasive throughout the mental health and social services arenas. Specific steps may need to be taken to revisit the mission, founding ideas, methodologies, theoretical approaches, and techniques that have been forgotten and overlooked within the organization.

In Tommy's story, the Sanctuary Model helped Glove House revisit the philosophy of their founder. Another creative approach to the problem of organizational memory, undertaken by New Vitae, a program for people suffering from chronic and severe mental illness, has been to set up a Committee for Institutional Memory. The committee is entrusted with regularly determining how institutional memory is being maintained and productively used. They document the problems and successes they encounter along the path to change; they also look at organizational tragedies that have affected the institution and how those tragedies may be continuing to affect policies in ways that are not helpful.

Earlier, we said that if we really understand clients' symptoms, we will realize that they were once adaptive. They represent the clients' best attempts to deal with an overwhelmingly stressful event or series of events. The same can be said about some of the irrational or dysfunctional processes we find in organizations. Often when we review the past, they represent the organizations' best effort to cope with overwhelming and stressful situations. These processes may no longer work, but they have become habits. As we know, habits are hard to break, and the organization can find itself stuck in the past, unwilling and unable to learn new tricks.

Implications for Social Learning Leadership

Moving to the Edge of Chaos

Building learning organizations requires a very different style of leadership than most people may be familiar with. Being a leader in a mental health or social service environment that requires constant adaptation to changing environmental circumstances, as well as staff who can constantly adapt to changing needs of the clients, requires an ability to deal with uncertainty and risk while modeling adaptive behavior for others. This very special zone, essential for any kind of individual or system transformation, is called "the edge of chaos." It is where life and creativity happen. Leaders in a social learning environment must resist telling people what to do while listening deeply to ideas that will help draw people out of their comfort zone. They must be able to manage the distress that uncertainty creates while at the same time conveying a sense of urgency.

Leaders Must Disturb the Equilibrium

All systems tend to stay in equilibrium and return to equilibrium if their balance is disrupted. This is a natural quality of living systems. In an organization, persistent social norms, corporate values, and orthodox beliefs keep the system in balance. These are the "attractors" in a system, the magnets that keep a system where it is and draws it back if it is disrupted. But when things need to change, the equilibrium must be disturbed and leaders must become "disruptive innovators" [168].

As the Chief Operating Officer of several child welfare programs, Brian is learning how to lead and disturb the equilibrium state of his managers:

Recently, the children in one of our cottages were really struggling and engaging in a variety of unsafe behaviors: running out of the building at night, breaking windows, damaging property, and fighting with each other. There had been three or four pretty serious incidents in the course of 48 hours, and there was an awful lot of hand wringing going on. I received a call from the Health Center telling me that things were out of control, but nobody could do anything because the Program Manager did not believe in behavioral plans, and clearly these kids needed to be on behavioral plans. I indicated that I was not convinced that a behavioral plan was the answer, but I thought the team should get together, talk, and figure it out. I agreed that I would make that happen. I contacted the Residential Director and asked him to call a meeting to get all the parties (clinical, residential, education, psychiatry, and nursing) in the same room to talk. Later that day he contacted everyone, and in the process of setting up the meeting he felt that he better understood the problem. Many of the staff wanted to take a more behavioral approach with the children and have clearer consequences for poor behavior, but they complained that the Program Manager has been taking a more trauma-based approach and did not want set limits for the children. No one knew what to do.

I told the Residential Director that I thought they did know what to do and would figure it out together. I also reminded the Residential Director that we did not punish kids. I had no problem with providing incentives for positive behavior and limit setting, but it would be inconsistent with our values to take a punitive stance with children who were struggling. At any rate, the behavioral problems decreased dramatically, not once the meeting took place, but as soon as it was set up. What happened here? I think two things happened. First, as the Residential Director contacted people to set up the meeting, they told him what they thought the problem was. They were able to talk about what was bothering them and put words and meaning to their upsetting feelings. The second gain was that they could relax a little knowing that the problem was going to be aired. The kids no longer had to act it out for us because we were ready to address it.

What I find myself doing now more than ever before is waiting to weigh in on the problems we are having with this child or that program. Instead, I end up mandating that a meeting take place. What I know is that when the wheels are coming off, it is because the adults do not have their act together. The kids are becoming unglued, and the adults often stand around them pointing fingers at each other. I am pretty confident that if we can get the key players in a room together, they can work out the issues. They resist being in the same room because this means that there is usually some conflict that needs to be worked out. Everyone is uncomfortable with the conflict, so they stand back and let the kids run wild and drive them crazy. They blame the kids, they blame their coworkers, and they exonerate themselves. I used to be much more likely to reach in and say "do this" or "do that," but that was generally not helpful. What I find I do have the power to do now is insist that people sit down and talk.

In Chapters 5 and 6 on the *Commitment to Nonviolence* and the *Commitment to Emotional Intelligence*, respectively, we talk a lot about the issues of trust in the organization. Trust needs to be built, and it is built piece by piece, in an honest and open dialogue. We experience a crisis, and our immediate thought is "Don't just sit there, do something." It's very hard to take the opposite position: "Don't do something, just sit there." Sit there and think, talk it through, figure out what to do next. When we feel stressed, we sometime confuse important things with urgent things. While an issue may be very important, it may not be urgent. It is not uncommon, when a problem seems crucial, to mistakenly think that we need to solve it NOW. Often we cannot stand the anxiety of leaving an important issue open. In our effort to manage our anxiety, we convince ourselves that it is urgent. In reality, far fewer issues need to be resolved NOW than we think. We spend a lot of time reacting to problems, and this creates a cascade of bad decisions. Our kneejerk reactions often make things worse, not better. When we are caught in a reenactment, just doing what comes naturally will make matters worse. Thinking through the law of unanticipated consequences takes some time and forethought. It is impossible for any one of us to anticipate all the possible consequences of a particular action. That is why making as many decisions as possible in democratic groups is desirable.

When leaders sit through these discussions, they need to listen and understand how others experience them and the organizational culture. Sometimes in this process leaders will desperately try to explain or justify behavior. We encourage leaders not to do that. It is better to just listen. When it is appropriate, they should apologize if someone's feelings got hurt. In most cases, we do not intentionally hurt or silence people, but if that is the consequence of our behavior, then our intentions don't matter much to the injured party. Sitting and listening, rather than explaining and defending, is something different. If we do something different, we are taking the first step toward changing the script, and that is a step in the right direction. We disrupt organizational learning by not engaging everybody in the process. Staff members who occupy lower rungs on the organizational ladder often hold their tongues in meetings with senior managers. They are afraid of looking stupid, being criticized, making somebody angry, or getting it wrong. They protect themselves. It's very difficult to develop the trust that is needed to really learn. Leaders have to work hard at establishing and maintaining trust, while the organization needs to develop processes for ensuring that there are opportunities for this to happen. Then leaders need to be careful not to sabotage these opportunities.

Sanctuary Toolkit

Encourage Double Loop Learning

The first thing we suggest to improve the level of social learning in the organization is to start talking about inflammatory issues. In the implementation process we ask organizations to develop a Core Team, which is a multidisciplinary, multilevel, diverse group of individuals who will be responsible for the ongoing implementation of the model. This Core Team is a microcosm of the organization and, as such, as the Core Team works together, the organizational story will begin to emerge.

One of the activities the Core Team engages in during implementation is a discussion about the elephants in the room—the undiscussables. We need people to talk about who gets to speak and who doesn't, who is heard and who isn't, which ideas are accepted and which are rejected. We need to examine how we experience each other. These activities feel risky, but they are necessary if we're going to rescript our organizations. Usually the cultural rules in the organization do not live in our conscious awareness. These rules are our default position and become "just the way things are around here." In most cases, the rules are made by people in power and tend to benefit them. As is often the case, people in power do not always see that the rules that benefit them may not benefit everyone. In following the steps of the Sanctuary implementation process, the Core Team is responsible for questioning the basic, but often thorny, assumptions upon which decisions are routinely made. That is double loop learning.

S.E.L.F. Psychoeducational Groups

The group dynamics theorist Kurt Lewin believed that the primary task of psychoeducation was to promote a change in the person's self-perception. He found that the change in the perception of oneself preceded changes in knowledge, values, and beliefs, and only when this change occurred would there be a lasting change in behavior [169]. In the original Sanctuary program, psychoeducation was an indispensable part of the program. After reading Lewin's work, we know why.

As a result of their experiences in the world, including previous experiences with the mental health and social service systems, many clients enter environments that are supposed to be therapeutic with very negative perceptions of themselves and the world around them. And largely because they have no other explanatory system, explanations become highly self-referential. Although it may appear that they are blaming other people for their circumstances, inside they blame themselves entirely. And the blame does not concern what they did or didn't do. It focuses on who they are: some basic overwhelming and indescribable defect that they perceive as permanent. Psychoeducation about the impact of psychological injuries changes that belief. By understanding how they came to be injured, people begin to develop hope that recovery from those injuries is possible.

Treatment changes when an entire staff shares the same knowledge base and can consistently share the same language and approaches. This is the outcome of structured psychoeducational groups, especially when those lessons are reinforced in informal interactions. Instead of drawing on their own folk psychology, which may or may not be helpful, all staff members can draw on a scientific knowledge base for why we do what we do and feel what we feel under conditions of extreme stress.

We have created a number of psychoeducational curricula that are organized around S.E.L.F., the fundamental tasks of recovery—safety, emotional management, loss, and future— that help clients to shift their understanding of what has happened to them, how they have responded to those events, and the role they must play in their own recovery.

In the fast-paced human service world that most of us function in today, for a curriculum to be useful it has to be simple enough to be delivered by staff members who have a minimum of training while still being applicable when used by more experienced professionals. In most cases, there can be no expectation that every client will have the time to experience the entire curriculum. Many treatment experiences are so brief that a curriculum that builds on previous lessons, as is typical in an educational setting, is simply not appropriate. Therefore, each lesson must embody at least part of the whole curriculum and the entire curriculum must be flexible enough so that each lesson can stand on its own. To be maximally useful in a treatment setting, it must be possible for a staff member to decide that "Today, we need to focus on loss" or "We are confronting some safety issues in the community, and I am going to do the lesson on social safety today" and not have to use the material in a set sequence.

Organizational Trauma Assessment

We know that organizational traumas—suicides, homicides, other deaths of key people, injuries, lawsuits, and media scandals—affect everyone in a group because when persons join a group, that group becomes part of their individual identity. But traumatic events are rarely adequately dealt with at the time, in part because people are advised by attorneys not to discuss the events that have occurred. Therefore, the experiences that people have had, and the emotions behind those experiences, are unlikely to ever be addressed. This results in what is often profound organizational memory fragmentation.

Part of the Sanctuary implementation process is having organizations do an assessment of their own traumatic experiences, and there is rarely an organization that hasn't been exposed to trauma. Dealing with the split-off memories may take time, however. Sometimes no one is around who remembers the events as they unfolded, even though those events may still be affecting organizational function. At other times individuals are there, but they are reluctant to revisit old bad memories, much like our clients. When an organization gets stuck, seemingly willing to move but unable to do so, we always suspect an unresolved traumatic experience.

S.E.L.F. Treatment Planning

Treatment Planning is the traditional method in the mental health sector for organizing what is actually going to happen in a treatment setting or relationship, although every component of the human service system will have its own version of planning to implement its mission with individual clients. Unfortunately, without effective Team Meetings and /or collaboration, Treatment Planning is likely to become a meaningless exercise done more to satisfy the desire of reviewers for documentation than as a real guide to day-to-day activities. Over time, efforts have been made to include clients and family members in the Treatment Planning process, but unless everyone shares a clear definition of what treatment actually is and has a common vision, language, and underlying assumptions, it is likely to end up as an exercise in futility that frustrates everyone involved.

S.E.L.F. Treatment Planning meetings are the time set aside to measure client progress and plan for the next step in treatment. In the interests of the *Commitment to Social Learning* and to avoid what is often a free-floating airing of opinions that doesn't necessarily accomplish what needs to be done, the S.E.L.F. framework provides an accessible way to evaluate goals, struggles, and progress by organizing this information into the categories of safety, emotion management, loss, and future and also fosters a shared language. It organizes the way we talk about treatment without minimizing any of the important aspects of treatment.

At the same time, it helps to guarantee that the issues surrounding the experience of adversity and trauma will not be overlooked or forgotten. The format compels the group to focus not just on current dangers but also on increasing levels of growth and change by giving equal time to recent successes, current challenges, and future commitments in all four domains of S.E.L.F. To be effective, the meetings must be nonhierarchical and create an environment that encourages discussion and collaboration between team members and that includes clients and families, rather than a rote reporting or reading from reports. Consistent with the Sanctuary *Commitment to Democracy,* all attendees are expected to participate in giving information and posing questions, and all participants have an equal voice. Instead of focusing most of the time on the problem, this methodology helps a group get to the solutions, and the bracketing question always is *"What happened to you?"* rather than *"What's wrong with you?"* Then more time is given to proposing and discussing solutions rather than problems.

Appointing a Devil's Advocate

Since dissent is so important for good decision-making processes, but for many people in an organization is too frightening and too risky to engage in, it can be valuable for a team to ask someone at each meeting to play the role of "devil's advocate." Traditionally, this is someone who takes a position he or she does not necessarily agree with just for the sake of argument. In taking such a position, the devil's advocate seeks to engage others in identifying weaknesses in a plan and considering unintended consequences. This helps the entire group to either improve the plan or abandon it altogether. Either way, it paves the way for much more frequent complex decision making.

The *Commitment to Social Learning* challenges us to reach better decisions by including all key stakeholders in the process of finding new solutions to the recurring problems of clients and the organization. Obviously, the only way we can accomplish this goal is to actually speak with each other. With that in mind, we move on to the *Commitment to Open Communication.*

Chapter 8

Commitment to Open Communication

We envisage the possibility of a flexible system in which open communication and learning as a social process can be maintained. Theoretically, this represents a system of checks and balances in which internal commitment, shared goals, and sensitivity to the outside world can be maintained.

Maxwell Jones (pp. 81–82), Maturation of the
Therapeutic Community [170]

SUMMARY: *A primary focus of the Commitment to Open Communication is on learning how to respond appropriately and avoid collective disturbance by understanding the nature of collective and unconscious processes, improving interpersonal communication, reducing the barriers that are created due to long-standing discriminatory practices, and enhancing organizational transparency.*

A Vision of Open Communication

- People mean what they say without being mean when they say it.
- Everyone communicates directly and, as much as possible, uses words to convey what they mean.
- When communication is unclear, people ask each other for clarification rather than making up their own story about what message was intended.
- There are ample opportunities for people to speak to each other face-to-face, and there is an expectation that people will share both thoughts and feelings about issues with each other.
- Failures in communication are seen as opportunities to improve, not to assign blame.
- Keeping secrets is seen as dangerous to the well-being of individuals and groups, but boundaries and privacy are understood and respected.

211

- People try their best to be consistent in using nonverbal and verbal forms of communication.
- Lying and deceit are seen as barriers to healthy individuals, groups, and societies.

What Do We Mean by Open Communication?

A Story of Collective Disturbance Resolved by Open Communication

This story begins about eight years ago at Andrus. By that time, the staff at Andrus had done a great job of reducing incidents of restraint on the campus. They had reduced restraints from 78 holds a month to fewer than 5. Brian had written a journal article about it and was being asked to present the results at conferences, and he was very proud of what they had accomplished. He thought the problem was solved.

In the summer of 2003 the reduction of holds had leveled off. It is harder to get from 5 incidents to 0 than it is to get from 78 to 5 for a number of reasons: when children first arrive they have not yet been acculturated to nonviolent norms, so if they come in with out-of-control behavior, which is usually the reason for admission, it takes some time to teach them a different set of cultural norms; a child can experience a particularly upsetting event that he or she has not yet developed the skills to manage properly; something can happen in one cottage that destabilizes the social norms, such as when a long-term staff member leaves, triggering reactions to disrupted attachment in the children, or when a new staff member arrives who has not yet developed sufficient safety skills to contain distress.

It is largely these somewhat unpredictable, but in our field natural, occurrences that help to explain the reluctance of professionals to absolutely prohibit the use of restraint. It's wrong to stand by and watch anyone get injured when it could have been prevented. At the same time, if, in an organization, you start equivocating about your values and start believing that five restraints (or forced administration of medications, or calls to the police, or administrative discharges) are acceptable, you are heading for trouble. In no time it's no longer 5 but 10 and then 15 exceptions that are acceptable. When this happens, the social norms change and the environment becomes progressively more coercive and violent.

Brian and Andrus's Residential Director routinely reviewed the incidents of restraints. In a meeting one week, they decided that it was time to "tighten the screws a little and push to eliminate restraints." They had spent part of the meeting reviewing the incidents that had occurred, and they came to a decision at the end of the meeting when they were feeling pressured to move on to the next pressing item on their agenda.

Their goal was a righteous one: eliminating restraints of children. They assumed that since the staff had done so well with the reductions they had made up to that point, they should, without much difficulty, be able to stop using restraints altogether. It was this flawed assumption that started the problem.

The process the two administrators used to implement their decision cannot really be considered much of a process. They just decided it was time to stop restraining children entirely. Let's look back at what they did not do: they did not consult the staff who would actually have to implement this policy; they did not think through the potential ramifications of their new policy; they did not seek buy-in; they did not think about what the staff might need to implement the change in policy (i.e., more training, backup overtime staff, more psychiatric consultation?); they did not schedule another meeting to consider all of the above.

This is where communication began going off the rails, although neither of them recognized it at the time. They both just went on to the next task in their busy day. But it had been left to the Residential Director to enact the change in policy with the milieu staff. He had concerns about how the staff were going to achieve zero restraints because he had been personally involved in all of the episodes of reducing holds, and he was aware of the incidents that were preventing a zero baseline. But he liked and respected Brian, and if that was what Brian wanted, he would do his best to deliver. In that moment, a critical loyalty conflict arose and was dissociated as the Residential Director stopped protecting his staff and instead complied with the desires of his own supervisor, Brian.

Similarly, Brian liked and respected his Residential Director, so when he went along with Brian's idea to eliminate restraints entirely, Brian took that as an indication of support. If, on that day, they had had more time to think about it, things might have turned out differently. Living systems are not predictable. Put a number of factors together one day and nothing happens. Put the same number of factors together on another day and you get an explosion.

The Residential Director went back to the staff and acquainted them with the new policy: "there will now be no restraints." The staff complied with the mandate to eliminate holds entirely. There was grumbling, and not all agreed. Some even expressed the belief that their leaders were taking away a tool without providing them with alternatives. But both administrators just chalked up the complaints to the usual griping that accompanies any kind of change. They provided no open forum for discussion about this issue and, as a result, open communication was shut down and went underground. The staff drew their own conclusions and added meaning to those conclusions. We know now that there was a growing belief among the staff that their leaders were out of touch with what was going on and that therefore the leaders did not care if staff members were hit by children. Underground discontent, frustration, and a feeling of betrayal were growing, but no one understood what was happening at the time.

Incidents of aggression directed at milieu staff gradually increased during the late fall/early winter of 2003. Up to that time there were typically 10 to 12 reported incidents a month involving aggression directed at staff, but most of those incidents were generally minor, like a child pushing past a staff person or pushing him or her away. At first there was a gradual increase in the number of incidents, but then the intensity of incidents started to increase. It got to the point that staff members were being routinely punched, slapped, and kicked.

At their next regular meeting, the Residential Director and Brian discussed this trend, but quickly dismissed it as the result of a particular child's reactivity to some event or a change in staffing in one of the cottages. They told themselves and each other that this situation would correct itself and no additional intervention was needed. But the number of incidents continued to rise. Internally, they were both feeling increasing anxiety. But instead of using the alarming trend to alarm each other, they each became protective of the other, calming each other down, rationalizing the causes, reassuring each other, and, in doing so, denying the magnitude of the problem. The communication between them had changed. It was no longer serving its rightful purpose of channeling vital information about what was happening to people lower in the organizational hierarchy for whom they were responsible. Instead of problem solving they were trying to help each other feel better and be less worried when actually there was a good cause for the worry and neither of them was sharing it with the other.

By January 2003, incidents of aggression directed at staff were occurring daily and were becoming more intense. In the middle of January, one of the residents hit a staff person in the eye with an attachment to a vacuum cleaner, sending her to the emergency room. Leaders failed to respond to the incident as they usually did, with serious concern. No one except a Human Resources assistant called the worker to check on her condition, and there was a perfunctory response to the child even though the behavior was clearly well outside the boundaries typically set for behavior. The two leaders seemed frozen, not adequately communicating with each other or anyone else. Protecting each other by protecting their faulty process took precedence over rationally addressing the problem and protecting the staff.

No one else did anything either. Every staff member, every clinician, and other administrators could see what was happening in the organization. Nonetheless, communication had become so stymied that no one called a special meeting, or went in alarm to either administrator, or sent a worried memo. This is what makes this kind of disturbance a *collective* disturbance. It isn't just the main characters who are in the grips of something that is paralyzing them—everyone is.

Over the next two weeks, incidents of aggression directed at staff continued to snowball, and by the end of January there were over 75 incidents reported across five cottages. This was more than *five* times the typical number of incidents. In addition to the sheer volume, four staff members ended up in the emergency room or missed work due to the injuries sustained. It was becoming clear (painfully so) that this was no blip on the screen. It could no longer be explained away by a single child's reactivity or a single staff person's resignation. The organization was looking at something bigger, uglier, and more complex. In a collective disturbance this is what typically happens: things get so bad that they no longer can be denied, but the situation can get pretty destructive before that happens.

Finally, at this point, the two leaders recognized that they were in the middle of a collective disturbance and they needed to act. With the wheels coming off and daily reports of mayhem and chaos, there seemed to be only one way to respond. When the going gets tough, the tough order pizza. Brian and the Residential Director decided to host two lunch events with milieu staff to discuss what was going on. They began by acknowledging that things were very difficult right now and that they had been remarkably ineffective in managing and responding to the difficulties. They apologized for this shortcoming. Then for the next 30 minutes or so the staff went to work on the two administrators, pointing out each misstep in excruciating detail. The two men listened carefully because they knew they deserved the angry response of the staff members, and they recognized that painful learning was taking place.

Once they had moved through this phase, they were able to talk about how difficult the work was, how vulnerable staff members sometimes feel, and how scary things can get at times. Staff members told stories, and some were even able to laugh about the difficult challenges they had encountered. They also discussed some potential solutions to the problems. There was clearly a need for more support and more communication. Although there were at first some calls for certain children to be discharged, by the end of the meeting staff were able to acknowledge that the children who were the most aggressive throughout this period were those who had been in the program for a long time but had not consistently acted this way. So, part of the learning for everyone was that when children who have not previously acted out do so, it can be a tipoff that a collective disturbance is afoot. They were also the most traumatized children and in many ways the most vulnerable to toxic interactions (or lack of interactions) between administrative and line staff.

The remarkable thing about a collective disturbance is how the simple act of opening up channels of communication changes things. At the staff meeting, the administrators decided that it would be valuable to the staff to add one support staff position. But that change did not happen for another couple of months because they needed to secure the funding and refine and develop the plan. Nonetheless, the incidents of aggression directed at staff ceased *immediately* after the meetings. In February, the organization was back to the usual 10 or so minor incidents per month.

Understanding Collective Disturbance

A "collective disturbance" is a form of organizational dissociation, a situation in which strong feelings get disconnected from their source and become attached to unrelated events or interactions. A conflict occurs at a higher level in an organization, and the emotional content and the cognitive content of the conflict separate. The emotional communication starts traveling downward, while the cognitive content of what is being communicated stays at the level of its original source. The people or parties that are in conflict do not consciously recognize what is going on. The dissociated feelings travel down to the most vulnerable members of the community, who then act out. The acting out escalates until the group finally recognizes that this is not an individual problem but a collective problem.

We can trace our story's collective disturbance to the process of change. The administration at Andrus had already spent several years trying to figure out what it means to become a trauma-informed system and on unlearning some of the time-worn attitudes toward staff using the Sanctuary Commitments that we were beginning to clearly articulate. The staff had responded by significantly improving the care that was being delivered to children, a sign of which had been the decrease in coercive measures and staff injuries. The organization had not, however, moved very far in the direction of the *Commitment to Democracy,* so it was fairly easy for the two administrators to just decide on their own that they wanted to eliminate restraints entirely, with no discussion, conversation, or recognition of the impact this might have on the staff.

Under the pressures of the day, Brian and his Residential Director started protecting each other and stopped looking at what was actually going on, but their internal and largely unconscious anxiety about what was happening in the organization did not disappear; it just became dissociated. Once dissociated, the information they needed to accurately address the problem was no longer accessible. Had they asked the staff why restraint incidents were still going on, or had they solicited suggestions for how to reduce the incidents to zero, the events that unfolded could probably have been prevented. But under the influence of a combination of previous organizational norms and ongoing stress, they did neither of these things. Instead, they withdrew from real engagement with each other but still communicated unrest to everyone else, but now indirectly, nonverbally, and emotionally. It's important to remember that emotions are contagious and that the emotions of leaders have a high impact on the people they lead—especially the emotions that are unconscious.

The message that the staff received from the administrator was that despite the significant improvements that had taken place, they still were not doing a good enough job of reducing restraints; after all their hard work, they needed to do more. There was no process for analyzing what the barriers, fears, and constraints were. The people at the top just thought that the situation could get better since it had so greatly improved already. It's a bit like saying to a child who has worked hard to get a B on a test, "That's nice but you should have gotten an A." Even in the description, the administrator records his thought as follows: "*we thought we would tighten the screws a little*," an attitude probably perceived by the staff as punitive (since it refers to tightening the screws on a rack, a medieval torture device).

The dissociated feelings started traveling downward. As illustrated by the story, group tension rose but it was ascribed to other, often inaccurate, sources, such as the clients, clients' families, another department, or another shift. In this case, the staff picked up the anxiety and felt variously vulnerable, angry, and overwhelmed. They then responded to those feelings by becoming more passive, and passive aggressive, in their dealings with the children. As the children sensed the anxiety of the staff, their anxiety increased as well. So did their acting out. The increased acting out only served to increase the staff's feelings of vulnerability and anxiety, which in turn fueled the emotional responses of the children.

A primary indicator that something was wrong was an increase in aggression directed at the staff. This was largely ignored. In truth, the first incidents may indeed have been the result of a particular child or a change in staffing, as the administrators concluded. Nonetheless, it was also an emotionally charged *nonverbal communication* that they ignored. It then became the failure to hear the message embedded in that communication, that "*we (milieu staff) need to talk to you about your insistence on eliminating restraint and leaving us powerless*," that created the snowball effect. As the authors who originally described a collective disturbance wrote, "*the failure in function of each person is integrated with the failure in function of the next one, and are integrated in such a way that the disorganization gains impetus like a snowball going downhill, with increasing size, spread, and seriousness of effects*" (p. 394) [171].

But none of these issues were addressed directly, so the emotional content of the communication went underground, becoming horizontal, nonverbal, informal, and unconscious while it snowballed emotionally. At first, these incidents were fairly well contained within one cottage. But then the grapevine activated, communication spread horizontally and vertically, verbally and nonverbally, formally and informally. The rumor mill was grinding out messages, and the level of anger and anxiety was increasing. As a result, the violence escalated dramatically across the whole campus. In any collective disturbance, it is the most vulnerable members of any community who will begin to act out, and in this case the most vulnerable are the children. And they will signal the distress they are feeling with aggressive behavior targeting the staff members they know. Staff members easily fall into the victim role in the child's reenactment because their leaders have signaled that they are indeed powerless, that their concerns are not valued, and that, yes, they are "cannon fodder." Thankfully, enough change had happened that in this case the staff did not become counteraggressive with the children, but the cost was an increasing level of staff injury that the administrators continued to ignore even when serious injuries occurred.

Both leaders denied what was going on and felt powerless to do anything about it, reactions that were not typical of either of them. Their apparent lack of concern and their response when a staff member suffered a serious injury were completely uncharacteristic, and although their reaction was ignored by both of them, it was a subject of much discussion and anger on the part of the staff. Blatant denial indicates the presence of dissociation. But at the same time, this very denial prevented them from exploring the etiology of the problem, which lay in their relationship with each other and the breakdown in communication between them. The lack of responsiveness and seeming powerlessness on the part of both leaders further fueled staff anxieties and the sense of vulnerability. *"First, they tell us we can't hold kids and then, when we get punched, kicked, and battered, the administration doesn't even respond."*

It was only when the incidents became impossible to ignore that the magnitude of the problem broke through the leaders' paralysis. It took many signals, from many places, over an extended period of time for the leaders to recognize that they had to do something and that they were trapped within a particularly difficult collective disturbance.

These kinds of collective events happen everywhere, and the more stressed the organization, the more likely they are to occur. Collective disturbances frequently illustrate that "the road to hell is paved with good intentions." They do not usually derive from anyone's malevolent desires but, as in our story, from a desire for something good that somehow goes wrong in the movement from thought to action. In part, they readily occur because we remain largely oblivious of group dynamics and collective unconscious processes. Compounding this problem is the reality that communication among human beings is multidimensional. Let's explore just how complicated communication is in a little more detail.

The Complicated Life of Messages in Organizations

Communication represents the flow of life in an organization. In our living systems analogue, communication is represented by the circulatory system that connects every part of the body to every other part and conveys the nutrients needed to stay alive. Imagine a picture of the human body that depicts the parts of the vascular system as completely interconnected. That's the way things should be operating in an organization. Information should be flowing through every part of the organizational body.

But as this story illustrates, that isn't what always happens. Do you remember playing "Whisper down the lane" as a kid (sometimes called "Telephone" or "Telegraph")? Remember how, in just a few passages through different ears, a simple message became garbled and unintelligible? Well, just because you grew up doesn't mean that communication has gotten any easier. It hasn't. Communicating with other people in an organization is a complicated process that involves minds and bodies, experience and memory, emotions, thoughts, intuitions, and beliefs.

There are many barriers to communication: physical barriers, such as geographically disbursed programs; psychological barriers related to each individual's understanding and interpretation of what the other person means; social barriers inherent in the structure of the organization, status, and power; and philosophical barriers about the underlying assumptions we make about what is right and wrong, good and bad. As a result of this complexity, communication of even a simple message between two people can go very wrong (Figure 8.1).

Multidimensional Communication

In human systems we communicate in many different ways. Some information is conveyed formally, such as in a meeting agenda, meeting minutes, or other written documents. Then there is the informal information that is shared in passing in the hallway, in a phone call or in a personal email. We also convey information in our looks and body posture in a meeting or in a face-to-face encounter. Since all of our organizations are built around fixed hierarchies, information travels up and down the hierarchy and moves across horizontal levels within the hierarchy. Complicating this process further is that we are always conveying both cognitive and emotional information, verbally and nonverbally, and some of this will be deliberate and conscious and some of it will be unconscious. The emotional tone of the sender has an impact on how the

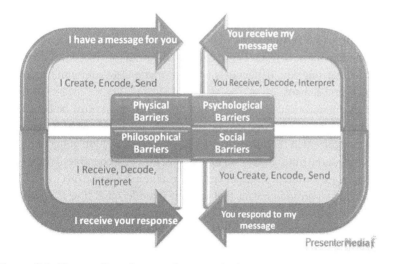

Figure 8.1 The complicated nature of communication.

message is encoded, as does the emotional tone of the receiver on how the message is decoded.

Given this complexity, consider how many things can go off the rails in an organization. Consider the potential barriers to accuracy. First of all, I have to use the words available to me and encode a message to you. If I put the words in a letter or an email, then I will have to be especially skillful as a writer if I want you to pick up not just the formal content of the words, but also what I am trying to convey to you emotionally. Let's say I can't be bothered with trying to write, because it is just too time-consuming; so, instead, I send the message to you through one, two, three, or more intermediary people (think of an upper-level manager wanting the line staff to do something differently with a client). If I send the message through one or more people, the message is vulnerable to the degradation of information that we experience whenever we play the Telephone game. The more important the message is, the more potentially problematic and ambiguous it is; and the more powerful I am, the more you are going to use your interpretive skills to figure out what I *really* meant. Your interpretations, like my message, will be affected by differences between us. The more alike we are in this range of diversity, the more likely we are to share basic styles and meanings and the more comfortable we may be with asking each other for clarification if we are not sure about what the message means. On the other hand, the more different we are, the more open every communication is to misinterpretation and the less likely it is that we will seek clarification.

As we see, nobody has to intentionally misconstrue information; it just happens. The more stress and pressure there are, the less likely the message is to be accurate. While the words in the message may be clear, the emotional content may be confusing. If I don't determine that you actually received the message that I intended, then all kinds of mischief may unfold that could negatively impact trust in our relationships for years. And all this happens without anyone intending any harm or even being consciously aware of what has happened! Throw in someone who deliberately wants to manipulate communication and the result can be chaos.

For an organizational body to be healthy, information must be constantly flowing around the organization, up and down, back and forth. It is important to recognize that there are many forms of communication going on in any group at the same time, and not all of it is conscious or recognized. When communication goes underground, all kinds of trouble can occur. The *Commitment to Open Communication* means that we have to understand how that happens and why, learn how to recognize it sooner rather than later, and know how to respond to it and get the flow of conscious communication going again.

Leaders must learn how to eliminate barriers that are blocking the flow of information, including making sure that people have the information they need to do their jobs. To know how to improve the flow of communication within an organization, we must know a great deal about what goes wrong in communication and develop some workable concepts about how to get the communication back on a better track.

We Are a Microcosm: Race, Class, Position, and Power

To understand what happened in the story we recounted, we need to look at the ways in which our organizations become microcosms of the larger world in which they are embedded. Every single person is a culture unto him- or herself. We each interpret messages we receive through the lenses of our own experience and differ based on age, gender, race, religion, ethnicity, education, experience, class, status, sexual orientation, gender identity, and region. Human service delivery systems tend to have structures that are similar across client populations and across geographic regions, so let's take a moment to look at those characteristics.

Agency leadership in social service organizations, especially in acute care programs, residential programs for children or adults, juvenile justice facilities, shelters, transitional living programs, and group homes tend to be made up of individuals who are better educated and more experienced than staff, earn more money, and have minimal contact with clients. In our neck of the woods, more often than not, they are Caucasian.

At the other end of the spectrum are the front-line workers (variably known as "milieu staff," "child-care staff," "shelter aides," "youth division aides," "youth counselors," "mental health aides," "therapy aides," "ward staff," "line staff," "sociotherapists," "mental health techs," "behavioral specialists," and "support staff"). They often earn very little money, work long hours (often doing a lot of overtime to compensate for the low wages), and have a high school diploma and maybe an associate's degree and sometimes even a bachelor's degree. They are often inexperienced, but there are usually a handful of very experienced workers. They spend 90% of their workday with clients and managing any number of challenging behavioral issues. And in our region, more often than not, they are people of color.

Between these two groups are a hybrid of professional staff and middle managers. They make a little more money than their milieu worker coworkers and a little less than senior managers. They tend to be more diverse in their cultural/racial makeup, and although they spend a lot of time interacting directly with clients, they have the option to retreat to their own space if overwhelmed. Teachers have prep periods, program managers have planning and paperwork time, and social workers have private offices.

This is not to suggest that any of these jobs are easy, but the milieu job is pretty relentless and offers the worker very little formal respite from what can only be characterized as a very challenging workday. Although milieu staff are the backbone of such programs, the pressures and challenges are enormous. Turnover is quite high, and many of them see themselves as foot soldiers. They are used to manage clients with very difficult behavior, and eventually they are chewed up and spit out by the system. On some level, the organization communicates to them that their value depends on their ability to contain difficult behavior. If things are out of control on their shift, they are viewed as incompetent, ineffective, or weak. Since their real value is their ability to control the environment, failing to do this seriously diminishes their value. So, if a child acts out, destroys property, hurts someone, or runs away on their watch, the attitude is "What do we need you for? If you cannot keep kids in check, you are not much help to us." They may not get such direct feedback, but they do get more subtle cues.

The race and class issues always percolate just under the surface or, in some cases, just above it. People of color, especially the milieu staff, feel very vulnerable in this structure. They feel that they are expendable. They receive not-so-subtle messages from those in power that their fortunes and longevity are tied to their ability to contain inappropriate behavior, and they do not have the luxury afforded their better-credentialed colleagues of retreating to their office or the staff lounge when things get dicey. In our story this attitude was inadvertently conveyed by the attitude of Brian and the Residential Director, who failed to discuss with the workers their assumption that they should just be able to reduce the holds with the children.

It is not uncommon for teams to develop plans for children who are struggling, plans grounded in having a milieu staff member shadow a child for the better part of a day. In some cases, this response becomes not an interim plan but *the* plan. Often the worker put in this position feels that he or she must just soldier on, because these kinds of assignments demonstrate how the workers add value and why they are valued. It also does not hurt that these kinds of assignments are generally the route to overtime and better compensation.

This dynamic is set up not because everyone has thought it through, but because no one has done so. It is set up because generations of significant power differentials between and among people become the default position in the organization and often end up being the latest reenactment in a lifetime of reenactments in this racially and economically divided country. In our story, when the administrators mandated change, it was not because they had a conscious, thought-out strategy about how the milieu staff should accomplish a reduction in restraint. They just wanted it to happen, and their meeting time was coming to a close, so they made a new rule. In doing so, they reverted to the traditional organizational methodology that had existed since the place had been founded: just tell the staff what to do and they will do it.

After days or weeks of trying to contain difficult behavior, the milieu worker may begin to fray around the edges. He or she will probably not ask for help because to do so will demonstrate that he or she might not be up to the task and might reduce the opportunity to earn a living. Other workers in middle management or professional positions may not pick up signs of distress in milieu staff. They may not feel the same level of pressure felt by milieu staff because they can get away to their office, a conference, or a staff meeting. The drain of this role on staff members is significant, but they do not acknowledge it and others may not notice it.

After managing very troubled children for prolonged periods, the milieu worker may begin to lose patience and perspective and may resort to more aggressive or punitive tactics to exert control. At some point the milieu worker burns out and blows up, and may end up either saying or doing something inappropriate with the child; alternatively, the worker begin to check out, perhaps calling in sick or becoming inattentive. The child or family complains and the worker is either spoken to, if the infraction is small, or disciplined and even terminated if the infraction is significant.

The disciplinary response then reinforces the sense that the milieu staff are vulnerable and are only useful when they can prevent problems from surfacing. The sense in the organization, at least among the milieu staff, is that they are spare parts. They are used up, worn out, and then dismissed. The professionals and the managers are not treated in so dismissive a fashion. Their level of exposure to toxic behavior is far better managed by them and for them. The power differentials are thereby reinforced and further embedded.

Addressing Diversity for Real

It is predicted that in the coming years, our workforce will become increasingly diverse. This is important for many reasons, not the least of which is that "diversity trumps ability" in solving many different problems. The greater the complexity of the problem, the more we need a wide variety of perspectives, interpretations, and abilities. But it also means that we must get better at communicating accurately with each other.

Brian gives an example of how miscommunication, particularly of values, can become embedded in the automatic reflexes that develop in a culture. It takes a *Commitment to Open Communication,* paired with the other commitments, for people to feel safe enough to have these kinds of conversations.

Several months ago, we held a large group meeting to discuss our organization's implementation of Sanctuary. We have been at this for almost a decade now and we still have our ups and downs, and we always will. We pulled together a large group of staff to talk about where we are doing well and where we are still struggling. As the discussion progressed, a staff member from one of our mental health clinics talked about the recent addition of some team-building activities at their staff meeting. She offered this as an example of an improvement. One of the clerical staff from that clinic, an African-American woman we will call Jane, said that she had made that suggestion a year ago at a staff meeting and nothing was done about it. Then, several weeks ago, a clinician made the same suggestion and the clinic leadership decided it was a good idea.

Immediately after Jane made the statement, a statement that suggested that people who are not clinicians or people who are not white are not always listened to in the organization. A senior manager, Bill, who is white, offered an explanation for why her suggestion might not have been heard. He said that perhaps Jane had not made her case persuasively enough, or perhaps the clinic was just not ready to act on her suggestion. A second manager chimed in and supported Bill's assessment of the situation. There was an audible rumble in the room and a good deal of side conversation, but no one challenged these two managers. Finally, a third manager, Mary, simply said, "I am wondering what just happened here. It seems there is a good deal of side conversation about something that was just said, and I am wondering if someone would be willing to say what that's about."

Shortly after Mary asked the question, several staff members spoke up. One of them said, "It always goes that way. A staff member shares a point of view; a manager offers an explanation that discounts that point of view, and then another manager supports the first manager. People feel shut down and discounted." Jane, who had originally raised the issue, indicated that this was the way she felt today and this was the way she felt about the reaction to her idea a year ago. This exchange led to a useful conversation in the group about race, class, position, and power.

What became evident was how easy it is to shut down conversation and shut down the dissenting voice. Additionally, it was clear that this conversation would not have happened if Mary had remained a bystander and had not invited the feedback.

An important shift for people in positions of leadership is the ability not just to handle dissent when it occurs but to actually search for it. When people begin to find their voice it is frequently clumsy, and they are prone to say what's on their mind in somewhat offensive ways. This is a problem that arises as a result of staff not being taught the skills necessary for participatory settings from childhood. Many adults have no idea about how to voice their concerns clearly, openly, and respectfully; persist even when they are ignored; listen deeply; welcome compromise and make concessions to get the job done; and then synthesize many different points of view. Instead, they grow up thinking that every conversation is a win-lose situation and that when it comes to complex groups processes, we all win or we all lose [172].

One of these conversations will not undo several hundred years of discrimination. We have to keep at it. That's why we call these things "commitments." No person or organization is going to get it right immediately, finally, or forever. The *Commitment to Open Communication*, like the other commitments, is a goal that we aim for, and on a good day we reach the goal.

The Transparent Organization—and That Means Everybody

The *Commitment to Open Communication* means doing the best you can to develop a "transparent organization," where there are as few barriers to open, direct, honest, and sensitive communication as possible and where there is no room for secrecy, backroom deals, herds of elephants in the room, and skeletons in the closet. As two prominent organizational consultants have pointed out, *"We won't be able to rebuild trust in institutions until leaders learn how to communicate honestly—and create organizations where that's the norm"* (p. 54) [173]

We make a *Commitment to Open Communication* because communication is crucial to building connections and a sense of community. If we cannot communicate our thoughts, opinions, and ideas, we remain isolated and cut off from each other. Open communication also allows for the possibility for self-correction and group problem solving. If we can state our opinion and challenge another point of view, then we can help make better decisions and better protect ourselves in the process. Open communication leads to better decision making and faster error correction. The transparency that occurs as a result of open communication protects against potential abuses of power and makes for a safer environment overall.

Conversations create culture, and to achieve a healthy organizational culture there has to be a "culture of candor" [174, 175]. Organizational transparency means that people can speak their minds freely without fear of retribution. Knowledge and information flow freely within acceptable legal and personal boundaries, allowing for ethically responsible decision making. Transparency means interacting with people honestly and authentically in a way that builds credibility. Tactical transparency means selecting tools and techniques to create such a culture of authenticity and openness [176].

Transparency does not mean sharing everything with everybody. There are ethical, legal, competitive, technical, and resource issues that have to be considered, but despite what may at times be barriers to transparency, openness is occurring more quickly than many of us might like to see. Blogs, social networking, and all forms of electronic media are exposing the inner workings of organizations more rapidly than ever before. The more transparent your organization is, the less likely it is that you will be trapped in deceit, cover-ups, or simple withholding of information that makes you look like a liar. Whatever you're worried about, it is probably going to be out there, somewhere in cyberspace, and it's better to plan ahead for how you want information to be disseminated rather than being surprised, misinterpreted, and misunderstood [176]. Here Brian describes a change in his own practice.

One of the practices we have begun in recent years is to share a summary of the budget with all staff. While we have made an effort to engage managers at all levels of the organization in the budgeting process, it is not practical to engage *everyone. What is possible, however, is to share with staff the priorities we have set and why we have set those priorities. People may not always agree with the decisions that we make, but if we can be clearer about all the competing priorities and objectives, at least they can understand the context. We have found that this practice goes a long way toward helping staff better understand the entire business and where that business is going. A crucial step in becoming more democratic is educating our staff by sharing more with them about the business we are in and how it works. Several years ago I was having lunch with several staff members, and we discussed the results of a fundraiser we had over the weekend. It was one of our most successful events, and we raised approximately $300,000. When I quoted the number, I could see people's eyes open and there was a lot of shifting of eyes among the group. I asked them what that was about and one of the staff bravely asked if that money would be reflected in pay raises. I indicated that I was not sure and went on to tell them that it was not a whole lot of money. They look confused, because $300,000 certainly is a lot of money. I told them that $300,000 was a little less than one week's payroll. There was an audible gasp. They had no idea of what kind of funds are needed to manage the operation.*

Workers often assume that the people at the top lack transparency. Their assumption may be right. Much of this goes back to the issue of nonviolence, trust, and maintaining a sense of moral and social safety. If people are afraid to say what's on their mind or fail to trust leaders or colleagues, they will keep important information to themselves. On the other hand, their attitude may become a self-fulfilling prophecy.

It's important to remember that the door swings both ways. An organization that makes a *Commitment to Open Communication* is not just making that commitment at the leadership level. It means that everybody has to be more authentic in their communications with everybody else. In an organization we are constantly building or betraying trust, and trusting relationships are a necessary component of everything we do. Figure 8.2 offers some general tips for building transparency.

The Commitment to Open Communication and Trauma-Informed Practice

Healing Organizational Dissociation

The *Commitment to Open Communication* aims at early identification of an evolving collective disturbance and, ultimately, prevention of the destructive aspects of a collective disturbance [171, 177]. To become more effective at managing these kinds of collective and emergent situations, staff members must realize that they exist. In our highly individualistic culture, this can be a hard sell. In general, we are not accustomed to perceiving unconscious motivations of individuals, much less those of entire groups. In the case of a collective disturbance, what occurs cannot

Figure 8.2 Building transparency.

simply be explained by the usual emotional contagion that occurs in groups. A collective disturbance has a structure that may not always be immediately visible, because so much is going on underground and often those who might be responsible for leading the team out of the mess are themselves deeply, though unwittingly, involved in creating the problem (Figure 8.3).

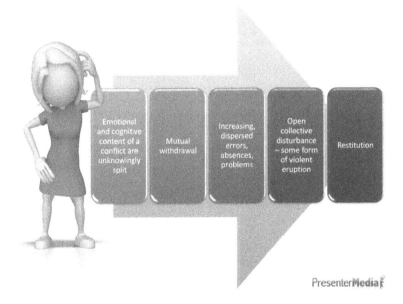

Figure 8.3 Stages of a collective disturbance.

In the story that opened this chapter, the collective disturbance originated in an unrecognized and unverbalized conflict between Brian and the Residential Director. It wasn't that they actually disagreed with each other; they both wanted to eliminate restraints. But they prematurely closed on a solution expressed as "let's tighten the screws and push." And it was the Residential Director who would have to implement that pseudosolution, hence the unspoken conflict. He was unknowingly trapped in a loyalty conflict. He wanted to please higher authority, but doing so required him to oppress those he was supposed to protect. Without conscious awareness that there even was a problem or a way to articulate it, he automatically dissociated the conflict while the feelings remained.

The feelings did not surface in their original meeting, but they became more evident when the Residential Director had to deliver the decision to the staff. But at that point, he had participated in making the decision and the goal was a worthy one, so the conflict became even more deeply buried. If the managers and staff members are able to confront their own unspoken conflicts, they can prevent or at least terminate a collective disturbance and, in doing so, reduce the level of violence within an organization. To prevent collective disturbance in a community, there must be a general recognition that group dynamics occur in any group, are largely unconscious, and must be identified as quickly as possible. There are early signs that a collective disturbance is emerging, as illustrated in Figure 8.4.

Figure 8.4 Signs of impending collective disturbance.

A group must become alert to these signs. The obvious signs in the story were first the staff complaints, which were only heard as griping, and then the widespread increase in staff injuries. Had other people besides Brian and the Residential Director been involved in reviewing those trends, the disturbance might have been more readily highlighted. Instead, the two main agents simply kept reassuring each other, further submerging the conflict and keeping the loyalty conflict dissociated.

In general, less experienced people will be more susceptible to the emotion surrounding an emerging disturbance, but are likely to mistake their anxiety for something else, and their attempts to remedy the situation may in fact make it worse. Meanwhile, more experienced members of the community will see the problem emerging, but may disavow their own perceptions simply because no one else seems to see it.

To fulfill the *Commitment to Open Communication*, a community needs a strong, critical mass of people who are able to look at the unconscious, shine some light into the shadows, and speak up about the problem. This is especially true when a group is under stress because of the impact of this stress on group functioning: perceptions narrow and the context of the situation is lost, while top-down communication increases and bottom-up communication decreases. As a result, feedback loops erode and groups regress to doing whatever they have done in the past, regardless of whether such strategies were effective. The organizational grapevine gets poisoned with destructive rumors and gossip, interpersonal conflict increases, and complex team behaviors decrease.

The first step in improving communication, and often the most difficult, is to determine that there is a problem. This requires that someone on the staff, not necessarily the leader, be prepared to call together the other members and see if there is a consensus that this is, in fact, a group problem and not an individual problem. We use Red Flag Reviews to accomplish this. While it is true that the emotions of individual patients and individual staff members may be triggered by their own unresolved issues, these may not constitute a group problem.

If a staff consensus is reached that a group problem is developing, the next step is to obtain an "outside" consultation with a member of the team not currently involved in the emerging conflict. The reason for an outside consultation is that it is extremely difficult to maintain objectivity when one is caught up in a collective disturbance, as our chapter-opening story illustrates. It is best to involve someone who is not in the immediate emotional situation as a sounding board and an objective voice. The "outsider" may be another staff member who has been on vacation and thus is not currently caught up in the drama, or it may just be someone who does not work with that particular group. The involved staff and the outside consultant then design an appropriate intervention that will restore safety, reestablish boundaries, and rebalance power.

There are no definitive rules for how to deal with a collective disturbance because every situation is different. But if we look at what the leaders
in our story finally did, we can draw some conclusions. Simple and obvious
things matter: Be nice to people when you know you have screwed up and do
something that is different from what you have been doing. Bring food; this is
a way of saying that you really mean to provide some comfort. If you are in a
position of leadership, admit your mistakes publicly and openly. Give people
a chance to talk about what they have been through, what they perceive, and
what needs to be different, and give airspace for the grievances. Apologize and
mean it.

These are powerful learning experiences, and if you have made the
Commitment to Social Learning, then you know it is important to share what
you have learned from the experience, widely and broadly. Once the emotions
have been integrated with the reasoning and experience related to the events, it
is time to formulate a plan. The staff then implement the plan, often by introducing the changes in a Community Meeting. Do not be surprised, however,
when things improve immediately. It's not magic but simply the result of paying
attention to collective group processes.

We have found that organizations in the process of Sanctuary implementation are prone to these collective disturbances because they are likely to arise
around any significant change. As you begin to change organizational beliefs
and practices, there will be periods of misalignment. People will be zigging
when they are supposed to be zagging. People will talk about the commitments
but will not always live them, because they are still unlearning old habits and
have not yet developed new ones. It can be unsettling when we are trying to
change; tensions can run high, and sometimes the organization can run off the
rails. If you keep talking and engaging, you can work through these difficulties.
It's also important to maintain a sense of humor and recognize that even the
smartest and most experienced individual can be trapped in complex group
processes and have no clue that this is happening.

Transparency When There Is a Crisis

When a crisis hits an organization, groups do what they have always done: they
"circle the wagons." Huddling together and figuring out what is going on, getting accurate information, and taking whatever emergency steps are necessary
is indeed important. But do not be too careful and thereby viewed as being
secretive or hiding something. Move ahead thoughtfully and as calmly as possible. Do not tell anyone that you are sure of things when you are not, but do
assure them you will tell them as soon as you have accurate information.

Be aware that there are different kinds of crises. A "meteor crisis" occurs
when something unexpected happens and lands on your organization like a

meteor. A "predator crisis" occurs when someone deliberately acts to harm your organization. A "breakdown crisis" happens when the organization, for some reason, simply fails to function [176]. Whatever the cause of the crisis, it is essential to stick to your principles, take the high ground, and stay as calm as possible. If you are in a leadership position, your employees are particularly likely to look to you as a guide when a crisis hits.

In a Sanctuary organization, we insist that everyone develop and carry a Safety Plan. We insist on this because we know that under stress we do not think clearly. It is best if we can think about what might go wrong and how we might react before something actually happens. This is why it is a good idea for organizations to develop emergency management plans and conduct drills on a regular basis. Communication often gets neglected when a crisis hits. Everyone involved works feverishly to manage the crisis at hand, but unless you really pay attention, it is easy to forget to communicate important information to people who need to know what is going on. Even when you work hard to manage a crisis, it is not really resolved until all the appropriate stakeholders have been notified and briefed on your efforts. In most emergency management plans, someone is assigned the role of communicator with key stakeholders. Unless this responsibility is clearly assigned, it is easy for it to be overlooked.

It is very difficult to maintain transparency in the face of a predator crisis. Such a crisis is caused by someone deliberately trying to harm your organization. In the case of an anonymous complaint, you can never be sure who is making the complaint and for what reason. Although our instinct in these situations is to circle the wagons, we are not sure how large a circle to form. The tendency is to form a tight circle, with just the immediate team or trusted colleagues. Although this approach is understandable, it can further undermine trust in the organization and drive staff members further apart. As in a terrorist attack, the real lingering casualty of these events is the impact they have on our trust and sense of well-being. This impact lingers long after the agency's reputation is repaired. Clearly, there are no absolutes, but in general, we have found more, rather than less, communication at these times to be desirable. Keeping secrets in organizations is generally not a healthy approach, and creates the potential for more misinformation and erosion of trust. Brian describes a predator crisis.

Some time back, we were confronted with several anonymous allegations of wrongdoing. Because these allegations were anonymous, we were not sure where they were coming from or who was responsible. We knew they were false, but we did not know how to defend ourselves and the organization. For many weeks, we senior leaders kept the information to ourselves and did not share it with our staff. Frankly, we did not know who we could trust. We became completely absorbed by the situation. As leaders we became isolated, withdrawn, and disengaged from the day-to-day events. Important details were ignored, and little if any joy was derived from the work. It was an awful time. It was the closest I have come to throwing in the towel and finding another line of work.

After careful consideration the Chief Executive Officer and I finally decided that we needed to share this information honestly and directly with the staff, and we conducted a series of staff meetings in which we reviewed what had been alleged. We described our take on the situation and the steps we had taken to investigate what had been alleged. Although we held these meetings with some trepidation, we walked away from them feeling liberated. We had taken a risk; we had decided to trust our staff and take a gamble that they fundamentally trusted us. We received feedback and positive support. We felt not only relieved but rejuvenated. It was a clear example of how debilitating a loss of trust can be in a system. Once we decided to put our issues on the table with our staff, things began to radically improve and we were all once again pulling in the same direction.

Implications for Open Communication Leadership

Leaders must believe that the free flow of information is constructive and vital to healthy organizational function. Just as in the Telephone game, the fewer links there are between sender and receiver, the less likely that the message will be distorted. Good leaders are good listeners; they listen for what is said and what is not said. In the *Commitment to Open Communication* transparency is everyone's responsibility, not just that of upper management. While we want our leaders to be more open and honest with us about their intentions and direction, we need to be open and honest as well. This is a difficult lesson to learn in an organization. When leaders are forced to speculate about what is really happening in a program they are just as likely to fill in the blanks as anyone else, and the conclusions they arrive at are likely to confirm their preconceived notions.

Collective Disturbance and Divided Loyalty

The story we have shared is a good example of how easily unaddressed issues such as divided loyalty can become a source of collective disturbance. The Sanctuary Model requires a shift away from the militaristic hierarchy that governs so many social service delivery settings to a more democratic mode of organization. But such a change does not come easily to most settings. In the traditional hierarchy, there is a chain of command that moves from top to bottom, with each lower level in the hierarchy following the orders of the one above and finding ways to get each subordinate level to obey commands. One essential job of each subordinate manager is to protect and defend the manager above. This may be a clearly articulated expectation or may be more subtly inferred from the organizational norms once a person is hired.

In Sanctuary, this expectation is at least partly reversed in that one of the essential responsibilities of all managers is to protect the people they manage while helping them achieve peak performance. This is more in line with the idea of Servant Leadership, wherein the highest priority of a servant leader is to encourage, support, and enable subordinates to live up to their full potential and abilities [178]. Such a reversal of the status quo often results in fundamental conflict between managers, and if this is not fully understood, middle managers especially will be fearful, will not reveal the conflict, and will instead dissociate, laying the groundwork for a collective disturbance to begin to unfold.

Keeping Your Grapevine Healthy

About 70% of organizational information flows through the grapevine. Several national surveys found that employees used the grapevine as a communication source more than any other vehicle. The grapevine is effective because messages sent informally tend to communicate information far more rapidly than formal systems of communication. Communication over the grapevine will never disappear, but managers can try to make sure that the information traveling over the grapevine is accurate and not malicious by providing abundant and accurate information as early as possible. Rumors thrive when there is not enough accurate information, especially when stress is high.

When managers become aware that misinformation is traveling over the grapevine, they must do their best to get out the real story. If the rumor mill is riddled with misinformation, it is likely that the leaders did not do a good job of communicating accurately. It is better to clear up misunderstandings later rather than never. Becoming angry and frustrated about misinformation is not useful. Managers set an example for open communication, and staff can observe in practice that there are few subjects that are undiscussable—no elephants in the room.

It is not only the line staff, or the low-level people, in the organization who gossip; managers do it as well. Just like line staff, managers gossip to fill in the blanks. There is a difference between telling stories and gossip. Stories can communicate rules and values, diffuse values, preserve the organizational tradition and history, strengthen interpersonal relationships, provide influence for those who have little voice in the organization, and serve as a vehicle for change [179]. But gossip can be used as a form of aggression. Instead of futilely attempting to get people to stop gossiping, it's probably better to focus only on gossip that becomes malicious, bullying, and abusive, thereby endangering the safety and well-being of everyone. A good rule of thumb when deciding what gossip is and what a story is to ask oneself how the main character of the gossip or story would feel if he or she suddenly walked into the room and heard it.

Keeping the Communication Flowing

In Sanctuary organizations there is a great deal of emphasis on communication. Treatment Reviews, Team Meetings, Community Meetings, and Red Flag Reviews should happen regularly to ensure that people are consistently talking with one another and solving problems together. In fact, we suggest that a sure sign that stress is getting the better of the organization is a reduction in the number of opportunities for sharing information and working together. When staff people begin to see efforts to collaborate and work together as a distraction from their work rather than as central to their work, leaders should make sure that people are connecting with each other. They should not just go with the flow and continue to allow the fragmentation to snowball.

Healthy organizations expect people to work together and should develop processes and systems to ensure that this is happening consistently. Managers and staff should make efforts to ensure that the system remains flexible and responsive to individual needs while still guaranteeing fair treatment for everyone. They do this by focusing less on making new rules for every new situation and instead by committing themselves to engaging in processes that examine, assess, and evolve adequate responses to complex individual and group problems. In this way, the organization remains open to new information and learning, and it can readily and spontaneously engage in processes of information sharing and knowledge creation that allow it to mobilize complex responses even in emergency situations.

Sanctuary Toolkit

Revealing the Elephants in the Room

Every organization seems to have undiscussable topics. These undiscussables are often the source of chronic collective disturbances. Some organizations have so many undiscussables that the elephants in the room crowd out everything else. The only thing that varies is which topic cannot be talked about and how paralyzing "organizational alexithymia," is to healthy function. We define organizational alexithymia as the inability at an organizational level to express distressing feelings that are already present. The undisussables can paralyze and completely block communication, suffocating the flow of organizational information (Figure 8.5).

Naming the elephant and determining how each person sees it is a good place to start. After looking at the organizational culture problems that the National Aeronautics and Space Administration (NASA) had after the Challenger disaster and the organizational dynamics that gave rise to the Enron scandal, two organizational development consultants made some suggestions for how leaders can encourage naming of the elephants. One of the suggestions was to

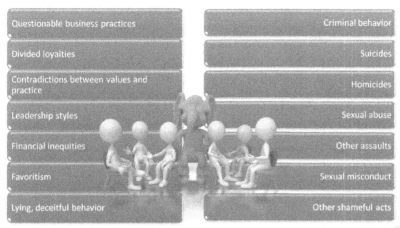

Figure 8.5 The undiscussables.

institute a Name-the-Elephant award so that people who have the courage to discuss the undiscussables are rewarded. Another suggestion was to create a "Naming Elephants" website where people can post comments anonymously (p. 83) [180]. Some people have suggested institutionalizing the tradition of a "corporate fool," someone who has free rein to say what most people can't—the traditional role of the fool under monarchy [174]. Here is one way Andrus is doing it:

> We have instituted an electronic suggestion/comment box at our organization. Staff can anonymously ask questions or post issues of concern to this box, and leaders periodically send an email with the concern and their response to the entire organization. Our only standard for questions or comments is that they be worded in a respectful manner and not be personal attacks. I think our willingness to distribute and answer all messages has been helpful and has indicated that we are willing to openly communicate. It has also been helpful by keeping us informed about what staff members are thinking and worrying about. There have been a fair number of surprises over the last year, and some issues have emerged that would not have occurred to me as being of significance. It has been a useful vehicle.

Many countries and organizations establish an ombudsman role. The traditional role of an ombudsman or ombudsperson, utilized far more often in Europe than in the United States, is to be the person whose job is to gather data and name the elephants. To do so, this person must be independent of the traditional hierarchy, and must maintain his or her own neutrality and guard everyone else's confidentiality. An ombudsperson can be an invaluable organizational asset for helping to resolve issues that are loaded with conflict.

One of the most important activities we do in the Sanctuary implementation process with organizations is to conduct a day-long retreat on this issue. It is impossible for an organization to move forward if it is mired in the past. It is crucial that the organizational elephants in the room be addressed and that the skeletons in the closet get put on the table, discussed, and then given a proper burial. In most cases these issues are hardly earthshaking, but the fact that we do not or cannot talk about them gives them more power than they deserve and prevents us from moving forward.

Using S.E.L.F. and Red Flags to Address Collective Disturbance

The key to addressing an evolving collective disturbance is to suspect that one might be going on. S.E.L.F. is a useful way to get at the deeper issues that may be the generative cause of the disturbance. If you look at the items in Figure 8.4, the signs of a collective disturbance are usually safety issues. Rising levels of safety concerns should give rise to a Red Flag Review. The Red Flag then provides the structure for looking at the emotions behind the erosion of safety, the losses that have happened and might continue to escalate if we continue on the same path, the losses we will have to address if we change, and a vision of where we want to go.

Communication Skill-Building

The process of improving communication requires skills that we often lack, even in executive positions, simply because we have never been taught them. Some formal systems have been developed that are quite useful and consistent with Sanctuary values. These can be introduced in orientation and taught to supervisors and staff, who then model these communication skills with clients.

Nonviolent Communication

Nonviolent communication is sometimes referred to as "compassionate communication." Its purpose is to strengthen our ability to inspire compassion in others and to respond compassionately to others and to ourselves [126]. Better communication skills can be learned, and an organization that embraces the *Commitment to Open Communication* may need to teach those skills and not just count on hiring people who are good communicators.

In his work on nonviolent communication, Rosenberg has offered some useful guidelines for improved listening and communicating skills that are consistent with a nonviolent approach. First, avoid using the verb *to be* without indicating that you are taking responsibility for what you are saying. It's better to say, "I think you were too harsh with that child" instead of "You were too harsh with that child." Second, try not to use words that are loaded with evaluation rather than just observation. Saying "You are irresponsible" does little but arouse the other person's defenses, whereas "I have noticed that you have been late three days in a row" guarantees that you are both observing something and taking responsibility for what you are saying. Third, don't confuse prediction with certainty. "You won't be on time tomorrow" would be better expressed as "I am concerned that you won't be on time tomorrow since you have been late three times this week." Finally, be specific in your communication and avoid generalities. Instead of making a specific complaint, such as "You always procrastinate and never get your reports in on time," try "I notice that you have not gotten your report to me on time in the last two months." Often when we listen to staff people talking about troubled clients, we hear the use of adverbs and adjectives that make what are actually personal observations sound very objective. "Jimmy is just a bad kid" is much different than "Jimmy really scared me today when he walked out and slammed the door." In the mental health professions, we often use diagnoses as a way of expressing an evaluation that sounds objective but that is not necessarily objective at all: "Susan is clearly a 'borderline'" or "Well, it's all you can expect from Timmy since he's a budding sociopath."

Being aware of how we say things becomes critically important when we need to confront negative behavior in each other (Figure 8.6). This is all part of creating a nonviolent environment where we can openly confront problems without intending to hurt, without retaliating, and with a clear intention to resolve our differences.

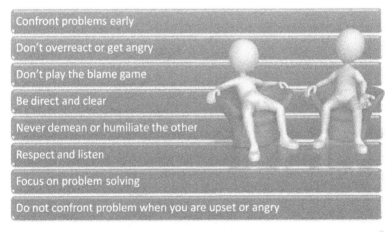

Confront problems early

Don't overreact or get angry

Don't play the blame game

Be direct and clear

Never demean or humiliate the other

Respect and listen

Focus on problem solving

Do not confront problem when you are upset or angry

PresenterMedia

Figure 8.6 Confronting negative behavior.

Authentic Conversations

In their book about having authentic conversations in organizations, the Showkeirs describe how to structure such a conversation [176]. Their ideas can be very helpful, particularly when the conversations you need to have are not necessarily conversations you want to have (Figure 8.7). These principles can be helpful regardless of who they are applied to: a peer, a supervisor, a supervisee, a client, a family member, or a friend. Such a structured conversation illustrates the connection between the *Commitment to Open Communication* and the *Commitment to Emotional Intelligence.* It also makes it more likely that both persons will learn something they didn't know before in such a conversation, and this honors the *Commitment to Social Learning.*

Making Room for Dialogue

Dialogue is a special form of conversation that goes beyond normal conversation, or at least what we think of as normal today. It is the kind of conversation we try to initiate in the Core Team process we described earlier. From the ancient Greeks to Native American tribal councils and Quaker practice, the capacity for dialogue has been recognized as a vital way of maintaining a peaceful community and arriving at better decisions.

The best-known descriptions of dialogue were presented by a quantum physicist, David Bohm. According to Bohm, dialogue encourages a group to learn collectively and produce new ways of thinking [181]. He thought that communication in human groups becomes blocked because of the basic cultural or

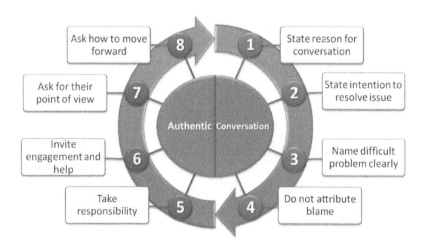

Figure 8.7 Authentic conversations.

subcultural assumptions that each person brings to any conversation. Groups of 20 to 40 people produce a microcosm of the larger world and will create their own microculture, along with their own shared meaning, language, and customs, if given the time to do so. To be productive, a dialogue must occur in an atmosphere of egalitarianism and the absence of coercive influences; is possible only when there is mutual trust and respect; requires deep listening with empathy; and involves bringing underlying assumptions out in the open in the absence of judgment and criticism.

Dialogue is the opposite of debate. In debate, the objective is to vanquish the opponent thus creating a win-lose situation. The objective of dialogue is to find some common ground, to establish shared meaning. Dialogue is also different from discussion, which also usually ends up as a win-lose conversation.

In the typical workplace, people from a wide variety of subcultures may need to interact and share a common purpose. Otherwise they will never be able to think together and work out complex problems and conflicts. As Bohm described the process, dialogue works best with 20 to 40 people seated facing one another in a single circle. He believed that smaller groups lack the diversity needed to reveal these tendencies and will generally emphasize familiar personal and family roles and relationships [182]. This speaks to the power of the Community Meeting and the Core Team, where typically at least 20 people are in the room.

The Sanctuary Model, the Seven Commitments, S.E.L.F., and the Sanctuary Toolkit all provide human service organizations with a trauma-informed, scientifically based shared meaning system that allows administrators, clinicians, line staff, children, adults, and families to get on the same page so that they can realistically and openly communicate. The Sanctuary Model itself was created through a multidecade dialogue with a wide variety of representative groups and cannot be attributed to a single author. Out of this dialogue, something new has emerged that could not have been predicted by its individual parts, and that is what is at the heart of the practice of dialogue—creating meaningful conversations from which new ideas, strategies, and tactics may emerge. The Core Team, comprised of 20–40 people, has many opportunities to practice the art of dialogue throughout the process of Sanctuary implementation.

Organizational Communication Plan

One of the first tasks of the Steering Committee while attending the Sanctuary Institute is to figure out what they are going to communicate, how they are going to communicate, and to whom they will establish communication about Sanctuary implementation when they return to their home organization. But planning and implementing the communication plan doesn't stop there; communication must be an ongoing process designed to spread the knowledge about the Sanctuary Model, the Sanctuary Commitments, and S.E.L.F.

In organization after organization, we have found that years of stress and strain have hampered the ability to think, plan, and work together. The stories are eerily similar from organization to organization, region to region, even country to country. The pressure of doing more and more with fewer and fewer resources has only pushed us further apart. It has somehow convinced us that this is the way it should be. Frequently, we hear staff members at our facilities suggest that a group problem-solving discussion is taking them away from their work. Time and again, we have found that the more stressed people are, the less they talk to each other and the more likely yesterday's failed solutions will be applied to tomorrow's problems. Now more than ever, we need to make a *Commitment to Open Communication*. We all need to see *Open Communication* as part of our *Commitment to Social Responsibility*. We sometimes need to say difficult things for the good of the community. Let's move on to our seventh and final commitment: the *Commitment to Social Responsibility*.

Chapter 9

Commitment to Social Responsibility

Injustice anywhere is a threat to justice everywhere.

Dr. Martin Luther King, Jr.
Letter from Birmingham Jail, April 16, 1963

SUMMARY: *The Commitment to Social Responsibility in the Sanctuary Model covers some very thorny issues that present difficult dilemmas within any organization and within our society as a whole. It is about the delicate balancing act between individual rights and responsibilities and the rights and responsibilities of the community. The issues of social justice and moral safety are at the heart of trauma, and the restoration of a sense of a "just world" is a critical component of healing.*

A Vision of Social Responsibility

- We recognize that fairly distributing individual and social justice is the key to having a peaceful, nonviolent, and safe organization.
- Shared ethical principles are the basis for our families, our institutions, and our society—in word and deed.
- We know that we must always balance our individual needs with the responsibility we have to our communities.
- We now know that our desire to punish is largely a desire for vengeance and that it produces a never-ending cycle of violence unless we stop it.
- At the same time, we recognize that the desire for retaliation is natural to our species, and that therefore we have an obligation to help each other manage the emotions associated with the desire for revenge and move each other toward restoration instead.
- We are committed to forms of justice that are restorative, not retributive.
- We recognize that all of the time we are either part of a solution or part of a problem; a healthy organization there are no bystanders.

- We have learned to recognize that injustice to one is injustice to all, that human rights are a critical determinant of human survival
- We realize that the only thing that sets humanity apart from the other forms of life we share this planet with is our power—and the responsibility that goes along with it—to decide whether to support destruction and annihilation or support life in its myriad forms

What Do We Mean by Social Responsibility?

Social Responsibility and the Team

A new child-care worker, Chuck, was hired for one of the younger children's units at Andrus. Chuck presented well in the interview. His resume showed good experiences, and he was a friendly, engaging young man. In the early days of his employment he seemed quite capable, and took to the work with enthusiasm and zeal. He said all the right things to his supervisor and followed up quickly and thoroughly on all assignments. He seemed to be a budding star.

About six weeks into his employment his coworkers raised a concern. Apparently over the prior weekend he had brought a movie in from home to show the children. The movie contained many adult situations and themes. The workers on his shift, Tanya and Roy, who had a very good relationship with their Program Manager, Larry, felt the film was inappropriate for the young children. The shift leader, Roy, decided to shut off the movie and move the group to a different activity. Chuck became quite annoyed and argued with Roy that the content was not inappropriate for the children. Chuck finally acquiesced, but Roy and Tanya were uncomfortable with the situation. On Monday, Roy reported the situation to Larry. Larry spoke with Chuck, who still felt that his coworkers had overreacted but indicated that he understood their point of view.

Two weekends later, Chuck came into work with a teen-rated video game. He was working with preteen and younger children. He spoke with Roy and Tanya about the game and was told that it was not appropriate for young children; he was advised to keep it in his bag. Later that afternoon, several children were out on a trip with Roy. Tanya was in the kitchen getting dinner ready, and Chuck was in the activity room with three of the boys leading an afternoon activity. After a while, Tanya left the kitchen and went to check on the activity group Chuck was leading. She found the door to the activity room locked. She unlocked the door and found Chuck and the three boys playing the video game that he had been told to keep in his bag.

Tanya asked to speak with Chuck in the hall and told him he that needed to put the game away and engage in the activity that was planned. Chuck became angry, told her that she was being unreasonable, and suggested that she was babying the children. Tanya remained firm and reminded him that they had discussed this earlier, and that he had taken it upon himself to undermine a team decision. Chuck went back to the room, turned off the video game, and announced to the children that Tanya didn't like it, so they had to stop playing. At the end of the shift, Tanya informed Chuck that she would be speaking with the Program Manager about the video game and Chuck's behavior.

The next day, Tanya spoke with the Program Manager. It was clear that Chuck had boundary issues and was not willing to listen to and learn from his more experienced coworkers. The Program Manager spoke to Chuck again, asked him what had happened, and explained why we do not expose the children to media with adult themes. Chuck indicated that he thought the team and the supervisor were being overly protective, and he made disparaging remarks about team members and how they coddled the children. It became clear to the Program Manager that this young man was not going to be a good fit with what they were trying to do on the unit. The Program Manager contacted the Residential Director and asked for a meeting. He recommended that Chuck be let go. Chuck was terminated later that day.

Although the outcome was not good for Chuck, it was clear that he was not cut out for the work on this unit. It was also clear that the staff had behaved in a socially responsible fashion and maintained their position in the face of unethical and inappropriate behavior on the part of a coworker. They understood clearly that their mission was to help and protect the children, not their coworker. They were honest with him, honest with their manager, and willing to do the right thing despite the difficulties. They recognized that it meant that they would end up being short-staffed for some time. It was likely that several agency staff, whom Chuck had befriended, would vilify them. Despite these barriers they still took the right, socially responsible action.

Social Responsibility Means Refusing to Be a Bystander

This story highlights a particularly challenging dilemma for social service delivery and a central focus of the *Commitment to Social Responsibility*. Throughout this book and in *Destroying Sanctuary,* we have discussed the powerful tendency of human beings and human service systems to respond to the mentally ill and socially disenfranchised with all manner of punitive, abusive, disrespectful, coercive, and condescending interactions. In *Destroying Sanctuary* we discussed how, in any institutional setting, we are both actors and bystanders [12]. When confronted with acts of dehumanization on the part of our colleagues, subordinates, or superiors, we must act to protect our clients, ourselves, each other, and our organizations. To do so, we need to know something about how to intervene as socially responsible helpers in order to make things better, not worse.

In our story, Tanya, Roy, and Larry were all acutely aware of their social responsibility to the children, to each other, to the team, and to the institution.

When they saw something wrong, they tried to correct it honestly and directly, and when their individual actions failed they didn't let the issue drop, as we so often do. They sought a constructive remedy. They made it their problem, not somebody else's. They refused to be bystanders.

To avoid being a bystander who tolerates unethical behavior, early intervention and prevention works best. The team worked promptly to intervene with Chuck's behavior before the children were hurt. The children then saw adults actively caring for them and setting limits even with each other. The outcome could have been different if the issue had been ignored, and we know of many times where dreadful things have occurred in organizations because it did.

The reason is that because bystanders become increasingly passive in the face of abusive and unethical behavior, action becomes increasingly difficult. Just as there can be a deteriorating spiral of perpetration in which each act of violence becomes increasingly easy to accomplish, there can also be a deteriorating cycle of passivity. As perpetrators assume control over a system, their power increases unless bystanders put up sufficient resistance to successfully counter it. At some point, however, resistance on the part of bystanders becomes extremely difficult because the perpetrator's power has become too concentrated, and unless sufficient numbers of bystanders organize and take action, one person alone will be overwhelmed.

Team treatment in our story was an advantage because none of the staff members had to confront this problem alone. They also knew that they each had a responsibility to act. That's important because when it comes to being a bystander or taking action, group influences are powerful. It has been repeatedly demonstrated that the more people there are who could respond to a situation, the less likely it is that anyone will. What follows is the emergence of a group norm of passive nonaction. Interestingly, however, all it takes is for one bystander in a group to take some sort of positive action against perpetration, and others will follow. Resistance to perpetration on the part of bystanders, both in words and in actions, influences others to become active instead of passive [183, 184].

Although leaders cannot act alone, it is crucial that staff consistently see their leaders stepping up and challenging unethical or inappropriate behavior. In our story, it was critical that Larry, the Program Manager, took the staff members' concerns seriously and that Larry's supervisors did the same. If leaders appear tentative or fearful, it is unlikely that the people who report to them will step into the breach. When a leader does not respond, it conveys a clear message that responding is dangerous or, even worse, that the behavior is not really a problem. When leaders become passive bystanders, all kinds of confusing and troubling messages are conveyed to people below them in the organizational hierarchy. By the same token, the response needs to be thoughtful and measured. Responses to unethical or inappropriate behavior must occur but should not be excessive.

At a basic, down-to-earth level, Tanya, Roy, and Larry were making decisions about social justice and the common good, the two important aspects
of the *Commitment to Social Responsibility*. That is the basic juggling act we all
perform when we have to balance our own interests with the interests of the
community. In the Sanctuary Model, "social responsibility" refers to the interactive ethical tension between individual needs and the needs of the group in
which each individual is embedded. Our *Commitment to Social Responsibility*
means that every member of the organization, from the Board of Directors to
the clients who seek help, are part of a larger living whole and that every individual therefore has an obligation to protect his or her own well-being AND the
well-being of the whole. However, this commitment is usually tested only when
there is conflict between individual and group needs.

For Tanya and Roy, and even Larry, doing nothing might have been much
easier and less time-consuming, although it never is in the long run. But they
each made an individual and a group decision that the potential harm to the
children, to the unit, and to the integrity of the program was being compromised, and they decided to act. Such conflicts arise in any caregiving setting
much more often than we would like to admit. So, what is it about us that
enables people like Tanya, Roy, and Larry to look at a situation, make a moral
judgment that something wrong is happening, and move to stop it? And even
beyond that, what makes people like Tanya, Roy, and Larry decide to work
in professions where they are called upon to make those kind of judgments
frequently, where they have to care enough about somebody else's children to
put the needs of the children and of the institution before their own individual
comfort? Trying to answer that question leads us into thorny deep territory
about human nature, justice, revenge, and altruism.

Reciprocity, Cooperation, Revenge, and Justice

*Reciprocity can exist without morality; there can be no morality without reci-
procity. If we accept this thesis, it is clear why the very first step in the direction
of the Golden Rule was made by creatures who began following the reciprocity
rule, "do as the other did, and expect the other to do as you did." (p. 136)*

Good Natured: The Origins of Right and
Wrong in Humans and Other Animals
Frans de Waal, 1996

The Kindly Emotions

Emotional connectedness, the arousal of empathy, and an appreciation of
another person's situation are at the heart of all social species, seen progressively in apes, dolphins, elephants, and certainly in healthy humans. As
Adam Smith pointed out, we are entirely capable of *"changing places in fancy
with the sufferer"* (p. 10) [185]. All of these species are known to engage in

"targeted helping"—engaging in altruistic behavior that is tailored to the specific needs of the other even in situations they have never seen before [186]. It is the retributive "kindly" emotions that arouse helping behavior, gratitude, forgiveness, benevolence, and pride. However, during the course of evolution, and certainly human evolution, these positive emotions became largely limited to members of our own group because in a social species, group survival is vital to individual survival, just as the survival of individuals is essential for the group.

As we look at organizations, we find that it is not uncommon for departments or work groups to protect each other and their own interests and be suspicious of or competitive with others in the organization. One of the challenges in treatment settings is figuring out how we can get professionals with a multitude of affiliations to organize themselves around the interests of a client rather than the interests of the group.

Likewise, the emotions associated with an absence of fair play—anger, outrage, and even shame—must be contained for the well-being of the group or, if not contained, at least directed outward. Injustice makes retaliation inevitable, and in mental health and social service delivery systems, we are serving people who have been exposed to conditions of significant individual and social injustice. *The Commitment to Social Responsibility* acknowledges this exposure and its accompanying desire for revenge as an important dynamic that we must address if we are to truly help people heal. So, let's look at how the social system of reciprocity and justice evolved.

Reciprocity and Retaliation

The primary basis of all social relationships is reciprocity. Chimpanzees, our closest genetic cousins, are a highly sociable species with a well-developed system of reciprocity, and the origins of the human justice system can be recognized in chimpanzee groups. It probably all started with the need to share food among social animals whose survival depended upon it. To avoid the dangers of violent free-for-alls and the dominance of the biggest animals, primates developed a system of retaliation for breaches in reciprocity, and out of this grew a *"system of revenge"* according to the noted primatologist Frans de Waal [187]. As de Waal points out, *"The first hints of moral obligation and indebtedness are already recognizable"* among primates (p. 136) [187].

As we have all experienced since early childhood, cheating, or dealing unfairly with someone who has dealt fairly with you, arouses indignation, moral outrage, and the perception of injustice; these reactions can be seen in chimps, in our own ancestors, and in us. Just as we experience outrage when we are treated disrespectfully or unfairly, de Waal has personally observed what appears to be retaliatory "outrage" and punishment among chimpanzees.

And like us, chimpanzees hold grudges until they find an opportunity to even the score [186, 187].

Retaliatory outrage can be traced throughout human history, a legacy of our animal-fighting, prehistoric past [188]. In its simplest form, revenge does what it does in the chimpanzee world; it warns the boundary violator to stay away and not cross over that boundary again or risk escalating and negative consequences. It also tells the other about one's power and place. The creature that does not fight back, in fact, may be marked as prey. To avoid this outcome, it makes sense to retaliate rapidly, efficiently, and definitively to any encroachment on one's territory. So, why is it that we don't always retaliate, even if we feel that we would like to? To understand this, we have to look at reciprocal altruism.

Reciprocal Altruism and Tit-for-Tat

"Reciprocal altruism" is an idea developed by anthropologist Robert Trivers in the early 1970s [189]. Reciprocal altruism is working when we remember who has done us a favor and what favor we should do in return. This is probably how cooperation between people and groups of people without a central authority naturally evolved eons ago. But with modern computer technology, we can test that theory, and that is just what the political scientist Robert Axelrod decided to do [40]. In a computer simulation of various interpersonal strategies called the "Prisoner's Dilemma," Axelrod invited game players from around the world to test what the best interpersonal strategy is.

There was one standout program that won the most points in the thousands of games that were played by many players around the globe and it turned out be the shortest of all the submitted programs: "Tit for Tat." This game uses a very simple strategy: Cooperate on the first move and, thereafter, do whatever the other player did on the previous move. Well-adjusted, socially competent people learn these basic relational rules at home and then at school and bring them into the workplace as just the way things should be (Figure 9.1).

In our story, Tanya and Roy had set a limit for Chuck, and he refused to be guided by their experience and concern for the well-being of the children. Initially, they were forgiving and simply chalked it up to inexperience, but when he betrayed their trust by appearing to go along with them and then doing what he wanted to do behind their back they responded clearly, directly, and consistently to him. Unfortunately, Chuck had not learned the most basic rules of the social game.

Revenge and Justice

The aspect of Tit-for-Tat, called "provocability," is essential for discussing the notion of revenge. It implies that retaliation, which at its best is limit-setting, may be a necessary though not sufficient strategy in interpersonal relationships.

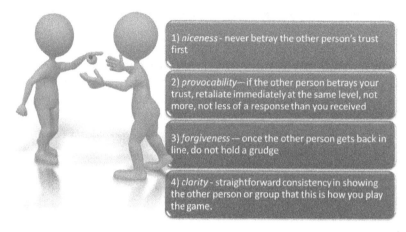

Figure 9.1 Basic rules of Tit-for-Tat.

But it also implies that there must be severe constraints on that retaliation. The injury and the response must be balanced. According to the Tit-for-Tat game, an overretaliatory response is bound to escalate conflict, while an under-retaliatory sets us up for being exploited. It may be not that revenge is so bad for people, but that we have no ongoing method for establishing balanced and fair retaliation, particularly when there is an unequal balance of power, as there is between parents and children, managers and employees, or someone who is armed and someone who is not. The situation is further complicated when the client you are working with has a long-standing history of mistreatment. Her or his perception of the fairness of a punitive response is likely to be far more distorted than we appreciate.

The evolution of the human sense of cooperative relationships, retaliation, and justice can be recognized in every child. Beginning at around 18 months of age and gradually evolving over the first years of life, children reach out and offer help and comfort to others; then they become concerned about issues of fairness. As early as 12 months of age children begin to protest about unfair treatment, and by age 4 they have learned how to treat others fairly [190, 191]. By age 9, children are making subtle discriminations between types of retaliation, the age of the perpetrator, and the relationship of the victim to the perpetrator [192]. In the course of healthy development, children learn how to modulate and manage the desire to "get even" for injuries they have suffered. They learn how to cooperate with each other as a fundamental social strategy, even when adults aren't around to tell them what to do. Healthy inhibitory responses to anger develop in the context of an empathic relationship with caretakers. In interaction with family members and peers, healthy children learn the rules of fair play, the role of apology, and how to cooperate with others [193].

For human groups to function effectively, justice concerns must be central concerns. These then are the main concerns with the *Commitment to Social Responsibility*, a shared concern for the welfare of the group that depends on justice and fair play. This is no less true in organizations than it is in whole societies.

Restorative Justice—Getting Off the Merry-Go-Round of Revenge

The basic programming for social behavior is reciprocity; do unto others as they do unto you. So, the normative response to violence is retaliation, which creates more violence. That's what we do and what we have always done. The desire to retaliate, supported by retributive systems of religion, law, cultural norms, and our very long memories, ensures the spread of violence everywhere to everyone and encourages the perpetration of violence across generations and throughout the centuries.

At the same time, the evolution of revenge has taken us from tribal justice based on kinship and hereditary blood vengeance to a world of laws in which the criminal justice system exacts its own form of legalized revenge. The unrelenting violence of the past century and, so far, of this new century may finally propel us to confront the cost of victimizing other people whether it occurs at home, in the streets, or in institutions. We may finally be coming to terms with the cost of retribution.

However, the continuing influence of tribalism can be found in the modern caregiving workplace. Staff members will sometimes gang up against a child who has injured another staff member. Clinicians may rally around another clinician who has been reprimanded by a supervisor, even if individually they believe the reprimand was deserved. Insisting that the cycle of violence be stopped, that we get off this apocalyptic merry-go-round of revenge, may, in the end, be our salvation.

Our present system of justice is based on the notion of retribution, revenge cloaked in social acceptability, backed up by laws. The primary questions to be answered under the present rules are *"What laws were broken?"* and *"Who broke them?"* and *"What punishment do they deserve?"* Not surprisingly, these are also the typical questions we ask in our treatment settings. Retributive justice is preoccupied with blame, pain, and punishment, and is primarily negative and backward-looking. The victim plays little if any role in achieving justice, nor is there much respect for the justice-seeking aspects of the perpetrator's behavior.

The challenge we face is that we work with clients whose life experiences have not squared with the rules of the game. They may believe that being nice will lead to being taken advantage of by others. Too frequently, our treatment settings are built on the belief that clients will learn the rules of the game if we respond to their rule-breaking behavior with retaliation and punishment. But for many people being served in our settings, retaliation never seems measured or fair because it is piled on top of years of hurt and abuse. As a result, our response only escalates the situation. We need to be able to help clients explicitly understand the rules of the basic social game and not assume that they will infer the rules based on our actions. Likewise, we must recognize that the tit-for-tat game is hardwired in our brains; therefore, staff working with traumatized clients need to avoid their own kneejerk response to punish rather than teach.

There is another way. Restorative justice may be the next phase in the evolutionary development of just communities. In this contrasting system of justice, the focus is on the restoration of relationship as well as individual and social healing [194–196]. The first question addressed is *"Who has been hurt?"* Once this is established, the next consideration is *"What are the needs of the victims, the offenders, and the community?"* The final question is *"What are the obligations and whose are they?"*

Under these guidelines, the aim of justice is to meet needs and promote healing, not to punish, although punishment, including imprisonment, can be recommended if it can be demonstrated to serve the purposes of the three involved parties—the victim, the perpetrator, and the social group. This is not an approach that can be reduced to a simple dichotomy of "liberal" versus "conservative" or "soft" versus "hard" on crime. It requires a radical shift in the basic assumptions we use to define what justice *is* and how justice is best obtained. In order to convince significant numbers of people that restoration, not revenge, should be the underlying principle for establishing justice, we need to help people better understand and appreciate the connections between childhood development and exposure to trauma and adversity.

Creating and Sustaining Just Organizations

Daniel Webster is quoted as saying that *"justice is the greatest interest of man on earth,"* and feelings related to perceived unjust treatment in the workplace are probably the dominant reason for most organizational conflict. Research has clearly demonstrated that the absence of justice provokes retaliation, lower performance, and harm to morale. Likewise, when employees perceive that their organization is just, they maintain respect for and trust in it, even when things do not go as they would like [197]. As one group of authorities on the subject has written, *"Organizational justice—members' sense of the moral propriety of how they are treated—is the 'glue' that allows people to work together effectively. Justice defines the very essence of individuals' relationship to employers. In contrast, injustice is like a corrosive solvent that can dissolve bonds within the community. Injustice is hurtful to individuals and harmful to organizations"* (p. 34) [197].

There is often a parallel process at play here. Too often staff members do what comes naturally, do what they are wired to do, and do this with the best of intentions. In a trauma-informed culture, we need our staff to better understand that our responses are often not aligned with the clients' experiences and what they need to change. Similarly, if managers are punitive to the staff, they are likely to replicate that behavior with the clients.

In *Destroying Sanctuary* we reviewed the three kinds of justice that need to be addressed in the workplace (see Figure 9.2). Because these three forms of justice interact with and influence each other, one component can be low, but if employees perceive that the other two forms are present, the negative effect can be offset [197, 198].

In the workplace it is important to reward high performance, but it is also important that people experience the workplace as providing rewards that are equal when individual performance depends on group performance. The key to resolving this perpetual dilemma is making sure that the procedures used to make these kinds of decisions are fair. Employees who report less pay satisfaction with pay are less satisfied at work. But when they feel that the methods for deciding on pay are fair, they have more positive reactions to their supervisors and are more committed to the organization. Everyone hates pay cuts, but when the methods for making decisions are perceived as just, employees are much more likely to accept the bad news and less likely to resign or engage in behaviors like stealing or sabotage. When workers understand why things have happened and are treated with respect and consideration, they are less likely to vent their anger on the organization [197]. This is also what makes

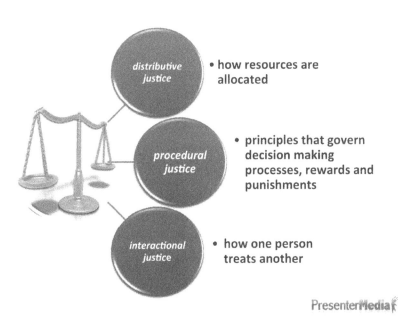

Figure 9.2 Justice in the workplace.

the *Commitment to Open Communication* so important; providing people with accurate information and increasing organizational transparency ensures a greater perception of organizational justice.

Managers spend much of their time managing conflicts between employees, and when both parties are intransigent, a manager may simply have to impose a settlement upon them. As long as any component of justice is present—distributive, procedural, or interactional (see Figure 9.2)—arbitration is likely to improve the situation. Managers can make hard choices, but they must do so in a just fashion. *"If you can't give people the outcome they want, at least give them a fair process"* (p. 43) [197]. Sufficient time and skill must be invested in management training and in the organization as a whole so that when inevitable conflicts arise, there is an ability to engage in conflict resolution and a willingness to learn from those experiences. In order for people in organizations to feel that the organization is just, there are certain characteristics of just processes that must be upheld (Figure 9.3). Even when we have done all we can to be fair and just, it is likely that some people will still feel aggrieved. In these cases, the *Commitment to Open Communication* permits us to continue to engage in dialogue with each other and improve our understanding and appreciation of each other's point of view.

In our story, the program staff tried to be fair, direct, and clear with Chuck. They recognized that he was just learning the rules, and they did not over-react the first time problems arose. But when Chuck did the same thing and then lied about it, they recognized that they were dealing with someone who could not follow the rules of just process, probably because he had never learned them.

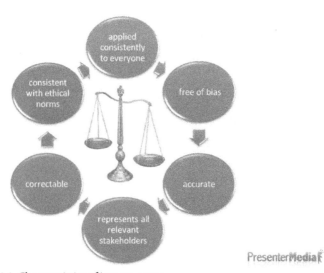

PresenterMedia

Figure 9.3. Characteristics of just processes.

The same principles of just process apply to performance evaluation and lay-offs. Performance appraisal is tricky and provides abundant fodder for feeling of injustice. It is important to approach performance evaluations with a clear understanding of their subjectivity. Researchers found that when employees had a voice in their reviews they were more satisfied, saw the process as more fair, and were more motivated to improve their performance. A "due process" approach to performance evaluations appears to offer the greatest possibility for the perception of fairness. In a Sanctuary program, our expectation is that staff will be engaged in performance review, and this process should be interactive and forward-looking.

In the case of layoffs, when a layoff is handled with procedural and interactional justice, staff members are less likely to put down their former employers and less likely to bring lawsuits. Sincerely apologizing to people for what's happening to them does not admit guilt. It shows compassion and may help the organization survive a crisis with its reputation intact [197]. When downsizing occurs, those left behind may be profoundly affected by a form of survivor guilt. If the organization provides them with accurate information and other forms of interactional justice in regard to those who are gone, the employees who remain are likely to respond less negatively. In a Sanctuary environment, dealing with organizational losses in a constructive and transparent way makes the *Commitment to Growth and Change* very relevant to the justice climate.

People perceive the nature and quality of the justice climate that is inherent in an organization from the first moment they set foot in the door to be considered for employment by the way they are introduced to an organization and the way they are treated at every level of interaction. Maintaining a just environment has been shown to profoundly affect organizational function in a number of key ways; trust predicts commitment, commitment predicts performance, good citizenship, and compliance with policies; and justice predicts trust.

The Commitment to Social Responsibility and Trauma-Informed Practice

Developmental Damage to the Belief in a Just World

The issue of justice cannot be avoided in human service organizations because it is at the heart of why a majority of people seeking services need to do so. Whether in interpersonal relationships or the workplace, human beings retaliate for perceived injustice if they continue to be treated poorly, if there is no apology for misconduct, and if they feel morally justified in their outrage. We know that the urge to retaliate for perceived injustice in childhood lingers throughout adulthood. All forms of physical, sexual, and emotional abuse provoke retaliatory behavior unless a sufficient number of mitigating factors impact on the desire to seek revenge. Victims of childhood adversity and other forms of interpersonal violence have experienced fundamental formative injustice, and this has powerfully influenced the way they view themselves, other people, and where they fit in the world.

Experiences with the family and the social environment form the child's maturing sense of justice, and justice becomes a central focus during adolescent development. Trauma, particularly interpersonal trauma, particularly that experienced at the hands of family members, often fragments or shatters the child's developing conceptual notion of a "just world"—the assumptions by which people orient themselves to their environment [199]. The image of manageability and predictability that arises from a belief in a just world is central to the ability to engage in long-term goal-oriented activity. Loss of this sense of manageability and predictability terrifies us. When you can no longer count on the basic reciprocal agreement on rules of conduct that we each rely on every day, life can become unendurable. When this process begins in childhood, the development of important social skills may be extremely disrupted.

As one group of investigators has pointed out, *"all acts of vengeance arise from an elementary sense of injustice, a primitive feeling that one has been arbitrarily subjected to a tyrannical power against which one is powerless to act"* (p. 9) [200]. The abuse of power by the perpetrator and the helplessness experienced by the victim are hallmark characteristics of interpersonal violence; therefore, we can expect that a victim will be highly motivated to seek revenge. The desire for vengeance/justice becomes a part of the response to trauma and may be directed at the original perpetrator or may be displaced onto others, often persons entirely innocent of the initial injury.

The consequence of this is that "hurt people hurt other people." It is around the issue of justice that our social divisions between "bad" people and "sick" people break down. People who hurt others are directly or indirectly trying to achieve an internal state of justice and are largely unaware of how their normal human drive to achieve justice has been perverted by the injuries they have received. As psychiatrist James Gilligan has pointed out, *"all violence is an attempt to achieve justice;"* in fact, *"the attempt to achieve and maintain justice, or to undo or prevent injustice, is the one and only universal cause of violence"* (pp. 11–12) [201].

Clients who have had these kinds of experiences will be hypersensitive to the empathic failures of the care staff. In most cases, staff members have not knowingly reinjured the client. The response of the client then seems way out of proportion. Because we fail to see our role in the conflict, we respond by punishing the behavior we inadvertently provoked and the situation escalates. Helping the staff to come to grips with the enormous power they have to reenact or rescript past experiences is a major staff development challenge.

Managing Punitive Impulses in a Sanctuary Program

One key issue that creates significant tension, ethical dilemmas, and safety concerns in many service delivery environments is the role of punishment as a form of, or at least an acceptable part of, intervention. There are strong currents within the larger culture that wax and wane around restoration versus retribution that then emerge in our criminal justice system, correctional institutions, juvenile justice facilities, mental health organizations, and school settings. The arguments for and the inclination toward punishment are as old as humanity; at the same time, an enormous body of scientific research makes clear the dangers of punitive responses that easily merge into abuse [202, 203]. We reviewed the current research on this issue of punishment and its effectiveness in *Destroying Sanctuary*. The bottom line is, it doesn't work very well at all.

The problem, of course, is that punishment is inevitably linked to justice, and if a person does not feel that the punishment is just, it tends to escalate his or her anger and the desire for retaliation, leading to a potentially endless cycle of escalating destructive behavior and similarly escalating punitive responses. This applies to the people who work in human service delivery environments as well. The typical response to some kind of infraction is punishment, although often the administration of punishment is actually distant in time from the actual infraction. The fear of punishment then drives other problematic behaviors like denial of responsibility, fear of taking any risks, lying, and covering up. And whenever people feel unfairly treated, they are likely to become vengeful.

We cannot travel along the same path we have always traveled and expect to blaze a new trail for the children, adults, and families we serve. Similarly, if we believe that most people find their way to treatment programs because they have been injured, it is hard to fathom how more of the same experiences that caused their problems will somehow solve their problems. For years, the response to problematic behavior in care settings was to induce some kind of pain based on the notion that problematic behavior needs to be punished and punishment will discourage future events. We believed this because this is what has been engrained in many of us, who remember being punished by our parents. We surmised that if punishment or pain does not solve the problem or modify the behavior, it is probably because the punishment was inadequate, the pain was insufficient to make an impression, and therefore the punishment needs to be ratcheted up. This is how things can begin to spiral out of control and how we easily become engaged in reenactment after reenactment. Remember the story in Chapter 7 of Tommy, the boy who had been physically abused by his father and tried to get the staff to punish him? For abused or neglected children, punishment is frequently part of a repetition of the past and very familiar, predictable territory.

But something is missing in our work, and it is easily overlooked. Many staff members and supervisors remember that they were punished as children, and they remember that it made an impression and often changed their behavior. They also underscore the fact that they punished their own children and it didn't hurt them. So, why isn't punishment effective in our settings? We need to remember that punishment may be an effective strategy if and only if it occurs in the context of a caring relationship and the punished person feels that his or her treatment was fair. It is easy to forget that what really matters, what really makes a difference in our lives and in the lives of our children is not punishment, but the love and attachment present in all those interactions and the threatened withdrawal of that positive regard. It takes a lot of time and effort for people who have been injured to feel that they are loved, and punishment without love is just coercion and abuse.

By the time many clients come to any kind of treatment setting, the cycle of infraction-misunderstanding-punishment-anger-revenge-infraction is likely to have been in place for many years in the relationship between the client and authority figures. It's usually "bad" behavior that brings a child or adult into an institution. The origins of the bad behavior reside in the disrupted attachment experiences, impaired emotional management, cognitive dysregulation, problematic relational schemas, and stunted moral development that are all a result of significant exposure to childhood adversity and trauma. But that fact is usually overlooked. Punishing people who have already spent a significant portion of their lives being punished in one way or another doesn't seem to make much sense.

The same can be said of the staff who work in human services and the way managers are treated by those to whom they report. We live in a blame culture, where affixing blame is a common substitute for solving complex problems. Knowing what we know about punishment and the impact of childhood adversity on our clients and our staff must lead to a change in the way the supervisory system and the organization as a whole manage the issue of discipline. We cannot expect to see change in our staff or clients if we remain resistant to change ourselves. How can treatment be successful if we continue to unwittingly reenact our own early childhood scarring experiences through negative behavior and punitive responses in the workplace?

However, this does not deny the reality that discipline is vitally important if anything positive is to be accomplished. But the discipline we all need to aim for is *self-discipline,* the acceptance of personal and social responsibility, the willingness to make personal decisions and follow through on the consequences of those decisions. But somewhere along the way, as a culture under stress, we have lost the notion of how people develop self-discipline and have come to believe the silly idea that the more you punish people, the more self-disciplined they will become.

We routinely encounter this attitude when we introduce the Sanctuary Model into settings, particularly those for children. Horrified staff members often ask, *"But does this mean these kids should be allowed to get away with bad behavior and not receive any consequences? Sanctuary is too soft!"* (p. 1). Once these questions are raised, they lead to some very interesting conversations. It is clear that there are, and perhaps always have been, very naive and dangerous assumptions about the way children develop, a mechanistic model of children not as young people but as wild beasts who will "get away" with whatever they can, related to that mental model issue we discussed earlier—human beings as basically bad. The problem with dehumanizing a human being—and, perhaps most importantly, a child—is that it is always a slippery slope. When an authority figure says it is the right thing to do, and when the dehumanizing behavior becomes part of a routine, people do not question whether it is right or wrong. This is how every human atrocity begins: dehumanization makes the subject an object, no longer truly human; authorization defines the situation so that the individual is absolved of the responsibility of making personal moral choices; through routinization, the situation is organized so that there is no opportunity to raise moral questions [204].

Obviously, children, like all humans, need limits. We need to know when we have "gone over the line," but the objective is not the external dependence on authority but rather the internalization of self-discipline, self-control, accountability, and a sense of both personal and social responsibility. Punishment does not build these traits; love and respect do. So, the key questions for treatment personnel should be *"What is the strategy most likely to help this child, adolescent, or adult internalize the lessons that we need him or her to learn?"* and *"If what we want to get is change, then how do we create processes that encourage that change?"* There is another way but it means, once again, changing our mental models of what justice really means.

Here is an example of a change in strategy that happened at Andrus. Several of the young children behaved very badly one Tuesday night. They were out of control, fighting with each other and with the staff. Several staff members, trying to protect the children from one another, were bit and scratched. Many workers from other programs were called to help out, and there was a general sense of outrage on the part of the staff. It was a very long and hectic night.

The following day, the staff members who had been most affected arrived at work and wanted to know what consequences or punishment would be doled out to the children. The Program Manager and Social Worker listened empathically to the staff concerns and then pointed out that a harsh punitive response was what the children would be expecting, and they suggested something else. They suggested that the staff and the children talk about what happened. That didn't mean making things *easier* for the children—because learning from your mistakes can be very difficult indeed—but it did mean making things *different*.

The staff canceled the activity for the afternoon and held a Community Meeting with the children, and they all talked about what had happened the previous evening. Each child spoke about what triggered the situation, what part he had in the situation, and how the script could have been rewritten with safety as the outcome. The children also were able to hear feedback from each other about the ways in which they had broken their commitment to having a safe community. At the end, each child involved in the fighting shared what he thought were appropriate restorative measures to use in contributing to accountability in the community. Staff members pointed out and praised the growth and change in the children. There was a lot of open communication, mutual respect, social responsibility, democracy, and a huge display of growth and change.

Many of the staff members commented that more learning and healing took place than would have occurred if they had just distributed consequences or punishment. While all the boys did restorative work, one boy stood out in the process. Michael, a very reactive and dysregulated child, who generally could not sit for more than a few moments, participated actively in the group and fully supported the plan for restorative work because, as he said, "it is important to take the bull by the horns." He was eight years old.

Helping Behavior Can Be Taught

Helpful bystanders have many characteristics in common that tell us a great deal about how we need to raise our children and model appropriate behavior for children and adults who seek help. Helpers have strong moral values that were transmitted to them by their caregivers. Among those values is empathy for others, which is applied to people in different social, ethnic, and religious groups. Bystanders who become helpers often have been marginalized or victimized themselves, but have been able to sustain connections with others rather than disconnecting from deep human bonds. Helpful behavior falls along a very long continuum and evolves gradually over time. Each successful attempt to help leads to more helping behavior, a trend that becomes self-reinforcing. This implies that helping behavior can be modeled, learned, taught, and reinforced [205, 206].

But even willing helpers can be derailed by social propaganda, by coercion, and by the influence of others who want to deny the perpetrator's behavior and who offer an alternative outlook on the victims of the perpetration. Explanations for unethical conduct on the part of staff such as "He deserves what he gets," "She's just trying to get attention," "Welfare recipients are just lazy and don't want to work," "There's more crime because we've gotten too soft on criminals," and "She's just manipulating us" reduce the humanity of the person or group that is targeted and excuses unethical behavior directed at them.

If helpers can get past the propaganda and see the flaws in thinking, they still have to feel that they have some responsibility for solving the problem and that they are able to choose something to do to help and put their plan into action. This sense of mutual responsibility can be taught later in life but is most easily modeled within the family system by what the children see in the behavior of their own parents toward other people.

The fundamental question is whether witnesses to the mistreatment of other people have an obligation to act. Are we, in fact, "our brother's keeper?" Until quite recently in human history, the family group or the tribe were the only groups to which we felt the kind of loyalty that demands protective action. In the Sanctuary Model we assert that we do indeed have an obligation to act. Not taking action when action is necessary has been termed a "sin of omission," while a "sin of commission" occurs when we do something we should not have done.

In the real world of our organizations, we frequently manage sins of commission differently than sins of omission. A staff person whose aggressive behavior results in injury to a client might lose his or her job, while another worker, who stands by passively while a coworker is struggling with a challenging set of behaviors flies under the radar. It is not acceptable to be abusive, but it is no more acceptable to be neglectful. The Sanctuary Model discourages aggressive, punitive, and coercive responses to challenging behavior, and at times, staff in agencies we work with might interpret this to mean that they should be passive. Sins of omission are no better than sins of commission. We cannot fight violence with violence, but we cannot simply stand by and watch. We all need to be brave enough to say and do the right thing, even when it means "speaking truth to power."

Social responsibility—being honest, ethical, fair, and just all of the time—is hard work, but it is crucial to helping our clients, and sometimes our staff, to discover a different reality. A *Commitment to Social Responsibility* is essentially an acceptance of the fact that we have the power to make a difference in our own lives and the lives of those around us. Often it is far easier to believe that we are powerless and that what we do, or fail to do, does not matter. In fact, what we do or fail to do is the only thing that does matter. We are all connected, and this means that the actions I take or fail to take can have an impact on other people; that other people matter and because my actions impact others, I matter as well. It is easy for us to abdicate responsibility when we are stressed and tired and not consider the impact of our action on others. A *Commitment to Social Responsibility* asks us to always consider our impact in the context of the community and what impact our choices and actions have on those around us.

Guard Your Social Immunity against Predators

The discussion of social responsibility would be incomplete without at least a mention of the risks associated with hiring someone who is a wolf in sheep's clothing. This is someone who is so concerned with his or her own well-being that he or she uses and manipulates clients and coworkers for personal gain. These persons may be predators.

People who are predators have something dramatically wrong with their emotional attachment system, which is intimately connected to their moral development. We don't develop a conscience because somebody tells us what is right and wrong. The basic wiring for moral development is built into our brains but needs to be stimulated by our relationship with others, with people we respect, listen to, love, and wish to emulate [35]. Moral development is relational.

We don't know precisely what goes wrong in the brain wiring of people who become predators, but we will probably find out that there is something wrong in the areas that are vital to attachment. From what we know so far, predators show deficits in autonomic arousal, in attention to meaningful social cues, in the orienting response, in sustained attention, and in electrodermal responses to distress cues. They demonstrate a lack of fear to adverse events, and both lower heart rate and lower skin conductance responses following punishment. These basic physiological changes appear to indicate that critical brain centers are involved in people diagnosed with antisocial personality disorder [207]. Whatever the case, they are good at faking normal responses, but they really do not feel love, shame, remorse, guilt, or empathy. As a result, they do not have a developed sense of conscience and concern for others. They want power over others, often show callous disregard for anyone they perceive as weak, enjoy exploiting and manipulating others, can be extremely charming in order to get what they want, and are very good at pretending that they feel things that they do not. Experts estimate that they represent 1 in 25 people but only about 20% of the prison population, which means that most of them are out in the world, operating in many different areas of our lives [208].

People who work in social services and clients in social service agencies are easy prey for predatory people. Workers in a socially responsible environment listen attentively to any warning signs that there might be a predator among them. Failing to do so can result in the unfolding of terrible events. But it's important to remember that there are all kinds of predators. Some of them are sexual predators who prey on children or anyone who is vulnerable. But since these people substitute a love of power for a love of people, they seek out and will often be given considerable power within institutional settings. We always need to be attuned to the signs and be prepared to collectively respond to predatory behavior.

Although we cannot offer any foolproof way of ferreting out such individuals in your organization, a system that makes everyone responsible for upholding the ethical standards of the organization is the best way to make it difficult for a predator who works there to survive. It might be possible for a predator to do the wrong thing with only one other person watching, but if everyone is watching it becomes increasingly difficult. Therefore, it is crucial to ensure that there is no one in your organization who is just a bystander. Everyone must have a stake in protecting the integrity of the organizations and the safety of its clients.

Implications for Socially Responsible Leadership

Taking the Lead in Creating Moral Safety

In Sanctuary the development of a positive moral climate is only possible when we are willing and brave enough to engage in the necessary and difficult conversations about these issues. The role of leaders in establishing such a moral climate is crucial. Leaders need to accept their social responsibility to reflect the desired values in both word and deed. Additionally, they need to have clarifying conversations when values are violated and praise others' best efforts to abide by organizational values. At the same time, leaders have to cocreate an environment with their colleagues and the people who report to them that allows for the open and honest discussion of important ethical questions. It is only though such discussion that an organization can become aligned behind a set of shared values.

Our expectation is that these discussions occur all the time, in supervision, Team Meetings, department meetings, leadership meetings, and Board meetings. The *Commitment to Social Responsibility* is consistently advanced by the other commitments as well. Communication has to be valued, power cannot be abused, people need to manage their emotions, and we need to see these conversations as opportunities to learn, change, and grow.

But it's not just formal leaders who have to wrestle with moral integrity. Decisions are made at every level of the organization every minute of the day, and everyone needs to take responsibility for ensuring that the decisions made are fair, ethical, just, and in the service of the mission. Given the *Commitment to Democracy*, there is an expectation that employees are not just waiting to be told what to do but are fully and consistently engaged in deciding on the best and most ethical solutions to the problems that confront the organization [209]. It is this engagement that conveys to the staff that they are trusted and expected to make important decisions. Sanctuary organizations create the necessary forums for these clarifying conversations to happen and encourage broad participation.

Strong, Nonpunitive Leadership Sets the Right Tone

Leaders have a social responsibility in times of high stress to sense and respond to the growing stress levels and intervene in ways that reduce rather than escalate the associated emotions. Bringing people together to talk and problem-solve is the most effective response. A lack of participatory structures lowers morale and is likely to lead to more disciplinary problems. Research has demonstrated that the lower performance gets, the more punitive leaders become. This may happen just when leaders need to be instituting positive reinforcing behaviors to promote positive change; instead, they become increasingly punitive [210].

Although there is a tendency for leaders to become increasingly punitive in times of stress, they may also move in the other direction as well. It is not uncommon for us to disengage from each other in times of stress. As a result, managers may become reluctant to take appropriate disciplinary action until the problem has grown so large that it can no longer be ignored. After all, having knowledge obligates us to do something. Embedding trauma assessments in routine evaluations has been difficult because the people asking the questions don't always want to know the answers. The same thing happens in leadership positions—captured beautifully in the ideas that "ignorance is bliss" and "what I don't know won't hurt me." The problem, of course, besides the lack of moral safety this engenders, is that problems that are not addressed tend to get worse. When management finally does respond, the response may be draconian. We have found that organizational stress can move us toward opposite poles, and we become either too passive or too aggressive in our approach. Managers need to be mindful and consistent in how they approach success, failure, and challenges in the workplace.

Sanctuary Toolkit for Social Responsibility

Socially Responsible Team Behavior: Assessing Our Moral Safety

The *Commitment to Social Responsibility* in the Sanctuary Model addresses our individual and group ethical response to the very difficult problem of creating and sustaining just environments. Some commentators believe that organizations must be designed and operated as ethical communities, and it is our intention that programs adopting the Sanctuary Model will be ethical communities. This means that we seek to honor our social contracts with each other and to prevent, avoid, or repair any harm; that we have a generally agreed-upon set of beliefs about preferable modes of conduct or desirable objectives to attain that are embodied in the Sanctuary Commitments; that there is a pervasive moral atmosphere in our organizations characterized by shared perceptions of right and wrong, what moral safety is and is not, as well as common assumptions about how moral concerns should be addressed (pp. 343–344) [211].

Unfortunately, many organizations are designed around, or have become skewed by, the few individuals who create problems rather than the majority of people who can be trusted [212]. In the story at the beginning of this chapter, the team as a whole took responsibility for ensuring that their program adhered to high ethical standards. Staff did not stand by waiting for someone else to do the right thing. They took the brave and appropriate step to ensure that the integrity of their program was protected.

One of the first orders of business in adopting the Sanctuary Model is to assemble a working group of leaders and line staff from all parts of the organization that we call a Core Team to engage in frank conversations about the organizational ethical system—what employees really believe and value in their organization—and determine if there needs to be some change in the value system based on what they now know about the impact of trauma and repetitive stress on clients, coworkers, and themselves. Once they understand clearly what their value system should be, they need to assess how those beliefs and values manifest themselves in the organization's policies, practices, and programs. They also need to identify where the gaps exist and how their beliefs may not always drive what they do. The clearer the organization's values and beliefs are, and the more consistently they can ensure that actions reflect those values and beliefs, the easier it becomes for all staff to do the right thing and create a morally safe environment.

Individual S.E.L.F-Care Plans

The work of doing human service delivery in any of its forms is demanding, often frustrating, exhausting, and underappreciated. To do this difficult emotional labor, it is essential for both direct care staff and leaders to practice good self-care. Part of the *Commitment to Social Responsibility* is taking responsibility for oneself and one's own well-being and, in so doing, appropriately responding to secondary or vicarious trauma – the impact of treating trauma survivors on staff – and preventing burnout. We take self-care very seriously and expect all of our staff to develop and implement an ongoing S.E.L.F.-Care Plan. Individuals need to rest, maintain relationships both in and out of the workplace, have fun, exercise, think, and relax. These plans need to address physical, psychological, social, and spiritual forms of self-care.

We also expect the organization to develop a plan for minimizing vicarious trauma and burnout as part of the organizational S.E.L.F-Care Plan. Healthy organizations acknowledge the importance of self-care, but all staff members must take personal responsibility for themselves as well. Studies have shown that leaders have a lot of influence on the emotional state of their staff, and this influence can either help or hinder performance.

CMRT: The Team Treatment/Self-Care Interface

The initial development of a researchable protocol for the Sanctuary Model occurred at the Jewish Board of Family and Children's Services in New York, a large multiservice mental health and social service agency with innovative programs aimed at trauma-informed care. A number of senior clinicians were on the team that worked on the Sanctuary project and then took steps to integrate trauma-informed knowledge more broadly throughout the organization. They recognized that their clinical staff were experiencing secondary trauma at alarming rates. They created Clinical Risk Management Teams (CRMTs) to address these problems on a routine basis. This format covered all the important aspects of the case, including what the clinician was dealing with emotionally, in a structured format that could be easily adopted in time-pressured environments that are in danger of losing any context for processing complex information in an emotionally intelligent way [213] (Table 9.1).

Table 9.1 Addressing secondary trauma as a team: Clinical risk management team, protocol outline (45 minutes)

Step	Time	Process
I. Case Presentation	10	Worker begins with "my concern in this case is that I…"
		Case summary that is brief, clear, and focused.
		Identify client strengths and coping abilities.
		Identify what is going well in case.
		Brief period for clarifying questions.
II. Trauma Issues	6	Explore worker's understanding of how the problem/symptoms are an expression of the person's having experienced trauma (e.g. flashbacks, dissociation, numbing, hyperarousal, affect dysregulation).
		Consider ways to talk with the client about how the problem/symptoms are an expression of his /her having experienced trauma.
III Exploration of Various Perspectives of the Case	6	(Worker listens but does not participate in this part of the discussion.)
		Give voice to different aspects of the client's ambivalence.
		Take the position of different people within the case.
		Use experiential exercises and/or role play as appropriate.
IV. Checklist of Issues	5	Identify whether and in what way these apply.
		Are there people in danger? actual/potential
		Is a report to Child Protective Services warranted, and what are implications?
		What health/medical factors? e.g. assessment and care of injury.
		What relevant cultural factors? (gender, race, religion, sexual orientation, ethnicity, class) (e.g. traditional modes of discipline, prohibitions against telling family secrets, how shame is expressed).
		What additional family resources? e.g. extended kinship.
		What additional community resources? e.g. hotline, shelter, justice system, order of protection, church/synagogue.

(continued)

Table 9.1 (*Continued*)

Step	Time	Process
V. Worker's Feelings About the Case	7	Worker discusses ongoing feelings about case and how these relate to the work.
VI. Case Concept- ualization	6	Responses from colleagues to what worker has presented. (Worker listens but does not participate in this part of the discussion). Each speaker gives case conceptualization as a rationale for specific treatment recommendations, including additional or alternate modalities, e.g. group, family.
VII. Worker's Reactions to the Team Process	5	Worker responds with which suggestions are usable and/ or useful and which are not

Source: Geller, J. A., L. H. Madsen, L. H., and Ohrenstein, L. (2004). Secondary trauma: A team approach. *Clinical Social Work Journal, 32*(4), 415–430. Used with permission.

S.E.L.F. Supervision

Although few of us would argue with the notion that good, consistent supervision is not only desirable but essential in an organization, we have to admit that it is also quite rare. That is why we have made the supervisory relationship a part of the Sanctuary Toolkit. Leaders and managers need to commit to their social responsibility to provide sound supervision. A strong, safe, responsive, and predictable supervisory relationship allows a manager to avoid many of the pitfalls that lead to an organizational perception that staff members are dealt with in a punitive and arbitrary manner. Strong, consistent supervision requires positive and consistent engagement. When present, an emergent employee concern will be addressed in a timely fashion, will be managed fairly and sensitively, will occur in the context of a warm and positive relationship, will be managed consistently, and will be contextualized. As a result, a positive supervisory relationship is likely to ensure that when discipline is necessary, it will be managed effectively.

The *Commitment to Social Responsibility* requires us to always balance our own needs and wants against the greater good of the community or the organization. It speaks to how we are all bound to each other and how injustice directed at anyone adversely impacts everyone. In the last chapter, we will describe the process we use to create the opportunity for the Sanctuary Model to emerge within each organization and share some lessons learned.

Chapter 10

Pulling It All Together

Tragedy and a Leap of Faith

September 11 may go down as one of the most tragic events in modern history not only because of the thousands of deaths it caused but also because it so seriously distorted American perceptions about itself and the world. It has knocked America down into a dank and dangerous cul de sac, making it susceptible to apocalyptic visions of darkness rather than motivating it toward high visions of human possibility. (p. 45) [214]

Jim Garrison, *America as Empire: Global Leader or Rogue Power?*

September 11, 2001, represents a collective trauma and a shared loss that has had profound effects on the way we all live in America over a decade later. It even changed the way we thought about our work and the work we were doing together. We began working on the Sanctuary process at Andrus in the summer of 2001, so very early in the process we were confronted with the terror and loss of the World Trade Center disaster. Andrus is located in Yonkers, New York, the first city north of Manhattan. Some people on the Core Team, as well as many other members of the staff, lost close friends and family members. All of us were stunned and shocked by the images we saw on television each night, and our sense of safety and security was shaken.

These events did, however, provide us with an experiential learning opportunity about the nature of trauma and the impact it had on each of us. The tragedy of the 9–11 attack and the national response to it are large-scale analogues to what frequently happens in the lives of clients and their families, to staff members who work in organizations, and sometimes even to the organizations as a whole [215–218]. We talked about how it was hard to concentrate, how it was difficult to sleep, how irritable some of us were. These events were imprinted on our minds, and many of us will never look at a clear blue sky in the same way again or hear a plane flying overhead without thinking about that day. For that reason, it became easier to imagine what life might be like for children and adults who have had daily experiences of shock, betrayal, loss, or devastation. These events changed how we looked at the world, how we looked at each other, and how we looked at the people in our care.

A Little Background

Andrus was founded in 1928 by the philanthropist John E. Andrus as a memorial to his late wife, Julia Dyckman Andrus. Julia Dyckman was an orphan who was adopted as a child and raised by the Dyckman family. Since the beginning, the Andrus credo has been "To Give Opportunity to Youth," and that continues to inform the mission today. The initial work on implementing Sanctuary at Andrus began with the campus programs that serve approximately 150 children ranging from 5 to 15 years of age. The Residential Treatment Program serves 73 children, and there is also a school-based Day Treatment Program with approximately 80 students. Since 2001, Andrus also acquired three outpatient mental health clinics and several community-based programs for children and families.

Over the years, the children at Andrus have changed and the field of residential care has changed as well. As an agency, Andrus has always tried to stay on the cutting edge of knowledge, and the initial interest in childhood trauma was just the latest manifestation of the wish to innovate. The former President and Chief Executive Officer, Gary Carman, was actually the first person to consider the compelling nature of research on brain development and the adverse impact that trauma has on childhood development. Dr. Carman's successor, Chief Executive Officer Nancy Ment, and Chief Operating Officer Brian Farragher, and other key administrators, spent about two years reading, attending conferences, and trying to figure out how to make the research findings fit with the programs they were running at the agency. They knew that over 75% of the children they worked with in the Residential Treatment Program and 40% of the children in the Day Treatment Program were victims of serious childhood trauma. They also knew that they were not doing enough to intervene in this area. As a result, many of these children were stuck, and despite their best efforts they were making only marginal improvements. At the same time, most of what they were learning about childhood trauma was theoretical, and they were struggling to determine how to integrate theory into actual practice.

Andrus struck up a relationship with Sandy and her team in the fall of 2000 after the Residential Director saw Sandy give a presentation on the Sanctuary Model at a conference in Philadelphia. What was most compelling about Sandy's work was that she had taken what was known about trauma theory and had developed models for use in residential settings. Andrus thought that these models were worth a further look, so we traded phone calls and meetings and finally agreed on a rather elaborate consultative arrangement, which began in earnest in June 2001.

To begin the Sanctuary process, Sandy and her colleagues, Joe Foderaro, RuthAnn Ryan, and Lyndra Bills, spent a week meeting with a wide variety of staff on the Andrus campus to learn about the organizational culture. Brian then selected 21 staff from key departments in the residential program and the school. We called this group of the best and brightest a Core Team. Our Core Team was made up of four senior administrators (Brian, the Campus Director at the time, and the leaders of the three major departments on campus: residential, education, and clinical), two clinical supervisors, two line clinicians, the Dean of Students from the on-campus school, four teachers, three school milieu staff, two cottage program managers, and three cottage milieu staff members. Once assembled, the plan was for the Core Team to meet two days a month for the next year and hammer out the new vision for how the Andrus campus treatment program could more effectively address the needs of traumatized children.

Getting Started: Making a Leap of Faith

As Sandy wholeheartedly admitted earlier in this book, she didn't really know what she was going to do when presented with the opportunity to work with Andrus. Her first book of what has turned out to be a trilogy, *Creating Sanctuary: Toward the Evolution of Sane Societies*, was a pioneering attempt to describe an approach to treating psychologically injured adults [2]. But Sandy is an adult psychiatrist with little experience working with children, and at that time she had no experience with children's residential programs other than the previous research project she had helped create at the Jewish Board of Family and Children's Services, which was still unfolding as the Andrus project began [50, 219–221].

What she did know was that she was on to something. She knew what things needed to happen to create change in people and in organizations. What was still not clear was the right sequence for creating change and how to organize such change. The right levers to pull and buttons to press were still a mystery. So, the Board of Directors and the administrative leadership at Andrus took a "leap of faith" in investing in an extensive two-year process of exploration. Neither Brian nor Sandy recognized it at the time, but as we look back on it now, we were doing two things at once. We were not just planning how to implement Sanctuary at Andrus; we were also figuring out how to implement Sanctuary in every organization we have trained since setting up the Sanctuary Institute. As we were grappling with presenting Sanctuary to Andrus staff, we were also building the foundation for the Sanctuary Institute. We were changing, and when that process begins, it is not always clear how it will evolve and where it will take you.

Our implementation process was very nonlinear and a lot of fun, emotionally demanding, and mostly revolved around process. The Andrus team was ready to learn a lot about childhood trauma and how to treat its effects, and they were ready to learn all the newest treatment interventions. What they were not ready for was the enormity of the undertaking. The problem with being an early adopter or trailblazer of anything new is that you have the opportunity to learn from your mistakes. But that only happens *after* you have spent considerable time, effort, and resources making those mistakes plus a little more time, effort, and resources convincing yourself and others that you really did not make any mistakes.

Learning by Doing

In spite of all the trials and tribulations of the year of preparation, we were finally able to agree that this was the way for us to go and that this Core Team could help lead the way. The initial year of the Core Team's work was spent talking about the concepts and looking at the way business was conducted in the organization. The second year activities of the Core Team focused on rolling out the training and the various Sanctuary Toolkit items. It required six full days of training for all of the staff to be trained, and the Core Team members led these training groups. They implemented Community Meetings, Safety Planning, and S.E.L.F. psychoeducational groups and trained all the staff on Sanctuary, neurobiology, parallel process, collective disturbance, reenactment, and a host of related topics. To accomplish all of this, the Core Team enlisted the help and support of other staff members who had not been part of the original team. In doing so, they began to expand the circle and engage others in the process of change. The greatest challenge in this whole process was being clear about what Sanctuary is and what it is not. Unlike many training programs, this one had no list of does and don'ts or some fancy acronym to help people remember the six steps of this or the seven rules of that. We discovered that Sanctuary can mean many different things to a lot of people.

The Sanctuary Institute

Our belief in the power of community led us to develop the Sanctuary Institute. The Sanctuary Institute is the gateway to the Sanctuary Network, a community of organizations committed to the development of trauma-informed services. The Sanctuary Network is a community of practice initially patterned after the United Kingdom's concept of a "Community of Communities."[1] We are all committed to the belief that we can do better for our clients and colleagues, as well as our society, if we can accept that the people we serve are not sick or bad,

1. See http://www.rcpsych.ac.uk/quality/qualityandaccreditation/therapeuticcommunities/communityofcommunities.aspx

but injured, and that the services we provide must give them hope, promote growth, and inspire change.

We believe that clients can change within a community that tolerates risk, values creativity, inspires hope, and believes that the future can be different from the past. We believe organizations require the same kind of community if they are going to improve, heal from their own stresses and injuries, and realize their full potential. As we all know, these kinds of communities do not exist in many places, but we believe that groups of committed people can change that situation if they understand the nature of trauma, have some basic group principles, and have a shared language and a clear system of values. In the process of doing this at Andrus and helping many other organizations take on the challenge of change, we have been participant-observers; our expertise in the area of Sanctuary-style institutional change is only a few years in advance of the programs we train.

It is hard to change your old patterns without help and support. It is not impossible, but it is hard. What we know about Trauma Theory indicates that our old patterns are difficult to break and that it is easy to slide back into established habits without even thinking about it. Oddly enough, we hatched the idea of the Sanctuary Network and the Sanctuary Institute while providing consultation to a sister agency, Parsons Child and Family Center in Albany, New York, that was interested in adopting the Sanctuary Model. We came to realize that by working with another agency, our own commitment to Sanctuary was strengthened. As we were confronted with the challenges faced by the agency we were training, we developed new strategies for meeting our own challenges at home. As we witnessed another agency breeze through challenges we found overwhelming and become overwhelmed by hurdles we took in stride, it became increasingly clear that we could learn from each other. We certainly did not have things figured out, nor did the agency we were working with. Together, however, we seemed to learn faster, push each other, and support each other. It became clear that the kind of community that helps clients heal could also be healing for the communities in which healing is supposed to take place.

Over the course of several months and several long car and train trips, we developed the idea of the Sanctuary Institute and the Sanctuary Network. But how do you make an idea a reality? It begins with the belief that you can do it, a sense of responsibility that you are obligated to do it, and a sense that you can, at least in part, determine your own future. Our process for developing the Sanctuary Institute adhered closely to the Sanctuary Commitments we have discussed throughout this book. We spoke openly, learned as we went, accepted criticism, followed through on our homework, and resolved disagreements by talking them through and reaching a consensus. As one of our former staff members used to say, "We got through it by going through it, not around it." Our work on this project was challenging, stressful, complicated, and, most important, fun. It was further proof to us that Sanctuary is a powerful tool, because this group was able to complete the task, deliver an exceptional product, and do it on time, even though none of us had ever done anything like this before. It was a clear illustration that great things can happen when you put a group of capable people together, create a safe working atmosphere that encourages creativity, and get them to pull in the same direction. It is our hope and our belief that the teams we work with in the Sanctuary Institute are capable of doing great things. If they work together, honor the Sanctuary Commitments, and share a vision of what they hope to become, they can do things they previously thought we well beyond their reach or even impossible.

We took our maiden voyage with our first Sanctuary Five-Day Training in the fall of 2005. When we started, out our intention was to train four or five agencies a year. We thought this might be a nice little project we could run out of our garage. In fact, we ended up turning three garages into a training center. Six years later, we have trained over 250 agencies nationally and internationally. Just as we learned from our first training experience, we continue to learn from the agencies we train. Each participant contributes in some small or large way to improving and refining the product. It is exciting to be part of this process from the ground up, and we consider ourselves incredibly fortunate to have the opportunity to work with so many talented and committed professionals and their organizations.

The introduction to the Sanctuary Institute begins with a five-day intensive training experience. Teams of five to eight people, from various levels of the organization, come together to learn from our faculty, colleagues from other organizations, and one another. They begin to create a shared vision of the kind of organization they want to create. These teams will eventually become the Sanctuary Steering Committee for their organization. The training experience usually involves several organizations, and generally these organizations are very different in size, scope, region, and mission. This diversity helps to provide a rich learning experience for the participants.

During the training, the Steering Committee engages in prolonged facilitated dialogue that serves to demonstrate the major strengths, vulnerabilities, and conflicts within the organization. By looking at shared assumptions, goals, and existing practice, staff members from various levels of the organization are required to share in an analysis of their own structure and functioning, often asking themselves and each other provocative questions that have never been discussed before. Many of these questions have never been raised because participants have never felt safe enough to say what has been on their mind or in their heart, even after many years of working together. Although the continual focus is on the fundamental question *"Are we safe?,"* participants quickly learn that in the Sanctuary Model, being safe means being willing to take risks by being willing to say what needs to be said and hear what needs to be heard.

Safety is understood as occupying four domains—physical, psychological, social, and moral safety—all of which must be in place for an individual or an organization to be truly safe. Participants look at the change process itself and are asked to anticipate the inevitable resistance to change that is a fact of life in every organization. They look at management styles, the way decisions are made and conflicts resolved. Through these discussions, they learn what it means for leaders, staff, and clients to engage in more democratic processes with a simultaneous increase in rights and responsibilities. They evaluate the existing policies and procedures that apply to staff, clients, and families and ask whether or not they are effective in achieving their shared goals. They are asked to learn about and become thoroughly familiar with the psychobiology of trauma, posttraumatic stress disorder (PTSD) and other trauma-related disorders present in the children, adults, and families they work with. They are challenged to begin thinking about the implications of that knowledge for treatment. They also learn how high levels of stress in the organization can impact relationships, emotions, and decision making at every level of the organization. They develop an understanding of the conceptual tool for organizing treatment—S.E.L.F. [222–224]. They learn about vicarious trauma, traumatic reenactment, collective disturbance, and the importance of understanding themselves and supporting each other. And they are introduced to the components of the Sanctuary Toolkit.

Participants report that the week-long training is a powerful experience, some have said even life-changing. It needs to be because they have a big job to go home to. They will need to go back to their respective organizations and begin to change the culture of the organization, as well as long-standing paradigms and patterns of behavior.

Assembling and Developing a Core Team

The members of the Sanctuary Steering Committee are instructed to go back to their organization and create a Core Team, a larger multidisciplinary team that expands its reach into the entire organization. It is this Core Team that will be the activators of the entire system and that we described in Chapter 4. The Core Team is armed with a *Sanctuary Implementation Manual*, a *Sanctuary Direct Care Staff Training Manual*, a *Sanctuary Indirect Care Staff Training Manual*, training materials, a S.E.L.F. Psychoeducation Curriculum, and ongoing technical assistance to guide them through the process of Sanctuary implementation. This process takes several years to take hold and then continues, hopefully forever. The Core Team should have representatives from every level of the organization to ensure that every voice is heard. It is vital that all key organizational leaders become actively involved in the process of change and participate in this Core Team.

As discussions begin in the Core Team, participating staff begin to make small but significant changes. Members take risks with each other and try new methods of engagement and conflict resolution. They feed these innovations and their results back into the process discussions. The Core Team must always maintain a balance between process and product. It is not enough to talk about how we will change things. We must also make actual changes in the way we do business. The Core Team therefore not only plans together how best to share what they are learning with the larger organization, but also plans how to train all agency personnel and clients in the Sanctuary principles, how to integrate the Sanctuary Toolkit into the day-to-day operation of the organization, and how to evaluate how these initiatives are taking hold in the organization.

It is essential to look at the implementation process on two levels. We want to ensure that people are behaving differently, but we also want to pay close attention to how we are implementing change. The Core Team is responsible for making sure that the Sanctuary Tools are introduced to staff, but they are also responsible for making sure that gaps in implementation are identified and addressed. For example, if Community Meetings are not happening in certain programs, they need to discover the reason. If Safety Planning is not taking place, what went wrong? Was the training done correctly? Is the leadership pushing the change? Confronting these problems together is an essential part of implementation. Always looking at what we do, as well as how we do it, is the key to lasting change.

We Think We Are Embarking on a Scientifically Based Parallel Process of Recovery

Scientific advances in understanding the biopsychosocial impacts of exposure to trauma, adversity, and disrupted attachment have great power and show promise for the work we do. We also have made the case that a trauma-informed approach not only helps our clients to recover, but also provides a parallel process of recovery for organizations and institutions.

As we discussed, we need to view clients not as sick or bad, but as injured, and we need to change the fundamental question from *"What's wrong with you?"* to *"What's happened to you?"* This shift brings the social context of all human experience back into the picture. People make bad choices because bad things have happened to them or because people around them have made bad choices in the way they have treated them.

Much of what we talked about in *Destroying Sanctuary* describes how human services have gotten far too good at dehumanizing people, and we need to put more "human" into human services [12]. This is where Trauma Theory really helps, but is also a hard pill to swallow. It is so much easier to see others as "the other." These labels serve to keep "them" there and "us" here. What Trauma Theory has taught us is that those of us who are "here" are lucky. We were fortunate to have people in our lives, and early in our lives, who thought we were special, great, gifted, and lovable. We have been able to form attachments that helped us develop the capacity to sooth ourselves, trust other people, and thrive as a result of these relationships. The only difference between us and our clients is often a few bad breaks.

The good news about Trauma Theory is that it confronts us with the fact that there is no "us" and "them"; there is only "we." If we are who we are because things, good or bad, have happened to us, then we can all be something else if something different happens to us. Although when we meet people to whom bad things have happened they often try to replay an old script with us, we can choose a different role. Unfortunately, we can only consistently do that when we are working in a community where others share the same understanding of humanity and help us to consistently draw on our better selves. Unfortunately, at every level of our caregiving system, the stresses that confront us each day have helped us become very good at demonizing each other, our clients, our coworkers, our direct reports and supervisors, and our regulatory bodies. It does none of us much good.

Measuring Results

It's hard to get there if you don't know where you are going. So, for the social service sector, what are the results we are trying to achieve? It's relatively easy to measure results in the for-profit world; it's the bottom line, the amount of profit expressed in dollars and cents gained, usually over the last quarter. But what is the "value creation" in the largely nonprofit human service world? The value in mental health services is not as easy to measure since it relates to human performance over a long period. It's true that enormous value is lost to a society by the toll that mental illness and social dysfunction takes on the individual and the social economy. Clinical and social services have value if they improve an individual, family, or group level of function.

But how often is that measured, and does knowledge about any of that economic result—or lack of it—ever get fed back into the industry that is supposed to produce the result? The answer is that it is rarely measured, and the results tend to be broad-brush, estimated, national results. And of course, it is easy to see that information like this has virtually no impact on the services that are provided until years after the fact—if at all. So, the feedback loops that should be in place that would regularly help us learn how to improve services based on the results we have or have not achieved are poorly designed or not present at all.

As professionals, we should have to be accountable for the outcome of our work. In real practice, only individually, as clinicians and service providers, do we have any idea of whether or not the work we do is effective. Only the people we provide service to can tell us whether or not they received the help they needed. There are few objective measures of any outcome and few controls because we are dealing with the enormous system of each person's life, a life that at any point in time is being affected by hundreds, even thousands, of influences. When someone drops out of treatment or stops coming for services, was it because what we did worked or because it didn't? When people improve, apparently as a result of what we do, was it that, something else, or simply what would have happened anyway? It's impossible to prove a negative, and for the most part, we are in the business of keeping worse things from happening, so how do you prove that what you did or said accomplished that, or didn't?

What happens instead is that treatment decisions are based largely on the simplistic idea of costs. If you cost an insurance company less, your services are more likely to be reimbursed. The improvement in the patient, whether his or her function has actually, realistically, and measurably improved, is not really a factor. And increasingly, reimbursement is becoming dependent on providing evidence-based practice. While this is certainly a move in the right direction, it also holds dangers. If we have evidence that a technique works, does this mean that other techniques do not work? Or are less effective? If a kind of therapy has been shown to be effective for one population, does that mean it is effective for other populations? And if it wasn't effective, was that because the treatment doesn't work or because the setting in which it was offered counteracted every possible therapeutic action? And if we have to send people who have apparently been successfully treated back to their former living situations and they fail, is this because the treatment did not work or because treatment alone cannot solve major social problems? And these are just a few of the questions that researchers must ask themselves when they evaluate any kind of intervention. When we deal with human lives, the research is very different from that used in dealing with human livers, hearts, or eyeballs. The determining factors are far more complex. Rarely does a research project study longitudinally the outcome of any intervention, and yet, to change things at the level of attachment requires very long-term research that looks at the next generation since we know that this is the basis of intergenerational transmission.

Struggling with Complexity

As an illustration of this issue, Sandy recently received an email from a former Sanctuary unit client who was treated in 1992. She described her hospitalization as a "watershed experience," and although she still suffers from depression and PTSD, she continues to use the tools she developed during her brief stay in the hospital 16 years ago. But she also described the intergenerational impact that brief hospitalization had on her and her family. Here is what she wrote:

I remember the first time I asserted to my sister's family (a niece shoving her sister) that violence was unacceptable in my home, and my sister acknowledging that I had changed. Three of the four of us have refused to follow the family pattern and have broken the chain. People are getting help decades ahead of schedule, including my two nieces and another sister. Even my father had his depression treated in his last decade of life—I knew that the way he abused us had stemmed from his own abusive childhood. It took years to forgive the man, but I am grateful that on his passing last year, I could freely grieve and own the good he had done to and for me.

The benefits of experiences like these are very hard to capture in routine research projects or quarterly reports. The human services field needs a significant investment in its approach to research and to cost-benefit analyses to answer pressing questions about effective interventions, strategies, approaches, and policies. At present, we have little research that addresses the issues surrounding complex PTSD [225–227]. The evidence-based practices that are held up as models for universal adoption have usually not been adequately investigated in clients with interactive complex problems. In fact, the severe comorbid problems associated with treatment seekers with complex PTSD, many of whom are high utilizers of social services, are frequently reasons to exclude these very clients from research studies!

Given the billions of dollars we are losing every year, wouldn't it make sense to make this investment? We invest in cancer research. We invest in research on heart disease. We need to have better valuation of the contribution that helping makes to the overall economy. This is particularly important when clear evidence exists that problems like cancer and heart disease are likely to have an intimate connection to the adverse experiences of childhood.

Lessons Learned

We thought it was fitting to end with a summary of the key lessons we have learned along the way as a result of our initial implementation at Andrus and the subsequent implementations we have facilitated across our network of agencies. We have learned from both our successes and failures, and we will be candid about what we did well and where we dropped the ball. It is comforting to acknowledge that we made our mistakes honestly. We only knew what we knew at the time. It is even more comforting to know that what we have learned from our mistakes has helped us to give other organizations a better start when we train them through our Sanctuary Institute

It Is Tough Out There, and Sanctuary Does Not Make You Bulletproof

Throughout this book, we have talked about some of the challenges that we faced as an organization over the last decade. At Andrus we have managed two mergers, an executive leadership change, board leadership changes, significant changes in our administrative team, program closures, program openings, tragic and sudden losses in the families of key staff people, and predatory behavior on the part of disgruntled former employees. We found through our work with other organizations that our experiences were typical for organizations like ours.

Sanctuary has not prevented bad things from happening. What Sanctuary has done is to help us more successfully navigate the hard times so that adversity does not result in trauma. Using Sanctuary has improved our social immunity. We talk more openly about the challenges, better understand the losses involved, support each other through the hard times, and do our level best to manage the difficult emotions associated with these changes and losses. We have not always managed the struggles successfully, because stress does cause you to return to some old bad habits, but we are getting better at this each day.

Record Keeping—Write It Down!

Neither of us kept very thorough or accurate records about the process that was unfolding. In retrospect, we wish we had. We were both feeling our way, and despite the fact that we are both fairly structured planners, it was impossible to structure something that hadn't happened yet and for which there was no clear prototype. So, what we both remember is determined by how each of our memories work. Fortunately, one of us tends to focus on what is missing and the other one on what is present, so the result is a pretty workable partnership. Still, we both wish we had kept better records.

We're Going to Change What?!?!?

Sandy had an inkling of the magnitude of change that would have to happen at an organizational level, but Brian did not. Organizational culture has been referred to as the DNA of the organization. It is the default position, the way we respond because it is the way we have always responded. Taking on a change like Sanctuary that goes to the heart of organizational culture is no small undertaking. The challenge is for us to always ask *"Why do we do the things we do?"* and *"Where did this practice, policy, or procedure come from?"* Getting leaders in an organization to change, to behave more democratically, to communicate more effectively is challenging, and if someone has already arrived at a leadership position by behaving one way, how likely is that person to radically change the way he or she does things so that the organization can become trauma-informed? Why should he or she change? What is the motivation behind this kind of change? The change we are talking about in this book is not the kind of change someone else will make; it is the kind of change *you* need to make: change *you* need to model. It is challenging for people who have achieved their position in the organization by behaving a certain way to suddenly pivot and go in a different direction. Change is not fun for any of us, wherever we are in the organizational hierarchy.

This, however, is the crux of the matter. It is hard to argue with the Sanctuary Commitments, but it is even harder to fully grasp the changes that are needed to achieve them. Most leaders come to this process thinking that "I need to change things in my organization," but what they mean is, "I need to change those other people"—those people who don't get it, those people who are punitive or reactive with clients. Few, if any, leaders begin the process by saying, "I have to change, I need to be different." In Brian's case, that lesson took about a decade to sink in. Creating the conditions for others to change first requires the leader to change, and change is hard.

It's All in the Pacing

We learned about pacing by not pacing things very well. The tensions in an organization are significant, and the challenges they pose to leaders are daunting. We need to understand that the changes we make in an effort to better manage organizational stress can also induce stress. We have found that the implementation of Sanctuary must closely mirror the process that happens in some of the cognitive behavioral therapies with traumatized clients. Many cognitive behavioral interventions are measured, exposing clients to increasing levels of stress as we teach new skills, a little at a time, so that we do not overwhelm clients with too much too soon. We have found that the process of Sanctuary implementation in an organization needs to be paced as well.

Some organizations can move more quickly, while others may need to move more slowly. Some issues are easier to manage than others. Some departments, programs, or work groups might each move at a different pace, depending on their tolerance for change, their ability to manage the stress that accompanies change, or the amount of support provided by leaders and colleagues. We built the *Sanctuary Implementation Manual* around a three-year, gradual, step-by-step process guided by both theory and practice in incremental steps that build skills and commitment progressively.

Getting Everyone on Board—the 20-60-20 Idea

In organizational change, we have all heard that 20% of the staff will be early adopters and embrace a new idea from the beginning. The ideas resonate with some people, and they accept the Sanctuary Commitments as truth. Whoever brought the idea of adopting the Sanctuary Model in the first place will be in this group, and he or she is likely to have recruited a few more people. They will leap at the opportunity to go to the Sanctuary Institute for training and therefore are likely to be members of the Steering Committee or the Core Team. It's important not to burn them out by expecting too much of them too soon.

The way in which they actually model the Commitments in their own behavior will have a great deal to do with how quickly they are able to recruit others.

At the other end of the spectrum are the never-adaptors. They also constitute about 20% of the population, and they like things the way they are and have no intention of changing. It is possible that some of them can be converted given some proper alignment of the stars, but they are unlikely to embrace the change. In most cases they actively fight the change or, through their behavior, demonstrate their disdain for the new way. This group need not be vilified for their unwillingness to accept these new ideas. In the Andrus process these were all good people, with no ill will; they just did not agree with our change of direction or were wedded to the old way of doing things. It is important that the staff members who fall into this group eventually be helped to exit the organization. It is preferable to help them discover that this is a place where they are no longer happy and have them decide to leave on their own, but if they fail to make this discovery they need to be shown the door. They do not need to be thrown through the door, but they do need to exit.

Then there is the 60% in the middle. Of this group, 30% are fairly pliable and given the right help, support, direction, and training, they will get on board and embrace the change. They may need to see that it works and that the organization is really committed to the change, but once they know this, they are ready to come along. The other 30% is more resistant. It takes them a little longer, and they are more easily influenced by the 20% of never-adopting resisters. A more sustained effort is needed to bring them along. They need more time, more support, and more evidence to change. In the early stages of change they can be a valuable asset because they are great at pointing out the gaps, failures, and shortcomings of the new system. Eventually, however, they need to embrace the changes. They may always be a little skeptical, but you cannot let them drift into the resister category. If they do, you need to manage them as resisters.

We All Pay a Price for Exclusion

From the point of view of diversity, the initial working group at Andrus that became the prototype for the Core Team was diverse in terms of race, gender, sexual orientation, age, experience, and education, except that we left out key component parts of the organization. We did not include a nurse or a psychiatrist. At the time, the agency outsourced its health center services, so the nursing staff were not actually agency employees. In retrospect, it was easier to leave it alone. We saw involving psychiatry as too expensive, also a faulty argument. On some level we did not know better, but it does tell us something when we chose to leave out an entire group of employees. It might suggest that their voice is not considered important or that they may be seen as resisters, and rather than deal with the resistance, we push it to the margins.

Sandy said that based on the notion of the therapeutic community, the departments that did not have direct contact with the children should still be included, like the maintenance staff, custodial staff, food service staff, business office staff, finance staff, and personnel staff. Brian disagreed and was reluctant to take those staff members away from their usual duties. In retrospect, we agree that this was a mistake. We corrected it in the Sanctuary Institute implementation process by creating staff trainings for both direct care staff and indirect care staff and by encouraging all organizations to include representatives of all departments in the Core Team.

Having to Do the Process—Don't Just Do Something, Sit Around and Talk

Brian and the staff at Andrus thought that we were gathering the team together to talk about treatment of the children and their families. The staff were used to training programs that are more like recipes—do this, don't do that, in five easy steps. This was nothing like that. Just as we urge clients to try something different to disrupt old patterns, we need to do the same with the organization, but no one fully recognized that at the time. The early steps were slow and painful. Brian remembers at one point saying, "This is excruciating." It seemed that there was a lot of talking and not much doing. Everyone was great at identifying the roadblocks but not particularly adept at figuring out how to get over them.

There was a lot of sparring and *a lot* of hurt feelings. We both remember several heated arguments, with people storming out of the room and then coming back, but neither of us can accurately recall what those arguments were about. Overall, it seemed that these emotional moments were prompted by one party devaluing the contribution or role of another. Throughout the process, considerable anger was directed at a couple of the leaders in the room. It was fascinating that these angry outbursts were not equally directed at all leaders. Two leaders, Brian and the Residential Director at the time, were the primary targets. In retrospect, people probably didn't have more issues with those two leaders than anyone else, but they were both safer targets because they were more willing and able to hear what was said and sit with criticism. Part of the organizational culture that emerged is that Andrus staff members were good at identifying what others should be doing but not particularly good at identifying what they themselves could or should be doing.

Resistance to Traumatic Origins

As part of this process, we also held several case conferences on some of the most traumatized children. What was remarkable was the team's collective difficulty in dealing with the issue of trauma in general. Here we were, working with Sandy, because of her expertise, to improve the way we worked with traumatized people, and none of us wanted to talk about or deal with the issue of trauma. Every time Sandy or her colleagues brought up the issue of trauma, the whole group would collude to change the subject. This was a powerful realization for Brian, Sandy, and the whole team because it taught us a lot about the nature of what we were up against and how hard it would be to change our practice in this area. It was both fascinating and disturbing to see how frequently we completely "forgot" about the traumatic histories of our children and their families and how seldom those histories played a role in determining what the child's patterns were or how we should respond to them. It was also disturbing to see how the resistance was entirely unconscious *and* shared as a group. In one moment, group members would "know" all about it, and the next they would promptly "forget." We now use that group forgetting process as an example of how difficult it is for all of us to change our mental models about how the world works.

This is not uncommon. The staff had a couple of hurdles to clear in this process. First, it is hard to accept that such terrible things had happened to the children in their care. No one enjoys listening to the stories and coming face to face with man's inhumanity to man. Additionally, once a client has told you his or her story, you have to do something about it. If you don't know what to do, it is easier not to know. Third, if you have operated for many years with the notion that clients are either sick or bad, it is hard to accept the idea that they are actually injured. They may tell you about their injuries, but you fail to appreciate that this is not a peripheral issue but rather the central issue.

Mission Accomplished—Oops, Maybe Not

After two years of planning and implementing, it seemed that we were ready to declare victory. We had implemented Sanctuary (meaning that we had trained everyone, had introduced the tools, and were using most of the tools most of the time). We were ready to stand on our aircraft carrier with the "Mission Accomplished" banner behind us and announce that we had prevailed. We were now a Sanctuary. Unfortunately, we were not done then, and we are still not done now, and we will never be done. Sanctuary is like life in that "it ain't over 'til it's over." Every day and every new experience provides an opportunity to move forward or slide back. We've done our share of both, as have all of the agencies we have trained.

It's about Leadership

While implementing Sanctuary is everyone's job in an organization, there is a special burden on the leaders. Several themes run through this book and the implementation process that are worth highlighting one more time. We are convinced that implementation begins with leadership, and we dropped the ball in this area. When we rolled out Sanctuary at Andrus, we rolled it out to all of the staff at the same time. We did nothing different or separate for the leaders. In doing things this way, we did not appreciate or anticipate that leadership is subject to the same 20-60-20 rule we described earlier. It is a mistake to think that all leaders are going to leap on board the change train any faster than the people who report to them. In fact, they might be even more reluctant. Without leadership behind the new initiative, it is unlikely that any of the middle 60% will fully get on board and it is unlikely that the 20% of resisters will be helped to the door. In fact, the resisters might become even more empowered because they support the leader's position. In this situation, the early adopters are likely to be the ones heading for the door and taking with them any hope of real change.

We engaged our senior leaders in the Core Team, but some were never really touched by the group. Brian believes now that they were not touched because the group knew they could not tolerate being challenged in any significant way. If you are a leader in a Sanctuary program, you'd better be ready, willing, and able to be challenged. We did not read this dynamic correctly, and we went to battle with two lieutenants who were not ready or willing to fight our fight. They were not opposed to Sanctuary, they were just not ready to make the personal changes required to lead the process. There is a big difference between saying you believe in something and actually behaving differently. The departments these two persons led never really got on board because their leaders never really got on board. Both have since found their way to the door, but life would have been easier if they had exited sooner or were challenged to adapt. To sum up, if we knew then what we know now, we would have started with the leaders, clarified the expectations for them, and tested their resolve in a different way. The good thing about many things in life is that there are do-overs. Do-overs are a good thing.

All of these activities are ultimately directed at creating a safety culture in the organization we work in. If people are to feel safe, we need to establish an optimum level of trust, which requires leaders to be ethical, honest, transparent, compassionate, and well regulated. Power needs to be used to advance an organization's mission, not the personal agenda of the leader. It is no small task to inspire trust in an organization and its members, but it is essential to healthy functioning and attachment. A crucial way we inspire trust is by ensuring that we are always reaching for more participation from all staff. Leaders need to value the ideas and opinions of all staff and clients and consistently look for ways to engage everyone in problem solving.

Additionally, leaders need to lead from the future. If we are to avoid falling into constant reenactments with clients, as well as with our staff, we need to have a clear vision of where we want to go and the change we hope to see. With that endpoint in mind, we can think about and plan for the potential losses associated with that different future and how these changes might disrupt people's feeling of safety. With a clearer sense of these challenges, we can more effectively help everyone manage the emotions associated with these changes.

The Sanctuary implementation process is challenging, nonlinear, messy, and ongoing. We have developed what we feel is an effective process, but we are constantly improving and refining it based on what we learn from the agencies we work with each day. We try to live by the principles we present in this book. We say that implementation is messy because even though there are some tools that we ask organizations to use, the process of discovery is often unpredictable, impossible to script, and deeply personal. Once an organization assembles its Core Team and begins to grapple with the gaps between what they are and what they hope to become, strange and wonderful things can happen. When leaders and staff begin to have conversations they never had before and begin to learn from each other, all kinds of new possibilities emerge. People begin to imagine what they might be able to accomplish together.

Ready Set Go, Ready Set Go Again, Ready Set Go Again...

The conversations that need to occur at all levels in the organization can be incredibly scary and challenging. Imagining what we can accomplish together raises the questions "What do we need to change to get there?" "What do I need to give up?" "What do I need to take on?" As possibilities emerge and new things begin to happen, the organization inevitably will end up in a state of disequilibrium, and the anxiety created by this state can either propel the organization forward or drive it back. Sometimes it will take many fits and starts before things begin to move in a better direction. Organizations that are already in a state of crisis may move quickly to a better place because they are ready for something new. They may also struggle more because they lack the leadership and basic systems to really change. More established, high-functioning organizations may move quickly because they have the systems and resources in place to implement change, but some may be stalled by a sense that their current mode of operation is adequate, so change might be resisted more intensely.

Like every client in our care, every organization is unique. Every leader of every organization is unique as well. Although we do have a process for implementation, we are willing to try something new when an organization gets stuck. We have repeatedly said in this volume that if a client is not changing, you need to try something different. We believe that the same holds true for organizations. If they are not getting where they want to go, then ask, "What can we change in ourselves to create the possibility of change in others?"

Democracy, Shmemocracy

Andrus has a long history of a top-down, hierarchical, autocratic management style, a kind of benevolent dictatorship. It has always been an institution that has cared for and about children, but it was far more invested in control and coercion as the vehicle of change and it had questionable faith in the ability of the staff working directly with the children to choose the proper intervention to effect change.

When we started discussing the Sanctuary Model there was a lot of talk about democracy, developing a constitution, and other subversive ideas. The notion of doing something different, managing or leading in a more open and participatory fashion, was both exciting and intimidating. When a leader introduces the Sanctuary Model and starts talking about democratic processes and shared decision making, the first reaction is that the person is either kidding or has totally lost his or her mind. Once people see that the person is displaying no other symptoms of madness (like wearing underwear on the outside or showing up at work dressed as a pirate), they begin to look for evidence that the organization is not really serious about this change. They look for evidence that contradicts what the leader is telling them: that Sanctuary is going to be the new world order. In the early stages of the change it is easy to see the inconsistencies and the gaps and easy to believe that this change is all talk. This change is also new to the leaders, and we are all prone to sliding back to our familiar ways of operating. How likely is it that an organization that used to operate the way we just described is willing to engage with staff in decision making? This is a total cultural shift.

Brian's initial frustration with the process was not about how tough it is for leaders to give up the reins of power; the hard part was that there was so little interest at lower levels of the organization in picking up the slack and taking more responsibility for decisions. It seemed that no matter what leaders said or how they behaved, Core Team members had enormous difficulty breaking away from old patterns. As a leader, it was very difficult to struggle through this process. While Core Team members complained about the evil and punitive autocracy, they took little initiative to start projects and make changes. Early on, Brian had difficulty resisting the impulse to jump in and overdirect the process or to criticize everyone for their passivity. Doing so would not have advanced the group process; it would only have confirmed their belief that as a leader he was a controlling and scary guy.

The initial challenge for Brian was to work with the Core Team in a way that indicated that he was willing to be more democratic and embrace a participatory management style. In order to demonstrate that he was willing to adopt this style of management, he had to sit and wait patiently for everyone else's participation. But leaders usually become leaders because they are action-oriented. Brian had to learn to bite his tongue but his face usually shows what he feels, so that was not always an effective strategy. It is clear now that the patient waiting he did was essential to moving. It is entirely possible for leaders to get too far ahead of their followers. Waiting for them sent a not-so-subtle message that he wanted them to come along.

What became apparent in this process is that the hierarchical culture at Andrus is firmly entrenched. Staff members send significant decisions upstairs and then complain about the awful decisions leaders make. Leaders happily make all the important decisions while grousing about the impotence and helplessness of the staff. These are the expected roles and patterns. Brian initially thought that if leaders changed, followers would quickly get in line. But what he found in this process was that when leaders change, the first response of the followers is skepticism, quickly followed by a frenzied effort to get leaders to behave the way they always have done. As a leader, Brian had to learn to be patient and maintain faith that the organization was going in the right direction even though it sometimes appeared stalled. In retrospect, Brian has also wondered whether he actually made the changes required in those early days. Although there was a lot of talk about being more democratic, there was probably not a significant shift in the kinds of tasks that were delegated to staff or middle managers. There remained a gap between what was said and what was done.

Turnover is another significant challenge faced by the organization, and it can be exacerbated by change. If you decide suddenly that it is time to move from an autocratic system to a more democratic system, you may think that this can only be a good thing. It is quite possible, however, that the persons who were hired to work in an autocratic environment might not thrive in a democracy. Making a major shift in philosophy and culture may result in higher turnover at first.

In addition to having patience, we learned that leaders need to model appropriate behavior at all times. If the leaders at Andrus were going to move their Core Team to a place where the team members could believe that the leaders were serious about their participation, it was essential for the leaders to get out of the way and try not to control the process. As leaders and facilitators, we had to listen to opposing points of view, avoid stepping on people's thoughts, welcome dissent, and do all of this in a respectful and civil fashion. This needed to happen for two fundamental reasons. First, line staff initially want to maintain the status quo. They believe that the leaders are going to misbehave, and we cannot validate that belief. Even more important, this is where we begin to send powerful messages about the kind of organization we hope to become. If we hope to develop a program based on respect and compassion, then leaders have to model these values for all community members. Power will always be unequally distributed in organizations like ours, but power does not give us the right to misbehave. If we believe we can treat our staff badly because we are more powerful, then what kind of moral authority do we have to ask our staff to treat clients respectfully? Leaders always need to be the best-behaved people in the organization.

Watch Your Front Door

We did not watch the front door closely enough, that is, we did not pay close enough attention to who we were hiring and how we were preparing our new hires. This mistake was in part exacerbated by the mistake we made about the leaders. If leaders are not clear about what changes they want to make, they do not consider those issues when hiring new staff. If they do not consider the desired changes when hiring, then they are likely to hire persons who would be successful in the old system, not the new one. These decisions make it even harder to implement the changes we hope to advance.

This mistake was also exacerbated by our declaring victory too soon. After we trained all of our existing staff, we did not build a robust system for ensuring that all new hires had a full and thorough orientation. We did not spend enough time in orientation reviewing how Andrus was different because we now employed the Sanctuary Model. We did not clearly articulate our values and expectations. Many of us on the Core Team thought that the Model was so compelling that it would just ooze out of the walls. In reality, very few of us have had much experience in organizations that operate democratically, encouraging open communication, social learning, and social responsibility. The assumption that people would embrace this regime implicitly was wishful thinking.

Our failure to properly shape leaders' behavior and properly orient new staff meant that our front door was wide open, and we were not hiring persons with different qualities and adequately trying to shape and reinforce these qualities in the early stages of employment.

Managing Paradox

In our first years with Sanctuary, we were neither clear enough nor brave enough to manage the paradoxes inherent in the Model. We talked endlessly about how important it is that the staff and children feel safe. The problem is, how do we square this sense of safety with the feeling that if you don't get on board, you will be out of work? Although this is not really a paradox, we think that for many leaders, who were reluctant anyway, it made disciplinary responses feel like threats and attacks. How could anyone feel safe when their teammate was being fired? On the other hand, how could anyone feel safe when their teammate was missing two or three days of work each month or actively working against the values we were trying to establish in the organization? At times, we allowed ourselves to be trapped in this situation and failed to exert leadership. Early in the implementation process we had this discussion and someone said, "We can't allow this to be a safe place for people who are not committed to making it a safe place." People who are not committed to the Sanctuary Commitments need to get on board or go.

When you begin to change the corporate culture, the process is very disruptive and creates numerous tensions within the organization. Staff members who have always been considered good at "controlling" the children may feel angry and displaced when their methods of control are challenged and called

"violent." Clients may escalate their acting out in order to prompt a familiar response. Understanding the response of our clients requires us to better
understand ourselves and accept that we need to change before we can hope to
inspire change the people with whom we work. Staff members are pulled out
of regular programming for training, leaving others to carry more responsibility. Community Meetings challenge all of us to connect with each other in a
different way and challenge staff members to call on or develop new skills and
capacities.

Problems that have been left unchallenged for a considerable period of time
may surface and compel a response. Adopting the Sanctuary Model is likely to
make things very uncomfortable for people who have been using the organization for some dubious motivations of their own. They may have created some
very difficult situations that will need to be addressed. Problems like bullying,
harassment, sabotage, anonymous threats, counteraggression, and sexual abuse
may come out into the open and need to be dealt with appropriately. Do not use
Sanctuary as an excuse to ignore unsafe behavior. If anything, use it as a reason
to address those problems immediately, directly, and thoroughly.

Our failure to deal with the leadership issues at times exacerbated our problems with implementation. If staff members see leaders who operate on the
margins, engaged in problematic behavior without consequences, then they
understandably grumble when they, or their colleagues, are criticized for the
same behavior. We need to be brave enough to hold everyone accountable,
including our cronies and ourselves, if we are going to make changes. We have
come to realize that safety is a relative term, and we cannot expect to be safe if
we do not do the things that are required by the organization. There is also a
great deal of confusion in differentiating between the words "safe" and "comfortable." Change is virtually never comfortable, but that does not mean that it
is unsafe.

Are We "Doing Sanctuary"?

In the second part of this trilogy, *Destroying Sanctuary: The Crisis in Human
Service Delivery Systems*, we gave a sobering account of what has happened in
the last few decades to service delivery. It was an attempt to explain what we
believed was, and still is, wrong with our human service and mental health
system and how it had gotten that way [12]. We attempted to explain why these
systems, which are supposed to help people change and recover, often seem to
make things worse for those seeking help. We explained how the system itself
has fallen victim to the impact of repetitive stress, adversity, and trauma and, on
many levels, had begun to look and operate much like the injured people it was
supposed to help. It was admittedly a difficult account and a rather sobering
tale. For many people who took the time and endured the pain of reading it, it
had the ring of truth. It described what helping professionals see and feel every

day but may not have the words to describe. Although it framed the problem, it did not provide much hope that things could be better.

In that volume we described how communication channels break down under stress, and we have seen it happen consistently at Andrus as we struggled to adopt the Sanctuary Model. We work intensively on an issue like budget planning or new program development, and because of the intensity of some of this work, we do not stop to keep people up to speed on the process. Even though we have good intentions, people really care more about the consequences. A sudden, abrupt announcement that surprises people ends up eradicating all of the good work that may have gone into planning. Although we have talked a lot about Sanctuary and have talked about the concepts for years, we still maintain a very black-and-white, good-or-bad, "we are doing it" or "we are not doing it" approach to the implementation process, and it constantly jams us up.

When we start working with other programs, particularly the most challenging ones, we often hear things like "Sanctuary isn't working," as if it were something that runs on batteries and the batteries are dead, so it isn't working. In truth, it's a process that each of us is either engaged with or not every moment of every day. But such a comment is worth listening to because it indicates that the process has become bogged down and, in all likelihood, so have the people engaged in that process. So, what is it that gets us out of the holes we find ourselves in? We need to envision being out of them and then starting to climb our way out. Otherwise, we just stay down there in the hole and starve to death.

Sometimes things get bogged down because organizations do not have the proper scorecards in place to determine whether the changes they are making are effective. The only scorecards we started with were numbers of incidents. But is that really how we should measure change? What are the outcomes we are hoping for as a result of our work? If we are not clear about that and don't have the measures in place to ensure that we are making progress, it is easy to get bogged down. We keep redesigning the implementation and the certification process as we get feedback about what prevents that bog-down effect. We have learned that for many organizations, outside technical assistance is mandatory. When there are so many immediate priorities, it is easy to forget where you are trying to go unless you have somebody else who is asking the right questions and directing you back on course.

In our Sanctuary implementation we sometimes lose the forest for the trees. The whole idea is that the work is complicated and stressful, and it takes all of us working together to figure it out and straighten each other out. What we encounter in our process is a good deal of back-and-forth discussion about whether we are really practicing Sanctuary. When all is said and done, we are not sure that anyone is ever "doing Sanctuary" any more than we are "doing life" or "doing love." We are always trying to get it right. We keep trying, but like anything that is hard, we often get it wrong. When we get it wrong, we should be able to talk about it, learn from it, and do it better (or "less wrong") the next time, but that does not always happen either. Something gets in our way, and we suspect that it is, more than anything else, our difficulties with forgiveness and letting go. Missteps can easily be seen as evidence that nothing has changed rather than evidence that we are all human and we pull up short from time to time. It is impressive how, at times, something that is so positive and compelling can be misused so consistently. We have often seen people hit over the head with the Sanctuary club. We might develop a new philosophy and language for how we talk about the work, but we apply the same old habits of blaming and shaming people who pull up short. You are probably not "doing Sanctuary" until you change that old habit.

The World of Bizarro

How does this happen? We think that it is hard to hold all of the commitments in our minds and hearts at the same time. We rail that someone is not making a *Commitment to Democracy*, but no one will say anything directly to that person. So, it is wrong for you to not include others in decision making but alright for me to not say anything to you about it. An organization's leaders make a unilateral decision that seems to fly in the face of democratic decision making. Such a gaffe may be subject to criticism. If, however, the criticism is only discussed in the "meeting after the meeting," then those who are critical of a lack of democracy are clearly not committed to open communication. Secrecy and gossip are acceptable when I engage in it but not when you do. We sometimes pick and choose which commitment we make on any given day.

Along the way, we have great difficulty giving each other a break or accepting that missteps are part of the process. So, when staff persons make a mistake, leaders can easily see them as incompetent rather than as good people who had bad reactions to high levels of stress. At the same time, when leaders make mistakes, as they often do, it is easy to say, "Sure, they talk about it, but they don't do it. If one of us screwed up like that, we would be fired." Both positions are extreme, and that is exactly what happens under pressure. We engage in either/ or thinking, but we do not see it as a stress reaction; we see it as justified. We see heroes and villains, perpetrators and victims.

In our Sanctuary Institute training we do an activity on the Bizarro World of the Sanctuary Commitments. For those of you who might not be familiar with Superman Comics, the Bizarro World was an alternate universe in which Superman was evil, at times rather dimwitted, and behaved in a manner opposite from the way Superman behaves in this universe. In our activity, we imagine a world where people are committed to stagnation instead of growth and change; to violence instead of nonviolence; to fascism instead of democracy; to insensitivity instead of emotional intelligence; to stupidity instead of social learning; to secrecy instead of open communication; and to "me" instead of social responsibility.

Looking at the Sanctuary Commitments in this way illustrates how absurd it is to consider any organization that would be opposed to making these commitments and instead chooses to live in the Bizarro World. Unfortunately, when we look at some of our practices and are honest with ourselves, we find that each day we actually live part of the time in the Bizarro World, doing the opposite of what we say we should be doing. We use coercion and fear to motivate, we make unilateral decisions about issues that affect others, we keep secrets, and we repeat failed strategies. We don't do it all the time, but we do it often. We do it because we are vulnerable to the impact of repetitive stress and because we are human.

None of the commitments stand alone. It is inconceivable that an organization could be democratic and not commit to social responsibility, social learning, and open communication. You cannot grow and change without learning. You cannot communicate effectively if you don't manage your emotions; you cannot speak your mind if you are fearful of retribution. The challenge here is that we *all* have to honor *all* the commitments *all* of the time. While this never happens perfectly in any organization, it is the goal. Grappling with the gaps is the route to getting better and moving further along the road to change. When leaders make unilateral decisions and someone confronts this behavior, learning and change are now possible. If no one confronts it, leaders should ask, "Why?" Really making these commitments means being willing to push each other to be better.

Often when confronted on these issues, it is easy to make an excuse. "That decision wasn't very democratic" might be met with "I am a leader, I'm leading!" Similarly, asking, "Why didn't you speak up?" might be met with "I was afraid the administrators will retaliate." If we settle for those canned responses, nothing changes and we continue to play our assigned roles with each other. By "commitment" we mean being morally obligated and emotionally compelled to follow through, as best we can, on what the commitment means. Earlier we discussed how important it is to provide hope for the people we work with. It is also crucial to be brave. Change is hard work and is not for the squeamish. We need to be brave enough to say what we have to say and hear what we don't want to hear and then make a change we may not want to make. When we make changes in ourselves, it not only inspires change in others, it compels change in others.

Not Seeing Positive Change

What we seem to watch for is evidence of how things have not changed rather than evidence of how things have changed. It is what we are programmed to see, and it is always possible to cite this evidence because there are always regressions in the process of change. It takes a long time for our patterns to change and take hold. If we point to every regression on either side as evidence that things really haven't changed, then they really haven't. The fundamental pattern remains intact: we are not on the same page, and we are not in this together.

The last seven years have been very trying times at Andrus. We have a new leadership team, we are trying to establish a new culture, and the agency has grown in size and complexity. We are trying to build systems to manage the increased complexity, and we have been trying to do a lot of catchup on this front. There is a great deal of pressure for everyone as we are trying to build a new structure. Large gaps still exist in our systems, and it will take time to close them. This is difficult when we are confronted on a daily basis with the 3, 6, 12, or 24 different things we still need to deal with. It is easy to focus more on the gaps that still exist rather than those we have closed. It is easier, for some reason, to think about the doom that may accompany our failure to solve a certain problem than it is to be proud of our accomplishments so far. But we cannot do everything at once and we need to be patient with the process, even if we are rattled by it. A huge part of leadership is the ability to contain the anxiety associated with gaps we see in our programming and practices. We want to create movement and urgency, not panic.

Problems with Power and Sliding Backward

The power differentials can also confound us in this process. Staff members often feel that they cannot speak frankly to people in power. There is the myth that if you say to someone in power "I think you are wrong" or "I think you made a mistake," you will be hurt. The feeling is that you will not be hurt today, or tomorrow, or next week, but it will happen, often when you least expect it. It is this sense that the organization is not safe that keeps us from speaking honestly to each other.

The way it used to work at Andrus was that senior leaders took care of all the nontreatment matters—things like budgets, billing, compliance, and crisis management The line staff worked with clients, but much of this work was directed by management as well. There was always some grousing about money, power, and position, but it was clear who did what. The program was simpler, the funding was simpler, and life was simpler.

Sanctuary has stood this system on its head, and the old order no longer applies. We are trying to find a new way, but it is difficult and painful and some people are wedded to the old order—not because it is best, but because it is what they are used to. It has not been particularly challenging to embrace the notion of democracy, but it has been challenging to sustain it. Democracy does not just imply that leaders are willing to share but that everyone is willing to share, and we are still working on that notion.

As we mentioned, moving from an autocratic system to a democratic system is not easy. Many years ago, the staff at Andrus were treated more like children than they are now. It is hard to take on more responsibility and ownership. It is even harder to do this when you are under considerable pressure. The clients are more challenging, the requirements are more challenging, and now we are trying to move people to a different level of involvement and decision making. In the process, people may reasonably wonder, "How is this reducing my level of stress and frustration? How is this helping me?" It becomes easy to slide back into the old patterns and keep them in place. The old way is our default position, and when we do not have time to think and plan, it is easy to fall back into old patterns. We are beginning to discover that the solution to all of our problems is more, not less, democracy. The more staff, clients, and other stake-holders feel a part of what we are trying to build, the more willing they will be to help us.

Using Sanctuary to Explore the Edge of Chaos

What we do have the power to do is to change ourselves; change the way we look at problems; change the way we think about our clients; and change the way we think about our organizations. We can create change in ourselves. We can do something different each day with our clients and avoid the harmful effects of continually replaying the past. Danger and the loss of safety are usu-ally the wakeup calls that urge individual survivors and organizations to rec-ognize that it is time for change. On the other hand, threat, dangers, and loss arouse individual and organizational anxiety, and stress and fear tend to drive us back to doing whatever is familiar.

The familiar is our "equilibrium state," and because it is familiar, that equilib-rium state often feels safer than anything else. It is the state we find ourselves in without even thinking about it. Great stress keeps us from thinking clearly; in fact, it may keep us from thinking altogether. We just keep doing what we have always done. As a species, we are fundamentally risk aversive. Deeply embed-ded in every organizational culture are the "equilibrium attractors" helping to guarantee that a system will return to its previous stable point, even after a radical divergence from that position. All change requires some degree of risk, and to help clients make the difficult but necessary changes in their lives, the organization as a whole needs to become less risk aversive and more mindful.

Once we start facing organizational problems, we find that they are generally bigger and more complex than they appeared at first, and it is difficult to know where to start. When faced with complexity, it is important to have a cohesive framework that helps structure the formulation of an action plan for change, knowing that change is normally resisted because maintaining equilibrium is what all living systems seek in order to stay viable. In a therapeutic, educational, or social service situation, it is essential that the client and the helper get on the same page so that their strategies for achieving identified goals are aligned. Similarly, in an organizational setting, it is critical that staff members, administrators, and, when relevant, Board members agree on basic assumptions and beliefs about their shared mission, desired outcomes, and methods for achieving their goals.

When an organization has at least a vague outline of another set of "attractors"—something they want to do or be in the future—then and only then does it become possible to begin moving the organization away from its stable equilibrium point, an equilibrium point that is likely to have become a situation of chronic crisis. In organizations adopting the Sanctuary Model, those attractors become things like "eliminating seclusion and restraint," "being more effective in treating traumatized children, adults, and families," "having fewer staff injuries," and "having less staff turnover." We need to become riveted on the future and constantly ask ourselves if this strategy, this behavior, or this pattern is actually taking us to that future or keeping us trapped in the past.

In chaos theory, the place of transformation, of true creative change, is "on the edge of chaos," and for individuals and organizations, that can be a very scary place to be. The Sanctuary Model is designed as a kind of organizational "spacesuit" that allows an organization to venture out into and explore unknown territory while remaining tethered to its own vehicle for sufficient safety to make the trip. Once the members of the community have found a "place" to which they want to go and the attraction of that place is sufficiently strong, they can let go of the tether and with some degree of reliability go to the new place.

The Holy Experiment, Moral Treatment, and Healing Communities

The key question that we are addressing in this book, and in the work that backs it up, is "What is a truly 'therapeutic community,' a group setting that promotes healing and health for everyone?" Part of the background for our work is the practice of the democratic therapeutic community that has its origins in the Moral Treatment movement of the eighteenth and early nineteenth centuries, as well as approaches to disadvantaged youth and combat victims of the twentieth century [228]. As Bloom and Norton wrote:

The therapeutic community is in many ways a subversive idea in that the goal of the TC is not to maintain an unhappy status quo but to create the "heat" that generates change. This change is generated largely through the democratically informed interactions between staff and clients and clients with each other. And today, the institutionally based practice of this "deep democracy" is itself a subversive notion in that it seeks to subvert the militaristic, hierarchical, and

frequently punitive and retributive control structures that typically character-
ize most of our social systems and replace them with an environment offering
different styles of relating that seek to avoid the repeating of past traumas.
(pp. 230–231) [229]

Nonviolent social and political movements emerged first among the Quakers in colonial North America. The founder of the Society of Friends, George Fox, believed that the civil war between good and evil was not external but internal, a spiritual war within every human being, and that the only way to overcome the external evils in the world is to overcome inner evil by following the Inner Light and choosing to act in loving, nonviolent ways. He believed that Truth is in everyone and that we each have a responsibility to listen, attune ourselves, and act on that Inner Light that he recognized as God [110, 126, 230]. The Sanctuary Model was developed in Philadelphia, where William Penn and the Quakers created their "Holy Experiment" (there being no word for nonviolence at that time) and demonstrated that nonviolence could work in every depart-ment of government from defense to criminal justice. The Experiment endured for 70 years until the vision faded and the Quaker Party lost its mandate at the ballot box. For those 70 years the Holy Experiment included a diverse collec-tion of colonists from many parts of Europe and with several religions who lived in relative harmony under Penn's "Great Law." The Great Law even abol-ished war on December 7, 1682 (the day of the attack on Pearl Harbor 259 years later—an interesting historical coincidence) [231].

We believe that creating safe communities is the answer to many of our social problems, what author Tina Rosenberg has described as the "social cure," in which communities of peers get together to solve big problems [232]. But experience tells us that we can only manufacture hope in communities that embody the principles and commitments we have discussed in this volume. Hope can flourish in a community where people are committed to making the future better, where they feel valued and appreciated, where they can listen and be heard, where they feel safe being who they are but challenged to be better, where they learn from experience, and where they feel some obligation to help others and get help for themselves when their well runs dry. We believe organi-zations that take on the Sanctuary Commitments are places where hope is alive and well, and as a result, transformation is both possible and necessary for our wounded world.

References

1. Rich, A . (1978). *The Dream of a Common Language: Poems 1974–1977*. New York: W. W. Norton.
2. Bloom, S. L. (1997). *Creating Sanctuary: Toward the Evolution of Sane Societies*. New York: Routledge.
3. Silver, S. (1986). An inpatient program for post-traumatic stress disorder: Context as treatment. In C. Figley (Ed.), *Trauma and Its Wake, Volume II: Post-Traumatic Stress Disorder: Theory, Research and Treatment* (pp. 215). New York: Brunner/Mazel.
4. Wilson, E. O. (1998). *Consilience: The Unity of Knowledge*. New York: Alfred A. Knopf.
5. Braun, B. G. (1988). The B.A.S.K. model of dissociation. *Dissociation, 1*(1), 4–23.
6. Bloom, S. L. (1994). The Sanctuary Model: Developing generic inpatient programs for the treatment of psychological trauma. In M. B. Williams & J. F. Sommers (Eds.), *Handbook of Post-Traumatic Therapy: A Practical Guide to Intervention, Treatment, and Research* (pp. 444–491). Westport, CT: Greenwood Publishing.
7. National Council on the Developing Child. (2006). *Perspectives: Early Influences on Brain Architecture: An Interview with Neuroscientist Eric Knudsen*. Retrieved 8/20/08 from http://www.developingchild.net
8. McEwen, B. S., & Gianaros, P. J. (2010). Central role of the brain in stress and adaptation: Links to socioeconomic status, health, and disease. *Annals of the New York Academy of Sciences, 1186*, 190–222.
9. Marmot, M. (2004). *The Status Syndrome: How Social Standing Affects Our Health and Longevity*. New York: Henry Holt.
10. Hubble, M. A., Duncan, B. L., & Miller, S. D. (Eds.). (1999). *The Heart and Soul of Change: What Works in Therapy*. Washington, DC: American Psychological Association Press.
11. Lipowski, Z. J. (1989). Psychiatry: mindless or brainless, both or neither? *Canadian Journal of Psychiatry, 34*(3), 249–254.
12. Bloom, S. L., & Farragher, B. (2010). *Destroying Sanctuary: The Crisis in Human Service Delivery Systems*. New York: Oxford University Press.
13. Smith, K. K., Simmons, V. M., & Thames, T. B. (1989). "Fix the women": An intervention into an organizational conflict based on parallel process thinking. *The Journal of Applied Behavioral Science, 25*(1), 11–29.
14. Bentovim, A. (1992). *Trauma-Organized Systems: Physical and Sexual Abuse in Families*. London: Karnac Books.

15. Gazzaniga, M. (2011). *Who's in Charge?: Free Will and the Science of the Brain*. New York: HarperCollins.
16. Silver, S. (1986). An inpatient program for post-traumatic stress disorder: Context as treatment. In C. Figley (Ed.), *Trauma and Its Wake, Volume II: Post-Traumatic Stress Disorder: Theory, Research and Treatment* (pp. 213–231). New York: Brunner/ Mazel.
17. Bowlby, J. (1988). *A Secure Base: Parent-Child Attachment and Healthy Human Development*. New York: Basic Books.
18. National Scientific Council on the Developing Child. (2010). *Early Experiences Can Alter Gene Expression and Affect Long-Term Development: Working Paper No. 10, http://www.developingchild.net. Working Paper 10*, Center for the Developing Child. Accessed October 2, 2012.
19. Schein, E. H. (1999). *The Corporate Culture: A Survival Guide. Sense and Nonsense about Culture Change*. San Francisco: Jossey-Bass.
20. Pascale, R. T., Millemann, M., & Gioja, L. (2000). *Surfing the Edge of Chaos: The Laws of Nature and the New Laws of Business*. New York: Crown Business.
21. Harris, M., & Fallot, R. (2001). Envisioning a trauma-informed service system: A vital paradigm shift. *New Directions for Mental Health Services, 89*, 3–22.
22. Anda, R. F. & Brown, D. W. (2010). *Adverse Childhood Experience and Population Health in Washington: The face of a Chronic Public Health Disaster. Results From the 2009 Behavioral Risk Factor of Surveillance System*. Washington State Family Council. Retrieved from http://www.fpc.wa.gov/publications/ACEs%20in%20 Washington.2009%20BRFSS.Final%20Report%207%207%202010.pdf. Accessed September 16, 2012.
23. Felitti, V. J., & Anda, R. F. (2010). The relationship of adverse childhood experiences to adult medical disease, psychiatric disorders, and sexual behavior: Implications for healthcare. In R. Lanius & E. Vermetten (Eds.), *The Hidden Epidemic: The Impact of Early Life Trauma on Health and Disease* (pp. 77–87). New York: Cambridge University Press.
24. Centers for Disease Control. (2010, December 17). Adverse childhood experiences reported by adults—five states, 2009. *Morbidity and Mortality Weekly Report, 59*, 1609–1613.
25. Bloom, S. L. (1995). The germ theory of trauma: The impossibility of ethical neutrality. In B. H. Stamm (Ed.), *Secondary Traumatic Stress: Self Care Issues for Clinicians, Researchers and Educators* (pp. 257–276). Brooklandville, MD: Sidran Foundation.
26. World Health Organization. (1948). *Preamble to the Constitution of the World Health Organization as adopted by the International Health Conference*, New York, 19 June - 22 July 1946; signed on 22 July 1946 by the representatives of 61 States and entered into force on 7 April 1948. Official Records of the World Health Organization, 2: p. 100.
27. Siegel, D. J. (2012). *Pocket Guide to Interpersonal Neurobiology: An Integrative Handbook of the Mind*. Norton Series on Interpersonal Neurobiology. New York: W. W. Norton.
28. Center on the Developing Child at Harvard University. (2010). *The Foundations of Lifelong Health Are Built in Early Childhood*. National Forum on Early Childhood Policy and Programs, Retrieved 7/8/12 from http://www.developingchild.harvard.edu
29. Wilkinson, R., & Pickett, K. (2009). *The Spirit Level: Why Greater Equality Makes Societies Stronger*. New York: Bloomsbury.
30. Public Health Agency of Canada. (2011). *What Determines Health?* Retrieved 5/12/11 from http://www.phac-aspc.gc.ca/ph-sp/determinants/index-eng.php# evidence

31. Ackoff, R. L. (2010). *Systems Thinking For Curious Managers*. Axminster, U.K.: Triarchy Press.
32. Hartmann, T. (2004). *What Would Jefferson Do? A Return to Democracy*. New York: Harmony Books.
33. Bloom, S. L. (2005). The Sanctuary Model of organizational change for children's residential treatment. *Therapeutic Community: The International Journal for Therapeutic and Supportive Organizations, 26*(1), 65–81.
34. Iacoboni, M. (2008). *Mirroring People: The New Science of How We Connect with Each Other*. New York: Farrar, Straus and Giroux.
35. Bloom, P. (2004). *Descartes' Baby: How the Science of Child Development Explains What Makes Us Human*. New York: Basic Books.
36. World Health Organization. (2002). *World Report on Violence and Health: Summary*. Geneva: World Health Organization.
37. Shonkoff, J. P., (2009). *Investment in Early Childhood Development Lays the Foundation for a Prosperous and Sustainable Society*. Encyclopedia on Early Childhood Development, Centre of Excellence for Early Childhood Development. Retrieved October 2, 2012 at http://www.child-encyclopedia.com/documents/ShonkoffANGxp.pdf
38. Iacoboni, M. (2008). *Mirroring People: The New Science of How We Connect with Others*. New York: Farrar, Straus and Giroux.
39. National Scientific Council on the Developing Child. (2007). *The Science of Early Childhood Development*, Retrieved 3/23/09 from http://www.developingchild.net
40. Axelrod, R. (1984). *The Evolution of Cooperation*. New York: Basic Books.
41. Gazzaniga, M. (2011). *Who's in Charge? Free Will and the Science of the Brain*. New York: HarperCollins.
42. Duhigg, C. (2012). *The Power of Habit: Why We Do What We Do in Life and Business*. New York: Random House.
43. Vidaver-Cohen, D. (1998). Moral climate in business firms: A conceptual framework for analysis and change. *Journal of Business Ethics, 17*(11): 1211–1226.
44. Bloom, S. L. (1994). Creating Sanctuary: Ritual abuse and complex PTSD. In V. Sinason (Ed.), *Treating Satanist Abuse Survivors: An Invisible Trauma* (pp. 285–291). London: Routledge.
45. Bloom, S. L. (1995). Creating Sanctuary in the classroom. *Journal for a Just and Caring Education, 1*(4), 403–433.
46. Bloom, S. L. (1996). Every time history repeats itself the price goes up: The social reenactment of trauma. *Sexual Addiction and Compulsivity, 3*(3), 161–194.
47. Bloom, S. L. (1998). By the crowd they have been broken, by the crowd they shall be healed: The social transformation of trauma. In R. Tedeschi, C. Park, & L. Calhoun (Eds.), *Post-Traumatic Growth: Theory and Research on Change in the Aftermath of Crises* (pp. 173–208). Mahwah, NJ: Lawrence Erlbaum.
48. Bloom, S. L. (1999). The complex web of causation: Motor vehicle accidents, comorbidity and PTSD. In E. Hickling & E. Blanchard (Eds.), *International Handbook of Road Traffic Accidents and Psychological Trauma: Theory, Treatment and Law* (pp. 155–184). Oxford: Pergamon Press.
49. Bloom, S. L. (2000). Creating Sanctuary: Healing from systematic abuses of power. *Therapeutic Communities: The International Journal for Therapeutic and Supportive Organizations, 21*(2), 67–91.
50. Rivard, J. C., McCorkle, D., Duncan, M. E., Pasquale, L. E., Bloom, S. L., & Abramovitz, R. (2004). Implementing a trauma recovery framework for youths in residential treatment. *Child and Adolescent Social Work Journal, 21*(5), 529–550.

51. McSparren, W., & Motley, D. (2010). How to improve the process of change. *Non-profit World, 28*(6), 14–15.

52. Banks, J. A., & Vargas, A. L. (2009). *Contributors to Restraints and Holds in Organizations Using the Sanctuary Model.* Andrus Center for Learning and Innovation, Yonkers, NY. Retrieved 9/16/12 from http://www.sanctuaryweb.com/PDFs_new/Banks%20and%20Vargas%20Contributors%20to%20Restraints%20and%20Holds.pdf

53. Banks, J., & Vargas, L. A. (2009). *Sanctuary at Andrus Children's Center.* Andrus Center for Learning and Innovation. Retrieved 9/16/12 from http://www.sanctuary-web.com/PDFs_new/Banks%20and%20Vargas%20Sanctuary%20at%20Andrus.pdf

54. Banks, J., & Vargas, L. A. (2009). *Sanctuary in Schools: Preliminary Child and Organizational Outcomes.* Retrieved 9/16/12 from http://www.sanctuaryweb.com/PDFs_new/Banks%20and%20Vargas%20Sanctuary%20in%20Schools.pdf

55. Stein, B. D., Kogan, J.N, Magee, E., Hindes, K. (2011). *Sanctuary Survey Final State Report, September 29. Unpublished data.*

56. Community Care Behavioral Health. (2011). *Assessing the Implementation of a Residential Facility Organizational Change Model: Pennsylvania's Implementation of the Sanctuary Model.* Retrieved 9/16/12 from http://www.ccbh.com/pdfs/articles/Sanctuary_Model_3Pager_20110715.pdf

57. Gall, J. (2002). *The Systems Bible: The Beginner's Guide to Systems Large and Small, 3rd Edition of Systemantics.* Walker, MN: General Systemantics Press.

58. Hardy, K. V. (2007). Untangling Intangible Loss in the Lives of Traumatized Children and Adolescents. In A. L. Vargas, & S. L. Bloom (Eds), *Loss, Hurt and Hope: The Complex Issues of Bereavement and Trauma in Children* (pp. 50–63). Cambridge Scholars Publishing: Newcastle, UK.

59. Hawken, P. (2009). *Commencement: Healing or Stealing?* University of Portland Commencement Address. Retrieved 8/25/11 from http://www.up.edu/commencement/default.aspx?cid=9456

60. Howe, D. Brandon, M., Hinings, D., & Schofield, G. (1999). *Attachment Theory, Child Maltreatment and Family Support: A Practice and Assessment Model.* London: Macmillan.

61. Hatfield, E., Cacioppa, J. T., & Rapson, R. L. *Emotional Contagion.* New York: Cambridge University Press.

62. Donald, M. (1991). *Origins of the Modern Mind: Three Stages in the Evolution of Culture and Cognition.* Cambridge, MA: Harvard University Press.

63. Angier, N. (2009, Aug 18). Brain is a co-conspirator in a vicious stress loop. New York Times, pp. 2-D.2. Retrieved from http://search.proquest.com/docview/434154848?accountid=10559

64. Hardy, K. V. (2007). Untangling intangible loss in the lives of traumatized children and adolescents. In A. L. Vargas & S. L. Bloom (Eds.), *Loss, Hurt and Hope: The Complex Issues of Bereavement and Trauma in Children* (pp. 50–63). Newcastle, UK: Cambridge Scholars Publishing.

65. Bloom, S. L. (2007). Beyond the beveled mirror: Mourning and recovery from childhood maltreatment. In A. L. Vargas & S. L. Bloom (Eds.), *Loss, Hurt and Hope: The Complex Issues of Bereavement and Trauma in Children* (pp. 4–49). Newcastle, UK: Cambridge Scholars Publishing.

66. Kanellos, M. (2010, October 19). *MIT Explains Why Bad Habits Are Hard to break.* CNET News. Retrieved 10/1910 from http://www.apa.org/pubs/journals/features/rev-1144843.pdf

67. LaPlanche, J., & Pontalis, J. B. (1973). *The Language of Psychoanalysis.* New York: Norton.

68. van der Kolk, B. A. (2006). Clinical implications of neuroscience research in PTSD. *Annals of the New York Academy of Science, 1017*(1), 1–17.
69. Dalenberg, C. L. (2000). *Countertransference and the Treatment of Trauma.* Washington, DC: American Psychological Association Press.
70. LeDoux, J. (1994). Emotion, memory, and the brain. *Scientific American, 270,* 50–57.
71. Van der Kolk, B. A., et al. (1985). Inescapable shock, neurotransmitters, and addiction to trauma: Toward a psychobiology of post traumatic stress. *Biological Psychiatry, 20,* 314–325.
72. Van der Kolk, B., Greenberg, M., & Orr, S. (1989). Endogenous opioids, stress induced analgesia, and posttraumatic stress disorder. *Psychopharmacology Bulletin, 25,* 417–442.
73. Van der Kolk, B. (1996). The body keeps the score: Approaches to the psychobiology of posttraumatic stress disorder. In B. Van der Kolk, L. Weisaeth, & McFarland. A. C. (Eds.), *Traumatic Stress: The Effects of Overwhelming Experience on Mind, Body and Society* (pp. 214–241). New York: Guilford Press.
74. Van der Kolk, B. (1996). Trauma and memory. In B. Van der Kolk, A. McFarlane, & L. Weisaeth (Eds), *Traumatic Stress: The Effects of Overwhelming Experience on Mind, Body and Society* (pp. 279–302). Guilford Press: New York.
75. Rothbaum, B. O., Ruef, A. M., Litz, B. T., Han, H., & Hodges, L. (2004). Virtual reality exposure therapy of combat-related PTSD: A case study using psychophysiological indicators of outcome. In S. Taylor (Ed.), *Advances in the Treatment of Posttraumatic Stress Disorder: Cognitive-Behavioral Perspectives* (pp. 93–112). New York: Springer.
76. Merton, R. (1968). *Social Theory and Social Structure.* New York: Free Press.
77. Rosenthal, R. (1968). *Pygmalion in the Classroom.* New York: Holt, Rinehart and Winston.
78. Hassabis, D., Kumaran, D., Vann, S. D., Maguire, E. A., et al. (2007). Patients with hippocampal amnesia cannot imagine new experiences. *Proceedings of the National Academy of Sciences, 104*(5), 1726–1731.
79. Senge, P. (1990). *The Fifth Discipline: The Art and Practice of the Learning Organization.* New York: Currency/Doubleday.
80. Karpman, S. B. (1973). *1972 Eric Berne Memorial Scientific Award Lecture. Transactional Analysis Journal, 3,* 73–76.
81. Bloom, S. L. (2007). Loss in human service organizations. In A. L. Vargas & S. L. Bloom (Eds.), *Loss, Hurt and Hope: The Complex Issues of Bereavement and Trauma in Children* (pp. 142–206). Newcastle, UK: Cambridge Scholars Publishing.
82. Bloom, S. L., Foderaro, J. F., & Ryan, R. A. (2006). *S.E.L.F.: A Trauma-Informed, Psychoeducational Group Curriculum.* Retrieved 9/16/12 from http://www.sanctuaryweb.com
83. Jeffreys, J. S. (2005). *Coping with Workplace Grief: Dealing with Loss, Trauma, and Change* (rev. ed.). Boston: Thomson Course Technology.
84. Roubelat, F. (2006). Scenarios to challenge strategic paradigms: Lessons from 2025. *Futures, 38,* 519–527.
85. Lummis, C. D. (1997). *Radical Democracy.* Ithaca, NY: Cornell University Press.
86. Gastil, J. (1993) *Democracy in Small Groups: Participation, Decision Making and Communication.* Philadelphia: New Society Publishers.
87. Mindell, A. (2002). *The Deep Democracy of Open Forums: Practical Steps to Conflict Prevention and Resolution for the Family, Workplace, and World.* Charlottesville, VA: Hampton Roads Publishing.
88. Beyer, L. E. (Ed.). (1996). *Creating Democratic Classrooms: The Struggle to Integrate Theory and Practice.* New York: Teachers College Press.

89. Kassing, J. W. (1998). Development and validation of the organizational dissent scale. *Management Communication Quarterly, 12*(2), 183–229.

90. Sanders, W. (1983). The First Amendment and the government workplace: Has the Constitution fallen down on the job? *Western Journal of Speech Communication, 47*, 253–276.

91. Cheney, G. (1995). Democracy in the workplace: Theory and practice from the perspective of communication. *Journal of Applied Communication Research, 23*, 167–200.

92. Cheney, G. (1999). *Values at Work: Employee Participation Meets Market Pressure at Mondragon*. Ithaca, NY: Cornell University Press.

93. Slater, P., & Bennis, W. G. (1990). Democracy is inevitable. Harvard Business Review Classic. *Harvard Business Review, 68*(5), 167–176.

94. Kerr, J. L. (2004). The limits of organizational democracy. *Academy of Management Executive, 18*(3), 81–95.

95. Rummel, R. J. (1997). *Power Kills: Democracy as a Method of Nonviolence*. New Brunswick, NJ: Transaction.

96. Surowiecki, J. (2004). *The Wisdom of Crowds: Why the Many Are Smarter Than the Few and How Collective Wisdom Shapes Business, Economics, Societies, and Nations*. New York: Doubleday.

97. Sawyer, K. (2007). *Group Genius: The Creative Power of Collaboration*. New York: Basic Books.

98. Shay, J. (1994). *Achilles in Vietnam*. New York: Atheneum.

99. Shay, J. (2003). *Odysseus in America: Combat Trauma and the Trials of Homecoming*. New York: Scribner.

100. Shay, J. (1995). *The Birth of Tragedy—Out of the Needs of Democracy. Didaskalia, 2*(2). Retrieved 10/8/08 from http://www.didaskalia.net/issues/vol2no2/shay.html

101. Gastil, J. (1994). A definition and illustration of democratic leadership. *Human Relations, 47*(8), 953–976.

102. Rahim, M. A. (2002). Toward a theory of managing organizational conflict. *International Journal of Conflict Management, 13*(3), 206–235.

103. Wilmer, H. (1958). *Social Psychiatry in Action: A Therapeutic Community*. Springfield, IL: Charles C. Thomas.

104. Rapoport, R. N. (1960). *Community as Doctor: New Perspectives on a Therapeutic Community*. London: Tavistock.

105. Jones, M. (1953). *The Therapeutic Community: A New Treatment Method in Psychiatry*. New York: Basic Books.

106. De Leon, G. (2000). *The Therapeutic Community: Theory, Model, and Method.* New York: Springer.

107. King, M. L. (1958). *The Current Crisis in Race Relations* (pp. 86–89). New South, March.

108. Bills, L., & Bloom, S. (2000). Trying out Sanctuary the hard way. *Therapeutic Communities: The International Journal for Therapeutic and Supportive Organizations, 21*(2, special issue), 119–134.

109. Bills, L. J., & Bloom, S. L. (1998). From chaos to sanctuary: Trauma-based treatment for women in a state hospital system. In B. L. Levin, A. K. Blanch, & A. Jennings (Eds.), *Women's Health Services: A Public Health Perspective* (pp. 348–367). Thousand Oaks, CA: Sage Publications.

110. Chernus, I. (2004). *American Nonviolence: The History of an Idea*. New York: Maryknoll Press.

111. Shepard, M. (1978). *Understanding Nonviolence from Tactical Nonviolence to Satyagraha*. Retrieved 7/2/08 from http://www.markshep.com/nonviolence/ Understanding.html
112. Cox, S., Jones, B., & Collinson, D. (2006). Trust relations in high-reliability organizations. *Risk Analysis, 26*(5), 1123–1138.
113. Jameton, A. (1984). *Nursing Practice: The Ethical Issues*. Englewood Cliffs, NJ: Prentice-Hall.
114. Austin, W., Bergum, V., & Goldberg, L. (2003). Unable to answer the call of our patients: Mental health nurses' experience of moral distress. *Nursing Inquiry, 10*(3), 177–183.
115. Lennick, D., & Kiel, F. (2005). *Moral Intelligence: Enhancing Business Performance and Leadership Success*. Upper Saddle River, NJ: Wharton School Publishing.
116. United Nations. (1948). *Declaration of Human Rights*. Available at http://www. un.org/en/documents/udhr/
117. UNICEF *Convention on the Rights of the Child*. (2005). Available at http://www. unicef.org/crc/
118. Tehrani, N. (Ed.). (2012). *Workplace Bullying: Symptoms and Solutions*. London: Routledge.
119. Gershoff, E. T. (2008). *Report on Physical Punishment in the United States: What Research Tells Us about Its Effects on Children*. Columbus, OH: Center for Effective Discipline.
120. Pfeffer, J. (1998). *The Human Equation: Building Profits by Putting People First*. Boston: Harvard Business School Press.
121. Kremer, J. F., & Stephens, L. (1983). Attributions and arousal as mediators of mitigation's effect on retaliation. *Journal of Personality and Social Psychology, 45*(2), 335–343.
122. Zillman, D., Bryant, J., Cantor, J. R., & Day, K. D. (1975). Irrelevance of mitigating circumstances in retaliatory behavior at high levels of excitation. *Journal of Research in Personality, 9*, 282–293.
123. Zillman, D., & Cantor, J. R. (1976). Effect of timing of information about mitigating circumstances on emotional responses to provocation and retaliatory behavior. *Journal of Experimental Social Psychology, 12*, 38–55.
124. Skynner, R., & Cleese, J. (1993). *Life and How to Survive It*. London: Methuen.
125. Twenlow, S.W, & Sacco, F. C. (1999). A multi-level conceptual framework for understanding the violent community. In H. V. Hall & L. C. Whitaker (Eds.), *Collective Violence: Effective Strategies for Assessing and Interviewing in Fatal Group and Institutional Aggression* (pp. 575–599). Boca Raton, FL: CRC Press.
126. Rosenberg, M. (2003). *Nonviolent Communication: A Language of Life*. Encinitas, CA: Puddle Dancer Press.
127. Pekrun, R., & Frese, M. (1992). Emotions in work and achievement. *International Review of Industrial and Organizational Psychology, 7*, 153–200.
128. Center on the Developing Child at Harvard University (2007). *A Science-Based Framework for Early Childhood Policy: Using Evidence to Improve Outcomes in Learning, Behavior, and Health for Vulnerable Children*. http://www.developingchild.harvard.edu. Accessed October 3, 2012.
129. Mayer, J. D., & Salovey, P. (1997). What is emotional intelligence? In P. Salovey & D. J. Sluyter (Eds.), *Emotional Development and Emotional Intelligence: Educational Implications* (pp. 3–31). New York: Basic Books.
130. Heery, E., & Noon, M. (2001). Emotional labour. In *Dictionary of Human Resource Management* (p. 95). New York: Oxford University Press.

131. Jehn, K. A. (1995). A multimethod examination of the benefits and detriments of intragroup conflict. *Administrative Science Quarterly, 40*(2), 256–282.
132. Jehn, K. A., Northcraft, G. B., & Neale, M. A. (1999). Why differences make a difference: A field study of diversity, conflict, and performance in workgroups. *Administrative Science Quarterly, 44*(4), 741–763.
133. Putnam, L. L. (1994). Productive conflict: Negotiation as implicit coordination. *International Journal of Conflict Management, 5*, 285–299.
134. Amason, A. C. (1996). Distinguishing the effects of functional and dysfunctional conflict on strategic decision making: Resolving a paradox for top management teams. *Academy of Management Journal, 39*(1), 123–148.
135. Cosier, R. A., & Rose, G. L. (1977). Cognitive conflict and goal conflict effects on task performance. *Organizational Behavior and Human Performance, 19*, 378–391.
136. Fiol, C. M. (1994). Consensus, diversity and learning organizations. *Organization Science, 5*, 403–420.
137. Schweiger, D., Sandberg, W., & Ragan, J. W. (1986). Group approaches for improving strategic decision making: A comparative analysis of dialectical inquiry, devil's advocacy, and consensus approaches to strategic decision making. *Academy of Management Journal, 29*, 51–71.
138. Sunstein, C. R. (2003). *Why Societies Need Dissent.* Cambridge, MA: Harvard University Press.
139. Krystal, H. (1988). *Integration and Self Healing: Affect, Trauma, Alexithymia.* Hillsdale, NJ: Analytic Press.
140. Goleman, D. (1995). *Working with Emotional Intelligence: Why It Can Matter More Than IQ.* New York: Bantam Books.
141. Lyubomirsky, S., King, L., & Diener, E. (2005). The benefits of frequent positive affect: Does happiness lead to success? *Psychological Bulletin, 131*(6), 803–855.
142. Barsade, S. G. (2002). The ripple effect: Emotional contagion and its influence on group behavior. *Administrative Science Quarterly, 47*(4), 644–675.
143. Barsade, S. G., & Gibson, D. E. (2007). Why does affect matter in organizations? *Academy of Management Perspectives, 21*(1), 36–59.
144. Humphrey, R. H., Pollack, J. M., & Hawver, T. (2008). Leading with emotional labor. *Journal of Managerial Psychology, 23*(2), 151–168.
145. Pirola-Merlo, A., Haertel, C., Mann, L., & Hirst, G., (2002). How leaders influence the impact of affective events on team climate and performance in R&D teams. *The Leadership Quarterly, 13*(5), 561–81.
146. Almond, R. (1974). *The Healing Community: Dynamics of the Therapeutic Milieu.* New York: Jason Aronson.
147. Leeman, C. (1986). The therapeutic milieu and its role in clinical management. In L. Sederer (Ed.), *Inpatient Psychiatry: Diagnosis and Treatment* (2nd ed.). New York: Williams and Wilkins.
148. Jones, M. (1968). *Beyond the Therapeutic Community: Social Learning and Social Psychiatry.* New Haven, CT: Yale University Press.
149. Calvert, G., Mobley, S., & Marshall, L. (1994). Grasping the learning organization. *Training & Development, 48*(6), 38.
150. Senge, P., Kleiner, A., Roberts, C., Ross, R., & Smith, B. (1994). *The Fifth Discipline Fieldbook: Strategies and Tools for Building a Learning Organization.* New York: Currency/Doubleday.

151. Chiva, R., Alegre, J., & Lapiedra, R. (2007). Measuring organisational learning capability among the workforce. *International Journal of Manpower, 28*(3/4), 224–242.
152. Denton, D. K., & Wisdom, B. L. (1991). The learning organization involves the entire work force. *Quality Progress, 24*(12), 69.
153. Kofman, F., & Senge, P. M. (1993). Communities of commitment: The heart of learning organizations. *Organizational Dynamics, 22*(2), 4–235.
154. McGill, M. E., & Slocum, J. W., Jr. (1993). Unlearning the organization. *Organizational Dynamics, 22*(2), 67–79.
155. McGill, M. E., Slocum, J. W., Jr., & Lei, D. (1992). Management practices in learning organizations. *Organizational Dynamics, 21*(1), 4–17.
156. Meen, D. E., & Keough, M. (1992). Creating the learning organization: An interview with Peter M. Senge; organization learning in practice. *The McKinsey Quarterly, 1992*(1), 58–78.
157. Pedler, M., Boydell, T., & Burgogyne, J. (1989). Toward the learning company. *Management and Education and Development, 20*(1), 1–8.
158. http://www.glovehouse.org/AboutUs.aspx. Accessed 9/15/12.
159. Akgun, A. E., Byrne, J. C., Lynn, G. S., Keskin, H. (2007). Organizational unlearning as changes in beliefs and routines in organizations. *Journal of Organizational Change Management, 20*(6), 794–812.
160. Kassing, J. W. (1997). Articulating, antagonizing, and displacing: A model of employee dissent. *Communication Studies, 48*(4), 311–332.
161. Kassing, J. W. (2002). Speaking up. *Management Communication Quarterly, 16*(2), 187–209.
162. Murphy, K. (2008). *Is Sanctuary "too soft " on kids?* Retrieved September 15, 2012 from http://www.sanctuaryweb.com/PDFs_new/Murphy%20is%20Sanctuary%20too%20soft .pdf
163. Kassing, J. W. (2001). From the looks of things. *Management Communication Quarterly, 14*(3), 442–470.
164. Mellers, B. A., Schwartz, A., & Cooke, A. D. J. (1998). Judgment and decision making. *Annual Review of Psychology, 49*, 447–477.
165. Dressler, L. (2006). *Consensus through Conversation: How to Achieve High-Commitment Decisions.* San Francisco: Berrett Koehler.
166. Whitaker, R. (2010). *Anatomy of An Epidemic: Magic Bullets, Psychiatric Drugs, and the Astonishing Rise of Mental Illness in America.* New York: Crown Publishing.
167. Argyris, C., & Schon, D. *Organizational Learning.* London: Addison-Wesley.
168. Dyer, J., & Gregersen, H. (2011). *The Innovator's DNA: Mastering the Five Skills of Disruptive Innovators.* Boston: Harvard Business Review Press.
169. Coghlan, D., & Jacobs, C. (2005). Kurt Lewin on reeducation: Foundations for action research. *The Journal of Applied Behavioral Science, 41*(4), 444–457.
170. Jones, M. (1976). *Maturation of the Therapeutic Community: An Organic Approach to Health and Mental Health.* New York: Human Sciences Press.
171. Stanton, A. H., & Schwartz, M. S. (1954). *The Mental Hospital: A Study of Institutional Participation in Psychiatric Illness and Treatment.* New York: Basic Books.
172. Goleman, D. (2006). *Social Intelligence: The New Science of Human Relationships.* New York: Bantam Books.
173. O'Toole, J., & Bennis, W. (2009). What's needed next: A culture of candor. *Harvard Business Review, 87*(6), 54–61.

174. Page, S. E. (2007). *The Difference: How the Power of Diversity Creates Better Groups, Firms, Schools, and Societies*. Princeton, NJ: Princeton University Press.
175. Bennis, W. G., Goleman, D., O'Toole, J., & Biederman, P. (2008). *Transparency: How Leaders Create a Culture of Candor*. San Francisco: Jossey-Bass.
176. Showkeir, J., & Showkeir, M. (2008). *Authentic Conversations: Moving from Manipulation to Truth and Commitment*. San Francisco: Berrett-Koehler.
177. Caudill, W. (1958). *The Psychiatric Hospital as a Small Society*. Cambridge, MA: Harvard University Press.
178. Spears, L. C., & Lawrence, M (Eds.). (2002). *Focus on Leadership: Servant-Leadership for the 21st Century*. New York: Wiley.
179. Noon, M., & Delbridge, R. (1993). News from behind my hand: Gossip in organizations. *Organization Studies, 14*(1), 23–36.
180. Hammond, S. A., & Mayfield, A. B. (2004). *The Thin Book of Naming Elephants: How to Surface Undiscussables for Greater Organizational Success*. Bend, OR: Thin Book Publishing Company.
181. Bohm, D. (1996). *On Dialogue*. New York: Routledge.
182. Bohm, D., Factor, D., & Garrett, P. (1991). *Dialogue: A Proposal*. Retrieved 7/27/05 from http://www.cgl.org
183. Staub, E. (1989). *The Roots of Evil: The Origins of Genocide and Other Group Violence*. New York: Cambridge University Press.
184. Staub, E. (1992). Transforming the bystanders: Altruism, caring and social responsibility. In H. Fein (Ed.), *Genocide Watch*. New Haven, CT: Yale University Press.
185. Smith, A. (1759/1937). *A Theory of Moral Sentiments* [1759]. New York: Modern Library.
186. De Waal, F. (2006). *Primates and Philosophers: How Morality Evolved*. Princeton, NJ: Princeton University Press.
187. De Waal, F. (1996). *Good Natured: The Origins of Right and Wrong in Humans and Other Animals*. Cambridge, MA: Harvard University Press.
188. Ehrenreich, B. (1997). *Blood Rites: Origins and History of the Passions of War*. New York: Henry Holt.
189. Trivers, R. (1985). *Social Evolution*. Menlo Park, CA: Benjamin/Cummings.
190. Bloom, P. (2010). *The moral life of babies, in New York Times* (pp. 44–49, 56, 62–63, 65). New York Times: New York.
191. Schulman, M., & Mekler, E. (1994). *Bringing Up a Moral Child*. New York: Doubleday.
192. Herzberger, S. D., & Hall, J. A. (1993). Children's evaluations of retaliatory aggression against siblings and friends. *Journal of Interpersonal Violence, 8*(1), 77–93.
193. Schore, A. N. (1994). *Affect Regulation and the Origin of the Self: The Neurobiology of Emotional Development*. Hillsdale, NJ: Lawrence Erlbaum.
194. Zehr, H. (1994). Justice that heals: The vision. *Stimulus, 2*(3), 5–11.
195. Zehr, H. (1990). *Changing Lenses: A New Focus for Crime and Justice*. Scottsdale, PA: Herald Press.
196. Bianchi, H. (1995). *Justice as Sanctuary: Toward a New System of Crime Control*. Bloomington: Indiana University Press.
197. Cropanzano, R., Bowen, D. E., & Gilliland, S. W. (2007). The management of organizational justice. *Academy of Management Perspectives, 21*(4): 34–48.
198. Ambrose, M. L. (2002). Contemporary justice research: A new look at familiar questions. *Organizational Behavior and Human Decision Processes, 89*(1), 803–812.
199. Lerner, M. J. (1980). *The Belief in a Just World: A Fundamental Delusion*. New York: Plenum Press.

200. Marongiu, P., & Newman, G. (1987). *Vengeance: The Fight against Injustice.* Totowa, NJ: Rowman & Littlefield.

201. Gilligan, J. (1996). *Violence: Our Deadly Epidemic and Its Causes.* New York: Putnam.

202. Grevin, P. (1990). *Spare the Child: The Religious Roots of Punishment and the Psychological Impact of Physical Abuse.* New York: Vintage Books.

203. Straus, M. A. (1994). *Beating the Devil Out of Them: Corporal Punishment in American Families.* New York: Lexington Books.

204. Zimbardo, P. (2007). *The Lucifer Effect: Understanding How Good People Turn Evil.* New York: Random House.

205. Fogelman, E. (1994). *Conscience and Courage: Rescuers of Jews during the Holocaust.* New York: Doubleday.

206. Staub, E. (2003). *The Psychology of Good and Evil: Why Children, Adults, and Groups Help and Harm Others.* New York: Cambridge University Press.

207. Strueber, D., Lueck, M., & Roth, G. (2006, December–2007, January). The violent brain. *Scientific American Mind, 17,* 20–27.

208. Stout, M., *The Sociopath Next Door: The Ruthless vs. The Rest of Us 2004,* New York: Broadway Book.

209. Cloke, K., & Goldsmith, J. (2002). *The End of Management and the Rise of Organizational Democracy.* San Francisco: Jossey-Bass.

210. Sims, H. P. (1980). Further thoughts on punishment in organizations. *The Academy of Management Review, 5*(1), 133–138.

211. Cohen, D. V. (1993). Creating and maintaining ethical work climates: Anomie in the workplace and implications for managing change. *Business Ethics Quarterly, 3*(4), 343–358.

212. Baucus, M. S., & Beck-Dudley, C. L. (2005). Designing ethical organizations: Avoiding the long-term negative effects of rewards and punishments. *Journal of Business Ethics, 56*(4), 355–370.

213. Geller, J. A., Madsen, L. H., & Ohrenstein, L. (2004). Secondary trauma: A team approach. *Clinical Social Work Journal, 32*(4), 415–430.

214. Garrison, J. (2003). *America as Empire: Global Leader or Rogue Power?* San Francisco: Berrett Koehler.

215. Bloom, S. L. (2004). Neither liberty nor safety: The impact of fear on individuals, institutions, and societies, Part I. *Psychotherapy and Politics International, 2*(2), 78–98.

216. Bloom, S. L. (2004). Neither liberty nor safety: The impact of fear on individuals, institutions, and societies, Part II. *Psychotherapy and Politics International, 2*(3), 212–228.

217. Bloom, S. L. (2005). Neither liberty nor safety: The impact of fear on individuals, institutions, and societies, Part IV. *Psychotherapy and Politics International, 3*(2), 96–111.

218. Bloom, S. L. (2005). Neither liberty nor safety: The impact of fear on individuals, institutions, and societies, Part III. *Psychotherapy and Politics International, 3*(2), 96–111.

219. Rivard, J. C., Bloom, S. L., McCorkle, D., & Abramovitz, R. (2005). Preliminary results of a study examining the implementation and effects of a trauma recovery framework for youths in residential treatment. *Therapeutic Community: The International Journal for Therapeutic and Supportive Organizations, 26*(1), 83–96.

220. Rivard, J. C., Bloom, S. L., Abramovitz, R. A., Pasquale, L., Duncan, M., McCorkle, D., & Fedel, S. (2003). Assessing the implementation and effects of

a trauma-focused intervention for youths in residential treatment. *Psychiatric Quarterly, 74*(2), 137–154.

221. Rivard, J. C. (2004). Initial findings of an evaluation of a trauma recovery framework in residential treatment. *Residential Group Care Quarterly, 5*(1), 3–5.

222. Foderaro, J., & Ryan, R. (2000). SAGE: Mapping the course of recovery. *Therapeutic Communities: The International Journal for Therapeutic and Supportive Organizations, 21*(2, special issue), 93–104.

223. Foderaro, J. (2001). Creating a nonviolent environment: Keeping Sanctuary safe. In S. Bloom (Ed.), *In Violence: A Public Health Menace and a Public Health Approach* (pp. 57–82). London: Karnac Books.

224. Bloom, S. L., Foderaro, J. F., & Ryan, R. A. (2002). *S.E.L.F.: A Trauma-Informed, Psychoeducational Group Curriculum*2006: Retrieved 9/16/12 from http://www.sanctuaryweb.com/self.php.

225. Spinnazola, J., Blaustein, M., & Van der Kolk, B. A. (2005). Posttraumatic stress disorder treatment outcome research: The study of unrepresentative samples? *Journal of Traumatic Stress, 18*, 425–436.

226. Courtois, C. A., & Ford, J. D. (Eds.). (2009). *Treating Complex Traumatic Stress Disorders: An Evidence-Based Guide*. New York: Guilford Press.

227. Briere, J., & Scott, C. (2006). *Principles of Trauma Therapy: A Guide to Symptoms, Evaluation, and Treatment*. Thousand Oaks, CA: Sage Publications.

228. Whiteley, S. (2004). The evolution of the therapeutic community. *Psychiatric Quarterly, 75*(3), 233–248.

229. Bloom, S. L., & Norton, K. Introduction to the special section: The therapeutic community in the 21st century. *Psychiatric Quarterly, 75*(3), 229–231.

230. Sharp, G. (1973). *The Dynamics of Nonviolent Action. Part Three of The Politics of Nonviolent Action*. Boston: Porter Sargent Publishers.

231. Nagler, M. N. (2001). *Is There No Other Way?: The Search for a Nonviolent Future*. Berkeley, CA: Berkeley Hills Books.

232. Rosenberg, T. (2011). *Join the Club: How Peer Pressure Can Transform the World*. New York: Norton.

Index